New Directions in American Political Parties

Our portraits of voters, their relationship to parties, and the behavior of elected party members have changed significantly within the last 10 to 15 years. Characterizations of dealignment and decreased importance of parties have been fairly rapidly replaced by a focus on party polarization. Voters are becoming more ideological and the debate is now about the relative role of ideology, religious attachment, views on immigration, and class in affecting party identification and voting. In a short period of time we have gone from concern that parties are not responsive or sufficiently different to whether polarization has become too great.

This volume, with contributions from some of the most noted scholars of political parties, brings together assessments of these changes to provide a comprehensive overview of current trends in the field. It serves as an excellent companion to courses on parties and elections, and a useful overview for scholars and students of American politics generally.

Jeffrey M. Stonecash is Maxwell Professor of Political Science at Syracuse University. He is the author of numerous books on political parties, polariza tion, and state politics.

New Directions in American Politics

The Routledge series *New Directions in American Politics* is composed of contributed volumes covering key areas of study in the field of American politics and government. Each title provides a state-of-the-art overview of current trends in its respective subfield, with an eye toward cutting edge research accessible to advanced undergraduate and beginning graduate students. While the volumes touch on the main topics of relevant study, they are not meant to cover the "nuts and bolts" of the subject. Rather, they engage readers in the most recent scholarship, real-world controversies, and theoretical debates with the aim of getting students excited about the same issues that animate scholars.

Titles in the Series:

New Directions in American Political Parties
Edited by Jeffrey M. Stonecash

New Directions in the American Presidency
Edited by Lori Cox Han

New Directions in Campaigns and Elections
Edited by Stephen K. Medvic

New Directions in American Political Parties

Edited by
Jeffrey M. Stonecash

Routledge
Taylor & Francis Group

NEW YORK AND LONDON

First published 2010
by Routledge
270 Madison Avenue, New York, NY 10016

Simultaneously published in the UK
by Routledge
2 Park Square, Milton Park, Abingdon, Oxon OX14 4RN

Routledge is an imprint of the Taylor & Francis Group, an informa business

© 2010 Taylor & Francis

Typeset in Minion and Gill Sans by EvS Communication Networx, Inc.
Printed and bound in the United States of America on acid-free paper by Sheridan Books, Inc.

Library of Congress Cataloging in Publication Data
Stonecash, Jeffrey M.
New directions in American political parties / Jeffrey M. Stonecash.
p. cm. — (New directions in American politics)
Includes bibliographical references and index.
1. Political parties—United States. 2. United States—Politics and government. I. Title.
JK2261.S862 2010
324.273—dc22
2009052328

ISBN 10: 0-415-80523-6 (hbk)
ISBN 10: 0-415-80524-4 (pbk)
ISBN 10: 0-203-86841-2 (ebk)

ISBN 13: 978-0-415-80523-0 (hbk)
ISBN 13: 978-0-415-80524-7 (pbk)
ISBN 13: 978-0-203-86841-6 (ebk)

Contents

PART III

Sources of Political Divisions, Realignment, and Current Party Differences

PART IV

Party Actions, Institutions, and Impacts

List of Tables

List of Figures

Preface

Our Changing Understandings of Parties and Their Supporters

It is a continual challenge to understand how politics is working. That challenge is particularly evident with regard to American political parties. In the mid-1990s it was common to read about the decline of political parties. The percentage of voters defining themselves as independents began to increase in the 1960s, and more of them engaged in split-ticket voting, or voting for candidates of different parties for different offices. During the 1970s and 1980s it was common to read that voters were becoming less attached to parties and dealignment was occurring. Voters were not seen as ideological and candidates were seen as seeking to build personal (nonpartisan) relationships to voters. It appeared that the rise of television and large campaign budgets were leading to a political world in which individual images were trumping broad party images. The widespread view was that candidate-centered campaigns were the norm. The parties in Congress contained considerable diversity and party unity was not high.

Then that line of interpretation began to seem inaccurate. The percentage of voters identifying with or leaning to parties began to increase. The percentage of those identifying with a party and voting for candidates of that party was increasing. Evidence began to emerge that partisan divisions around ideology, religion, and class were becoming more important. Republicans took over the House in 1994 and in a cohesive fashion engaged in a clearly partisan struggle with President Bill Clinton about a broad array of policy issues. From 2001 to 2006 Republicans held the presidency and Congress and they strongly differed with Democrats in Congress over matters large and small. Something was changing and the challenge for students of parties is to understand how important partisanship is becoming and what is creating those divisions.

The chapters that follow are an effort to offer the latest in what we know about the changes unfolding before us. The author or authors of each chapter have spent considerable time studying their particular field. The first chapter provides a brief summary of the changes occurring in partisan behavior in recent decades. The next chapter reviews changes in American society that create the context that parties must respond to. Then the broad responses of parties are analyzed—their strategies, their efforts to cope with a changing media and get their message out to voters, and their organizational efforts. The next chapters focus on the matters that seem to be dividing Americans the most—race, class, ideology, religion and morality, immigration, and region. Finally, the analysis turns to the effects of this growing partisanship on the presidency, Congress, and public policy. Together these chapters provide an overview of what we know now about American political parties.

Syracuse, New York
December 2009

Contributors

Alan Abramowitz is the Alben W. Barkley Professor of Political Science at Emory University in Atlanta, Georgia. He received his BA from the University of Rochester in 1969 and his PhD from Stanford University in 1976. Dr. Abramowitz has authored or coauthored five books, dozens of contributions to edited volumes, and more than forty articles in political science journals dealing with political parties, elections, and voting behavior in the United States. Dr. Abramowitz's newest book, *The Disappearing Center: Engaged Citizens, Polarization and American Democracy*, will be published in 2010 by Yale University Press.

John Aldrich (PhD, Rochester) is a Pfizer-Pratt University Professor of Political Science at Duke University. He specializes in American politics and behavior, formal theory, and methodology. Books he has authored or coauthored include *Why Parties, Before the Convention, Linear Probability, Logit and Probit Models*, and a series of books on elections, the most recent of which is *Change and Continuity in the 2008 Elections*. His articles have appeared in the *American Political Science Review, American Journal of Political Science, Journal of Politics, Public Choice*, and other journals and edited volumes. He has served as coeditor of the *American Journal of Political Science* and as a Fellow at the Center for Advanced Study in the Behavioral Sciences and at the Rockefeller Center, Bellagio. He is past President of the Southern Political Science Association and of the Midwest Political Science Association, and is a Fellow of the American Academy of Arts and Sciences. Current projects include studies of various aspects of strategic voting, campaigns and elections, political parties, and Congress.

Mark D. Brewer is Associate Professor of Political Science at the University of Maine. His research interests focus generally on political behavior, with specific research areas including partisanship and electoral behavior at both the mass and elite levels, the linkages between public opinion and public policy, and the interactions that exist between religion and politics in the United States. Brewer is the author of a number of books and articles in academic journals, with the most recent being *Party Images in the American Electorate* (Routledge, 2009), *Dynamics of American Political Parties* (with Jeffrey M. Stonecash, Cambridge University Press, 2009), and *Parties and Elections in America* (with L. Sandy Maisel, Rowman & Littlefield, 2010, 5th edition, revised).

Marika Dunn is a doctoral candidate in political science at Rutgers University-New Brunswick. Her research areas focus on political representation in the United States within the context of race, ethnicity, and immigration. Prior to Rutgers, she managed programs for a women's legal advocacy organization in Washington, DC. She holds a BA from Hampshire College in Amherst, MA, where she concentrated on political theory and legal studies.

Diana Dwyre is Professor of Political Science at California State University, Chico. She conducts research on political parties, political money, and legislative politics, and her most recent book, with Victoria Farrar-Myers, is *Limits and Loopholes: The Quest for Money, Free Speech and Fair Elections* (CQ Press, 2008). She is the 2009–2010 Fulbright Australian National University Distinguished Chair in American Political Science, and she served as the William Steiger American Political Science Association Congressional Fellow in 1998.

Danny Hayes is assistant professor of political science in the Maxwell School of Citizenship and Public Affairs at Syracuse University. He has published more than a dozen articles on media coverage of campaigns, voting behavior in presidential elections, political participation, and other topics in *the American Journal of Political Science, Political Research Quarterly, Political Behavior*, and *Political Communication*, among others. He is currently at work on a study of the dynamics of media coverage and public opinion in the lead-up to the Iraq War and a project examining the effects of redistricting on political participation.

Kerry Haynie is an associate professor of political science and codirector of the Center for the Study of Race, Ethnicity, and Gender in the Social Sciences at Duke University. His publications include *New Race Politics in America: Understanding Minority and Immigrant Politics* (2008, coedited with Jane Junn); *African American Legislators in the American States* (2001); and *The Encyclopedia of Minorities in American Politics*, volumes 1 and 2 (2000). He received his PhD in political science from the University of North Carolina at Chapel Hill.

Jane Junn is Professor of Political Science at the University of Southern California. She is the author of *Education and Democratic Citizenship in America* (with Norman H. Nie and Kenneth Stehlik-Barry, University of Chicago Press,

1996), which won the Woodrow Wilson Foundation award from the American Political Science Association for the best book published in political science. She is also the author of *Civic Education: What Makes Students Learn* (with Richard G. Niemi, Yale University Press, 1998), and *New Race Politics: Understanding Minority and Immigrant Politics* (edited with Kerry L. Haynie, Cambridge University Press, 2008). Her research articles on political behavior, public opinion, racial and ethnic politics, the politics of immigration, gender and politics, and political identity have appeared in journals including *Perspectives on Politics, The DuBois Review, Politics & Gender, American Politics Research*, and the *American Behavioral Scientist*.

Rebekah E. Liscio is a PhD candidate in political science at Syracuse University, specializing in American and comparative politics. Her research focuses on political communication, public opinion, and political parties. She is author of "The Consequences of Republican Party Strategy" (with Jeffrey M. Stonecash and Mark D. Brewer) in *The State of the Parties* (2010) and has presented a conference paper on "A Convergence of Framing Effects and Candidate Images" (2009). She is a research affiliate with the Campbell Public Affairs Institute and holds an MA in political science from Syracuse University, a BA in political science from the University of Vermont, and a certificate in political psychology from Stanford University.

Sidney M. Milkis is the White Burkett Miller Professor of the Department of Politics and Assistant Director for Academic Programs at the Miller of Public Affairs at the University of Virginia. His books include: *The President and the Parties: The Transformation of the American Party System Since the New Deal* (1993); *Political Parties and Constitutional Government: Remaking American Democracy* (1999); *Presidential Greatness* (2000), coauthored with Marc Landy; *The American Presidency: Origins and Development, 1776–2007* (2007, 5th edition), coauthored with Michael Nelson; and, most recently, *Theodore Roosevelt, the Progressive Party, and the Transformation of American Democracy* (2009). He is the coeditor, with Jerome Mileur, of thee volumes on twentieth century political reform: *Progressivism and the New Democracy* (1999); *The New Deal and the Triumph of Liberalism* (2002); and *The Great Society and the High Tide of Liberalism* (2005).

Laura Olson is Professor of Political Science at Clemson University. Her work has appeared in *Political Research Quarterly, Social Science Quarterly*, the *Journal for the Scientific Study of Religion*, and other scholarly journals. Recent books include *Religion and Politics in America: Faith, Culture, and Strategic Choices* (Westview, 2010) and *Women with a Mission: Religion, Gender, and the Politics of Women Clergy* (University of Alabama Press, 2005).

Howard L. Reiter is Professor Emeritus of Political Science at the University of Connecticut, where he taught from 1974 to 2009. He is the author of *Selecting the President, Parties and Elections in Corporate America*, and, with Jeffrey M. Stonecash, the forthcoming *Counter Realignment: Political Change in the Northeast*. In 2001–2002, Professor Reiter held the Fulbright Distinguished Chair at Uppsala University in Sweden, and in 2010–2011, he will be president of the New England Political Science Association.

David Rohde is Ernestine Friedl Professor of Political Science at Duke University, and Director of the Political Institutions and Public Choice Program. He received his PhD from the University of Rochester in 1970. He is the author of books and articles on various aspects of American national politics, including *Parties and Leaders in the Postreform House*, and a series of 15 books on national elections since 1980 coauthored with Paul Abramson and John Aldrich.

Jeffrey M. Stonecash is Maxwell Professor in the Maxwell School, Syracuse University. He does research on political parties, changes in their electoral bases, and how these changes affect political polarization and public policy debates. His recent books are *Class and Party in American Politics* (2000), *Diverging Parties* (2002), *Political Polling* (2003; 2008, 2nd edition), *Parties Matter: Realignment and the Return of Partisanship* (2006), *Governing New York State* (2006), *Split: Class and Cultural Divisions in American Politics*, (2007), *Reassessing the Incumbency Effect* (Cambridge University Press, 2008), and *Dynamics of American Political Parties* (Cambridge, 2009). He has just completed *Counter-Realignment: Political Change in the Northeast* (Cambridge, 2010) with Howard Reiter (University of Connecticut) about the decline in Republican support within the Northeast from 1900–2008.

Candis S. Watts is a PhD candidate in political science at Duke University.

Part I

Overview

Voters and Parties in Recent Decades

Chapter 1

Changing American Political Parties

Jeffrey M. Stonecash

Changing Voting Patterns: Increasing Partisanship

American political parties are often defined as a collection of individuals with common interests. The extent of this commonality, however, varies considerably from time to time as change unfolds. Parties are loose and changeable collections of candidates, party officials, organized groups, and groups of unorganized voters. Candidates seek voters and groups seek policy commitments. Elites—candidates and party officials—seek to connect with organized groups (NRA or the Sierra Club) and unorganized "groups" (those pro-life or pro-choice) to attract their support (Aldrich 1995). Groups simultaneously seek policy commitments from candidates in exchange for the group's endorsement and support. These interactions are complicated by social change which can alter group interests and shift what specific groups want from candidates (Karol 2009).

In recent decades the outcomes of this dynamic of social change and interactions between candidates and the electorate have changed American political parties. Our interpretations of what is occurring have also changed and this book presents our latest views. As late as the 1990s we had a rough consensus that parties and the attachment of voters to them were on the decline. Now partisanship is on the rise. The evidence has sometimes been hard to be certain about, but it is becoming clearer as time passes. The behavior of voters indicates the pattern. Surveys in the 1960s and 1970s found that voters were less and less attached to parties. Higher percentages of voters were saying they did not identify with a party. Those who did identify with a party were less likely to vote for candidates of their party. There was an increase in split-ticket voting, or voting Democratic for one office and Republican for another. The conclusion was that voters were voting for individuals and not parties, and that we had entered a world of candidate-centered campaigns. A vast amount of research emerged to document all these changes. In the 1970s and 1980s it was common to encounter titles such as David Broder's *The Party's Over* (1972), William Crotty's *American Parties in Decline* (1984), and Martin Wattenberg's *The Decline of American Political Parties, 1952–1996* (1998).

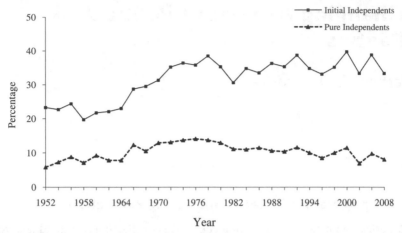

Figure 1.1   The Presence of Independents, 1952–2008.

Then evidence began to accumulate that things were changing again and that partisanship was increasing. When respondents were asked if they identi-fied with a party, about one third responded initially that they were independents, as shown in Figure 1.1. But when a follow-up question was asked about whether the person leaned to either party, far fewer said they were independent. After those leaning to a party were removed, the percentage of "pure" independents was much lower. Further, after peaking at 13 to 14 percent in the 1970s it was declining and reached 8.1 percent in the 2008 election.

Not only do most Americans identify with or lean to a party, but the evidence indicates that individuals identifying with a party are increasingly inclined to vote for candidates of that party (Bartels 2000). Figure 1.2 presents the percentages of those who identify with either the Democratic Party and

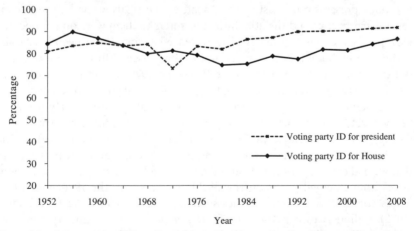

Figure 1.2   Percentage of Major Party-Identifiers Voting for Candidates of their Party. Sources: NES Cumulative Data File, 1948–2004 and 2008 study..

voted Democratic or identify with the Republican Party and voted Republican. Those who lean to either party are defined as identifying with a party because they generally vote strongly for that party (Keith et al. 1992). From 1952 through the 1970s it appeared that partisanship was of declining relevance. But from the late 1970s onward there has been a steady increase in the extent to which those with a partisan identity engage in partisan voting.

The same pattern has prevailed for straight-ticket voting, or voting for presidential and House candidates of the same party. In the 1950s about 85 percent of voters chose candidates of the same party for these two offices. From 1968 to 1976 this percentage was in the low 70s. In 1980 it was 64.3 percent. Since then the percentage has been rising, reaching 82.3 in 2004 and 77.3 in 2008. Something was changing. Partisanship was becoming more important (Stonecash 2006). It was clear that conclusions about the decline of parties, at least as embodied in the attachment of voters, needed to be reconsidered.

The behavior of individuals was also affecting the consistency of election results across the nation. Figure 1.3 presents the correlation[1] between presidential and House results across all House districts. A high correlation indicates that results are very similar across districts. When the Democratic presidential candidate receives 70 percent, the House candidate receives a very similar percent. When the Democratic presidential candidate receives 40 percent, the House candidate receives a very similar percent. When there is a decline in the similarity of partisan voting percentages for these two offices, the correlation declines. In the early 1900s the correlation was high. It then plummeted in 1948, came back in 1952 and 1956, then declined again and was relatively low in the 1960s and 1970s. The result was that in House districts the winners of the presidential and House vote began to differ, resulting in an increase in what we call split outcomes, or different partisan winners within a district.

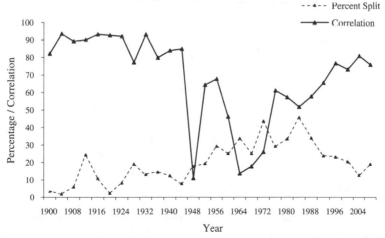

Figure 1.3 The Association of Democratic House–President Results: Correlation and Split Outcomes, 1900–2008.

Then, much as with the individual level data, the consistency of partisan outcomes began to increase. Enough voters were voting for the same party that the correlation between presidential and House percentages was increasing and the percentage of House districts with split outcomes gradually declined. Partisanship is again becoming more important both at the individual and aggregate level.

Party Change and the Emerging Sources of Division

These increases in partisanship did not just occur. The parties were responding to and actively pursuing and attracting specific voters. As Mark Brewer indicates in chapter 3, the parties were listening to shifting concerns within the electorate, deciding which concerns to respond to, and formulating strategies to connect with and appeal to the voters they wanted to attract. In chapter 4 Danny Hayes examines how the parties were seeking to get messages about their concerns through the changing media so that voters would see the differences in the way the parties wanted them seen. As Diana Dwyer indicates in chapter 5, they were raising money, recruiting volunteers, and developing organizations to connect with and mobilize voters. Their next challenge was to establish an image of their party and get it to specific voters.

Change came about because of concerted efforts by groups and candidates to create strong support among some groups and not others. The efforts involved fundamental issues. While party leaders seek to exploit short-term issues, they also have substantive concerns that create somewhat enduring attachments among voters. Each party was coping with a changing society, with what concerns to pursue, and with whether it could shed some of its less valued base and acquire a new base. The changes occurring within each party had long histories. By the late 1900s the dynamics of the interaction between groups and parties were producing greater clarity of party positions and electoral bases. Chapter 3 provides more detail on these changes, but in brief, the parties were changing their geographical bases and clarifying their electoral bases. The lengthy process of change at first reduced the clarity of electoral bases. Beginning in the 1970s the results of party actions on voter allegiances began to gradually be evident. From 1870 through the 1920s the Democratic Party was largely based in the South. It was generally in the minority and was seeking to expand its electoral base. It first sought to increase its support in Northern cities among workers and was eventually successful in the 1930s (Andersen 1979; Plotke 1996). That gave the party a larger base, but it created a coalition that was Southern and for segregation and a Northern delegation that was increasingly for equal opportunity for blacks (Feinstein and Schickler 2008; Schickler, Pearson, and Feinstein 2009). The party sought greater support in the North, and as they succeeded the tensions within the Democratic coalition increased (Brewer and Stonecash 2009). The conflicts eventually set off a major realignment with much of the South abandoning the Democratic

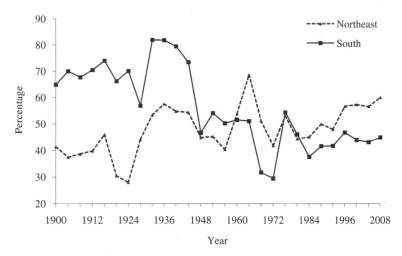

Figure 1.4   Percentage Voting for Democratic Presidential Candidates, South and Northeast, 1900–2008.

Party while its success in the North increased (Ware 2006). The Democratic Party became a consistently more liberal party on a host of issues.

Republicans were undergoing their own changes. In the first half of the 1900s the Republican Party was largely based in the Northeast. Beginning in the 1950s conservatives within the Republican Party began to push the party in a more conservative direction (Rae 1989). They wanted the party to oppose a growing role for the federal government and advocate lower taxes. By the 1970s social conservative groups were emerging and voicing concerns about morals and traditional norms (Hetherington and Weiler 2009; Hunter 1991). The Republican Party responded, seeing it as compatible to advocate less government in the economy while also using government policies to affirm traditional values (Dionne 1997). They pursued Southern voters, who were more conservative, eventually doing very well in the South (Black and Black 1987, 2002), but losing the Northeast (Reiter and Stonecash 2010).

These dynamics shifted where the parties drew their greatest support, with the major changes being the shift in partisan support within the South and the Northeast. Figures 1.4 and 1.5 indicate just how much change has occurred. In the early 1900s the South was overwhelmingly Democratic and the Northeast was Republican. Over time the two regions have reversed positions. That lengthy process of change created the appearance of party "decline" in the 1960s and 1970s, but it was a result of a gradual process of voters shifting their allegiances (Key 1959). As change continued and the older base of each party gradually moved to another party, voter alignments became clearer. Chapter 11 provides more detail on these changes.

These changes were driven by the interaction between groups and candidates. Groups sought policy commitments and party candidates responded.

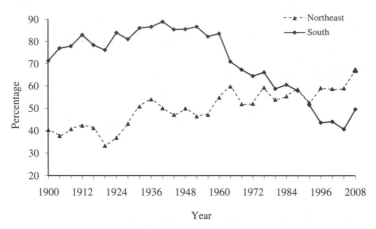

Figure 1.5   House Democratic Voting Percentages, by Region, 1900–2008.

Race emerged as a major source of division and as chapter 6 indicates it remains as such. Issues of class (chapter 7) have seemed to be important but how much they matter remains unclear. Ideological divisions have clearly become more important, as chapter 8 documents. Religion and normative values (chapter 9) and immigration (chapter 10) have also emerged as major issues dividing the parties. For the most part these divisions have developed gradually, and our efforts to understand why and how these divisions have developed are ongoing. These chapters present our most current understandings.

Party Differences: Congress and the Presidency

The evolving divisions discussed in these chapters have affected the differences between parties. Academics have developed measures of the ideological placement of Members of Congress based on how they vote (Poole and Rosenthal 1997).[2] It is then possible to create an average score for Republicans and Democrats in the House and the Senate, and then determine the difference between those averages. Figure 1.6 indicates the difference between these party averages over time. In the early 1900s there were relatively large differences. Then the differences declined in the 1960s and 1970s and led to the conclusion that parties were in decline. Since then the creation of greater clarity as to whom identifies with each party and the policy differences between the parties have resulted in greater differences between the parties in their voting records.

The parties are also now more unified. Figure 1.7 tracks the tendency of Senate members to vote with their party, when a majority of one party votes against the majority of the other. Since the late 1970s there has been a steady increase in the willingness of party members to line up and vote with their

Figure 1.6   Average Congressional Party Differences, 1856–2006.

party against the other. The same pattern prevails in the House of Representatives. The development of these differences is discussed in chapter 13.

The same trends that have created differences in congressional party bases have affected the role of the president and in how the president is seen. Since the 1950s the differences in how Democratic and Republican voters see the president have steadily increased. From the 1950s through the 1970s differences in presidential approval ratings between Democrats and Republicans averaged about 40 percentage points. During George W. Bush's administration differences were generally 80 percentage points. Among Democrats 10 percent might approve while among Republicans it was 90 percent (Jacobson

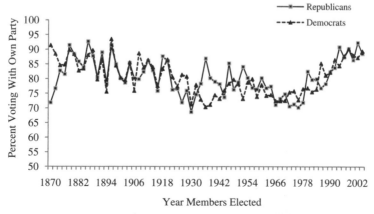

Figure 1.7   Average Party Unity Score by Party, Senate, 1870–2006.

2007, 7). Again, partisanship was coming to mean more in American politics. How this has affected the role of the president is discussed in chapter 14.

Finally, all these changes have had significant effects on how we discuss public policy, the differences that parties advocate, and the consequences that follow when one party gains power. As chapter 12 indicates, there are now more battles over how to think about or discuss policy. The parties begin discussions further apart then in the past, and it matters a great deal who has power in Congress and the presidency.

The processes that have led us to this point are complicated. The chapters that follow provide considerable depth as to what has happened to create the current state of political parties in America.

Notes

1. In this case the correlation is multiplied by 100 so it can be on the same scale as the percentage of split-outcomes. For this analysis the correlation is Democratic percentages.
2. A higher score is more conservative and a lower score is more liberal.

Part II

Social Change and Party Response

Chapter 2

Social Change in America
The Context for Parties

Jeffrey M. Stonecash

The political process is a mechanism that we hope creates representation and response to the concerns of voters. Parties are central to this process. They seek to bring together groups with some commonality of interests to forge coalitions. This task is never easy for politicians because social change is ongoing in American society. That change creates new constituencies, new concerns, and new conflicts to deal with. Representatives are continually faced with a society in flux. In the late 1800s a rural small-town society was being transformed into an urban one. Farming was being steadily displaced by manufacturing and there was considerable anxiety about the impact of change on rural communities. A largely Protestant society was struggling with steady immigration of Catholics from Europe, economic inequality was high, and there were numerous conflicts between labor and management.

These conflicts continued to play out in the early 1900s and then in the 1930s the Great Depression created vastly greater unemployment and poverty and prompted conflicts about what role the national government should play in responding to those problems. Economic collapse created real problems that politicians had to cope with. Then following World War II economic inequality declined, but there was great concern about the spread of communism in other countries, which created conflicts about what size military we should fund, how much we should confront the spread of communism, and how much government should engage in pursuing suspected communists within America. In the 1950s and 1960s the civil rights movement became more forceful, followed by the women's movement advocating for more equality in the treatment of women. All of these changes generated new political divisions within the society.

Social and economic change has continued in recent decades and that has created new issues for politicians to respond to. The purpose of this chapter is to provide a brief overview for recent decades of the social and economic changes that have and are continuing to create political concerns and conflict. These changes provide the context within which politicians must operate. As a new concern emerges, politicians must decide how salient it is likely to become. Will it displace older conflicts or be added to them in some fashion? Will taking a position on a specific change create conflict with a party's existing constituency or bring it new voters? Is the change and its accompanying conflict likely to persist or is it short-term in nature? Change creates numerous dilemmas for politicians. How the parties have responded to these issues is covered in subsequent chapters.

Population Growth and Its Location

In 1950 the population of the United States was 150,528,000. Of that total, 51.5 percent was in the Northeast and the remainder of the North. Most of the manufacturing and wealth of the society were in those two regions. The South was the poorest region of the nation. Since then there have been remarkable changes that are reshaping America. The population has been moving to the South and the West and those regions are experiencing the major growth in population. Table 2.1 indicates just how much difference in population growth there has been since 1950.

The population in the Northeast has grown the least, increasing 38.2 percent since 1950. The major increases have been in the South (141.9%) and the West (149.3%). These shifts have had enormous impact. States in the Northeast have a history of higher state and local taxes and services. Now they are experiencing less population growth to help sustain those taxes and services and are seeking help for various services. The regions of the South and West are also experiencing pressures, but largely from population growth. There is greater pressure to raise taxes to provide for schools, water systems, and roads and bridges. In response to these very different changes, the congressional representatives of each region seek federal aid to help reduce the state and local taxes that otherwise would have to be imposed to support services.

Table 2.1 Population Change by Region, 1950–2004

| Region[1] | Total Population (In thousands) | | | Average % |
	1950	2004	% increase	State Increase
Northeast	39,478	54,572	38.2	58.7
Remaining North	38,049	59,337	55.9	69.7
South	37,587	90,911	141.9	134.4
West	35,414	88,284	149.3	205.7

1 The regions are defined as follows. Northeast consists of Connecticut, Maine, Massachusetts, New Hampshire, New Jersey, New York, Pennsylvania, Rhode Island, and Vermont. North consists of Delaware, Illinois, Indiana, Maryland, Michigan, Minnesota, Ohio, West Virginia, and Wisconsin. South consists of Alabama, Florida, Georgia, Kentucky, Louisiana, Mississippi, North Carolina, South Carolina, Tennessee, Texas, and Virginia. West consists of Alaska, Arizona, Arkansas, California, Colorado, Hawaii, Idaho, Iowa, Kansas, Missouri, Montana, Nebraska, Nevada, New Mexico, North Dakota, Oklahoma, Oregon, South Dakota, Utah, Washington, and Wyoming.

Table 2.2   Percentage of U.S. Population in Urban, Suburban, or Rural Areas

Year	Area		
	Urban	Suburban	Rural
1950	32.8	23.3	43.9
1960	32.3	30.6	37.0
1970	31.4	37.2	31.4
1980	30.0	44.8	25.2
1990	31.6	48.2	20.2
1998	30.2	49.9	19.9
Change	−2.6	26.6	−24.0

There are other population shifts that have significant political implications. In the late 1800s and early 1900s the major change involved the shift from a rural to an urban society. That, combined with immigration into cities, created a base that Democrats eventually won over in the 1930s and which gave them a national majority and the New Deal coalition. In the decades since the 1950s there has been an equally important shift with the growth of suburbs. Table 2.2 indicates the shifts that have occurred over time. Those data stop with 1998 because that was the final year when the Census Bureau used this classification.

In 1950, 56.1 percent of Americans lived in urban or suburban areas, with the remainder living in rural areas. Since then there has been a steady decline in the percentage of the population living in rural areas and a significant increase in the percentage living in suburbs. These population shifts have created new political demands. Rural areas, faced with declining population and a declining or stagnant tax base, want aid to help support existing services. Cities, and particularly those in the North and Midwest, are facing declining populations, and want federal aid to help them support services and social programs. Those in the suburbs are more likely to see themselves as individualists, somewhat successful, and less likely to see the need for national social programs (McGirr 2001). They are much more likely to support local services, but oppose federal programs, and be Republican (Lang, Sanchez, and Berube 2008, 30–32). These differences are then represented by Members of Congress and become the source of major conflicts over policy priorities in Congress.

As the population moves from region to region and within metropolitan areas, there has also been considerable geographical "sorting" or clustering of the population. Using counties as the basis for analyses, over the period since the late 1980s there has been an increase in the percentage of counties with a landslide in presidential elections, or counties where one candidate wins by more than 20 percentage points. Apparently people tend to move to places where those of like minds live. That trend is creating political environments where people talk to those with similar views, reinforcing their perceptions of the world. These moves are creating a basis for greater polarization, with people running into fewer people who hold opposing views (Bishop and Cushing 2008).

Economic Changes

As populations move there are also changes in the types of jobs they hold. Perhaps the most significant change has been in manufacturing activity, which provides jobs with good income levels for workers, which in turn are a source of state and local taxes, and contribute to the general prosperity of areas. Table 2.3 summarizes the changes in this regard. In 1950 the Northeast and remaining Northern states had about one third of its labor force in manufacturing, with the other two regions between 16 and 18 percent. Since then manufacturing has dropped in all regions, but the greatest declines have been in the Northeast and remaining North. The Northeast has declined from 35.0 to 9.1 percent. The remainder of the North declined from 33.5 to 13.4 percent. The declines elsewhere have been less.

These changes have great significance for states and Members of Congress. The loss of jobs means residents either move elsewhere in search of jobs or have less income. Members representing districts and states in the Northeast and remaining North are more concerned about the competition from foreign factories, and they become advocates of protectionist legislation, while areas in the sunbelt that have fewer factories to protect are more supportive of free trade. Northern states have generally had more generous welfare programs and Members of Congress who are representing those states want more money to help support these programs. Southern states have more growth occurring, have traditionally provided less welfare, and are less supportive of federal aid for these programs (Mellow 2008; Karol 2009). The consequence of these regional shifts is ideological divisions over the role government should play and how much individualism should be emphasized.

The decline of manufacturing has also affected union membership, as shown in Table 2.4. Unions are important because they affect the existence

Table 2.3   Manufacturing Employment by Region, 1950–2004

Region	Percent Employment in Manufacturing			Average %
	1950	2004	% Change	State Change
Northeast	35.0	9.1	−25.9	−27.1
Remaining North	33.5	13.4	−20.1	−18.3
South	18.4	9.9	−8.5	−7.3
West	16.1	9.2	−6.9	−3.2

Table 2.4   Union Membership by Region, 1964–2007

Region	Percent in Union		Average %
	1964	2007	State Change
Northeast	29.1	15.0	−14.1
Remaining North	35.6	14.3	−21.3
South	15.7	5.6	−10.1
West	25.3	11.1	−14.2

of work rules, pensions, and health care insurance programs. They also affect prevailing wage rates. They provide contributions and volunteers for political parties, with most, but not all, of these resources going to Democrats. In the mid-1960s, the Northeast and remaining North had sizable percentages of their labor force in unions. Since then there have been significant declines in union membership across all regions, which has resulted in fewer well-paying blue-collar jobs. It also means that union advocacy for better treatment of workers is less than in prior decades and that supporters of unions have fewer resources to draw upon for campaigns.

As the economy has changed there has also been a steady increase in inequality in the distribution of income since the 1970s. As Table 2.5 indicates, the major change has been that those in higher income groups have gained while those in the lower income groups have not experienced much in the way of gains. This growing difference in resources has created more atten tion to issues of access to college, health care, and pensions. The types of jobs being created and the pay they provide are changing and creating questions about whether government can play some role in stimulating job growth. The answers provided by liberals and conservatives differ a great deal, but it is clear that the context within which politicians operate is changing.

Table 2.5 Pre-Tax Average Household Income by Income Groups (2004 dollars), 1979–2004

Income quintile	1979	2004	% Change 1979–2004	Dollar Change 1979–2004
Lowest fifth	15,100	15,400	2.0	$300
Second fifth	32,700	36,300	11.0	$3,600
Middle fifth	49,000	56,200	14.7	$7,200
Fourth fifth	66,300	81,700	23.2	$15,400
Top fifth	127,100	207,200	63.0	$80,100

Source: Congressional Budget Office, Effective Federal Tax Rates, 1979 to 2004, Table 4C, December 2006. Data from: http://www.cbo.gov/publications/bysubject.cfm?cat=33

Immigration and Political Reaction

As population movement amongst native born Americans occurs, there has also been an increase in the number of immigrants. These additions to American society create political issues. Many immigrants, just as in the past, come to the United States in search of a better life: some are legal immigrants and some are undocumented. Figure 2.1 indicates the historical pattern of legal immigrants to the United States since 1900. After relatively loose immigration rules in the early part of the century, immigration restrictions were imposed in the 1920s. Then they were loosened in the 1960s and since then there has been a steady increase in legal immigration (Tichenor 2002). In addition to legal immigration there has also been considerable illegal immigration as people seek jobs. By some estimates there are now roughly 12 million illegal immigrants in the country now, with many of them coming from Latin America.

This rise in immigration has created new political issues. Some welcome immigrants as part of America's tradition of providing opportunity to those who seek it. Many businesses welcome the workers and rely on them to staff their businesses. But others are not receptive to: Many immigrants have low incomes and do not speak English. Some voters are concerned that the presence of non-English speaking immigrants means that immigrants will not assimilate and will change the character of American society. They worry that they will have to pay for social services and schools for immigrants who do not contribute much in the way of taxes.

The distribution of immigrants across the nation has surprised many and changed the politics of some states. Many immigrants have gravitated to northern urban areas and reinforced the Democratic base in large cities where there is support for liberal policies. But immigrants have also come to be a significant factor in many Sunbelt states, those stretching from California to Florida. In many of those states the population of immigrants is of sufficient size to make significant changes in the politics of the states. In other states

Figure 2.1   Legal Immigration to the United States, 1900–2006.

they are less of a presence but enough that conservative voters are reacting to them and expressing their opposition to providing social services and allowing illegal immigrants to stay. As Dunn and Junn discuss in chapter 10, the presence of immigrants creates significant divisions within American society that were not present 20 years ago.

Changing Social Behaviors

As if all these changes are not enough, the consensus about social norms that seemed to prevail prior to the 1960s changed after that decade. Beginning in the 1960s there were numerous challenges to existing norms. In a series of decisions in the early 1960s the Supreme Court banned school prayer. It then legalized abortion in 1973. Births out-of-wedlock began a steady increase and abortions increased. Sex became much more present in movies and television. Figure 2.2 provides trends for two matters that greatly trouble social conservatives, or those who believe in traditional values. One trend is for the percentage of children that are born out-of-wedlock.[1] Over time the percentage of all births occurring without the mother being married has steadily increased. To social conservatives this is not only fundamentally immoral, but it is likely to create enormous social problems later. If marriage does not follow the birth, the child will likely be raised by a single parent, who will probably have less money and be in a situation of stress. The prospects for the child diminish considerably. The other trend is abortion. Immediately after abortion was legalized in *Roe v. Wade* the rate of abortion increased and then began to gradually decline. To social conservatives (and even to a lesser degree among many who support abortion rights) this rate is unacceptable. Even the recent decline is not acceptable because to critics there are still too many abortions. The abortion issue prompts passionate reactions from both sides. To

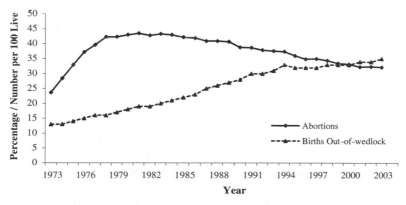

Figure 2.2   Percentage of Births Out-of-Wedlock and Abortions per 100 Live Births, 1960–2004.

opponents, abortion is murder, immoral, and a sign of significant social decay. To supporters of abortion rights it is a matter of whether women have a right to control their own bodies rather than state or federal laws controlling what happens to them.

The combination of the two trends is even more troubling. Some women, and particularly younger women, are having children without a family structure to provide for and help children. Society is likely to end up having to provide for many of these children. Other women are having abortions. Social conservatives view these trends as indicating a decline in morality and individual responsibility.

These trends are not the only ones that have agitated social conservatives. They are troubled by increases in divorce, crime, the number of people receiving welfare, the presence of sex on television and in movies, and the lack of a prominent role for religion in American society. Faced with all these trends, social conservatives have mobilized to seek changes in public policy that will do more to reinforce traditional morals.

Foreign Policy Issues

Finally, how to conduct foreign policy has become a source of division. For much of the post-World War II era, there appeared to be a bipartisan consensus about foreign policy. There were those who wanted the United States to be more aggressive militarily and those who wanted more emphasis on diplomatic negotiations to solve conflicts. Over time, however, foreign policy and whether to conduct wars have become sources of partisanship (Fordham n.d.; Kupchan and Trubowitz 2007). Many conservatives believe that America has a unique role to play in the world and also think that the nation should act unilaterally to protect its interests. In contrast, many liberals think that the United States should operate as a partner in the international community and should work through cooperative arrangements with other nations to try to resolve international conflicts. The former view emphasizes military action while the latter view emphasizes negotiation.

Those with differing views have increasingly come to be aligned with a particular party: conservatives on this issue have moved to the Republican Party and liberals have moved to the Democratic Party. The result, and particularly after 9/11, is that foreign policy has become a source of partisan divisions. In prior years, there were modest differences between Democrats and Republicans on whether and how to conduct wars (G. C. Jacobson 2005, 2007). Issues of how to handle matters like wars in Iraq and Afghanistan and how to handle a "War on Terror" are now highly divisive and partisan issues. They raise questions of what patriotism and loyalty to nation mean and what behaviors constitute manifestations of these traits. To many conservatives patriotism means support of America in foreign endeavors and no dissent. Liberals, in contrast, often argue that the highest sign of adherence to American ideals is to be willing to question decisions. Needless to say, they often are very far apart in reacting to issues involving national security.

Summary

Social change is unlikely to cease. It creates new issues that politicians struggle to respond to. Sometimes a party has to find a way to add a new issue to existing ones to maintain or expand a coalition (Karol 2009). The subsequent chapters examine the political responses to these issues and how those responses have affected partisan policy differences.

Notes

1. Source: Centers for Disease Control and Prevention, National Center for Health Statistics, National Vital Statistics System. Data for 1960–1999 are drawn from Stephanie J. Ventura and Christine A. Bachrach, "Nonmarital Childbearing in the United States, 1940–99," *National Vital Statistics Reports*, 48, no. 16 (October 18, 2000). Data for 2000–2001 are drawn from Joyce A. Martin, Brady E. Hamilton, Stephanie J. Ventura, Fay Menacker, Melissa M. Park, and Paul D. Sutton, "Births: Final Data for 2001," *National Vital Statistics Reports*, 51, no. 2 (December 18, 2002). Data for 2002–2003 are drawn from Brady E. Hamilton, Joyce A. Martin, and Paul D. Sutton, "Births: Preliminary Data for 2003," *National Vital Statistics Reports*, 53, no. 9 (November 23, 2004). Data for 2003 are preliminary.

Chapter 3

Strategic Maneuvers

Political Parties and the Pursuit of Winning Coalitions in a Constantly Changing Electoral Environment

Mark D. Brewer

Introduction

Although political parties are indeed complex and multifaceted institutions, their primary motivations, their very reasons for existence, are quite simple. In the American two-party system, political parties—at least the two major parties—have two goals that override all other considerations and shape all decisions and actions: the parties desperately want to win elections so they can exercise government power and make public policy as they see fit. These twin goals must be kept front and center at all times when considering parties in the American context.

While the goals of the parties are simple, achieving them is anything but. The American electoral environment is constantly changing, and in order to have any chance at success political parties must recognize, interpret, and respond to these changes. American society is highly dynamic, a characteristic that unceasingly shifts the playing field under the parties' feet. New groups emerge and enter the social arena while old ones decline. New issues rise to prominence and demand a place on the political agenda while former concerns fade from relevance. The economy rises and falls, evolving all the while. This causes the financial fortunes of various groups and interests in the United States to wax and wane, a process that of course immediately becomes political. Sometimes outside events occur that no one could possibly have foreseen, and these events require a political response. In American politics, a political response is inevitably a partisan response. These partisan responses, however, are always formulated amidst high levels of uncertainty and ambiguity, in a political environment whose boundaries and realities are to a certain extent unmarked and regularly shifting.

This combination of change and uncertainty has created something of a pattern in the partisan dynamic of American politics. Party leaders and activists always agree on the primary goals—win elections and exercise government power. But due to varying levels of diversity within parties—ideological differences have been most important in recent years, but over time region, class, religion, and race and ethnicity have served as important sources of intraparty division as well—parties struggle to come to agreement on how best to achieve these goals. The process of resolving these internal debates tends to look something like this:

- What is the proper plan for victory on Election Day?
- What is the appropriate strategy to implement this plan?
- What results are produced by the chosen strategy?
- What are the implications of these results?

The dynamic outlined above is usually more urgent for the minority or "out" party because they are shut out of power at that particular moment in time. But it is also in play for the majority party as even the most successful strategy (and often the most successful strategy) increases the diversity of the party's electoral coalition, setting the stage for the development of greater intraparty tensions in the future. This chapter will untangle this dynamic. We will discuss the changes the Democrats and Republicans have faced over the past sixty years, how they have responded to these changes along with the reasoning behind the responses, and demonstrate how the combination of change and partisan response has shaped the American electoral environment.

The Long Shadow of FDR

Although he has been dead now for over six decades, it is undoubtedly the case that no one individual has affected American partisan politics more over the last half of the twentieth century and the first years of the twenty-first than has Franklin Delano Roosevelt. Roosevelt's win in the 1932 presidential election did far more than end a three-plus decade period of Republican dominance in American electoral politics. That win laid the groundwork for a radical altering of the partisan coalitions in the United States, alterations that to a certain extent remain in place to this day.

Coalition construction is central in determining whether a party will meet with success or failure on Election Day, and ultimately whether the party will be able to control government and dictate policy outcomes. In their attempts to cobble together a winning coalition parties compete with one another for the votes of individuals. But they appeal to these individuals through their identification with and membership in some combination of the myriad social and demographic groups that are present in American society. As Petrocik (1981) correctly notes, American electoral politics is by and large a group-based politics. Individuals' group identities and affiliations play a large role in how they view and interpret the political world, a fact that parties have long recognized (Green, Palmquist, and Schickler 2002; Lazarsfeld, Berelson, and Gaudet 1948). Party leaders engage in the complicated and often contentious process of trying to pull together a coalition of various groups and interests that will put them over the top at the polls. Success in such an endeavor is never easy. The dynamic nature of American society makes the construction of party coalitions an uncertain and at least somewhat speculative process, and determining the correct mix of groups and devising the proper appeals to make to these groups is a tricky business.

The Democratic Party of the late 1920s and very early 1930s was the clear minority party in American politics, comprised of a dominant Southern wing and little else. They possessed a three decade long record of mostly dismal failure, but the party did have grounds for optimism as it approached the 1932 election cycle. By 1932 the United States was over two years into the Great Depression, by far the most significant economic downturn in American history. The Republican Party was in control of both the presidency and Congress when the Depression began, and the general pattern is that voters punish the party in charge when the economy goes bad. This happened to a certain degree in the 1930 congressional elections, and the Democrats had every reason to believe they could translate this success to the presidential race in 1932.

Democratic optimism extended beyond the economic suffering presided over by the GOP. The American electorate had experienced a great deal of change in the first three decades of the twentieth century. Immigration had substantially altered the demographic complexion of American society. The American electorate in 1932 was much more Irish, more Italian, more Polish, more a number of other white ethnic groups than it was in 1896. These changes also made the electorate more Catholic, and to a lesser extent more Jewish. This same influx of immigrants (and their progeny) combined with a massive internal migration from the farm to the city to make America a much more urban nation in 1932 than it had been in 1896. The United States became a majority urban society for the first time according to the 1920 Census, and the political clout of urban populations was clearly on the rise during the 1920s. Many of those moving to the cities were taking jobs in the expanding industrial sector of the American economy, and the American economy was rapidly transforming from agrarian to industrial. A growing number of these industrial workers were at least attempting to form organized labor groups, although they routinely met with stiff resistance from both business ownership and management and the Republican-controlled federal government. Each of these developments contributed to a society in flux. Some of the basic markers of American society—ethnic, religious, community type, economic—were undergoing dramatic change in the 1920s.

These changes provided the Democratic Party with opportunities for political gain, and the chance to escape minority status. The groups described in the above paragraph—white ethnics, Catholics, Jews, urbanites, organized labor—were groups that were at best ignored and at worst treated with hostility by the majority Republican Party. These groups were open to appeals from the Democrats, if only the party decided to make such appeals. After bitterly debating this issue internally for most of the 1920s, the Democrats finally made up their mind when they gave their 1928 presidential nomination to New York Governor Al Smith (Burner 1968; Ware 2006). The selection of Smith—grandson of immigrants, New York City-born, family roots and personal experience in the working class, Roman Catholic—signified that the party was indeed going to go after the votes of these newly emerging groups. While Smith lost quite badly in 1928, he did much better than previous Democratic candidates in the urban areas of the Northeast and Midwest, exactly the areas where there were large concentrations of ethnic, non-Protestant, industrial workers (Clubb and Allen 1969; Lubell 1956; Sundquist 1983).

Democratic leaders in general and Franklin Roosevelt in particular hoped to build on Smith's success and finally craft a winning electoral coalition, one that preferably had some staying power. Roosevelt saw the potential in Smith's 1928 defeat. He mapped out strategies to appeal to the urban working class, to the Catholic and Jewish ethnics. At the same time, Roosevelt made sure to cultivate the Southern wing of the party. The South, of course, had been strongly Democratic since the end of Reconstruction, but some southern Democrats had abandoned the party in 1928, due in large part to Smith's Catholicism. FDR, himself safely Protestant, wanted to make sure the Democrats' Southern base stayed in the fold.

Roosevelt won the 1932 Democratic presidential election, and the Democrats expanded their majority in the House and regained control of the Senate. FDR and the rest of his party repeated, even expanded this success in the 1936 election cycle, and it is in the 1936 results that one can see the full flowering of the famous New Deal Coalition. Roosevelt's win in 1936 made it clear that he and his fellow Democrats had been able to substantially transform the composition of the party. The Democrats had taken their traditional Southern base and added enough other elements to it to make themselves the majority party in American politics, and to do so by a comfortable margin. In the course of two presidential election cycles—three if one gives Smith the credit he is likely due—Roosevelt and his fellow party leaders transformed the Democratic Party from a minority, regionally based institution to a dominant majority party rooted in nationwide support among the economically disadvantaged and underprivileged (Allswang 1979; Leuchtenburg 1963; Schlesinger 1960; Sundquist 1983). To achieve their goals of winning elections and exercising government power, FDR and the Democrats decided to try to add the votes of Northern working class urban ethnics to their Southern base, and successfully did so through a series of ethnoreligious and policy appeals (Social Security, public works programs, prolabor legislation, etc.). The successful execution of these plans essentially guaranteed the Democrats electoral dominance for at least a generation (Milkis 1993; Moley 1979; Shefter 1994; Ware 2006). But this success also increased diversity within the Democratic Party, a development that gradually caused intraparty tensions to rise and eventually provided the Republicans with an opportunity to mount a comeback.

Republican Efforts to Escape Minority Status: The GOP in the 1950s and 1960s

As the Republican Party surveyed the electoral landscape in the aftermath of the 1948 election cycle they had to have been quite discouraged. The party lost its fifth straight presidential election and also gave back control of Congress after holding it for only two years. Republican problems during this time went beyond the ballot box, as the party suffered intense internal divisions. A moderate, internationalist faction centered in the Northeast consistently battled a conservative, isolationist wing with its strength in the Midwest for control of the party (Rae 1989). In recent years the moderate faction had won the intraparty battles (Wendell Willkie, the party's 1940 presidential nominee, and Thomas Dewey, the GOP nominee in both 1944 and 1948, belonged to the moderate Northeast wing of the party) but badly lost the interparty wars. This served as a double source of irritation to conservatives, who believed the only way to defeat the Democrats and break up the New Deal Coalition was to move the party clearly to the right.

The conservative faction of the GOP had a plan to return the party to victory on Election Day, but they could not get the rest of the party to go along. One of the primary reasons for this was some evidence that the Republicans' situation in the early 1950s was not as desperate as it may have seemed at first blush. While there was no doubt that FDR and the Democrats had built a formidable coalition with the support of the working class white ethnics of the urban areas in the Northeast and Midwest (as well as blacks in these regions), there was also no doubt that the real key to the Democrats' success, what enabled them to win presidential elections and even more so to obtain congressional majorities, was the party's overwhelming dominance in the South. In the other regions of the country Republicans were almost on par with the Democrats in terms of votes (Brewer and Stonecash 2009; Ware 2006). The plan for GOP success then, or at least one possible plan, was to improve the party's performance in the South.

Table 3.1 demonstrates both the Democratic advantage in the South as it existed in 1952 but also the potential for Republican inroads in the region. The top row of the table presents the breakdown of party affiliation first for the nation as a whole, and then for the non-South and the South separately. The Democrats held an impressive edge in party identification nationwide, but their advantage in the South was overwhelming, and contributed a great deal to the party's overall lead. But when one turns to the presidential vote in 1952—the next row in the table—the Republicans appear to be in much better shape, not only nationwide and in the non-South, but in the South as well. Dwight Eisenhower was the Republican candidate in 1952 (once again the choice of the moderate faction), and while there is little doubt that his own immense personal popularity helped him and his fellow Republicans in 1952, it was also difficult to write off the GOP's improved performance—especially in the South—as an Eisenhower-only phenomenon.

Table 3.1 1952 Party Identification and Presidential Vote for Nation, Non-South, and South

Party Identification

Nation		Non-South		South	
Democrat	Republican	Democrat	Republican	Democrat	Republican
57	34	51	40	75	14

Presidential Vote

Nation		Non-South		South	
Democrat	Republican	Democrat	Republican	Democrat	Republican
44	55	43	56	52	48

Sources: Party identification data from the ANES Cumulative Datafile, 1948–2004. Presidential vote data from Rusk (2001).
Note: South defined as the eleven states of the Confederacy.

While the potential for Republican gains in the South was real, and clear to many party leaders, the party as a whole was somewhat divided on how best to pursue the opportunity the South presented. Some Republican leaders, primarily within the party's moderate faction, believed the proper course of action was to continue to present the party as a somewhat but not dramatically more conservative option to the Democrats. Under this plan the Republicans would not threaten the basic changes brought about by the New Deal, but rather would promise to run the programs more efficiently and on a smaller scale. They would reduce taxes on the more affluent and would scale back some of the gains made by organized labor. These latter two points could be seen as appealing to at least some white Southerners, as the region had a long history of antiunion bias and was beginning to develop economically, as will be discussed below. Conservative Republicans, on the other hand, wanted to take a much harder line against what they saw as the excesses of the New Deal, and also against what they viewed as the emerging racial liberalism of the Democrats under the leadership of Harry Truman. Racial conservatism would gain the party votes in the South, conservatives argued, while a message of overall conservatism would attract New Deal opponents across the nation.

Eisenhower's victories in 1952 and 1956 seemed to vindicate the views of the moderate faction of the GOP. However, after Republican presidential nominee Richard Nixon—whose selection had been engineered by the party's moderates—lost the 1960 election and the party failed to register any significant improvement in that year's congressional elections, conservatives within the party were emboldened to make their case for changing the direction of the party in a much more aggressive fashion. Conservatives worked hard to stoke resentment to what they saw as the threatening growth in the scope and power of the federal government that was a result of the New Deal. The long-simmering issue of race also reached a rolling boil in the 1960s, and as it did so it became connected to arguments over the proper role of the federal government. Following Nixon's defeat conservative elements within the party began organizing from the ground up, hoping to finally gain the upper hand in the party's internal affairs. Within a relatively short period of time they were able to do just that, and in 1964 the conservative faction of the Republican Party was finally able to seize control of the party. They produced a very conservative platform at their convention that year, and more important, in Arizona Senator Barry Goldwater they nominated an unambiguous, dyed in the wool, no excuses conservative for president. After a long time on the outside looking in, the conservative faction was in charge of the Republican Party and installed a pull-no-punches spokesman in Goldwater to make their arguments and express their views. Seemingly overnight the Republican Party moved significantly to the right across the board.

Goldwater is perhaps most known for conservative stands on states' rights and civil rights issues, but his conservatism extended far beyond these areas. Goldwater was a fierce detractor of the New Deal on any and all fronts. He revived the strong fiscal conservatism that the Republican Party had last championed in the early 1930s, and attacked the welfare state at the federal level. He was opposed to government involvement in the economy, and was no friend of organized labor. He argued for a return to what he saw as the rugged individualism of America's past, and called for an end to the intrusion of the federal government into the affairs of the states and of individuals. He was also, as Leege and his colleagues (2002) note, the first Republican presidential candidate to emphasize culturally conservative themes, although not nearly to the degree we see among contemporary GOP politicians. Goldwater was the epitome of the views of the 1940s and 1950s Republican conservatives, with one crucial difference. Where the conservatives of those years were isolationist on American foreign policy, Goldwater was aggressively interventionist. He was a strong advocate for the use of American power in the global arena, even going so far as to say that he would use nuclear weapons in the pursuit of American interests. This was an important change, one that would have lasting influence on partisan conflict in the United States.

Goldwater of course lost badly in 1964, with Lyndon Johnson defeating him in one of the largest landslides in American history. But Goldwater did win five states in the South (plus his home state of Arizona), and he was a clear messenger for conservative positions. His candidacy was the critical juncture both for conservatives directing the Republican Party and for the growth of the GOP in the South (Black and Black 2002; Carmines and Stimson 1989; Rae 1989; Stimson 2004; Sundquist 1983). Richard Nixon learned a great deal from Goldwater's 1964 campaign and used the themes of racial conservatism, states' rights, and opposition to an activist federal government, albeit carefully, to win the presidency in 1968 (Perlstein 2008; Phillips 1969; Rae 1989). Since Goldwater, no Republican with the exception of Gerald Ford in 1976 has been able to win the party's presidential nomination without at least giving a good deal of lip service and exhibiting a high level of deference to conservative themes and viewpoints. In 1964 the Republican Party decided that the key to the party's success lay in the South, and that the way to build support in the South was to present a clear and firm conservative choice. The strategy worked, as the GOP dramatically increased its success in the South, and also attracted conservative voters from other parts of the United States. Once again, however, these successes also produced implications that the Republicans would have to struggle with down the line.

The Democrats from 1952 to 1972: Trying to Keep the New Deal Coalition Together

Five presidential election victories in a row, combined with control of Congress by large margins for almost the entirety of that same period, would seem to indicate that a political party is in pretty good electoral shape. But that was not the case for the Democrats in 1948. The party's long running success and current unified control of the federal government obscured some serious tensions mounting within the party. Since the end of Reconstruction, the South had been two things: strongly Democratic in its politics and extremely different socially from the rest of the United States (Woodward 1951). Race, of course, was the primary source of Southern difference, but economics played a role here as well. The South had traditionally been the poorest region of the country, and the South of the 1940s was still an agrarian, economic backwater in a nation that was rapidly becoming the industrial giant of the world economy. Southern poverty predisposed the region to favor the redistributionist economic policies of the New Deal, and as long as party leaders left Southern Democrats alone to deal with the issue of race as they saw fit, white Southerners could be counted on to remain safely in the Democrat fold.

By the late 1940s and early 1950s things began to change on both the economic and racial fronts. The South began to develop economically. As this development progressed, the incomes of some native Southerners rose at the same time growing numbers of non-Southerners with managerial and professional occupations began migrating into the region. This provided a class-based decline for Democratic support in the region (Lublin 2004; Rae 1989; Shafer and Johnston 2006). But by far the bigger threat to Democratic hegemony in the South came from the changes related to race. Blacks outside of the South were among the groups brought into the Democratic coalition by FDR and the New Deal. The number of non-Southern African Americans continued to grow throughout the New Deal era (Judd and Swanstrom 2008), and by the late 1940s they were a significant element of the Democratic coalition. As the number of Democrats in Congress with sizable black constituencies rose and the influence of blacks with the party grew, it became increasingly difficult for the Democrats to finesse the issue of race internally. Northern liberals within the party—whose numbers grew each year—pushed harder and harder for the party to adopt positions and work for policies that were favorable for civil rights for black Americans. White Southerners—who occupied many key positions of power within the party—fought tooth and nail against such positions and policies. The internal dispute over race bubbled within the Democratic Party in the 1940s, and came to a head during the Truman administration. Truman lacked FDR's caution on the issue of race, and some of his actions as president—such as establishing a presidential commission on civil rights, becoming the first president to ever address the NAACP, and perhaps most important, desegregating the U.S. military by executive order—produced the first meaningful crack in the New Deal coalition (Carmines and Stimson 1989; Ladd with Hadley 1975; Leuchtenburg 2005; Lubell 1956; Rae 1992). A number of white Southerners abandoned the Democratic Party, at least at the presidential level, and instead supported the States' Rights/Dixiecrat campaign of South Carolina Governor Strom Thurmond, and many of them never came back (Frederickson 2001).

At the same time that the Democrats' support was declining in the South, more and more Northern liberals were moving into Democratic ranks, changing the internal makeup of the party, and pushing the party further to the left on race and other issues as well. By the 1960s it was clear that the non-Southern wing, concentrated in the major urban areas of the Northeast and Midwest, was the dominant force within the Democratic Party (Brewer and Stonecash, 2009). The increasing power of liberals within the party can in many ways be seen in both the personal transformation of and the policies pursued by the most influential Democratic public official during that decade, Lyndon Johnson. Johnson began his political career in the House as a typical New Deal Southern Democrat; populist on economic issues but conservative on race. This continued in LBJ's early years in the Senate. But by the late 1950s Johnson took note of the increasing Northern, liberal tint of the party and began to shift his positions on race. By the time he became president in the wake of Kennedy's assassination in 1963 Johnson was convinced that the future of the Democratic Party was outside of the South, and that the Democratic Party of the future would be a liberal one (Leuchtenburg 2005).

Having made this determination, LBJ committed the party to an aggressive liberal agenda dealing with a host of race and class issues, and Democratic liberals in Congress delivered the policies Johnson sought. The Civil Rights Act of 1964, the Voting Rights Act of 1965, Medicare and Medicaid, expansion of Food Stamps, Aid to Families with Dependent Children (AFDC), and other programs too numerous to list here were in many ways the height of the liberal ascendancy in the Democratic Party, and in the middle of 1965 many Democratic leaders believed that they had successfully interpreted and responded to changes in American society. By doing so they believed they had ensured that they would retain their majority status in the American political universe. By shifting their core message from what John Gerring (1998) labeled their "populist" theme, focused on trying to end special economic privilege, to a core message that was "universalist," aimed at bringing all previously discriminated against and oppressed groups into equal citizenship, the Democrats thought they had successfully adapted their New Deal coalition to address the social, economic, and political changes that had taken place since the end of World War II.

Unfortunately for them, the Democrats were wrong. Before 1965 was even over the backlash against LBJ and liberal Democrats in Congress had begun. The party lost seats in both houses of Congress in 1966, and Johnson's approval ratings were declining. Riots became a regular feature in minority neighborhoods in seemingly every major American city, and as images of rioting African Americans replaced those of peaceful black civil rights demonstrators being beaten by white police officers public opinion on racial issues began to shift. Increasing numbers of Americans began to question the dramatic expansion of the welfare state in particular, and growth in the activism and intrusiveness of the federal government in general. Rising public unhappiness with the rapidly worsening quagmire that was Vietnam also hurt Johnson and his fellow Democrats. By 1967 thousands of people all across America were turning out to hear Alabama Governor George Wallace rail against meddlesome federal judges and bureaucrats, lazy welfare recipients, and know-it-all academic and government elites who in his view were trying to tell Americans what they should think and how they should act (Carter 1995). The same was true of Richard Nixon, although he was always much more careful and opaque in his language (Perlstein 2008). By Election Day in 1968, millions of Americans had voted for Wallace or Nixon over Democratic nominee Hubert Humphrey, who had tried unsuccessfully to hold the older elements of the Democratic coalition while at the same time appealing to the newer, more liberal groups now demanding attention from the party. Many white Southerners and also a good many white ethnics abandoned the Democrats in 1968, and more would do so in the future (Baer 2000; Petrocik 1981). In the aftermath of the 1968 election cycle, the Democrats were a party in turmoil. Their plan for maintaining their majority status—increase their support outside of the South by moving to the left on racial and social issues—did not work as envisioned, and the party paid the price for its miscalculation.

The Republicans Take Advantage: 1968 and Beyond

Richard Nixon and the Republicans won the 1968 presidential election, but the margin of victory was razor thin. Nixon received 43.4 % of the popular vote, Humphrey 42.7%, and Wallace 13.8%. Nixon's edge was larger in the Electoral College with 301 electoral votes compared to 191 for Humphrey and 46 for Wallace, but even these figures are indicative of a close contest. Given the fact that Humphrey was the sitting vice president in an incredibly unpopular Democratic administration, Nixon and other Republican leaders realized that the 1968 presidential results did not ensure or necessarily even suggest future success for the party. The GOP still had significant work to do if it wanted to take advantage of the opportunity to finally move past the Democrats and become that nation's new majority party. What was the appropriate plan, and what was the best strategy to successfully carry out that plan?

Richard Nixon could be accused of many things, but no one could ever claim that he was a stupid or unobservant politician. He watched carefully as the conservative wing of the party secured Goldwater the 1964 presidential election, and paid even greater attention to Goldwater's success in the South. Nixon began carefully courting Southern and conservative Republican leaders, going to great lengths to curry favor with them while at the same time being careful not to alienate the more moderate, Northeastern wing of the party. After winning the 1968 presidential election, Nixon carefully studied both his campaign and that of Wallace. Nixon believed that if he could attract Wallace's supporters without losing any of his own, his reelection would be guaranteed. Nixon was right. In his 1972 reelection Nixon drew heavy support from the Southern whites and blue collar ethnics who Wallace appealed to in 1968, but also kept the party's moderates strongly behind him (Carter 1996; Perlstein 2008). Republican leaders realized that a base of Nixon and Wallace supporters would leave the party well positioned for future success. To that point Southern whites and blue collar ethnics had really only abandoned the Democratic Party at the presidential level, for the most part remaining loyal to Democratic candidates in congressional and state elections. But Republican leaders had some hope that this would change. The presidential vote is generally a leading indicator of partisan change in the electorate, followed at some later point by shifts in vote patterns for other offices and eventually party identification.

If Nixon's impressive 1972 victory furthered Republican leaders' hopes of once again becoming America's clear majority party, the Watergate scandal and Nixon's resignation in 1974 quickly dampened such optimism. The public's anger at Nixon spread to other Republican politicians and really to the party in general. The party lost 46 seats in the House and four in the Senate in the 1974 elections and Nixon's replacement as president, Gerald Ford, lost the 1976 presidential election to the relatively unknown Democratic nominee, Georgia Governor Jimmy Carter. The party seemed to be struggling once again, but in reality the negativity surrounding Nixon and Watergate proved to be a remarkably short-term obstacle to the party in its pursuit of electoral success. Ford's loss to Carter (50% to 48% in the popular vote) was not nearly as large as it could have been given the taint of Nixon and Ford's pardon of the disgraced president. Carter's relatively weak performance as president also benefitted the Republicans, and as Carter's term wore on GOP leaders had reason to become increasingly optimistic about their chances in the 1980 election cycle.

A weak incumbent of the opposing party is always helpful to a party trying to retake the presidency (or any other office), but the Republicans had far more going for them in 1980 than a Democratic Party led by Jimmy Carter. America had seen rapid and large scale social change on a number of fronts since the 1960s, and an increasing number of Americans were uncomfortable with at least some elements of this change. In addition to the race-related changes discussed previously, a number of other dramatic shifts had taken place in American society, many of them having to do with cultural or moral issues. Religion was largely removed from public schools, at the same time sex education was brought in. The national norms on sexuality were radically reoriented as the discussion and presentation of sex in the popular media increased dramatically and homosexuals ratcheted up their efforts to obtain equal rights. The American family underwent large changes as the number of women working outside of the home rose, out-of-wedlock births increased, and divorces skyrocketed. Perhaps most important, the Supreme Court's decision in *Roe v. Wade* (1973) legalized abortion nationwide, a development that ignited the most explosive cultural debate of the late twentieth century. By the mid-1970s socially conservative Americans—a relatively large percentage of the citizenry—had plenty of reasons to be concerned about the direction of American society (Brewer and Stonecash 2007). This provided the Republicans with an incredible opportunity for political gain, and the party was primed and ready to take advantage.

At first there were not clear differences between the parties on cultural issues. As is often the case when a new issue or set of issues first emerges on the public agenda, the parties were unsure of where the public stood on the various cultural questions entering the public debate, and were therefore cautious and unsure of where exactly they should stand on these same issues. But over time public opinion in these issues began to crystallize, and the parties were able to get a sense of where various groups in American society—groups inside and outside of their electoral bases stood on cultural issues. As this happened the parties began to differentiate themselves on these new social concerns, and they began to incorporate cultural issues into their strategic thinking. Gradually the Democrats moved in a liberal direction on questions of culture, while the Republicans moved in a conservative direction. This decision on the part of the GOP to move right would prove to be one of the most beneficial the party ever made.

Many social conservatives were then and are still today white evangelical Protestants, a group that has historically been heavily concentrated in the South. As previously discussed, by the 1970s many Southern whites were already questioning their traditional Democratic loyalties for class or racial reasons. The entrance of cultural issues into the public dialogue, and the Republican Party's move to conservative positions on these cultural issues, gave many Southern whites one more reason to abandon the Democratic Party and embrace the GOP. Some members of the Republicans' conservative wing such as Phyllis Schafly, Richard Viguerie, and Paul Weyrich—all of whom had worked on the 1964 Goldwater campaign—reached out to prominent and influential evangelical leaders such as Jerry Falwell, Timothy LaHaye, and Pat Robertson in the effort to bring them into the Republican fold. These efforts were ultimately successful and this new partnership worked at the grassroots level to bring cultural conservatives—most prominently white evangelicals but also other groups such as traditionalist Catholics and more conservative mainline Protestants—into the Republican coalition and get them active in electoral politics (Berlet and Lyons 2000).

Ronald Reagan, the GOP's 1980 presidential candidate, proved especially appealing to social conservatives with his support for returning prayer to public schools, and his opposition to the Equal Rights Amendment and abortion. Indeed, Reagan's 1980 victory was due at least in part to the support of social conservatives, establishing a relationship that still exists today. Social conservatives—voters who oppose abortion, favor prayer in public schools, are uneasy with questions surrounding homosexuality, attend religious services regularly, and place a good deal of importance on religion in their day-to-day lives—have become a critical element in the Republican Party coalition since 1980 (Brewer and Stonecash 2007; Layman 2001; Leege et al. 2002; Rae 1992). Many political observers would go even further, and argue that social conservatives are the single most important component of the current Republican Party, and such a claim would be difficult to dispute. Contemporary Republicans universally venerate Reagan, and they do so with good reason. Reagan's win in 1980 was also the ultimate victory of the conservative wing of the Republican Party. Never again would the moderate wing mount a challenge for internal supremacy. Reagan was able to unite conservatives of all stripes—economic, racial, cultural, and foreign policy (if one considers an aggressive foreign policy conservative)—behind one candidate, and more important bring these various types of conservatives securely into the Republican Party. All of the successes the Republicans have had since 1980—Reagan's landslide reelection in 1984, George H.W. Bush's election in 1988, the Newt Gingrich-led Republican Revolution of 1994 that allowed the GOP to take control of both houses of Congress for the first time in over four decades, and George W. Bush's election in 2000 and reelection in 2004—would have been unthinkable and unattainable without the overwhelming support the party has received from conservative voters (Abramowitz and Saunders 1998; Saunders and Abramowitz 2004).

The Democratic Muddle: 1972–?

The Democrats followed their very close defeat in the 1968 presidential election with a loss of epic proportions in 1972 as the very liberal George McGovern was steamrolled by Nixon on Election Day. This defeat caused many Democrats to ask a very simple question: What did the party need to do in order to win elections? Coming up with a correct answer was anything but straightforward. Part of the problem was that the question itself was at least somewhat misleading. Democrats in Congress in the 1970s and 1980s were doing just fine at winning elections. The party controlled the House for the entirety of these two decades, usually by large margins. The same was true for the Senate in the 1970s, and even when the Republicans gained control of the Senate from 1981 to 1987 their margins over the Democrats were slim. So at least until 1994, the more appropriate question for Democratic leaders was what did the party need to do to win presidential elections? Watergate put off the need for serious thought on this matter in the mid-1970s, and Carter's win in 1976 indicated to some that the party could achieve a workable balance between older New Deal economic liberals and the racial and cultural liberals that rose to prominence in the party in the 1960s and 1970s. Carter did well in the urban areas of the Northeast and he also carried every Southern state with the exception of Virginia. But the 1976 presidential election was an anomaly, due in large part to Watergate and to a lesser extent incorrect perceptions of Carter due to his Southern roots. The 1976 results offered virtually nothing in terms of predicting the actual future directions of either party.

Following Carter's failed reelection attempt in 1980, the Democrats continued to drift, lacking much of anything in terms of direction. It was clear that the national party was liberal across the board and becoming more so all the time, but the Democrats still had a good many Southern conservatives within their congressional ranks. These southern congressional Democrats often ran their campaigns in a very different fashion from the party as a whole conducted its presidential campaigns, and they usually won. Meanwhile, the party as whole spent the 1980s offering liberal policy positions and nominating liberal politicians as their presidential candidates—Walter Mondale in 1984 and Michael Dukakis in 1988—and watched as their policies were seemingly rejected by voters and their presidential candidates were badly beaten on Election Day. The party kept offering liberal platforms and candidates, and a majority of Americans kept rejecting them.

By the late 1980s it was clear to some Democrats that the direction of the party had to change. A number of Democratic politicians came together to form the Democratic Leadership Council (DLC), a group dedicated to reining in—but not necessarily abandoning—the emphasis the party had been placing on racial and cultural issues in favor of a return to a traditional New Deal focus of using the federal government to provide economic assistance for average Americans. When Arkansas Governor Bill Clinton secured the Democratic presidential nomination in 1992, it seemed that the DLC wing of the party had won out, and when Clinton won the election, it seemed that the DLC vision was vindicated. Clinton's campaign focused heavily on economic issues, and what he would do as president to help the average person. Clinton went out of his way during the campaign to make the case that he was a new kind of Democrat, very different from some of the party's previous presidential offerings like McGovern or Mondale (Baer 2002). Clinton's reelection in 1996 only seemed to confirm that the DLC's more centrist, more economic focused party was the path to electoral success in the new political world created by the massive social changes of the 1960s and early 1970s.

There were, however, some pretty big holes in such an argument. The first had to do with Clinton's win in 1992. That contest of course was a three-person race, and there was a good deal of thinking that Clinton would not have able to defeat George H. W. Bush without the third party candidacy of Ross Perot. Another problem was the Republicans' takeover of Congress in 1994, a development that virtually no one outside of Newt Gingrich saw coming. Clinton's reelection in 1996 even demonstrated the weakness of the Democratic Party to a certain extent. Clinton was a popular incumbent president, running during good economic times against a Republican opponent—Bob Dole—who was regarded by most as a very weak presidential candidate, and even then Clinton could not get a majority of the popular vote. Losses by the Democratic nominees in 2000 and 2004—Al Gore and John Kerry respectively—combined with the party's failure to take back Congress[1] indicated that the Democrats still needed to figure out the proper recipe for constructing an effective coalition and actually winning elections. Some voices within the party argued that Clinton and the DLC were correct, and that toning down cultural issues while focusing on traditional bread and butter economic concerns was the way to go. Other voices disagreed, believing that the path to electoral success was a move to even more liberal positions on all fronts—economic, racial, and cultural. The Democrats stumbled along, seemingly a party without much direction because neither side was able to carry the day. And as they stumbled, they continued to lose elections to the Republicans. The Democrats could not agree on a plan to return to majority status, much less any strategies that would assist in achieving their goal.

The Current State of Affairs

Things have of course improved for the Democrats over the past two election cycles. The party was able to regain control of both houses of Congress in 2006, and they increased their margins in both chambers as a result of the 2008 elections. Barack Obama's victory in the 2008 presidential election also improved the outlook of the party. Obama became the first Democratic president since Carter in 1976 to get a majority of the popular vote at 53%, a figure that was the highest for a Democratic presidential nominee since LBJ in 1964. His primary and general election campaigns produced millions of newly registered Democrats, resulting in an increased edge for the party over the Republicans in terms of party identification figures.

The developments outlined above are obviously all major positives for the Democratic Party. Nonetheless, one must be careful not to read too much into them at this point. Certainly Obama's victory was impressive, as was the Democrats' ability to retake Congress and subsequently increase their majorities in both houses. But why the party was able to accomplish these things is not yet clear. Are the Democratic successes a result of majority of Americans endorsing their plans for governing? Or do the 2006 and 2008 election results represent nothing more than a majority of Americans disliking what they had and thus opting for something different? George W. Bush was after all an incredibly polarizing figure, and by the end of his presidency his approval ratings had sunk to the lowest on record (Abramowitz and Stone 2006; Jacobson 2007). When the low opinion of Bush is combined with the unpopular Iraq War and the onset of the largest economic meltdown since the Great Depression, it is not much of a stretch to argue that the Democrats' successes in 2006 and 2008 were nothing more than a rejection of the status quo rather than a majority endorsement of a Democratic vision of governance. What the Democrats have right now is the chance to make meaningful changes to the American party system. Whether they are able to do so will depend on what the party does now that it is in power and how voters ultimately respond to the Democrats' actions. The Republicans too face uncertainty as a result of the 2008 elections. Were their failures simply a reaction of public disgust with Bush, or were they a more meaningful rejection by voters of the fundamental positions and policies of the parties? Both parties currently find themselves struggling to interpret change and respond in such a way that will result in electoral success.

There are a few things that we can state with much more certainty about the current state of partisan affairs in the United States. We know that partisanship in the electorate is as strong as it has been since at least the 1950s, and that the importance of party identification on vote choice has risen as well (Bartels 2000; Hetherington 2001; Stonecash 2007). It is clear that at the elite level the parties are extremely polarized in terms of where they stand on issues, and that this polarization at the very least has had an impact on voting behavior at the mass level (Brewer 2005; Brewer and Stonecash 2007; Layman and Carsey 2002a, 2002b; Sinclair 2006; Stonecash, Brewer, and Mariani 2003).

It is also the case that voters today have much clearer and more detailed images of the parties than they did twenty, thirty, or forty years ago, as Table 3.2 demonstrates. Every four years the American National Election Study (ANES) asks respondents if there is anything they like and dislike about both the Republican and Democratic Parties. Table 3.2 presents these partisan likes and dislikes grouped into seven substantive categories[2] and pooled by decade for easier interpretation. The first thing that jumps out from this table is that in recent years Americans are seeing more to like and dislike about both parties than they were in the more muddled years of the 1970s and 1980s. It is also clear that the New Deal economic cleavage is still alive and well (Brewer 2009; Green et al. 2002). Economic images remain the most prominent for both parties, with the Democrats being seen much more positively for economic reasons (because they are seen as the party of the common person) than are the Republicans (because they are seen as the party of the rich and big business). The increased ideological divide between the parties is also evident in

Table 3.2 Positive and Negative Images of the Democratic and Republican Parties by Subject Area and by Decade, 1950s–2000s

Decade	No Mention		Economic		Non-Economic Domestic		Party Philosophy		Government Management		General Party Image		People in the Party		Foreign Policy	
	Pos.	Neg.	Pos.	Neg.	Pos.	Neg.	Pos.	Neg.	Pos.	Neg.	Pos.	Neg.	Pos.	Neg.	Pos.	Neg.
Democratic Party Images																
1950s	42	56	34	6	5	3	4	8	1	5	9	9	4	7	1	7
1960s	45	56	26	4	6	5	4	11	2	3	13	12	4	4	1	6
1970s	59	64	22	6	2	1	6	12	1	4	7	7	2	4	1	3
1980s	53	62	22	7	4	2	11	12	1	4	7	7	2	3	1	3
1990s	55	57	20	7	6	4	11	15	1	5	6	8	2	2	0	1
2000s	45	56	22	5	10	6	14	15	1	4	6	9	2	3	1	2
Republican Party Images																
1950s	53	51	6	25	2	5	7	3	4	1	8	7	13	5	6	2
1960s	59	54	4	16	2	4	12	5	2	1	10	12	6	6	5	2
1970s	69	60	5	19	1	1	10	6	3	2	6	7	4	3	3	1
1980s	62	58	9	19	2	4	10	6	4	2	6	5	4	2	5	4
1990s	62	52	7	19	4	6	12	9	4	4	5	7	2	2	3	1
2000s	55	49	8	18	6	8	15	10	3	4	6	9	2	1	3	2

Note: Percentages sum across, and may not sum to 100 due to rounding. See endnote 2 for information about the make-up of the categorization scheme utilized here.

Source: American National Election Studies, respective years. First mentions only.

the images reported in Table 3.2. Beginning in the 1960s and growing steadily since then, both parties have come to be seen in more ideological terms (see the party philosophy category). This has tended to benefit the Republicans more than the Democrats, but it is clear that the public now knows which party is liberal and which party is conservative. The growing importance of racial and cultural issues in the images of the parties—represented in the noneconomic domestic category—is also evident, as to a lesser extent is the tendency of the Republicans to be seen more positively on foreign policy than the Democrats. But the primary story told by Table 3.2 is the dominant positions of class and ideological divides in the public's images of the parties. Indeed, since 1964, the number one like of the Democratic Party is because they are the party of the working class while the number one dislike of the Republicans is that they are the party of big business and the upper class. Turning the tables, the number one like of the Republican Party is the party's conservatism, while the number one dislike of the Democrats is some variation on the party's liberal nature, if one is inclined to count a dislike of George McGovern in 1972 as a reference to liberalism (Brewer and Stonecash 2009). The increased depth and clarity of party images has allowed Americans to more accurately identify the party that best fits their views and register their policy preferences on Election Day.

We can also present a relatively clear picture of each party's current electoral bases. This chapter has described how each party has responded to social, economic, and political change over the past six decades. Tables 3.3 and 3.4 present how these responses have affected each party's electoral coalition. Beginning first with the Democrats, Table 3.3 presents Democratic Party identification and presidential vote by decade for ten groups that at some point since the New Deal have been important elements of the party's base. The figures are presented separately for 2008 for the sake of comparison. The first seven groups were all components of the original New Deal coalition, while the last three have become important at some subsequent point.

Table 3.3 indicates that much of FDR's New Deal coalition has remained strongly Democratic even long after his death. Those in the bottom third of the income distribution, union households, urbanites, and Jews are still critical components of the party's base. The importance of African Americans has increased over time. Two New Deal elements have declined within the Democratic coalition. Southern whites have dropped dramatically in their support for and presence in the Democratic Party, while Roman Catholics have declined in a less steep but still important manner. Table 3.3 also presents the figures for three more recent entrants into the Democratic coalition—women, individuals with low religious salience, and Latinos. All three groups are now crucial elements of the Democratic base.

Table 3.4 presents similar figures for the Republican Party. The first four groups—those in the top third of the income distribution, non-Southern white Protestants, rural dwellers, and those employed in professional and managerial occupations—represent the Republican coalition (such as it was) during

Table 3.3 Democratic Party Identification and Presidential Vote for Key Groups by Decade, 1950s–2000s, and 2008 Separately

Decade	Bottom Income Third		Southern Whites		Union Households		Urban Dwellers		Roman Catholics		Jews		African Americans		Women		Low Church Attendance		Latinos	
	PID	PV	PID	PV	PID	PV	PID	PV	PID	PV	PID	PV	PID	PV	PID	PV	PID	PV	PID	PV
1950s	55	43/31	74	51/19	64	54/36	59	47/34	65	49/28	78	75/7	59	72/7	52	39/48	54	43/39		
1960s	58	56/31	64	45/15	67	66/32	63	64/31	68	72/32	80	88/6	75	94/13	56	54/55	56	53/37		
1970s	58	50/30	54	32/13	61	52/31	61	52/32	64	47/28	73	70/4	82	90/18	53	44/58	52	45/46		
1980s	58	55/30	48	33/14	58	55/30	61	59/34	55	47/28	69	63/4	82	90/22	53	46/60	49	43/45	61	61/6
1990s	58	63/31	42	40/15	62	59/23	62	62/32	54	52/26	80	83/4	80	93/20	54	55/59	53	56/49	63	69/7
2000s	56	58/33	36	34/15	60	62/20	69	68/37	47	50/26	79	84/5	84	90/21	52	54/59	53	55/48	54	57/6
2008	59	69	36	33	60	60			49	57	81	85	86	100	54	57	55	64	61	77

Source: Decade data from the ANES Cumulative Datafile, 1948–2004. 2008 data from the ANES 2008 Time Series Study. Note: For presidential vote, the first figure is the percentage of the group that voted Democratic for president and the second figure is the percentage of all Democratic presidential voters who possessed the characteristic in question. Urban includes data from 2000 only. The 2008 study is a preliminary release, and some data are not yet available, and party coalition percentages are not able to be determined.

Table 3.4 Republican Party Identification and Presidential Vote for Key Groups by Decade, 1950s–2000s, and 2008 Separately

Decade	Top Income Third		Non-South White Protestants		Rural Dwellers		Professional and Managerial		Southern Whites		White Men		White Evangelical Protestants		High Church Attendance		Roman Catholics		Suburban Dwellers	
	PID	PV	PID	PV	PID	PV	PID	PV	PID	PV	PID	PV	PID	PV	PID	PV	PID	PV	PID	PV
1950s	40	62/42	52	71/60	34	60/42	43	67/21	18	48/13	34	58/45	n/a	n/a	35	59/42	25	51/20	39	63/32
1960s	38	47/44	49	59/65	34	46/47	43	52/25	24	43/18	35	45/45	29	48/21	34	54/46	22	26/14	38	46/33
1970s	41	63/43	47	68/51	35	61/43	41	62/27	29	68/20	36	63/44	34	68/23	35	62/33	23	51/23	35	59/36
1980s	47	63/41	52	67/45	38	58/35	44	56/32	38	66/22	45	63/44	42	69/23	40	57/31	32	50/24	41	61/48
1990s	49	42/43	53	46/40	39	38/32	44	39/33	45	49/26	48	43/46	37	43/35	45	48/40	35	33/24	44	39/47
2000s	47	53/35	53	58/30	51	36/31	42	44/37	53	63/29	51	57/42	57	69/29	51	58/34	42	49/27	48	44/49
2008	52	59	50	56	51		52		49	67	46	58	51	71	52	62	38	43	48	

Source: Decade data from the ANES Cumulative Datafile, 1948–2004. 2008 data from the ANES 2008 Time Series Study. Note: For presidential vote, the first figure is the percentage of the group that voted Republican for president and the second figure is the percentage of all Republican presidential voters who possessed the characteristic in question. Rural and suburban contain data from 2000 only. The 2008 study is a preliminary release, and some data are not yet available, and party coalition percentages are not able to be determined.

the New Deal era. We can see that more affluent Americans have consistently been critical elements within the Republican base, and that rural dwellers and professional/managerial workers have been as well, although to a lesser and more inconsistent extent. Non-Southern white Protestants have remained relatively consistent in their GOP party identification and presidential vote, although the percentage of the Republican presidential coalition they account for has declined steeply. For the Republicans, the real story of the past sixty years is the groups that they have been able to bring into their coalition. The last six groups in Table 3.4—Southern whites, white men, white evangelical Protestants,[3] those for whom religion is highly salient, Roman Catholics, and suburbanites—have all increased their presence in and support for the Republican party over the past sixty years. The growth for the Republicans among the first four of these groups has been particularly impressive, a result due at least in part to the party's adoption of conservative positions on racial and cultural issues.

Conclusion

The central theme of this chapter is change. American society is constantly changing, and political parties must correctly interpret these changes and respond to them with changes of their own if they hope to win elections and exercise political power. Party leaders must act strategically to achieve their goals, but successfully doing so is a difficult task. For the Democrats, the struggle of the past six decades has been to try to maintain its coalition of economic have-nots while at the same time satisfying the voices of racial and cultural liberalism within the party. For the Republicans, the initial difficulty was remaking the party as a thoroughly conservative option to the increasingly liberal Democrats. Bringing fiscal, racial, social, and foreign policy conservatives together under one partisan roof was no easy task, but ultimately one that Republican leaders were able to achieve. Now the GOP has to determine if a solely conservative party is enough to win elections in a society that grows more religiously, racially, and ethnically diverse by the day. The futures of both parties are uncertain, but that is the very nature of American partisan politics. Change happens, and the parties must determine how to respond.

Notes

1. The Democrats did control the Senate for two separate periods in the 107th Congress (2001–2003), the first due to a fifty-fifty tie-in seats while Al Gore was still the vice president and the second resulting from Vermont Senator James Jeffords' switch from Republican to an independent caucusing with the Democrats.
2. The categorization scheme utilized here is somewhat different from the scheme contained in the NES data, but is relatively self-explanatory and straightforward. The "people in the party" category is made up of individuals in the party (e.g., Bill Clinton or George W. Bush), along with responses such as "They have

good leaders" and "I don't like their ticket." The "general party image" category contains responses such as "I've always been a Republican" or "I just don't like them." "Government management" is also straightforward, consisting of responses referring to efficiency, corruption, or taking care of problems (nonspecific). The "party philosophy" category is made up of ideological references (e.g., too liberal, or not conservative enough), references to the parties' views on government, and other responses that speak somehow to what the respondent thinks the party stands for or believes in, such as a party being for equality, or compassionate, or socialist. The "economic" category consists of any response mentioning a type of economic group (e.g., "They are for the common man" or "They help business") as well as specific economic policy mentions such as references to taxes or unemployment policy. "Noneconomic domestic" consists of almost all domestic policy mentions such as agriculture, civil rights, abortion, and veterans' affairs. The "foreign policy" category contains all references to relations with other nations, mentions of a general policy stance (e.g., isolationist or for a strong military), mentions of a specific policy, such as SALT II, and all mentions related to military spending. The vast majority of likes and dislikes fit quite cleanly into one category or another and the few that do not are mentioned by so few people as to be irrelevant with one significant exception. A number of respondents give likes and dislikes that the NES places in a response labeled "For government activity, believe government should take care of things, for big government, supports social programs and spending." A similar response exists for those opposed to such things (this is the current wording, in place since 1972). The wording—but not the substance—is somewhat different from 1952 to 1968). After much consideration (and waffling as well) I decided to place these responses in the "party philosophy" category. Of course a case can be made that these responses could also fit into the "economic" category. There are a relatively large number of these responses, especially in recent years, so moving them into the "economic" category would obviously change the results presented here. The full categorization scheme is available from the author on request.

3. For the 1960s to 1980s evangelical Protestant religious tradition (and Roman Catholic as well) is determined using vcf0128a in the NES Cumulative Datafile. This classification scheme is not without problems. The most significant has to do with the classification of Baptists. Prior to 1972 the NES survey instrument did not differentiate among Baptists, meaning that during this period some Baptists are misclassified in the division of Protestants into mainline and evangelical traditions. There is simply no satisfactory way to deal with this problem. For the 1990s, the revised classification scheme represented by vcf0128b is utilized. Beginning in 1998, NES officials stopped dividing Protestants into "mainline" and "evangelical" categories as they began a review and reevaluation of the construction of the religious tradition variable. This review apparently has yet to be completed, and thus the last four versions of the NES Cumulative File offer no variable differentiating Protestants by religious tradition after 1996. In an attempt to provide at least some differentiation among Protestants for 2000 and 2004, white Protestants were identified as evangelical by denomination *only*. For 2008, evangelicals were identified by denomination, and for those respondents identifying as simply Protestant or Christian, self-reported born-again status. Full classification schemes are available from the author upon request.

Chapter 4

Parties and the Media
Getting Messages to Voters

Danny Hayes

Parties must communicate messages to voters. Otherwise, they cannot maintain and mobilize their base, expand their electoral coalition, persuade swing voters, and build a long-term party image. The information and messages to which citizens are exposed affect what they think about issues, candidates, and the parties themselves. And in an era of an unceasing flow of political information, parties and candidates that are unsuccessful in communicating with and persuading the public will have little chance of winning elections and turning their proposals into policy.

Just 20 years ago, the political communication game consisted largely of developing television advertising strategies and direct mail campaigns and convincing print and broadcast reporters to deliver the messages the parties wanted the public to hear. By no means easy, the process was well understood. Not so today.

In the early years of the twenty-first century, the transformation of the media environment that has altered American society is also presenting unprecedented challenges for political parties and candidates. The number of news outlets has exploded. Audiences are gradually moving away from traditional media and toward newer venues, like 24-hour cable news channels, a sea of Web sites trading in political information, and seemingly every day a new kind of social media—YouTube, Facebook, Twitter. With the news audience increasingly fragmented, political parties must navigate a communications landscape whose contours are continually shifting.

This chapter provides an overview of the transformation of the media environment in recent decades, highlights the consequences for parties, and discusses their emerging responses. My primary argument is that the new media environment presents parties with new opportunities to communicate with their core, committed supporters. This has facilitated fundraising, the recruitment of volunteers, and mobilization. But the persuasive value of these new venues is limited because their audiences tend to be comprised largely of partisans, not independents and swing voters. To win over uncommitted voters, parties must continue to rely on traditional forms of media communication—

new media connects with partisans
To reach swing voters ~~pants~~ needs old media

television advertising and attempting to communicate to the larger public through the mass media, whose audiences continue to be large. A strategy that effectively pairs messages with the appropriate venue and audience is central to party success.

The Current Landscape: A Media Environment in Transition

As late as the early 1980s, American consumers had just a handful of choices for political news. They could subscribe to their local newspaper. They could buy a national newspaper, like the *New York Times*. They could read Time or Newsweek. They could listen to brief news summaries on the radio. They could watch their local evening news, or they could tune in to one of the broadcast networks to see Dan Rather, Tom Brokaw, and Peter Jennings report the day's political developments. At a glance, such a menu may seem ample. But compared to what the public has at its disposal today, the media fare of just a few years ago looks downright paltry.

Today, political information is available at any time of the day, from a dizzying array of outlets. No longer do Americans wait for the slap of the newspaper on the driveway or until 6:30 p.m. for a TV news update. Cable news channels blare their headlines 24 hours a day. Major news Web sites update their content nearly every minute. There is an ever-growing roll of Internet sites and blogs trading in political news and commentary. The Huffington Post, Drudge Report, and Politico, to name three, claim millions of visitors each month (Kafka 2008; Shea 2008; Sherman 2009). Consumers can access political information at home on TV, and at the office or the gym on their Blackberrys and iPhones. This is not to say that the current environment offers political news of superior quality. But political information is today more voluminous and more accessible than at any time in the history of the world.

Data from the Pew Research Center in Figure 4.1 reveal the significant changes in Americans' media habits over the last two decades. In 1993, 58 percent of Americans claimed to have read a newspaper the previous day, 44 percent listened to the radio, 42 percent said they regularly watched the national network news, and more than three-quarters (77 percent) regularly watched their local news. While the absolute levels of media exposure are inflated—Americans tell pollsters they pay more attention to the news than they actually do (Prior 2009)—the over time trends illustrate the extent to which traditional forms of news have ebbed from people's daily routines. By 2008, 34 percent of Americans reported to be newspaper readers; just 35 percent listened to the radio; network news consumption had declined to 29 percent. And local news viewership was down to a slim majority, 52 percent. In the mid-1990s the average American claimed to be a newspaper reader and national television news viewer. No longer is that true.

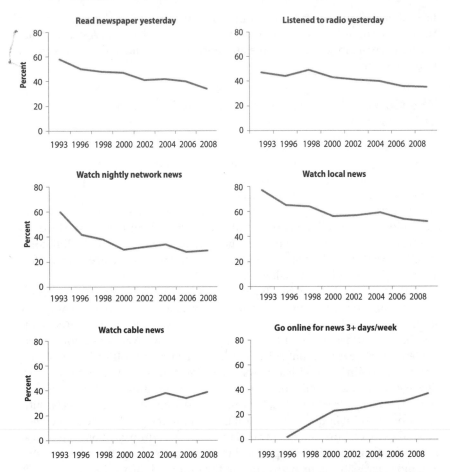

Figure 4.1   Americans' Changing News Consumption Habits. Source: Pew Research
Center Surveys, 1993–2008. Data are compiled in the Pew Research
Center report "Key News Audiences Now Blend Online and Traditional
Sources" (http://people-press.org/report/444/news-media).

Citizens have not abandoned the news, but they have turned to new outlets.
CNN, the first all-news cable network, broadcast its first newscast in 1980, and
cable expanded as a source for political news with the entrance of Fox News to
the market in the mid-1990s. The Pew data presented here track Americans'
cable news consumption only since 2002, and the major growth in market
share occurred earlier. But, the proportion of Americans, even in the last six
years, who regularly watch cable news, has risen on average about a percentage
point each year, from 33 to 39 percent. At the same time, the increase in online
news consumption has been dramatic. In 1996, when few news organizations
had a web presence, 2 percent said they went online for news at least three

days a week. By the summer of 2008, more than one third of the country—37 percent—was getting its news fix on the Internet. As the number of sources of political information has proliferated, the news audience has gravitated to them.

What are the consequences of these changes for political parties? Why does it matter where Americans get their news from? In what ways have these developments provided new opportunities for parties to communicate their ideas?

Direct and Mediated Communication with the Public

Parties find themselves confronting an ever-evolving media landscape that requires complex and diversified communication strategies. The splintering of the news audience makes it harder to reach large segments of the electorate through mass media (Tewksbury 2005). Individuals can selectively attend to information sources that cater to their political taste. And some people may opt out of political news entirely, preferring to spend their leisure time perusing a rich menu of entertainment choices (Prior 2007). As a result, parties must not only continue to use tactics of an older era—a heavy emphasis on television advertising and courting the media in the hopes of generating "free" news coverage that has a wide audience—but also tap into the technological capabilities of new media. Success in both of these endeavors is required to mount effective communications campaigns.

We can understand the challenges parties face by considering two types of communication—direct and mediated communication. Direct communication involves messages that are created by party elites, primarily party leaders and candidates, and communicated directly to citizens. Traditionally, these have been comprised of television advertising and direct mail, but technological developments have allowed parties to engage in new forms of electronic direct communication. Mediated communication consists of messages that emanate from party elites but are transmitted to voters by someone else, most importantly journalists. Despite the waning of mass media audiences, this type of communication remains critical for parties and candidates. The new media environment has also created a new venue—what I will call "allied media"—that provides another outlet for candidate and party messages.

Direct Communication

Direct communication is especially valuable because it allows parties and candidates to disseminate messages precisely in the form they want, when they want, to whom they want, and without distortion. The most important form of direct political communication is television advertising. When Barack Obama's 2008 presidential campaign wanted residents of Cleveland to see an ad about the Illinois Senator's economic plan, for instance, they didn't have to wait for the *Cleveland Plain-Dealer* to publish an article about his ideas. All they needed to do was buy air time in the Cleveland market and run an ad—many times—about his proposals to bring jobs and prosperity to the region.

Television advertising, the single biggest expense for national campaigns, has contributed to the increasing, and astonishing, cost of political campaigns. In 2008, the Obama campaign spent an estimated $230 million on television advertising (Schouten 2008), breaking the 2004 record of $188 million set by George W. Bush's presidential campaign (Rutenberg 2008). The McCain campaign and the Republican National Committee spent around $130 million on TV ads. Obama won about 70 million votes on Election Day, meaning that he spent about $3.20 per vote in advertising dollars; McCain spent about $2.15 in TV advertising for each of his 60 million votes. When House, Senate, and state campaigns are included, the total advertising budget for political campaigns in 2008 was in the billions.[1]

Television advertising strategies have become increasingly sophisticated and fine-tuned in recent years, with campaigns designing ads to target specific segments of the electorate (West 2005). Not only do campaign ads give candidates unparalleled control over their messages, but they also give them valuable flexibility in directing their messages to audiences where they will be most effective. Ads about unemployment run in Ohio, for instance, and ads focusing on immigration and the environment run in Colorado. In presidential campaigns, candidates rarely spend money advertising in uncompetitive states, allocating their resources to media markets in battleground states, where vote shifts have a bearing on Electoral College support (Shaw 2006). Consultants also design strategies to run ads on particular programs with particular audiences. Turn on the local news during campaign season, and you're likely to see a political ad. Watch MTV for an hour, and you probably won't see any ads at all. Parties and candidates hunt where the ducks are, airing messages that will be seen by potential voters. People who watch television news tend to turn out at high rates; young people—the vast majority of MTV's audience—do not, so candidates run ads during the local news, not *The Hills*.

Television advertising and direct mail have been augmented in recent years by new forms of electronic communication. Party and candidate e-mail lists, Web sites, and, more recently, social networking sites like Facebook are now used to reach out to voters. These tools have been rapidly incorporated into modern campaigns in large part because of their cost: They're cheap. Compared to television advertising, messages can be made available on a Web site or e-mail list for a pittance.

All the major presidential campaigns since 1996 have operated Web sites. Candidates for other offices rapidly followed suit. By 2004, Web sites had become "virtually mandatory" for candidates running for Congress (Druckman, Kifer, and Parkin 2007, 426), with 81 percent of U.S. House candidates and 92 percent of Senate candidates maintaining web pages (Foot and Schneider 2006), a figure that had climbed even higher by 2008. Politicians have even begun to embrace Twitter, a site where users post 140-character updates throughout the day.[2]

These methods permit politicians to efficiently communicate with their base. Most of the people who visit candidate Web sites, sign up for party e-mails, or join candidate social networking communities are supporters of the party or candidate—otherwise, they would not be inclined to seek out online communication with politicians. During campaigns, candidates and parties regularly send "campaign updates" and appeals for donations over their e-mail listserves. John McCain and Barack Obama's supporters were regularly updated on the candidates' activities during the 2008 campaign. And Obama pioneered what will probably become a common tactic of making important announcements to his supporters online—such as his choice of Joe Biden as his vice presidential running mate—before announcing them to the press and wider public.

These electronic communication efforts have assisted parties in raising money from activists and supporters and mobilizing and organizing geographically disparate supporters across the country. Howard Dean's Democratic primary campaign in 2004 was the first example of the organizing power of the web to spur the "netroots"—the online equivalent of traditional grassroots supporters—to action.[3] The research on Internet political communication is still in its nascent stages. But some work has shown that the Web has assisted campaigns in raising money, recruiting volunteers (Hindman 2005), and mobilizing supporters (e.g., Kreuger 2006). A recent study suggests that text messaging may hold promise as a way to get out the vote, with turnout being higher among young people who were sent text message reminders to vote (Dale and Strauss 2009).

The Internet and the growing availability of electronic information have also allowed parties to more narrowly target their appeals to specific voters. Both the Republican and Democratic parties, and several prominent consultants, now maintain large voter databases that include information about Americans' turnout and donation history, as well as demographic information and consumer profiles. The goal is to use this information to narrowly tailor communications campaigns with messages that parties think might appeal to specific individuals. Known as "microtargeting," the tactic allows candidates to design messages based on what surveys or consumer behavior data tell researchers those individuals are likely to be concerned about.

For example, survey data may tell a campaign that married mothers in suburban East coast cities tend to be concerned about terrorism. A campaign can then use its voter information databases to design a piece of direct mail or e-mail message about terrorism to only the people who fit this profile. Another message—on, say, gun control—can be sent to voters who fit a different demographic or political profile. Parties even greet visitors to their Web sites with different content, depending on the user's geographic location or other personal information (Howard 2006). Hillygus and Shields (2008) suggest that microtargeting helps campaigns use "wedge" issues—issues that drive a stake between a party supporter and their party's candidate—to try to peel off weakly committed voters from an opponent. The effectiveness of microtargeting remains uncertain—one of the pioneers of the method, Mark Penn, presided over Hillary Clinton's 2008 Democratic primary defeat—but there is little doubt that technological capabilities and the growing stores of information about voters at parties' disposal will make the tactic a part of the political toolbox in the years to come. Hillygus and Shields (2008, 198) write, "[A]s technological advances continue to change the political landscape at an exponential pace, we expect to see candidates attempting to find and use even more detailed information about individual voters."

The Communications Limitations of New Media

Technological developments have facilitated direct communication with the most engaged and informed segments of the electorate (e.g., Boogers and Voerman 2003; Xenos and Moy 2007), people who tend to have the most stable and well-formed political attitudes (Zaller 1992). These individuals tend to be faithful partisans, whose support for a candidate or party is largely immune to political messages, no matter the communications venue. But using the new media to reach independents and swing voters, whose loyalties candidates covet, is much harder.

Data from a Pew Research Center survey conducted in November 2008 confirm the largely partisan profile of the online political community. Table 4.1 presents the percentage of Americans who reported interacting in various ways with political campaigns on the Internet. The data are broken down by

Table 4.1 Americans' New Media Use, by Partisanship

	Dem	Lean Dem	Ind	Lean Rep	Rep
Visited Obama/Biden web site (N=1,487)	41%	40%	15%	26%	21%
Visited McCain/Palin web site (N=1,487)	16	21	13	24	31
Received e-mail from candidate or party (N=1,495)	44	39	26	35	38
Got political information from Facebook or MySpace (N=416)	29	24	2	7	25
"Friended" a candidate or party on Facebook or MySpace (N=416)	18	16	0	2	9

Note: N of respondents to Facebook/MySpace questions reflect only respondents who said they used social networking sites. Independents are defined only as respondents who said they did not lean toward one party or the other.
Source: Pew Research Center Survey, November 2008.

party identification, with categories for self-described Democrats and Republicans, independents who reported "leaning" toward one party, and independents who expressed no preference for either party.[4] This allows us to examine the relationship between partisanship and online political activity.

Two patterns are evident in the table.[5] First, partisans are far more likely to interact with the parties online than are independents. For each activity, the percentage of respondents visiting candidate Web sites, receiving e-mails, and engaging with the candidates on Facebook or MySpace is lowest among self-described independents. The fraction of partisans doing so is much higher. For example, while just 15 percent of independents visited the Obama/Biden Web site, 40 percent of Democrats (and leaners) did. Even about a quarter of Republicans and GOP leaners visited the Democrats' site. The divide is evident, though less pronounced, for McCain/Palin's site and receiving e-mail from a candidate or party. But the key point is that about 85 percent of independents avoided the candidates' Web pages, and three quarters said they never received e-mail from a campaign or party.

The Pew surveys also asked respondents whether they used a social networking site, such as Facebook or MySpace. Those who did were asked about their political activities on the pages. While 29 percent of Democrats and 25 percent of Republicans said they had gotten political information from a social networking site, a paltry 2 percent of independents said they had. And the pattern is even clearer when Facebook and MySpace users were asked about their engagement with the party and candidate pages. Not a single independent in the survey said they had "friended" a candidate or party during the campaign. The candidates' Facebook friends might be better termed family members.[6]

Second, the more partisan a voter is, the more likely he is to be exposed to party communications. In all but two cases, self-avowed partisans were more likely to say they had interacted with the parties and candidates online than those who leaned toward one of the parties. This is partly because partisans tend to be more interested in politics. Thus, they are more engaged with politics, online or otherwise. But the Internet also provides unparalleled opportunities for "selective exposure," a concept that describes people's tendency to seek out information that confirms beliefs they already hold and avoid information that challenges those attitudes (Festinger 1957; Klapper 1960).

Visits to the candidate Web sites illustrate how politically motivated Internet users can wall themselves off from information that challenges their attitudes. First, the percentage of Democrats saying they had visited the Obama/Biden site—41 percent—was about twice as large as the share of Republicans (21 percent). The reverse was true for McCain/Palin, with 31 percent of Republicans and 16 percent of Democrats reporting a visit. Just as interesting, Democratic leaners were more likely than Democrats to visit the McCain/Palin site, and Republican leaners were more likely than Republicans to visit Obama/Biden's page. On every other question, more partisans reported online activity than leaners. But not when it came to looking at their party's opponent's Web site. Some citizens may use the Internet to gather information from a variety of political perspectives. But most probably do not. Instead, the Web serves as a nearly perfect selective exposure machine.[7]

Clearly, what parties can accomplish with these emerging direct communications technology is limited. New tools help parties deliver messages to their core supporters, or to other activists and journalists (Druckman, Kifer, and Parkin 2007). But because it is nearly impossible to reach independent and swing voters through these channels, the persuasive value of new forms of direct communication is currently minimal. If more independents in the future turn to these sites for information, they may prove useful for winning over uncommitted voters. But given the well-documented tendency of undecided voters to rely primarily on information they encounter serendipitously in their daily lives—through the news and entertainment media and conversations with acquaintances, for example—the utility of new media will remain limited for reaching voters whose minds parties want to change. To communicate with these people, campaigns must continue to use television advertising as well as traditional forms of media communication, especially the news media, which possess a broad reach.

Mediated Communication

We come now to the second form of party communication, mediated communication. Its key characteristic is that parties relinquish control over the dissemination of the message—they can't dictate whether, or the manner in which, information is portrayed to public. The most important type of mediated communication involves party messages that are transmitted to the public through the news media. But the success in getting the media to disseminate messages depends on parties' ability to tap into journalistic preferences and standards of newsworthiness. Two anecdotes from the 2004 presidential campaign illustrate just how seriously parties take this process.

In the late summer, Democratic nominee John Kerry and his campaign aides undertook an unusual strategy to win the attention of the news media. Rather than adhering to the time-honored tactic of delivering the same stump speech day after day, Kerry's campaign rolled out several of its major policy initiatives—on health care, national security, and the like—in a series of "issue weeks" (Benedetto 2004; Nagourney 2004). Knowing that the media are apt to ignore oft-repeated policy statements, the campaign's hope was to guarantee at least some coverage of their chosen issue by concentrating attention on it within one or two news cycles. The strategy presumably emerged from the Kerry camp's view that special measures were needed to overcome the tendency of reporters to ignore the issues that candidates talk about (Lockhart quoted in Jamieson 2005, 140–49).

Meanwhile, the Bush campaign was just as acutely aware of the preferences and incentives of the news media, and, critically, the way they influence coverage. Mark McKinnon, George W. Bush's chief media advisor, told PBS that the campaign's choices about how to publicize issues were directly related to its understanding of what the press considers newsworthy: "We can go out in campaigns, and we'll try and strategize: 'Let's go do a press conference on our policy on the environment. Let's go to a manufacturing plant and talk about our economic plan'—zero coverage, or the back of page D17," he said. "But we do the story attacking Kerry—page 1."[8]

Campaigns view the news media as major players in communicating with the public. And with good reason: The mainstream news audience is huge. Even with the proliferation of new media outlets, more than 23 million people each night still watch one of the three network newscasts, dwarfing the prime time cable news audience. In 2008—a year of widespread newspaper closures and newsroom cuts—48 million Americans still subscribed to a daily paper.[9] And those figures do not include people who regularly read a national network's Web content or visit mainstream newspaper sites, a group that is substantial.

Moreover, in contrast to the audience for candidate Web sites and e-mail lists, the mass media audience contains large numbers of persuadable voters. Table 4.2 shows American National Election Studies (ANES) data on respondents' exposure to traditional media.[10] The survey, conducted in the fall of 2008, asked how many days in the previous week respondents watched national network news, afternoon/evening local news, read a newspaper, and listened to news on the radio. To simplify things, I present the percentage of respondents who reported at least three days per week of exposure, which strikes me as a reasonable indicator of habitual viewing.[11] The data are broken down by level of partisanship, using the traditional seven-point party identification scale. Unlike the Pew data in Table 4.1, the ANES distinguishes between "strong" and "weak" partisans.

Just as in Table 4.1, Table 4.2 reveals two patterns. First, there is again evidence that the citizens most attentive to the news are also the most partisan. About 70 percent of self-identified strong Democrats said they regularly watched national network news, 68 percent said they watched the local news, and 41 percent said they read a newspaper. About 70 percent of strong Republicans reported watching national news, 54 percent said they watched local news, and 47 percent said they read the newspaper and listened to the radio. In most cases, these figures were the highest for any of the partisan categories. As noted earlier, the absolute levels of exposure should be interpreted cautiously, because Prior (2009) has shown that self-reported measures of media exposure reveal an "immensely inflated" news audience when those data are compared to Nielsen ratings data. But since the focus here is the comparison across categories—not the precise levels of exposure—we can be confident that the more partisan a person is, the more likely he is to pay attention to the news.

Second, unlike online forms of communication, traditional media have a substantial audience of independents. While independents are less interested

Table 4.2 Americans' Use of Traditional Media 3+ Days Per Week, by Partisanship

	Strong Dem	Weak Dem	Lean Dem	Ind	Lean Rep	Weak Rep	Strong Rep
National network news (N=1,108)	70%	50%	49%	45%	62%	45%	68%
Early local news (N=1,111)	68	46	47	35	56	41	54
Read newspaper (N=1,111)	41	40	40	30	35	44	47
Listen to radio news (N=1,110)	33	42	35	39	35	54	47

Note: Figures represent the percentage of individuals in each partisan category saying they used traditional media at least three days per week.
Source: 2008 American National Election Studies.

in public affairs than partisans, 45 percent report watching the national network news at least three days a week, 35 percent watch local news, 30 percent read a newspaper, and 39 percent listen to radio news. These numbers are substantially higher than for independent visits to candidate Web sites or Facebook pages. For example, compare Table 4.2 to Table 4.1, where the percentage of independents interacting with politics online was never higher than 26 percent. If a major part of campaign strategy involves peeling off voters who are not fully committed to one candidate (Hillygus and Shields 2008; Shaw 1999), then parties have a substantial incentive to attempt to use the mass media to send messages to these people.

Do the Media Pay Attention to Party Messages?

But it is not only the news media's reach that makes them valuable. News coverage carries credibility with the public that a candidate ad or party-sponsored message does not. Citizens often have a skeptical view of statements from politicians—their messages are, after all, self-serving—but may be more receptive to information that emanates from the news media, at least among those who view them as trustworthy sources (Hayes 2008; Ladd 2009; Miller and Krosnick 2000). Thus, having the news media transmit strategic messages is of considerable value for political parties.

The problem for politicians, however, is that the media are unreliable messengers, as the tactics of the Bush and Kerry campaigns should make clear. Sometimes the media reflect candidate messages, sometimes they distort them, and sometimes they ignore them entirely. Only when party messages are perceived as newsworthy will journalists pay attention to them. This produces constant conflict between the two groups, which are faced with the persistently frustrating reality that they need each other.

Parties want the media to deliver their preferred messages, unfiltered and unaltered. They want news that places the focus on the issues and events that they believe will benefit their cause. They want news that portrays their candidate in a favorable light and the other side in a negative light. In other words, parties want one-sided, biased news coverage that emphasizes their preferred issue agenda.

The norms and practices of journalism, however, demand that news be two-sided and balanced (Bennett 2009; Graber 2006; Tuchman 1972). Reporters are not interested in serving as tools of politicians. This means that only in rare circumstances will the news reflect one side's preferred agenda. This is not to say that journalists ignore everything parties want them to hear. To be sure, the media need politicians to make news for them; candidates' statements and actions are the raw material for news stories. But party and candidate messages are likely to get through the media filter only when those messages can be transmitted as part of large newsworthy narrative. This is why the Kerry campaign sought to portray its issue announcements as "new" developments each week, and why the Bush campaign made sure to attack Kerry when they wanted front-page coverage for an event. Novelty and conflict are two central parts of the definition of newsworthiness, and those standards have a lot do with when party messages get through, and when they don't.

Realizing this, candidates and parties expend considerable energy trying to get reporters to reflect their campaign messages. Modern campaigns are replete with "pseudo events" (Boorstin 1961)—events, activities, and photo-ops created largely for media consumption. Examples abound. Consider a camouflaged John Kerry in October 2004 parading out of an Ohio wood, dead goose in tow, in an effort to communicate (through the resulting news photos) his embrace of ordinary Americans' values and to dispel notions that he was an elitist. Or John McCain's June 2008 visit to a Bagdad market to highlight the success of the American troop "surge" in Iraq, which the Arizona Senator had advocated. Barack Obama's entire July 2008 trip abroad, including a widely publicized speech in Berlin, was as much a media event as a foreign policy junket. And though not explicitly a campaign event, George W. Bush's tailhook landing on an aircraft carrier in May 2003 was designed (prematurely, it turned out) to underscore the success of the Iraq War and his wartime commander-in-chief image (Bennett 2009, 45–48).

These events were staged primarily for the benefit of the media, whose stories and images the parties hoped would amplify the same messages each camp was also emphasizing in its advertising campaigns. The strategy seems well-founded, as candidate messages are more likely to be effective in shaping voter attitudes when the news media reflect those themes (Hayes 2008; though see Ansolabehere and Iyengar 1994). If candidates hope to set voters' agendas and shape their views of candidates, they will benefit when their messages are amplified by the news media.[12] "Campaigns that are successful are able to couple those," says Democratic consultant Joe Lockhart (Jamieson 2005, 146).

While the media are rarely consistently faithful to candidate agendas (Farnsworth and Lichter 2006; Patterson 1994; Vavreck 2009; though see Dalton, Beck, Huckfeldt, and Koetzle 1998 and Just et al. 1996 for an alternative conclusion), variations in the type of media outlet, campaign activity, and electoral context can increase the likelihood that candidates will have their messages transmitted to the public.

For instance, print outlets are much more responsive to candidate discourse than broadcast media (Hayes forthcoming; Ridout and Mellen 2007), in part because they have more space and are less reliant on visuals.[13] Paradoxically, the media also appear more responsive to candidate agendas when an election is less competitive. When races tighten, the level of convergence between candidate and news agendas declines, because the media find other topics to report on—the horse race, campaigns' strategic maneuvering, the importance of wedge issues—rather than what the candidates are saying on the campaign trail (Hayes forthcoming).

The potential for conflict and drama also may influence when the media reflect candidate agendas. When candidates stake out diverging positions on the same issue, the resulting conflict lends itself to the narrative storytelling that is the cornerstone of political journalism (Jamieson and Waldman 2003; Schudson 1996). Being able to "pit" candidates' statements against one another increases the news value of campaign discourse, making it more likely that a candidate's message will be reported (Hayes forthcoming). For example, in June 2008, the first extended reporting of Barack Obama and John McCain's issue positions in the postprimary period occurred as each candidate criticized the other's economic policy in speeches on the same day. While other factors, such as rapidly deteriorating economic numbers, contributed to the high level of convergence, the candidates' attacks on one another no doubt made the story irresistible to reporters. As Tucker Eskew, senior strategist for the 2004 Bush campaign, puts it, the media are "biased for conflict" (quoted in Jamieson 2005, 156).

These findings suggest that it is not fruitful to think of media responsiveness to candidate agendas as an "either/or" proposition. The extent to which the media transmit candidate messages depends on a variety of factors, including the political context and the strategies of the candidates themselves. The next question, then, is so what? Why does it matter whether the media attend to or ignore party and candidate messages?

The Effect of Media Messages on Voter Attitudes

For decades, political scientists believed that the media served only to reinforce people's views—they had little power to alter political attitudes, beliefs, or behaviors. Despite the thorough penetration of American society by the mass media, the dominance of the "minimal effects" paradigm (e.g., Klapper 1960)—what Bartels (1993, 267) calls "one of the most notable embarrassments of modern social science"—persisted into the latter decades of the twentieth century. But there is now consensus that the media messages matter greatly for voter attitudes and behavior, making it imperative for parties to try to influence news content (e.g., Hetherington 1996; Iyengar and Kinder 1987; McCombs and Shaw 1972; see Graber 2006, 182–217). The ability of parties to get the media to carry those messages can have major consequences.

The more attention the media devote to an issue, the more likely the public is to view that issue as important. This is the well-established agenda setting effect (Iyengar and Kinder 1987; McCombs and Shaw 1972). Agenda setting on its own matters greatly—what problems voters believe are important can shape perceptions of presidential mandates, legislative activity, and policy outputs. But in thinking about elections agenda setting is especially important as an antecedent to priming. Priming occurs when an issue or candidate characteristic that has been made salient to a voter—when that consideration has been "primed"—takes on greater weight in a political judgment, such as a vote choice (Iyengar and Kinder 1987; Kinder and Krosnick 1990). When the media focus heavily on an issue such as the economy then economic considerations are made more accessible in voters' minds. Their vote decisions are more likely to reflect an evaluation of which candidate they believe will more effectively handle inflation and unemployment than if economic issues had not been primed. The importance of priming in campaigns has received considerable attention in recent years from political scientists and communication scholars, who have found it to have important consequences (Claibourn 2008; Druckman 2004). Theories of agenda control are premised on the idea that what people think about when they go into the voting booth shapes who they vote for (Budge and Farlie 1983; Petrocik 1996; Riker 1996).

Though it is still too early to precisely discern the role of the media in the 2008 campaign, it is likely that the issue agenda, dominated by the economy, was important to Obama's victory. McCain, a war hero with a widely known story of heroism from his time in Vietnam, would have preferred to focus the media and voters' attention on terrorism, foreign affairs, and questions of leadership. But his attempts to set the public's agenda throughout the summer of 2008 were stymied by a news media more concerned with the Obama campaign's hammering away at the Republican Party's responsibility for a faltering economy. Obama's message on the deteriorating economy appears to have been reported at a louder volume than McCain's leadership and foreign policy messages, a fact that was reflected in opinion polls that showed voters much more concerned with the economy than any other issue.[14] As a result, voters in 2008 were probably more likely to cast a ballot based on economic concerns than any other issue. Had the attention of the media been focused more on questions of leadership than the economy, it is conceivable that McCain would have fared better (though it seems unlikely he would have won, given the dismal state of the economy and voters' association of him with George W. Bush). Early research into the 2008 campaign suggests the economy was indeed central to the outcome (e.g., Holbrook 2009; Linn, Moody, and Asper 2009).

It is not only issue salience that parties and candidates concern themselves with. The portrayal of candidates in the media can affect voters' attitudes toward them (Druckman and Parkin 2005; Hetherington 1996; Kahn and Kenney 2002; Shaw and Roberts 2000). Let's take an example from the 2000 presidential campaign. In that year, the Bush campaign made use of a series of questionable events Democrat Al Gore was involved in—the 1996 Buddhist temple fundraising scandal, a statement about his role in the development of the Internet, his comparison of his dog's prescription drug costs to his mother-in-law's, among others—to paint the Vice President as an untrustworthy politician willing to say anything to get elected (Jamieson and Waldman 2003, 41–60). The attacks ultimately ended in a major opinion shift, as voters in large numbers began to question his honesty and integrity (Johnston, Hagen, and Jamieson 2004).

Interestingly, it was not the Bush ad campaign or speeches that moved public opinion. Rather, the Bush attacks "supplied language that then infused news coverage of Gore in late September," Johnston et al. (2004, 119) write, "and a series of negative stories about Gore caused many citizens to reevaluate him." The news narrative "permanently transformed the terms of competition to Al Gore's disadvantage." In the razor-close election of 2000, the shift arguably cost Gore the presidency. The dynamic suggests that campaign communications are more effective when the messages are amplified by the press (Hayes 2008), which many citizens view as more credible sources than politicians themselves.

Ultimately, parties know that the media play a powerful role in shaping voter attitudes. The media can set voters' agendas, influence the criteria by which they choose candidates, and shape the favorability of perceptions of candidates. As a result, parties have an incentive to expend considerable effort trying to get the media to reflect their issue agendas, a task that requires constant strategizing, as evidenced by the Kerry and Bush campaign anecdotes noted above. A candidate who is successful in transmitting his or her messages through the media is more likely to reap benefits on Election Day than a candidate who cannot use the mass media to his or her advantage. This is especially true when candidates are in pursuit of swing voters who are not (yet) reachable in large numbers through new media outlets.

A New Form of Mediated Communication: Allied Media

The complicated dance between politicians and journalists has been a standard feature of modern campaigns for decades. But the proliferation of outlets in the new media era has created a second type of mediated communication, distinct from the traditional, nonpartisan journalism of the sort described above. The new category—what I will call "allied media," partisan or ideological information sources designed to amplify and promote party messages—has created a new venue for party communication. These sources include talk radio, ideological and partisan blogs, and overtly partisan media outlets or programs (e.g., The O'Reilly Factor, Countdown with Keith Olbermann).

In many ways, the current era is beginning to offer hints of the politics of the nineteenth century, a time when independent, nonpartisan journalism was not the norm. Most newspapers were affiliated with one political party or the other, and their content was designed to promote the party's ideas and fortunes. Editors were chosen not for their command of the language, but their loyalty to the party. News outlets were agents of partisan warfare. Such outlets are increasingly common today.

Beginning with the rise of political talk radio in the 1980s, and in particular the popularity of Rush Limbaugh's conservative talk show, continuing with the entrance of Fox News and its distinctively conservative brand of political coverage, and after consolidating the development of the Internet, there are now media outlets dedicated not to nonpartisan, balanced journalism, but a form of party advocacy (Jamieson and Cappella 2008). In recent years, MSNBC's prime time lineup—featuring former Democratic staffer Chris Matthews, Bush tormenter Keith Olbermann, and former Air America host Rachel Maddow—has developed into a liberal challenge to Fox News' conservative programming. And the left-leaning blogosphere has become to liberals what talk radio is to conservatives. To be sure, these outlets are not official organs of political parties and candidates—and importantly, they do not necessarily adhere to party doctrine or talking points—but they represent new venues for partisan communications to which citizens have access.

While these outlets are no doubt a relevant feature of the political environment, it is important not to overstate their importance. The average prime time cable news audience (combining Fox News, MSNBC, and CNN) in 2008 was about 4 million viewers, just a fraction of the broadcast networks' news audience.[15] In addition, their viewership is heavily populated by committed partisans. A Rasmussen Reports press release titled "News You Watch Says a Lot about How You'll Vote" reported that a survey in August 2008 showed that 87 percent of Fox News viewers planned to vote for John McCain. At the same time, 63 percent of MSNBC viewers and 65 percent of CNN viewers said they would vote for Barack Obama.[16] Perhaps useful for generating enthusiasm among hard-core party supporters, these outlets are unlikely to help parties expand their coalitions or win over swing voters.

The same limitations apply to the expanding blogosphere, which has become a forum for ideologically driven takes on the news. The vast majority of political blogs fall on the right or left—there are very few that offer a nonpartisan or centrist take on the news (Lawrence, Sides, and Farrell forthcoming). And the audience for political blogs remains relatively small—just 14 percent of the public in 2006 said they read a political blog—so their relevance for the overall information environment is not clear. What is certain, however, is that these sites represent the increasing "balkanization" (Jamieson and Cappella 2008) of information sources in the media era. The proliferation of news sources has given partisan commentators a place to propagate their views, and a place for committed ideological followings to receive a friendly take on politics.

Consequences of the Transformed Media Environment

Compared to the communications environment even two decades ago, the media landscape faced by political parties today is strikingly complex. The transformation of the media environment—and Americans' increasingly diverse media habits—has forced parties and candidates to develop new methods to communicate with voters. New media have provided opportunities to communicate with supporters who want to engage with the party in ways not seen since the era of machine politics. But because these new venues have only a limited capacity to reach swing voters and weaker partisans, traditional communications strategies—television advertising and the use of the news media, especially—remain critical to party communications efforts.

As we consider the future of political communication in the United States, we can envision several consequences of the changes in the media environment. First, as it grows ever more complex, parties will need to refine their communication strategies further. Increased segmentation of the electorate and the use of microtargeting (Hillygus and Shields 2008) may be a major part of that process. Parties will also likely develop new ways to use the Internet, including creating more opportunities for interactive communication between party leaders and the party faithful.

Second, news audiences will likely continue to fragment. As recently as the 1980s, Americans got their political information from the same few places. Today, consumption patterns are increasingly diverse—one person may watch Fox News, read the Wall Street Journal, and occasionally listen to NPR. Another person may watch ABC's World News Tonight, read a local newspaper, and the liberal blog Talking Points Memo. Another person may get all of his news from Google News. The new era of heterogeneity in media consumption means that reaching large audiences through a single outlet or medium is increasingly implausible.

Third, a result of that fragmentation may be growing informational polarization. To the extent that partisans increasingly receive their news from sources that present ideologically tilted—as opposed to balanced, independent—information, voters may slowly lose shared frames of reference. People with different predispositions are increasingly likely to be exposed to competing information, frames, and interpretations of political events. If consumers of different political stripes are exposed to different messages, even shared vocabularies (think "torture" vs. "enhanced interrogation techniques") may become relatively rare. The realities of new information environment suggest that deliberation between people of different political stripes may become more difficult, just as evaluations of and attitudes toward political figures and issues have polarized along partisan lines in recent years (e.g., Jacobson 2007).

Fourth, because entertainment options have expanded just as rapidly as news choices, there is a slice of the electorate that will be inclined to opt out of political news altogether. Prior (2007) suggests that the expansion of entertainment options has already contributed to a widening of the political knowledge gap in the United States and lower voter turnout. A 2008 Pew survey found that the proportion of Americans regularly going "newsless" was 19 percent, up five percentage points since 1998. The increase was about twice as large among young people between the ages of 18 and 24.[17] If some individuals are increasingly difficult to reach through the media, old or new, then parties may see a shrinking pool of persuadable voters.

These possibilities, of course, amount to informed speculation. The media environment is rapidly changing, making prediction difficult. Every day seems to bring a new technological development that gives people access to more political information, faster, quicker. For parties to be able to succeed in this environment, they will need to continually update their communications strategies. Of that, we can be sure.

Notes

1. This, at least, was an early prediction by TNS Media Intelligence/Campaign Media Advertising Group, which tracks spending on political advertising. See http://www.cnn.com/2007/POLITICS/10/15/ad.spending/index.html (accessed August 13, 2009).

2. Among the most famous political "tweets"—as Twitter messages are known—in the site's short history was delivered by Iowa Republican Sen. Charles Grassley While on a June 2009 diplomatic trip in Europe, President Obama had called for action by Congress on health care reform. Grassley, evidently miffed by the transatlantic directive, posted on Twitter, "Pres Obama you got nerve while u sightseeing in Paris to tell us 'time to deliver' on health care. We still on skedul/ even workinWKEND" (National Public Radio 2009).

3. In recent years, the term netroots has become most associated with the online community on the liberal end of the ideological spectrum.

4. Pew does not distinguish between "strong" and "weak" partisans as do many surveys, including the American National Election Studies, which I rely on later. The Pew question asks respondents, "In politics today, do you consider yourself a Republican, Democrat, or Independent?" Respondents who call themselves independents are then asked, "As of today, do you lean more to the Republican Party or more to the Democratic Party?" Only independents who say they do not lean toward either party are included in the "Ind." category in Table 4.1.

5. Question wordings for Table 4.1 are as follows: "Now thinking about some campaign websites, did you ever go to The Obama/Biden campaign website to get news or information about the 2008 elections?"; "Now thinking about some campaign websites, did you ever go to The McCain/Palin campaign website to get news or information about the 2008 elections?"; "Over the past several

months, how often did you receive email from a candidate or political party?";
"Thinking about what you have done on SNS like Facebook and MySpace, have
you gotten any campaign or candidate information on the sites?"; "Thinking
about what you have done on SNS like Facebook and MySpace, have you signed
up as a 'friend' of any candidates on a social networking site?"

6. Because these questions were asked only of Facebook/MySpace users, the percentage of the total population visiting the candidates' pages is much lower even
than the percentages in the table.

7. The similarity of leaners to partisans underscores the point that people who call
themselves independents but admit to having a preference for a party should be
considered to be more like partisans than independents. Political scientists have
documented this tendency in voting behavior and political attitudes (Keith et al.
1992), and it appears the principle applies to new media consumption as well.

8. A transcript of the interview with McKinnon on the PBS show Frontline is
available here, http://www.pbs.org/wgbh/pages/frontline/newswar/interviews/
mckinnon.html (accessed June 23, 2009).

9. These figures come from the Project for Excellence in Journalism's 2009 State of
the News Media Report, available here: http://www.stateofthemedia.org/2009/
index.htm (accessed June 23, 2009).

10. Question wordings for Table 4.2 are: "How many days in the past week did you
watch the national network news on TV?"; "How many days in the past week did
you watch the local TV news shows such as 'Eyewitness News' or 'Action News'
in the late afternoon or early-evening?"; "How many days in the past week did
you read a daily newspaper?"; "How many days in the past week did you listen to
news on the radio?" The numbers reflect the percentage of respondents reporting three or more days of exposure.

11. Slicing the data in other ways—for example, looking at the percentage that
reported watching news or reading the paper seven days a week—yields the
same conclusions.

12. Recent evidence from Ladd (2009) about the decline in trust in the media suggests this effect wanes as trust in the media erodes.

13. A story about the late CBS anchor Walter Cronkite underscores the difference
in the "carrying capacity" between TV newscasts and newspapers. Shortly after
Cronkite's death in July 2009, the broadcaster Robert McNeil told PBS that
Cronkite "had tried to get an hour on CBS and repeatedly failed. Once, he had
the entire text of a CBS half-hour show reprinted as though it were on the front
page of the New York Times and it covered less than three columns, which he
thought was very illustrative of how little information could actually be given,
however important it was in context at the time." See http://www.pbs.org/news-
hour/bb/media/july-dec09/cronkite_07-20.html (accessed August 14, 2009).

14. For example, a representative result was the one in a USA Today/Gallup Poll
taken in early September of 2008. Even before the financial crisis had reached
full boil, 42 percent of respondents said the economy would be the most important issue to their vote. By comparison, 13 percent said the situation in Iraq, and
12 percent said terrorism. These data were retrieved from pollingreport.com.

15. This figure comes from the Project for Excellence in Journalism's 2009 "State of
the News Media" report.

16. See http://www.rasmussenreports.com/public_content/politics/elections2/elec-
tion_20082/2008_presidential_election/news_you_watch_says_a_lot_about_
how_you_ll_vote (accessed July 23, 2009).

17. See "Key News Audiences Now Blend Online and Traditional Sources" at http://
people-press.org/report/444/news-media (accessed August 16, 2009).

Chapter 5

Party Organization and Mobilization of Resources

Evolution, Reinvention, and Survival

Diana Dwyre

James Madison asserted in the *Federalist Papers* that "both the public good and the rights of other citizens" could be sacrificed to the "ruling passion or interest" of a majority faction, or political party (Madison, *Federalist No. 10*, 1787). Further, he argued for adoption of the Constitution that would establish a separation of powers and various checks and balances in the new federal government to protect the rights of the people by making it difficult for a majority to take control of the entire government (Madison, *Federalist No. 51*, 1788). George Washington warned in his Farewell Address (drafted for him by Alexander Hamilton) of "the baneful effects of the Spirit of Party," and his successor, John Adams, asserted that "a division of the republic into two great parties...is to be dreaded as the greatest political evil under our constitution" (quoted in Hofstadter 1969, 2, 22). Given the Founders' fear of and disdain for political parties, it is not surprising that there have been many concerted attempts to chip away at the power and influence of these potentially powerful organizations. Yet, one of the enduring features of U.S. party organizations is their ability to survive, and sometimes thrive, by adapting to changing and often hostile circumstances (Aldrich 1995; Brewer and Stonecash 2009; Kolodny and Dwyre 1998).

Party organizations have evolved, and sometimes transformed, in order to serve the needs of the politicians who utilize them to attain their goals (Aldrich 1995; Pomper 1992). While these goals vary, the most basic ones have been well-articulated by Richard Fenno: that politicians desire a long and successful career in politics and thus work to be reelected or rise to higher office; that they aim to achieve preferred policies; and that they want to gain power and prestige within government (Fenno 1973). When achievement of these goals is threatened, politicians often turn to parties to get back on track. Indeed, various political actors, such as the Progressives and contemporary campaign finance reformers, have altered the regulatory and political environment in ways meant to limit the role of political parties in U.S. politics, only to find that these resilient and malleable organizations reemerge from often quite challenging circumstances. Other hurdles, such as technological developments and the rise of nonaligned, independent voters, have presented parties with additional challenges to which they have adapted.

Parties have been through many transitions as they have struggled to adapt to changing and often challenging circumstances. This chapter first examines their formation and initial struggles to attract and mobilize voters and create an identity and organization. The ways parties have reacted to and sought to adapt to the remarkable social changes that have occurred over time are then reviewed. The impact on the functioning of parties by movements critical of parties is also discussed. Finally, the focus is on the transition to an organization that supports rather than controls elected officials.

Why Did Parties Emerge?

Given the Founding Fathers disdain for political parties, why did parties emerge in the first place? In fact, it was some of the Founders themselves who began to organize groups of like-minded lawmakers during the very first Congresses after ratification of the Constitution. On one side were Treasury Secretary Alexander Hamilton and Vice President John Adams; on the other were Secretary of State Thomas Jefferson and Representative James Madison. In 1790 Hamilton arranged the first legislative caucus of lawmakers identified as Federalists. By 1795, those opposed to Hamilton and the Federalists had organized as the Jeffersonian Republicans, and by then legislators' "voting patterns can be identified as polarized, broadly along party lines" (Aldrich 1995, 77). The two sides disagreed about the broad issue of just how strong and active the new federal government should be, with the Federalists arguing for more power and vigor at the national level, and the Republicans advocating for a more limited centralized government.

These leaders realized how inefficient and unpredictable it was to organize a winning coalition for each issue that arose in Congress. Many of the issues of the day, such as the assumption of the states' Revolutionary War debt and Hamilton's proposed creation of a national bank, predictably divided lawmakers according to their views on the strength and reach of the federal government (Aldrich 1995, 70). Later, foreign policy issues, such as the French Revolutionary War, divided the nascent parties, as the Republicans supported the expansion of democracy and equality inspired by the French, and the Federalists sided with the British in advocating policies to maintain domestic order, trade with Britain, and protections for private property.

However, these were organizations that existed only at the elite level, and they were primarily parties in government with little connection to voters in the states. Eventually, the two emerging parties began the difficult task of organizing outside of government to build support among the electorate. They used a variety of tools to do so. For example, partisans in Congress formed committees of correspondence to communicate with partisan elites in their states, patronage was used to build loyalty among supporters, local partisan caucuses and societies were formed, and disloyal partisans were even purged from office (Eldersveld and Walton 2000, 52). The new party organizations also were supported outside the halls of government by an emerging partisan press that eventually featured newspapers on both sides, and "by 1800 elections were publicly and undeniable partisan" (Aldrich 1995, 77). As these efforts to mobilize voters increased, voter turnout also increased from around 24 percent of the white male population from 1792 to 1798, to 39 percent in 1800 (Eldersveld and Walton 2000, 47).

Partisan polarization became so intense by 1798 that President John Adams and the Federalist-controlled Congress acted to stifle their opposition with use of the Alien and Sedition Acts, a series of laws to control the activities of foreigners in the United States, which were enacted under the threat of war with France. The Sedition Act, for example, allowed for fines and imprisonment of individuals who criticized the government, Congress, or the President in print or in speech, and a number of Republican newspaper publishers were arrested and their newspapers shut down in this concerted attempt to put the Jeffersonian Republicans out of business. Many questioned whether these Acts were constitutional. Public opposition to them and the fear of Federalist tyranny helped Jefferson defeat Adams in the 1800 presidential election and helped the Republicans take control of the House of Representatives (Nichols 1967, 201–2).

The rise of the Jeffersonian Republicans was a shift from much of the history of democracy because they were a group organized not to overturn or conquer the government in power but to challenge it peacefully by building stable majorities in government and winning the public's support in elections. Indeed, past instances of party competition, in Great Britain, for example, sometimes resulted in violent conflict where losers were exiled or even put to death (Hofstadter 1969, 12). Thus, in spite of the tradition of antipartyism in the early days of the republic, there was a gradual acceptance of and recognized need for legitimate opposition in the form of competing political parties.

After 1800, the Federalists faded as a party. They had "advanced little in developing a capacity for organization...," relying primarily on "their press to develop a propaganda which was both venomous and scurrilous in its attacks upon Jefferson's morals and ethics, even accusing him of scientific animal vivisection" (Nichols 1967, 204). Indeed, the business owners and wealthy people who benefited most from the Federalists' policies were far outnumbered by the Jeffersonian Republicans' constituency of small farmers and the less wealthy in the mid-Atlantic and Southern states who supported the Republicans' more egalitarian and states' rights approach to governing. The Federalists also diminished their prospects with their opposition to and behavior during the War of 1812. Federalist New Englanders clandestinely traded with Britain and withheld funds and soldiers from the war effort, and it was rumored that the Federalists supported secession of New England states from the Union. The decline of the Federalists led to a period of one-party dominance by the Republicans, rather inaccurately described as the "Era of Good Feelings," from 1808 to 1824.

As political parties emerged in the new nation, the ability of partisans to organize outside of government eventually determined which faction would survive. In a relatively short period of time, partisan elites transformed internal governmental coalitions into organizations that developed partisan newspapers, utilized patronage to strengthen their support, and began to reach down into the grass roots.

Building a Grassroots Political Party: Jackson's and Van Buren's Democratic Party

Although most elected officials were Jeffersonian Republicans in the early 1820s, the rapid and extensive growth of the party created a diverse membership that eventually developed into various factions within the organization. For instance, the 1824 election featured five Republican candidates for president, each representing a different faction of the party and with support from different parts of the country.

The same important principle that divided the Jeffersonians and the Federalists twenty-five years earlier also divided these candidates and the nation in 1824. The role and power of the federal government relative to the states, particularly on the issues of economic development and slavery, was the matter that created such sectional cleavages within the Republican Party in 1824 (Kolodny 1996, 144–46). For example, the older regions of the country, such as the Eastern seaboard, favored the traditional "elitist republican" view of the Founders and mostly supported the antislavery, strongly nationalist John Quincy Adams; while the proslavery, state's rights Southern states split their support between elitist William Crawford and the more "egalitarian republican" Andrew Jackson (Kolodny 1996, 144–55). Out of these different views and sectional cleavages grew the divisions that would emerge out of the unusual 1824 election: the egalitarian republicans would grow into the Jacksonian Democratic Party; and the elitist republicans opposed to Jackson and his supporters would become the Whigs (144).

The population of the new nation had grown, and various states had moved to expand democratic participation. A few states had loosened the requirements for voting so that the electorate was no longer confined to the few white men who could meet the property requirement. Some states began to hold conventions for presidential nominations instead of allowing the state legislature to select nominees. Well-developed party organizations already existed in a few states, particularly in New York and Pennsylvania, and the 1824 election featured many new and intensified methods of mobilization:

> Money was raised, old newspapers took new stands, and new ones were established. Pamphlets and broadsides were printed and distributed. Voters were solicited more vigorously and variously than in any previous campaign. Electors were nominated and campaigned before the voters; tickets were printed which voters took to the ballot boxes. (Nichols 1967, 271)

While these activities were not nationally centralized or coordinated, they represented the beginning of a shift from an elite-focused system with few efforts to mobilize voters, to an organized national partisan operation designed to win the most votes from the expanding voting public.

Amid an economic downturn that ended the so-called Era of Good Feelings, Andrew Jackson won the popular vote in 1824, but not a majority of the Electoral College votes. So, the election was thrown to the House of Representatives, where Clay gave his support to Adams after Adams promised to name Clay his secretary of state, and, in what some charged was a "corrupt bargain," John Quincy Adams was selected president. Jackson and his followers were determined to reverse what they saw as the usurpation of the presidency.

Jackson's prospects improved significantly when, in 1827, Senator from New York Martin Van Buren joined Jackson's presidential campaign. Van Buren was a savvy and effective political operative who had managed a well-organized political machine, the Albany Regency organization. Jackson had built a following of "Jackson Men" during and after the 1824 election, and they remained loyal to their hero "Old Hickory" and committed to undoing the results of the 1824 election. They too helped shape the organization that would forever change electoral democracy in the U.S. Jackson, Van Buren, the Jackson Men, and other democratically oriented activists built the first national grassroots political party in history. Van Buren's efforts in particular led to the creation of this first mass-based party, the Democratic Party. Van Buren mobilized elites to support Jackson and convinced them to provide resources to create a new type of party organization that mobilized voters to elect Jackson president in 1828.

The importance of preexisting political organizations, such as Albany's Regency, and of well-developed competition in some states should not be underestimated as an important factor in the development of the new type of party (Hofstadter 1969, chapter 6; Nichols 1967, chapter 18). These activities in various states had emerged, in part, out of a new view of parties and partisanship: that legitimate political opposition was not only *necessary* as a nonviolent check on power but also *natural*, for it was "foolish to expect free men to exist in politics without contention" (Hofstadter 1969, 250–51).

Out of a history of antipartyism and then an era of one-party rule, this acceptance of parties and party competition as positive was developing alongside increased demands for greater democratic participation and rejection of elite aristocratic rule, a slow revolution that began with Jefferson. Indeed, the new party men were of a different breed than the elite leaders of the past. Van Buren and his Regency colleagues were "middle class or lower middle class, often self-made men or the sons of self-made men. There was a distinct edge of class resentment in their attitude toward patrician politicians who assumed that office was a prerogative of social rank that could be claimed without the expenditure of years of work in party-building and without the exacting discipline of party loyalty" (Hofstadter 1969, 241). Thomas Jefferson was their hero, and they were political professionals energized by the Jeffersonian democratic promise. They believed that "negotiation and management of opinion were better than leadership through deference" (Hofstadter 1969, 242). The goal was to reinvigorate and reorganize Jefferson's old Republican Party.

The conscious development of a new type of political party on the national level sprang not from some theoretical preference for such an institution, but from what Hofstadter calls "one of those pragmatic American innovations, based upon experience and experiment, which one usually finds keyed closely to changing institutional necessities" (1969, 252). While no new states entered the union after 1821 until Arkansas joined in 1836, the population of the country continued to disperse, and the addition of many new communities, especially in the Western regions, necessitated a more complex and structured political organization to manage communication, mobilize voters, and promote a candidate for a nation-wide presidential election. The logistical context had improved enough so that better communication and transportation made these expanded and more strategic activities possible.

A major change in the way presidential candidates were nominated also motivated creation of a new kind of party. While the franchise had not been significantly expanded, by 1828, over 90 percent of states were choosing presidential electors by popular vote rather than having state and national legislative caucuses choose them, increasing *presidential* suffrage (Aldrich 1995, 106; McCormick 1967, 104–6). Indeed, white male turnout increased significantly from 26.5 percent in 1824 to 56.3 percent in 1828 (Aldrich 1995, 104). The ability to influence the presidential nomination process in new ways and the resulting desire to organize this new electorate created a ripe environment for organizational entrepreneurship.

The generally more democratic and egalitarian nature of American society during this era contributed to this fertile context for party building. In addition to the changes in the presidential nomination process, more states began popularly electing governors, the number of popularly elected local officials increased, printed ballots were being used, and various elections were consolidated to take place on a single day (McCormick 1967, 110). These changes presented both challenges and opportunities for the nascent mass parties, shaping their structure and activities to focus almost exclusively on electoral matters.

Aldrich argues that Van Buren and his colleagues were motivated by a classic problem of collective action: how to reduce the costs of participation by both voters and politicians (Aldrich 1995, 100–4). Some voters faced higher participation costs in the early 1800s than voters do today, such as getting to distant polling places and having free time to vote. Moreover, literacy rates were lower, making it difficult to become informed about political matters.

Party activities were designed to build enthusiasm for the election and the party's candidates. The parties organized speeches, rallies, bonfires, marches, and other party hoopla. Jacksonian Democrats, for example, raised hickory poles to advertise Old Hickory's candidacy in 1828. Such party activities "provided information about the election, the contenders, and the stakes involved, lowering decision costs," thus making participation "worthwhile" (Aldrich 1995, 101). Campaign activities also provided opportunities for social interaction and entertainment, building interest and enthusiasm that resulted in mass participation. For example, as McCormick has noted,

> ...the varieties of experiences that parties in this era afforded to the electorate went beyond the political sphere. Those tens of thousands of men and women who attended the mammoth Whig festival at Nashville in 1840; those untold millions who carried torches, donned uniforms, chanted slogans, or cheered themselves hoarse at innumerable parades and rallies; those puffed-up canvassers of wards, servers of rum, and distributors of largesse; and all those simple folks who whipped themselves into a fury of excitement and anxiety as each election day approached, were thrilling to a grand dramatic experience, even a cathartic experience. There was no spectacle, no contest, in America that could match an election campaign, and all could identify with and participate in it. (McCormick 1967, 108)

Jackson and Van Buren also helped lower participation costs for candidates, elected officials, and benefit seekers, and convinced these elite political actors to provide the resources needed to enable the new party organization to deliver on its promise. This was a truly national party system, not based on sectional differences, but one that united the regions of the country behind the Jeffersonian Republican principle of states' rights, a principle that had previously united North and South behind Jefferson. Indeed, this new party system was present in every state. Widespread opposition to Adams and the growing popularity of the war hero Jackson, who played up the "corrupt bargain" of the 1824 election, helped Van Buren convince political leaders from various regions to rally around Jackson and the new Democratic Party.

Moreover, supporters were *not* asked to make any commitments to particular policy stands (for or against slavery, for example), only to help defeat Adams by building a truly national party organization based on Jeffersonian

Republicanism. This allowed Van Buren to bring together a coalition he called the *Alliance* that included both Southern planters and Northern bankers, and he argued in his correspondence to potential supporters that "the renewal of party would set aside sectional interests and in particular the slavery issue" (Aldrich 1995, 108).

In return for their support and assistance, Van Buren noted that Jackson's victory would help those running for office on the same party ticket, propel those elected to leadership positions in government, and allow them to share in the significant spoils of office that came with Jackson's election, such as patronage jobs, government contracts, and other federal funds. They would not have to make any policy commitments and they could ride the tide of Jackson's popularity.

Van Buren also created a centralized party organization in Washington, DC. The *Caucus* "oversaw fund-raising, established and subsidized a chain of newspapers throughout the nation, and determined how and where to focus their efforts" (Aldrich 1995, 111). By 1848, the Democrats had established a permanent central committee with one member from each state to insure that party operations would continue between presidential elections (Nichols 1967, 371). At first, the resources needed to fund the Caucus came from the various party leaders. Eventually, however, the great expense of building party organizations in the states would require much more money, and parties eventually turned to "high-level benefit seekers" such as bankers and corporate leaders to fund the party organizations and mobilization efforts (Aldrich 1995, 112).

Both Jackson and Adams ran as the standard-bearers of different factions of the Democratic-Republican Party in 1828. The larger electorate, extensive Democratic Party voter mobilization efforts, and the passion Jackson and his supporters had for his candidacy, combined to deliver victory and to change forever the course of party politics in the United States.

Van Buren had built the party into a powerful electoral force. A huge influx of immigrants added to the party's ranks, and their political participation helped them assimilate into American life (White and Shea 2000, 44). Yet, it was the extensive "spoils system" based primarily on government jobs that also helped the party maintain its electoral power. Van Buren argued that filling government jobs with party loyalists, or what he called "rotation of office," promoted public accountability. If the party's mail carriers, street cleaners, and post office workers did not run the government well, voters could hold the party accountable in the next election and the new government would give those patronage jobs to *their* loyalists. Holders of patronage jobs were motivated to work hard for the party or risk losing their jobs. The spoils system increased the number of nonelites participating in politics, and, combined with the partisan activities such as parades, rallies, and community events that provided opportunities for social interaction and entertainment, the parties developed truly mass-based political participation.

By 1834, the various groups and leaders that opposed Jackson and his policies had combined, leading to formation of the Whig Party. By 1840, the Whigs had successfully imitated the Democratic Party's strategies and had developed into a full-fledge, nation-wide, mass-based party as well. This additional organizing and voter mobilization further increased participation. Indeed, presidential election turnout rose sharply with real party competition, rising from 58% of the voting age population to 80% from 1836 to 1840 (see Table 5.1).

The newly competitive environment encouraged further party organizational development. During the 1848 Democratic national convention, the Democrats established the Democratic National Committee (DNC), the first formal national party organization to arrange and direct the presidential campaign and organize future conventions. This national organization provided a common focal point for party activities throughout the states, allowing for greater coordination of presidential election efforts and an efficient use of party resources to promote the party's choice. U.S. national party organizations were (and are) primarily electoral organizations that are not much involved in the development of policy or the activities of their elected officials in government, unlike their counterparts that developed later in other Western democracies (Epstein 1986).

Table 5.1 Voter Turnout in Presidential Elections, 1824–1876

Year	Percent Turnout of Voting Age Population
1824	26.9%
1828	57.6%
1832	55.4%
1836	57.8%
1840	80.2%
1844	78.9%
1848	72.7%
1852	69.6%
1856	78.9%
1860	81.2%
1864	73.8%
1868	78.1%
1872	71.3%
1876	81.8%

Source: Gerhard Peters, "Voter Turnout in Presidential Elections, 1824–2004" in the American Presidency Project at UC Santa Barbara at http://www.presidency.ucsb.edu/data/turnout.php

Later, the Democratic Party tried to institute a more stable system of funding the party. In 1852, the Democrats created a party fund and proposed that each of the 233 congressional districts give at least $100 to be used mostly for printing campaign materials (Nichols 1967, 375). Yet they turned to a wealthy New York banker, August Belmont, to fund most of the enterprise (375). Congressional representatives also provided themselves with resources to help them campaign for reelection, such as printing copies of their speeches at government expense and distributing them widely using their franking privilege. Yet organizational success could not withstand the force of the divisive issue of slavery, which led to a realignment of the American political system and another transformation of the political parties.

The Civil War Realignment and More Party Organizational Development

This party system, with two parties competing effectively in all states, remained functional and healthy until the 1850s, when sectional antagonisms divided both camps. The Whig Party collapsed in much of the South over the slavery issue. The Whigs were weakened in the North by the anti-immigrant activities of the Know-Nothings, whose campaign against Catholic Irish immigrants convinced many Whigs to join the Know-Nothings' American Party. The Democratic Party split into North and South factions, and a new Republican Party (Lincoln's party) emerged in the North in the midst of this partisan chaos.

The nascent Republican Party introduced new fund-raising techniques in its first campaign in 1856. The new party was backed by businessmen from the Northeast, and one of the wealthiest, New Yorker Edwin Morgan, headed up the newly established national party committee, the Republican National Committee (RNC). Morgan tapped his fellow business owners for campaign money and set up a system of exchange to gain their support: he "operated a scheme of contingent gifts, subscriptions payable if [Republican presidential candidate] Fremont won. Newspapers were bought or subsidized, and presumably 'understandings' were arrived at, to be honored in the event of victory" (Nichols 1967, 376). Like Van Buren before them, the Republicans were building a system of exchange to insure the continued strength of their party. What would eventually become the powerful yet corrupt political party machines were being developed during this pre-Civil War era.

In the realigning election of 1860 the Democratic Party's northern and southern factions each nominated separate candidates for president, splitting the Democratic vote and allowing Republican candidate Abraham Lincoln to win with only 40 percent of the popular vote. Before Lincoln even took office, seven Southern states had seceded from the union, seeing his election as a threat to the institution of slavery and to their sovereignty. While a competitive party system continued to operate in the North, the bloody Civil War disrupted politics in the South and a new national party system did not emerge until the 1870s.

Yet, as we have seen, political setbacks or crises often motivate politicians to turn to and redesign their parties to help them achieve their goals (Aldrich 1995). Indeed, partisans in Congress established the congressional campaign committees amidst this political chaos in which the factional conflicts in both parties led congressional incumbents to be insecure about their own electoral fortunes. The national party committees were focused primarily on the presidential contest and not very active during congressional midterm elections (Kolodny 1998). The National Republican Congressional Committee (NRCC) was formed in 1866, and the House Democrats followed soon thereafter to establish the Democratic Congressional Campaign Committee (DCCC). Senate party leaders created their own party electoral committees (the National Republican Senatorial Committee [NRSC], and the Democratic Senatorial Campaign Committee [DSCC]) after ratification of the Seventeenth Amendment in 1913 that required the direct election of senators by subjecting them to popular election rather than selection by their state legislatures. In the U.S. system of the separation of powers that is designed to make it difficult for parties to gain too much power or coordinate activities, it is not at all surprising that the parties eventually separate in the same fashion (Burns 1963; Kolodny 1998). James McGregor Burns has argued that this "four-party politics" stifles the exercise of democracy in the United States by making it difficult for the people to hold those in government collectively responsible (Burns 1963; see also Fiorina 1980).

West v. East: Agrarian Revolt and Republican Ascendance

This next era of party politics was marked by two powerful developments: the rise of a radical agrarian movement, and the emergence of powerful and potent urban political party machines. First, we will discuss the farmers and the impact their movement had on the course of party development. In the wake of the Civil War and through the unusual political era of Reconstruction, the new partisan divisions were highly sectional. In the South, the Republicans' support came almost entirely from blacks, who were eventually disenfranchised by Jim Crow laws enacted by white Southerners in spite of the Fifteenth Amendment to the Constitution (e.g., poll taxes, literacy tests, and white primaries). The Democrats had strong support from white Southerners and from only those Northern cities controlled by Democratic Party machines, such as New York City's Tammany Hall. These partisan divisions were economic as well. Northeastern and Midwestern industrialists supported the GOP (Grand Old Party, the nickname adopted by the Republicans) during this time of great industrial expansion, and the party supported them with protective tariffs on imports, economic development for the West, and expansion of the railroad system. The Democrats drew support from farmers and the working class, who were largely left out of the prosperity from rapid economic expansion during the Industrial Revolution.

In the 1890s, a third party movement developed out of the discontent of distressed farmers in the South, Great Plains, and far West. The emergence of the People's Party highlighted the tensions between the economically booming urban areas in the East and the depressed rural regions elsewhere, as neither major party addressed the problems faced by the agrarian community. Farmers were confronted by falling prices for their goods, tight and expensive credit, growing debts, unprofitable reliance on merchants and middlemen, and monopolistic railroad rates. They opposed the gold standard for currency and called for the unlimited coinage of silver as a way to loosen credit. They saw both parties as captured by the Eastern moneyed establishment of industrialists and New York bankers. Populist senator William Allen of Nebraska expressed the farmers' discontent well:

> We feel that, through the operation of a shrinking volume of money, which has been caused by eastern votes and influences for purely selfish purposes, the East has placed its hands on the throat of the West and refused to afford us the measure of justice which we, as citizens of a common country, are entitled to receive. (quoted in Sundquist 1983, 140)

A severe economic downturn in 1893 under Democratic President Grover Cleveland further split the Democratic Party. Cleveland further alienated many already dissatisfied voters by, for example, refusing to support any move away from the gold standard, and using federal troops to put down the 1894 Pullman strike. The recession deepened as railroads, banks, and factories failed, and coal and railroad strikes continued. The House of Representatives switched from Democratic to Republican control in the 1894 midterm elections. Then the prosilver Democrats captured the splintered party as the 1896 presidential election approached, and they effectively absorbed the Populist agrarians to nominate Congressman William Jennings Bryan for president. They adopted a platform that challenged the existing industrial order, and the parties were again aligned on opposite sides of important national issues, not just silver versus gold, but also big corporations and bankers versus farmers and workers.

Such polarization once again provided incentive for party organizational development. The Republicans were terrified by Bryan's nomination and the radical Democratic Party platform, and the GOP fought back with "a massive and crushing counterattack" (Sundquist 1983, 156). This effort was managed by Ohio industrialist and experienced Republican operative Mark Hanna, who used new fundraising and organizing techniques to mobilize support for GOP candidate William McKinley. At a time when there were not yet any restrictions on corporate contributions to political campaigns, Hanna raised an unprecedented amount of money by simply "assessing major corporations at a rate of one-fourth of one percent of capital" (156). Big business, banks, and insurance companies gladly contributed, and the GOP reported spending $3.5 million for the 1896 election, yet the actual amount is thought to be many times higher, while Bryan raised a mere $650,000 (156–57). Armed with this mass of resources, Hanna mounted an extensive and highly organized voter mobilization campaign. These mobilization efforts became overtly coercive toward the end of the campaign, as "employers threatened their employees, creditors their borrowers, buyers their suppliers," and even the clergy joined the effort by preaching against Bryan (156–57).

Turnout was high in the election of 1896, with 13.9 million voters casting ballots, about 79% of the voting age population (Peters 1999–2009; Sundquist 1983, 157). The contest realigned the electorate as the Republicans added to their post-Civil War coalition the support of many working and middle class urban dwellers, with McKinley winning the nation's largest cities in the East and Midwest. The gravitation of workers to the GOP was not due solely to threats from their employers, for earlier in the late 1880s and early 1890s some industrial workers had shifted toward the Republicans because of the party's protectionist tariff policies, which they saw as job protection. Thus, the new party alignments proved durable once the GOP returned to more normal campaign tactics. The Democrats were unable to compete nationally, and the Republicans controlled federal politics almost exclusively from 1896 to 1928. The Democrats elected only one president during this period, in 1912 when Woodrow Wilson became president due to a split in the Republican Party coalition.

Marching the Masses into the Public Forum: The Urban Party Machines

The political party machines that thrived in America's big cities in the late nineteenth and early twentieth centuries were both Democratic and Republican. Yet neither flavor was particularly ideological, for both parties' machines were "interested only in power, jobs and profit" (Pomper 1992, 71). The urban party machine emerged and thrived as an adaptation to the many political and economic strains produced by the industrial revolution in an environment of no real governmental activism to deal with the challenging consequences of such dramatic change. Millions of immigrants and migrants poured into the big cities in search of work and prosperity. This immense and rapid population growth created a huge need for an expanded infrastructure of housing, transportation, schools, hospitals, and other services, as well as a need to socialize and assimilate the vast number of new urban dwellers.

Machine politicians saw an opportunity to enhance their power and profit, as Tammany Hall district leader George Washington Plunkitt proclaimed in explaining the difference between "honest graft and dishonest graft,... I seen my opportunities and I took 'em" (Riordon 1963, 3, 5). The party machines were well positioned to meet some of the needs of the urban working class and poor, and they did so because such activities helped them attract loyal partisans, enabling them to mobilize those voters to win elections and thus fulfill their desire for power and profit.

Pomper notes that the machines worked to accomplish their true goals by performing "'latent functions,' unintentionally meeting essential societal needs" (Pomper 1992, 71). For example, in exchange for payment to the party, party bosses cut through government red tape for contractors who would then recoup this cost of doing business from lucrative government contracts. In order to insure that the machine's candidates were elected, the party politically socialized and mobilized millions of new voters. Crenson and Ginsberg (2002) point out that the parties

> contending for office and influence were virtually compelled to organize and mobilize citizens. Popular support was the currency of power, and in the struggle to acquire power, political leaders produced the high rates of participation that persisted until the start of the twentieth century... [citizens] became active because vigorously competitive leaders marched them into the public forum. (4–5)

The machines were funded by the industrial, corporate, and banking interests that benefited from the policies enacted by machine-elected officials. Party bosses hand picked nominees to insure loyalty to business interests and mobilized the masses to support those candidates. The party bosses and the corporate leaders had a mutually supportive relationship: "Sharing individualist, acquisitive goals, the machine and the local robber barons were natural allies" (Pomper 1992, 80).

The support of voters and activists was secured with the promise of patronage jobs and government contracts for some, but certainly not all. Rather, the party machines provided something of a social safety net and help in times of great need, such as the death of the family breadwinner or an apartment fire, services that garnered gratefulness and votes on Election Day. White and Shea note that "overt corruption was tolerated because party leaders had such a devoted following. If someone's house burned, a child was arrested, or there was no food in the pantry, it was the boss who came to the rescue" (White and Shea 2000, 51). Moreover, newly arrived immigrants were socialized into American politics and assimilated into their new communities through machine politics. The machines secured the funding to build the urban infrastructure so needed by their voters because they could benefit from kickbacks and payments. Thus some of the needs of the fast-growing cities were being met not by government but by the party bosses who helped fill elected posts with politicians who would do their bidding.

While the urban party machines were successful in many respects, they were inherently contradictory and unstable, particularly so in the face of efforts to restrict their power and influence: "an elite focus versus a mass base; individualistic, coalitional goals versus social collective needs; ethnic particularism versus class needs" (Pomper 1992, 82). For example, the parties promoted the interests of the corporate elite while courting the support of their overworked, underpaid, and unrepresented workers. The machine also focused on one ethnic group over another, such as the Irish over the Italians, which led to a succession of coups and rocky transitions. Yet, some party machines remained quite strong, such as the powerful Chicago machine, well past the Progressives' efforts to dismantle them. What they could not survive, however, was the rise of the American welfare state that began under the New Deal.

The Progressive Movement: An Assault on Parties

The most serious, most direct and most successful challenge to party organizations and majoritarian politics in the United States has been the Progressive movement. Beginning at the end of the nineteenth century, as the political party machines had harnessed powerful majorities in the context of the Industrial Revolution, the Progressives pointed to what they saw as "excessive political expediency and increasingly sordid partisan manipulation of democratic politics" (Silbey 2002, 11). The corrupt party machines became the focus of all that was wrong with turn-of-the-century American politics. While the Progressives certainly wanted to reduce the role and influence of big business in politics, as their standard-bearer Teddy Roosevelt demonstrated with his crusade to "bust the trusts," they did not focus primarily on business as the culprit of the corrupt and dysfunctional system. They instead concentrated their efforts on reform of the political parties and of various political processes controlled by the parties: "reform required dethroning the political bosses who in alliance with the holders of concentrated economic power defended the status quo" (Sundquist 1983, 172).

The Progressives aimed to replace collective majoritarian politics, which, under the party machines, was indeed corrupt and unrepresentative, with an individualistic politics, whereby political decisions would be made by autonomous individuals, the sum of which would theoretically be a collective decision reflective of the public interest (see, for example, Pomper 1992, 116–21; Ostrogorski 1902). To break the machines' power, the Progressives successfully enacted legislative measures "that attacked and ultimately destroyed several of the links between parties and voters" (Silbey 2002, 11). The Progressives aimed to regulate a variety of political processes, transforming parties from private associations into "public utilities" (Epstein 1986, chapter 6): "the general purpose of these reforms was to remove impediments that allegedly obstructed voter control of government and public policy" (Pomper 1992, 118).

First, the Australian (i.e., secret) ballot was introduced in the states from about 1888 to 1890 to replace party printed ballots. The move was designed to address voter intimidation and ballot-box stuffing. Yet, the parties were not excluded entirely, for most states' ballots listed nominees for office by their party. Government involvement in the ballot, and the decision to include the party label on the new secret ballot, made it easier to later further regulate the nomination of candidates for office and eventually take it out of the hands of the parties altogether by establishing the direct primary. Some municipalities, especially in the West, adopted nonpartisan ballots and still have them today.

The Progressives also introduced registration requirements for voting, which effectively disenfranchised millions of mostly working class and immigrant voters (Epstein 1986, 165; Crenson and Ginsberg 2002, 56). Voter turnout declined sharply after the 1890s, when states began to institute registration requirements (see Table 5.2). Voters are required to register many days before an election, when interest in a contest is generally not high. Until late in the twentieth century a number of states only allowed voters to register at particular public offices during weekday working hours, requiring many would-be voters to lose a day's pay to register.

Crenson and Ginsberg view voter registration requirements as a purposeful effort by the Progressives to exclude the masses: "Progressives not only objected to the corruption that was unquestionably an aspect of party politics during this era but also opposed the growing political power of the big-city

Table 5.2 Voter Turnout in Presidential Elections, 1880–1924

Year	Percent Turnout of Voting Age Population
1880	79.4%
1884	77.5%
1888	79.3%
1892	74.7%
1896	79.3%
1900	73.2%
1904	65.2%
1908	65.4%
1912	58.8%
1916	61.6%
1920	49.2%
1924	48.9%

Source: Gerhard Peters, "Voter Turnout in Presidential Elections, 1824–2004" in the American Presidency Project at UC Santa Barbara at http://www.presidency.ucsb.edu/data/turnout.php

parties and their working-class and immigrant supporters as a corruption of the democracy envisioned by the founders" (Crenson and Ginsberg 2002, 56). In recent years, some efforts have been made to lower the hurdle to participation posed by registration requirements. For instance, some states, such as Minnesota, have reduced this effect of registration requirements by allowing for same-day registration, whereby a voter can show up to a polling place on Election Day to both register and vote. The 1993 Federal Motor Voter Act makes it easier to register by allowing one to do so while applying for a driver's license, renewing a vehicle registration, or visiting a social assistance office. Yet, the United States remains the only advanced democratic country that requires voters to register before voting, and registration continues to depress U.S. voter turnout.

To break the party bosses' access to and use of patronage, the Progressives instituted the merit system (later called the civil service system). The ability of the party bosses to reward loyal party workers with jobs was an important element of the machine's power. The Pendleton Act of 1883 established the U.S. Civil Service Commission, making competency and merit the qualifications for government positions and designating thousands of jobs as permanent, whose occupants would remain in their positions regardless of which party controlled the White House. The states and localities also established merit systems for many government jobs, and the party bosses lost a powerful means of keeping their partisan troops in line and working on the party's behalf. Party leaders viewed the civil service system as an impediment to democratic accountability, for civil servants would not be held accountable for their job performance when the elected leaders were swept out of office.

The Progressives also sought to bypass partisan elected officials by replacing various political processes with direct democracy. The initiative and referendum allow voters or the legislature, respectively, to place legislative matters and constitutional amendments on the ballot for a direct vote of the people. While such measures were intended to give more power to the people rather than the powerful and wealthy, initiatives and referendums today are big-money undertakings that are not generally very representative of majority opinion (Broder 2000; Streb 2008, chapter 4). Moreover, once a policy is enacted or a constitution amended with a ballot measure, there is no way for the voters to hold anyone accountable for these often dramatic changes, and new voters often try to undo what voters did in a previous election.

The Progressive reform that most weakened the power and influence of parties was the introduction of the primary election. The direct primary took the ability to nominate candidates for office away from the party leaders and gave it directly to the voters. The power to nominate allowed the party bosses to insure that only *loyal* politicians (those loyal to the machine's goals) would get elected to office. This control over who could run for office was an important cog in the party machine, whereby the corporations funded the campaigns of party politicians who would do their bidding in government, and the party machines would turn out the voters to elect them. Taking this power away from the party bosses also meant taking power away from organized and cohesive party majorities and replacing it with individual action. Parties no longer have a means to encourage party loyalty among its partisans in government, thus freeing elected officials from some measure of *collective* accountability for their official action or inaction. Thus, unless embracing the party label is a clear benefit, candidates can appeal directly to voters for support and potentially insulate themselves from the wrath of voters if their party is out of favor since they no longer have to follow the party's program to earn the party's nomination.

The Progressive reforms of the late 1800s and early 1900s did not generally have an immediate effect on the activities, functions, and strength of party organizations, but they gradually eroded the various connections between parties and voters in the effort to replace those links with a direct connection between citizens and government. The direct primary in particular "accomplished its intended aim, the substitution of individualist political action for that of cohesive party majorities" (Pomper 1992, 120). An extended period over which the role of parties changed and diminished, only briefly interrupted by something of a party resurgence during the New Deal, followed the series of Progressive reforms. Slowly but surely the nation moved into an era that some have called "postparty" in which the parties had to adjust to a changing and often hostile environment (Silbey 2002, 13–18).

A Brief Pause in the Efforts to Chip Away at the Parties: The New Deal

During the New Deal, Franklin Roosevelt and his allies reenergized the Democratic Party, and their activity motivated the Republicans to gear up in response. The Democrats realized that their initial electoral victory was due to the Depression, and that "Democratic electoral success in 1932 might not survive the crisis that caused it or bring any lasting change in the distribution of political power" (Crenson and Ginsberg 2002, 59). The Roosevelt administration used its governmental power to strengthen friendly Democratic organizations, including the still vital party machines in cities such as Chicago and Pittsburgh, by giving them some control over the vast resources of the New Deal. Thus, as with the old party machines, desperate unemployed working class voters owed their income and security to the party, and they "willingly gave their political support to the party organizations that provided them with crucial jobs or emergency relief funds" (Crenson and Ginsberg 2002, 60). Roosevelt also worked with labor unions to strengthen their hand in dealing with business by, for example, supporting the Wagner Act to protect workers' right to organize. Union members turned out for the Democrats, and the Congress of Industrial Organizations (CIO) gave nearly $2 million to help reelect Roosevelt in 1936 (60). These mobilization efforts had a long-term impact. Indeed, the newly mobilized voters remained Democratic voters, and the New Deal coalition enabled the Democratic Party to control American politics for a generation.

Yet, the New Deal mobilization did not last forever. After World War II, the labor unions and urban party machines that fueled Democratic Party resurgence during the New Deal lost influence. The unions suffered from internal divisions, and corporations organized politically against them. Party organizations eventually lost their hold on urban voters when their services were effectively replaced by the welfare state created by Roosevelt and the Democrats: "The demand for welfare became overwhelming with the collapse of the economy.... As a local, 'retail' supplier of relief, the machine could not compete with the federal government's 'wholesale' supply of housing, jobs, and income subsidies" (Pomper 1992, 81). The government in effect replaced ethnic politics with class politics, so the machine's appeal to ethnic loyalties no longer worked very well either.

Once the economic crisis was over, Southern Democrats, who had been another important part of the New Deal coalition, became less comfortable in a party that began to focus more on civil rights and liberal economic policy. As early as 1939, Southern Democrats and conservative Republicans worked as a *Conservative Coalition* in Congress that dramatically cut funds for relief, reduced business taxes, and investigated labor activities (Crenson and Ginsberg 2002, 63). Because they did not face any real electoral competition in their one-party region, Southern Democrats rose to many of the leadership positions in Congress under the strict seniority system. With their Republican conservative allies, they prevented passage of liberal economic and social policies such as national health insurance and civil rights through the 1940s and 1950s, and into the 1960s. After World War II, during another era of dramatic social, economic, and technological change, we see party organizations again working to adapt to a new and challenging environment.

Postwar Parties: Finding a Place in Modern Politics

Postwar America was a time of general economic growth with a newly activist government fully in place. The expansion of the government created many new points of access to policymakers. A great number of new nonpartisan interest groups, particularly economic groups, formed and used these points of access to establish direct links to government independent of the parties that used to mediate the political demands of the public: "By the 1960s, every policy impulse had its own organization that moved readily into the legislative and administrative arenas, largely as if parties did not exist" (Silbey 2002, 14). This diversity of political voices each representing narrow interests often results in fragmented policy making rather than a process that revolves around majority coalitions built on compromise and cooperation such as those the parties had built in the past (Lowi 1979; also Crenson and Ginsberg 2002). Thus the development of the activist federal government further diminished the relative power of parties in the political process.

Additionally, many interest groups began to engage in electoral activities previously conducted by the parties, such as mobilizing voters, financing candidates, and articulating issue positions. Candidates themselves also began hiring campaign professionals not attached to a party organization to conduct surveys, raise money, craft political messages, coordinate volunteers, and mobilize voters—activities the parties had performed in the past (Agranoff 1972; Sabato 1981). The parties no longer had a monopoly over the electoral arena, as there was a gradual transition from party-centered to candidate-centered politics in the United States from the 1950s to the 1980s.

The transmission of political information also changed dramatically and to the detriment of the parties. The partisan press was replaced first by sensationalist and often antipolitical newspapers and then by a trend toward *objective* journalism in reaction against such *yellow* journalism. While the latter development may have been an improvement over the former, both types of news reporting took away one of the parties' most powerful political tools with which to communicate with voters. In the 1920s and 1930s, radio emerged as another powerful communications tool used so effectively by FDR to speak directly to the American public in his Fireside Chats. By the 1960s, candidates for various offices at all levels were using the radio and some began to use television to campaign directly to voters. On television, candidates tend to present themselves as individuals, not as members of a political party, and focus on personal characteristics rather than partisan appeals, further eroding the voters' connection to the parties (Ranney 1983). This ability to communicate directly with voters enabled candidates to win their elections without relying so much on the party's voter mobilization efforts.

Indeed, party identification declined during the 1960s and 1970s, as the number of voters who identified themselves as independents (not affiliated with a particular political party) increased from 1968 to 2000. Voters began splitting their tickets after World War II, voting for one party's nominee for president and the other party's nominee for the U.S. House of Representatives or the Senate. Figure 5.1 shows the correlation between Democratic presidential and congressional voting from 1900 to 2008; that is, the extent to which the percentage vote for Democratic presidential candidates was associated with the percentage vote for Democratic congressional (House and Senate) candidates. For example, after Democratic president Harry Truman alienated Southern white voters by advocating for civil rights during his first term from 1945 to 1948, Southern voters continued to support Democratic House and Senate candidates in the 1948 election but did not vote for Truman to the same extent, thereby decreasing the correlation between the presidential and congressional results (Brewer and Stonecash 2009, 23, 80). The correlation between presidential and congressional voting rose slightly after 1948,

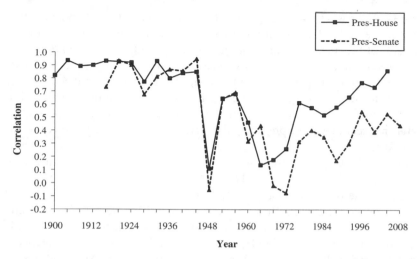

Figure 5.1   Correlation of Presidential Results, with Results in Senate (by state) and House (by district), 1900–2008. Source: Brewer and Stonecash 2009, 23.

but until the 2000s it did not reach the high levels experienced before the war, as Figure 5.1 shows.

By the late 1950s, the parties were sorting out in different ways as new issues emerged that divided the Democrat's New Deal coalition and the Republicans struggled against the drive toward a larger and more activist government. Southern whites were increasingly uncomfortable in the Democratic Party, as the liberal wing of the party pushed civil rights, workers' rights, and anti-poverty measures. However, Southern Democrats did not immediately gravitate toward the Republicans, particularly after Republican president Dwight Eisenhower sent U.S. Army troops and federalized the Arkansas National Guard to protect black students while Little Rock integrated its public schools in 1957. At the same time, liberal Democrats were not making much headway on their policy agenda as the Conservative Coalition continued to block their bills in Congress.

The election of John F. Kennedy emboldened the liberals in the Democratic Party. More liberal Democrats were elected to Congress, and they worked to push the party further to the left. Yet, the Democrats still needed Southern votes to remain in charge. In light of the party's leftward movement and the likelihood that this shift would cause Southern whites to leave the party, Kennedy worked to expand the Democrats' base to include more Northern black voters (Ranney 1983, 90). Then, Kennedy's assassination in 1963 changed the landscape for the Democrats.

Vice President Lyndon Johnson assumed the presidency, and although he had been a traditional anticivil rights Southern Democrat in the past, "by the late 1950s, he was becoming increasingly convinced that the Democratic Party's future success lay less with southern conservatives and more with liberals outside of the south, including blacks" (Ranney 1983, 93–94). By 1963, Johnson was committed to a civil rights and an antipoverty agenda, and he quickly pushed Congress to pass the 1964 Civil Rights Act that required equal access to private establishments and barred racial job discrimination. In 1964, Johnson proposed his War on Poverty and Great Society programs, and he went on later that year to win the presidential election in a landslide against conservative Republican candidate Arizona Senator Barry Goldwater. The Democrats also won the largest House and Senate majorities they had seen since 1930 even though they lost seats in the South. The influx of 41 House members from outside the South changed the Democratic Party's overall ideological character with a quick shift to the left (Ranney 1983, 96–97). Johnson and the congressional Democrats then passed a series of laws that significantly expanded the role of the federal government in an effort to achieve equality of opportunity, such as Medicare (health care for the elderly), Medicaid (health care for the poor), the Voting Rights Act of 1965, and scholarships and loans for college students (98).

By the next presidential election, however, the Democrats were not riding so high. Race riots in cities across the country, increasing problems with and protests against the Vietnam War, and demands by party regulars to have a larger role in the party's activities and decision making fragmented the party. Both Martin Luther King and Democratic presidential candidate Robert Kennedy were assassinated in 1968, slowing the momentum of the civil rights movement and the liberal wing of the Democratic Party. Mired in the Vietnam War and urban strife, Johnson did not run for reelection in 1968. The Democratic national convention erupted into chaos as convention delegates tried to deal with Southern states that sent two delegations to the convention, one all white and one that was mixed race. Outside the convention hall, Chicago police attacked antiwar protesters. Inside the convention, delegates nominated Hubert Humphrey as the party's presidential nominee. Humphrey's nomination was the result of a backroom political deal worked out by the old-guard party leaders. Humphrey went on to lose the 1968 presidential election to Republican Richard Nixon, as states' rights American Independent Party candidate George Wallace took white Southern votes from the Democrats. The New Deal coalition was eroding.

The controversial 1968 Democratic convention led to calls for a larger role for policy-motivated activities or "amateurs," and a smaller role for the party machine "professionals" who had secured Humphrey's nomination (Wilson 1962). In 1969, the Democratic National Committee established the Commission on Party Structure and Delegate Selection (the McGovern-Fraser Commission), which designed reforms to make the presidential nominating process more representative of the party membership and more open to wider participation. The delegate selection process was changed and required states to choose at least 90 percent of their convention delegates by either voting during a convention or via a primary (rather than being selected by the state party committee). The reforms took much of the power to nominate the party's presidential candidate away from the party leaders and helped liberal candidate George McGovern win the party's nomination in 1972, presumably a candidate the party leaders would not have chosen because of his ideological distance from the bulk of voters in the middle. The Republicans also adopted reforms to open up their nomination process, but the Democrats' more far-reaching efforts had a more significant and detrimental effect on the party's strength and capabilities.

Democratic Party amateurs and professionals battled over whether winning elections or pursuing particular policy goals was more important. The policy "purists' heavy focus on the agendas of specific candidates and special interests, also resulted in the neglect of the parties' organizational needs" (Herrnson 2002, 51). The parties had already lost a good deal of influence in electoral politics due to the direct primary and other Progressive reforms, and this intraparty fracas further diminished the Democrats' ability to build an effective coalition among very diverse interests and to coordinate the party's activities to win elections.

Another major development a few years later was passage of the 1971 Federal Election Campaign Act (FECA) and subsequent amendments. The FECA required parties to separate their federal election activities from their state and local party activities, which curtailed state and local party participation in federal elections. Limits were put on contributions to and from the parties. Moreover, the FECA encouraged the proliferation of political action committees (PACs) that quickly became a primary source of funds for congressional candidates: "The amount of money a House or Senate candidate can collect from possibly hundreds of PACs easily eclipses the amount that parties are permitted to give to and spend on behalf of a candidate" (Farrar-Myers and Dwyre 2001, 139). Thus as candidates searched for resources to run for office, they became less dependent on their parties for financial and other support.

During the candidate-centered politics of the 1970s and 1980s the parties were limping along with ineffective organizations and a diminished role in electoral politics. Many scholars and other observers declared the sad state of party politics in a series of books, such as *The Party's Over* (Broder 1972), *American Political Parties in Decline* (Crotty 1984), and *The Decline of the American Political Parties* (Wattenberg 1990). Yet, as they had done in the past when their influence was waning, the parties responded by working to reinvent themselves to regain a place of relevance in electoral politics. In the wake of the Watergate scandal, for example, there was a large decline in the number of voters who identified with the Republican Party and huge Republican losses in the 1974 and 1976 elections. Herrnson notes that this Republican "crisis of competition drew party leaders' attention to the weaknesses of the Republican national, congressional and senatorial campaign committees"

(Herrnson 2002, 52). So, after a battle for the leadership, the GOP elected new entrepreneurial leaders, such as RNC chairman William Brock, who focused on party organizational development. The Democrats followed with similar efforts to renew their national party committee's institutional and electoral capabilities.

The parties emerged from this period of transition as stronger, more professional, and financially secure organizations that are diversified in their activities and staffing. They evolved from organizations that *did the work* to elect their candidates to organizations that *provided the resources* to their candidates to get *themselves* elected. Aldrich discusses this evolution: "over time… the parties as organizations have adapted to the changing circumstances, and a new form of party has emerged, one that is 'in service' to its ambitious politicians but not 'in control' of them as the mass party sought to be" (Aldrich 1995, 273; see also Herrnson 1988). The national parties' committees began to raise significantly more money, allowing them to invest in their organizational infrastructures, such as permanent headquarters, expanded professional staffs, advanced technology for fundraising, polling, and accounting, and extensive party-building efforts to strengthen the state parties (Herrnson 2002).

The parties' new financial strength was the key to their transition to the institutionalized professional organizations they are today. Table 5.3 illustrates the fundraising success of the national parties since 1976 (figures are adjusted for inflation in 2009 dollars to show real changes over time). It shows the national party committees' federal, or "hard" money receipts, money raised under the FECA contribution limits and source restrictions (e.g., until 2010, before the Supreme Court's decision in *Citizens United v. Federal Election Commission*, 558 US (20100 corporations and banks were not permitted to spend money in federal elections; instead they had to create a PAC and raise money from individuals to spend in elections).[1]

Moreover, during this time the parties found other creative ways to raise large sums of money. For instance, the parties also raised nonfederal, or "soft" money, until it was banned by passage of the Bipartisan Campaign Reform Act (BCRA, also known as the McCain-Feingold Act) in 2002. Soft money is money raised and spent largely outside of federal campaign finance limits and regulations. The national parties began to raise large amounts of soft money in the early 1990s from wealthy individuals, corporations, labor unions, and other organizations (see Table 5.4; figures are adjusted for inflation in 2009 dollars to show real changes over time).

Technically, soft money was not to be used for federal elections. However, the parties found ways to use these large soft money donations to help federal candidates, such as transferring the money to state parties that would then fund so-called issue ads to help the party's federal candidate (Dwyre 1996). Issue ads are not permitted to expressly advocate the election or defeat of a candidate for office. Yet the soft-money funded issue ads produced by the par-

Table 5.3 National Party Hard Money Receipts, 1976-2009 (in millions of constant 2009 dollars)

	Democrats				Republicans			
	DNC	DCCC	DSCC	Total	RNC	NRCC	NRSC	Total
1976	49.7	3.4	3.8	56.9	110.5	45.9	6.8	163.2
1978	37.4	9.3	1.0	47.7	113.3	46.7	36.1	196.1
1980	40.4	7.6	4.5	52.4	203.9	53.2	58.4	315.6
1982	36.9	14.5	12.5	64.0	188.2	129.8	109.4	427.5
1984	96.9	21.6	18.5	137.0	220.1	121.2	169.8	511.1
1986	33.9	24.2	26.4	84.5	165.1	78.4	169.7	413.2
1988	95.5	22.8	29.8	148.1	166.1	63.3	120.3	349.8
1990	24.0	15.0	28.9	67.9	113.5	54.9	107.6	276.0
1992	101.3	19.7	39.3	160.2	131.5	54.2	113.6	299.2
1994	60.9	28.3	38.5	127.7	127.4	38.9	95.2	261.4
1996	149.2	36.6	42.4	228.2	265.7	102.1	88.8	456.6
1998	85.9	33.4	47.2	166.4	137.8	96.3	70.8	304.9
2000	155.5	60.7	50.8	267.0	266.9	122.0	64.6	453.5
2002	81.0	55.7	58.1	194.8	204.2	148.4	71.1	423.7
2004	462.3	106.6	101.4	670.3	448.1	212.3	90.3	751.3
2006	140.1	149.9	130.1	420.1	260.3	188.9	95.1	544.3
2008	260.9	176.7	163.3	601.0	429.0	118.7	94.7	642.3

Source: Federal Election Commission press releases.
Note: Figures reflect funds raised from January 1 of the year preceding the election through December 31 of the election year. Figures adjusted for inflation using www.usinflationcalculator.com

ties and many interest groups were usually indistinguishable from campaign ads and often more negative (Herrnson and Dwyre 1999). Soft money was much like the money the party bosses collected from wealthy corporate leaders in an era with no real campaign finance regulations. Indeed, reformers who passed the BCRA characterized soft money donations to the parties as a corrupting influence on elections and governing, for such substantial sums of money might be able to buy elections and sway votes in Congress (Dwyre and Farrar-Myers 2001).

Soft money made the national party committees superrich, and allowed them to do even more to help their candidates win. In fact, some legislators (e.g., Republican Senator Mitch McConnell and Democratic Representative Martin Frost, who chaired the DCCC at the time) and scholars (see, for example, La Raja 2003) argued against the ban on soft money in the McCain-Feingold bill. They asserted that ending this stream of funding for the parties would weaken

Table 5.4 National Party Soft Money Receipts, 1992–2002 (in millions of constant 2009 dollars)

	Democrats				Republicans			
	DNC	DCCC	DSCC	Total	RNC	NRCC	NRSC	Total
1992	48.3	6.8	0.9	56.0	55.3	9.4	14.0	78.7
1994	64.0	7.4	0.6	72.0	65.4	10.8	8.2	84.4
1996	104.3	16.9	19.5	176.7	155.7	25.5	40.5	221.6
1998	75.2	22.4	34.3	132.2	99.1	35.6	50.2	185.0
2000	171.3	71.1	79.9	322.3	208.4	59.3	56.1	323.8
2002	113.6	67.7	114.0	295.3	136.7	83.7	79.7	300.1

Source: Federal Election Commission, "Party Committees Raise More than $1 Billion 2001–2002," press release, March 20, 2003.

Note: Figures reflect funds raised from January 1 of the year preceding the election through December 31 of the election year. Figures do not include transfers among the committees. Figures adjusted for inflation using 2009 dollars to show real changes over time.

the parties relative to special interest groups, and that this would be detrimental to our system of representative democracy in which the parties are the only funders of campaigns that promote the interests of majorities (La Raja 2003, 2008, esp. chapter 6; Milkis 2003; see also Dwyre and Farrar-Myers 2001, 157, 219). Some observers also thought that the ban on soft money would be far worse for the Democrats than the Republicans, calling it "The Democratic Party Suicide Bill," because of the Republicans' traditional financial edge over the Democrats, as can be seen in Table 5.3 (Gitell 2003; see also Dwyre and Farrar-Myers 2001, 157). However, as Table 5.3 shows, the parties did just fine after the ban on soft money took effect in 2004, particularly the Democrats, by raising record amounts of hard money.

The parties have used their financial strength to enhance their role in contemporary elections, and their activities may have contributed to the recent resurgence in party identification and party voting (both by the electorate and by legislators in Congress). Indeed, since the 1970s, the incidence of ticket splitting has declined significantly—see Figure 5.1 above that shows the correlation between presidential and congressional voting rising since the 1990s. These developments may be due in part to a major effort of both parties to invest in advanced technology to more effectively target voters for mobilization. Sophisticated techniques, such as data mining of data sets with different types of information on potential voters, have helped the parties better identify which voters are more likely to support their candidates based on policy preferences, lifestyle, demographics, and other factors. The parties have used this information in combination with low-tech and somewhat old-fashioned voter mobilization techniques, such as door-to-door voter contact, phone banking and direct mail, in successful get-out-the-vote (GOTV) programs in recent elections (Dwyre and Kolodny 2006).

The parties also have invested in Internet and e-mail programs and information technology professionals to conduct targeted fundraising, voter education and GOTV operations. One of the results of these computer-based techniques has been a rise in small donations to both parties and their presidential candidates. This has expanded the *number* of campaign contributors, which may diminish the influence of big-money contributors as parties and candidates continue to improve this low-cost means for raising campaign cash in small increments. Indeed, in the 2008 election both John McCain and Barack Obama raised more of their money from small donors than past presidential candidates had done (Malbin 2009). This is certainly a trend in a positive direction, but it is not a sea change in the role of big money in elections.

While contemporary political parties are certainly not as strong and influential as the mass-based parties of Van Buren's time, they have found a meaningful place in American politics. Party identification among voters and party voting in Congress and state legislatures are up. Parties provide important campaign services to their candidates, and they continue to develop new techniques of fundraising and voter mobilization. However, both major parties face new challenges. Barack Obama ran his presidential campaign as an independent enterprise with little input (yet much assistance) from the Democratic Party organization. The Republicans are struggling to build a winning coalition from diverse factions within their party. How each party addresses its challenges will determine how it fares in an ever-changing environment.

Conclusion: Of Evolution, Reinvention, and Survival

U.S. political parties emerged and evolved by continually reinventing themselves to survive challenges from the forces of societal change as well as from outright enemies. They developed and changed in response to evolving opinions about the role and nature of parties; in response to major crises such as the Civil War and the Great Depression; and they responded to significant advancements in science and technology such as the Industrial Revolution, the advent of broadcast communications, and the introduction of the Internet. They were not destroyed by the Progressives or overtaken by the rise of interest groups politics, because strategic politicians found them useful and continue to this day to turn to parties to help them achieve their goals (Aldrich 1995; Pomper 1992).

The strength and influence of political parties have varied over time. The heyday of party power was when the mass-based, grassroots party developed by Martin Van Buren and the Jacksonian Democrats transformed elite partisan organizations into genuinely participatory democratic institutions. During the early to mid-1800s, party organizations (the Democrats and the Whigs) were truly competitive as the idea of peaceful and legitimate party opposition became accepted. This evolution of thought about parties, whereby legitimate opposition and true competition are eventually considered not only acceptable but also necessary, is a crucial development that made it possible for U.S. parties to become a powerful vehicle for majority opinion to overcome the governmental separation of powers that divides the majority's influence. Offering a meaningful choice to a wide range of voters allows the people to truly rule.

Party change and development is also linked to major transitions in the alignment of voters (Brewer and Stonecash 2009). As we have seen, surviving as a political party is not just about the mechanics of running and winning elections. Parties continually adjust to the changing views of voters to maintain or build coalitions that can win elections and achieve majority status. Voters often sort out differently when new issues emerge. For instance, the issues of slavery and immigration split the Whig Party beyond its ability to survive because it could not build a stable coalition of voters.

The New Deal coalition began to dissolve when civil rights, poverty, and the Vietnam War replaced the economy as the primary issue. A major crisis, the Depression, and a virtually singular focus on its solution, the New Deal, brought Democrats of all stripes together for a generation. Eventually, however, the advent of new issues and the Democratic Party's focus on them led many voters to feel more comfortable in the Republican Party. The Democrats then had to seek voters from different groups in order to remain relevant and competitive in the new electoral and policy environment. Expansion of the role of government during the New Deal and later in the 1960s, the issue that originally distinguished and continues to divide the parties, as well as the emergence and candidates' use of new technologies such as radio, television, direct mail, and computer communications, proved to be particularly difficult hurdles to party cohesion and organizational strength. Through it all, however, the parties have remained consistent in one respect—they have focused on winning elections.

As so many adept scholars have concluded and party leaders throughout time have known, political parties must first win elections before any other goals can even be pursued. Thus the story of U.S. political parties will continue to be one of evolution and reinvention that succeeds when parties focus on winning. This is not to say that politicians will or should embrace *any* position that could win them votes, but in order to survive they will eventually adjust their appeals to build winning (and they hope lasting) coalitions.

Note

1. In January 2010, the Supreme Court invalidated restrictions on corporate and union independent expenditures as a violation of free speech, allowing them to now spend independently from their treasuries, rather than having to create a PAC to advocate election or defeat of a candidate for office, see *Citizens United v. Federal Election Commission*, 558 US (2010). While this is a dramatic change in campaign finance law, it is likely to have little effect on party fundraising, because the decision does not directly affect corporate and union giving to political parties.

Part III

Sources of Political Divisions, Realignment, and Current Party Differences

Chapter 6

Blacks and the Democratic Party
A Resilient Coalition

Kerry L. Haynie and Candis S. Watts

According to a 2008 American Nation Election Study Poll, 71 percent of blacks[1] who are registered to vote self-identify as Democrat. In contrast, just 2 percent of registered blacks identify as Republican, and 23 percent as Independent.[2] This makes blacks the most asymmetrical of the major political subgroups in party identification terms. Blacks are also the only large racial or ethnic subgroup in which more than half of its members identify with one party. The 69 point advantage that blacks give to the Democrats is significantly larger than that given to either party by any other segment of the electorate. For example, the distribution pattern of Latinos across the parties is somewhat similar to the pattern for blacks, with an advantage for the Democrats over the Republicans of 34 percent. This advantage, however, is half the advantage blacks give the Democrats.

Blacks are not only overwhelmingly Democratic in their partisan identification, they also consistently vote for Democratic candidates by overwhelming margins in elections at all levels. In the 2004 presidential election, for example, the Democratic candidate, John Kerry received 88 percent of the votes cast by blacks, while incumbent Republican candidate George W. Bush received only 11 percent of the black vote.[3] The margin was even greater in 2008, when Democrat Barack Obama received 95 percent of the black vote compared to just 4 percent going to John McCain.[4]

This severely unbalanced black identification with the Democratic Party has been a consistent pattern over the past four-and-a-half decades. However, blacks have not always been so strongly Democratic in their party affiliation. From just after the Civil War until the 1950s, most black voters and officeholders aligned themselves with the Republican Party. In the early years, this affiliation with the Republicans was a profitable one. For example, during Reconstruction fifteen black Republicans were elected to the U.S. Congress, thirteen to the House of Representatives and two to the Senate (Haynie 1991). In addition, between 1865 and 1877, close to two thousand black Republicans were elected to state and local offices and appointed to important party leadership positions throughout the South (Foner 1996; Gurin, Hatchett, and

Jackson 1989; Philpot 2007; Walton 1972). Another indication of black prominence and success in the Republican Party was the appointment of John R. Lynch, a state legislator from Mississippi, as temporary chairman of the 1884 Republican national convention (Gurin et al. 1989).

Why then, do the vast majority of blacks today identify with the Democratic Party? What led to the shift in black allegiance from the Republicans to the Democrats? What are the political ramifications of this severe party identification imbalance for politics, the political system, and blacks as a group? How likely is the near monolithic black identification with the Democrats to change in the future?

In the Beginning: Blacks as Republicans

Given its openness to and support of black participation, as well as some of the specific policies it advocated, it is easy to understand why the Civil War and Reconstruction era Republican Party was attractive to early black political participants. President Abraham Lincoln's Emancipation Proclamation of 1862 was responsible for immediately freeing thousands of slaves and laying the legal foundation for an end to slavery. The Republican controlled Reconstruction congresses supported black interests and promoted black well-being through legislation such as the Civil Rights Acts of 1866, 1871, and 1875; as well as through the enactment of the Civil War amendments to the Constitution—the Thirteenth, Fourteenth, and Fifteenth Amendments. However, the seeds of the black exodus from the Republican Party were planted as early as 1872, in the midst of internal party conflict over the extent to which the party should continue to support Reconstruction policies that alienated white Southerners (Philpot 2007; Walton 1972).

The presidential election of 1876 led to the Compromise of 1877, which effectively ended Reconstruction and signaled the end of Republican advocacy of black interests, especially in the South. The 1876 presidential election ended with neither Samuel J. Tilden, the Democratic candidate, nor Rutherford B. Hayes, the Republican candidate, having enough electoral collage votes to be declared the winner. In the Compromise of 1877, southern Democrats agreed to allow Hayes to become president in exchange for Hayes and the Republicans agreeing to remove all federal troops from the former Confederate states. This was a devastating blow for blacks. As Barker, Jones, and Tate (1999) put it, the Compromise:

> ...led to widespread feeling among blacks that they had been abandoned by the Republican party and once again offered up to the whims of their former slaveholders. Consequently, black Republicans who had prospered during Reconstruction were brushed aside both by the reemergence of the Democratic party as well as by southern Republican leaders who wanted to rid the party of its black image. (217)

The Compromise resulted in the resurgence of white supremacy and "a new period of lily-white Republicanism in the South" (Walton 1972, 24). The end of Reconstruction ultimately led to the disenfranchisement of black Southerners and ended their influence in the region's social, economic, and political affairs. Blacks' primary response to their diminished power and the growing "lily-white Republicanism" was to form regional Republican Party factions, known as Black and Tan organizations, which were intended to provide them with the institutional means to maintain a presence in national party affairs (Gurin et al. 1989; Philpot 2007; Walton 1972). Nationally, Republican Party elites were unwilling to take up the cause of black Republicans. As Gurin et al. (1989) observed:

> As for national politics, blacks in the North were increasingly shunned by the Republican party, owing to its candidates' preoccupation with the South. The Republican Party treated black Republicans as expendable, since a relatively small number of blacks lived in the North, and southern blacks generally could not vote. (25)

Consequently, blacks became increasingly alienated from the Republicans. Their situation in the party continued to decline for the remainder of the nineteenth century and into the twentieth century.[5]

The Transition to the Democrats

The shunning of blacks and their interests resulted in significant black support for Woodrow Wilson, the Democratic Party candidate for president in 1912. This was the first time blacks displayed substantial interests in the Democratic Party on a national level (Gurin et al. 1989; Philpot 2007; Walton 1972). This support for the Democrats came with great reluctance on the part of black elites. For example, although *Crisis*, a publication of the National Association for the Advancement of Colored People (NAACP), endorsed Wilson, the endorsement, according to Gurin et al. (1989), took place "largely as a choice of desperation and with many misgivings" (26).

President Wilson and the Democrats proved to be a disappointment for blacks. Early in his term, Wilson issued executive orders that instituted segregation and required separate toilet and food service facilities in federal government departments. Thus early into the twentieth century, blacks found themselves in a political no-person's land, having been rejected by both parties' national agenda. In 1936, blacks rallied around Franklin D. Roosevelt's first presidential reelection bid. Roosevelt's economic and social policies led to overwhelming black support for the Democrats. As Walton (1972) describes it:

> Roosevelt's social policies were an attractive lure for politically root-less Black voters searching for a viable party: his welfare programs, his

appointment of a "Black Cabinet," and his creation of the Fair Employment Practices Commission captured the imagination of the majority of
Blacks and set the stage for their strong swing to the Democratic party.
(27)

Hence, the conversion of blacks to the Democratic Party came to fruition
with the implementation of FDR's New Deal.[6]
The death of Roosevelt in 1944 revealed that black loyalty to the Democratic
Party was tenuous. The fact that Harry S. Truman, Roosevelt's successor, had
to campaign vigorously for the black vote in the 1948 election demonstrated
that blacks' loyalty was tied more to FDR than to the party itself. As part of his
effort to attract black voters, Truman inserted a civil rights plank in the 1948
Democratic Party platform (McClain and Stewart 2010). The inclusion of civil
rights on the party's national agenda strengthened the support the Democrats
had among blacks.[7] For example, during the 1952 presidential election, 78 percent of blacks who voted, voted for the Democratic Party candidate (Gurin et
al. 1989). Moreover, 1952 marked the beginning of a more than five-decade
long increase in Democratic Party identification among blacks (Table 6.1).

Table 6.1 Partisan Identification by Race, 1956–2008

	Black			White		
	Democrat	Republican	Independent	Democrat	Republican	Independent
	%	%	%	%	%	%
1956	61.3	22.7	16.0	38.2	30.9	25.1
1960	55.4	24.1	20.5	47.9	30.6	21.5
1964	81.0	6.0	13.0	49.6	26.8	23.6
1968	86.8	2.7	8.5	41.0	26.9	28.7
1972	67.4	7.5	13.5	37.0	25.4	29.9
1976	71.2	4.5	16.2	35.5	26.5	29.6
1980	72.2	4.8	13.9	35.7	25.6	25.9
1984	63.6	3.6	15.3	32.9	31.5	26.0
1988	62.2	6.4	24.7	29.2	32.8	32.4
1992	66.3	5.8	20.2	31.9	31.5	30.2
1996	65.7	3.4	22.2	35.2	30.9	26.8
2000	66.8	3.4	18.3	29.2	29.3	28.4
2004	60.8	1.7	33.5	25.4	36.2	31.8
2008	70.9	1.8	22.6	27.1	30.5	35.2

Sources: American National Election Studies, 1956–2008
Note: Each year's data comes from the corresponding American National Election Study taken
during that year.

Although in the 1950s there were few substantive differences between Democrats and Republicans on racial issues, President Eisenhower's refusal to endorse the Supreme Court's 1954 decision in *Brown v. Board of Education of Topeka*, and the Republican Party's refusal to embrace the burgeoning civil rights movement, did not provide blacks with any incentive to break away from the Democrats and return to the GOP. Two political occurrences in 1964 solidified blacks' alliance with the Democratic Party. One was that President Lyndon B. Johnson became the champion of black civil rights and led a successful battle to have the 1964 Civil Rights Act enacted into law. The second occurrence was that the Republican Party nominated Senator Barry Goldwater, an opponent of the Civil Rights Act, as its party's candidate for president. These two events redefined and clearly distinguished the parties' position on matters of race and civil rights:

> Before 1964 the electorate saw little difference between the two parties in terms of race. After 1964, however, the electorate developed a clear perception of the Democratic Party as more favorable to black interests. Just as important, this perception was closely related to reality. Not only did the 1964 presidential candidates take divergent positions on civil rights, but House Democrats also became more liberal on civil rights issues than House Republicans. Senate Democrats had become almost as liberal as Senate Republicans after the 1958 elections, but they became even more liberal in 1964. In short, the events of 1964 served to restructure permanently the relationship between the parties on issues of race. (Huckfeldt and Kohfeld 1989, 11)

A new political coalition was brought into being in 1964, one that remains fully intact more than forty-five years later. Although there have been episodes of serious internal racial conflict and strife within the Democratic Party, blacks have been the most loyal and reliable subgroup in the party coalition for this entire forty-five-year period.

Black Party Identification Today

As we learned from the data in Table 6.1, blacks today remain overwhelmingly Democratic in their party affiliation. Party identification among blacks has been relatively static in recent years. The 72 percent to 4 percent advantage currently held by the Democrats is virtually the same advantage the Democrats had in 2000, when 71 percent of blacks who were registered to vote self-identified as Democrats, and just 5 percent as Republicans.[8]

Blacks' identification with the Democratic Party does not vary as the most politically salient and relevant demographic characteristics vary. With regards to gender, there is some evidence of a slight gender split within the black electorate. According to 2008 American National Election Study data, 73 percent

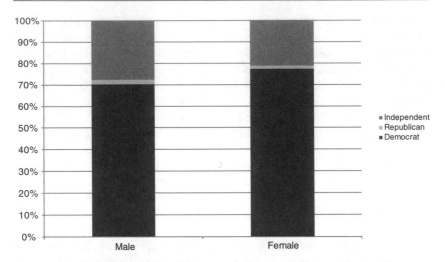

Figure 6.1   Black Partisan Indentification by Gender. Source: American National
Election Study, 2008.

of black women self-identify as Democrats, while only 68 percent of black men
do so (Figure 6.1). This divide is also present when we look at the intensity
with which men and women identify with the party. Black women are more
likely than black men to identify strongly with the Democratic Party.[9] Interestingly, although black men are less likely than black women to identify with
the Democratic Party, they are not significantly more likely than them to be
Republicans.

A longstanding finding in political science research is the lack of significant
partisan and ideological cleavages among blacks of different economic means.
Unlike with other racial and ethnic groups, blacks from all class backgrounds
demonstrate remarkable agreement on most political, social, and economic
issues (Dawson 1994; Gurin et al. 1989). On no issue is this more apparent
than party identification. As the data in Figure 6.2 show, there are virtually
no differences in the party identification propensities of blacks in the highest
income brackets and those in the lowest. Blacks of all income groups identify
overwhelmingly with the Democratic Party. Similarly, we see no major differences in party identification among blacks with different educational backgrounds. Blacks of all educational levels are much more likely to be Democrats
than either Republicans or Independents (Figure 6.3). By comparison, there are
significant differences in party identification among whites based on income
and education. For example, in 2008 there was a 10 point difference between
the percentage of whites in the highest income bracket who identified with the
Democratic Party and those in the lowest income brackets. Thirty-one percent
of whites with incomes of $30,000 or less self-identified as Democrats, while
just 21 percent of whites with incomes of $75,000 or more did.

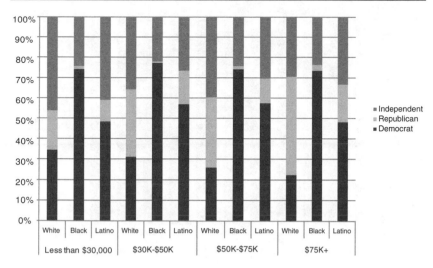

Figure 6.2   Partisan Identification by Income. Source: American National Election
Study, 2008.

While large proportions of black adults in all age cohorts are affiliated with
the Democratic Party, there is evidence of some generational differences. A
much smaller proportion of younger blacks (18- to 29-year-olds) identify as
Democrats when compared to older blacks (>49 years olds) (Figure 6.4). These
data suggest that, in the future, the Democratic Party might not be able to
count on the party identification advantages it receives from Blacks today.
This issue is discussed in more detail below.

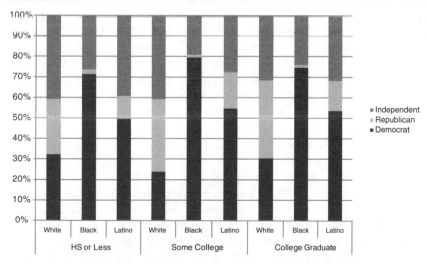

Figure 6.3   Partisan Identification by Education. Source: American National Election
Study, 2008.

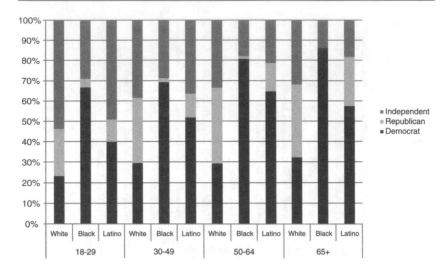

Figure 6.4   Partisan Identification by Age. Source: American National Election Study, 2008.

A Growing Racial Divide

According to the Census, blacks, in 2009, constituted 12 percent of the U.S. adult population, but just 2 percent of Republicans were black. These percentages were unchanged from what they were almost a decade earlier (Table 6.2). The percentage of U.S. adults who are white fell from about 73 percent in 2000 to an estimated 68 percent in 2009, yet during this same period, the percentage of Republicans who are white (88%) stayed the same.[10] For the Democratic Party, the share of its members who are white declined from 64 percent in 2000 to 56 percent by 2009, well below their representation in the overall population.[11] These data indicate that there is a wide and widening racial divide when it comes to party identification. The growing overrepresentation of whites and the growing underrepresentation of blacks (and other ethnic minorities) in the Republican Party, and the growing overrepresentation of blacks and the growing under representation of whites in the Democratic Party are trends that deserve our attention.

The overrepresentation of blacks in the Democratic Party has had beneficial consequences for the party and for blacks. The migration of blacks from the South in the 1920s and 1940s resulted in large concentrations of blacks in cities like Chicago, Cleveland, Detroit, Newark, Philadelphia, and St. Louis. This concentration of blacks, along with waves of white flight created influential black Democratic enclaves. These black political strongholds have contributed to the election of thousands of Democrats, including a large number of black Democrats, to various state, local, and municipal positions. The election of black mayors in all of these and other cities is perhaps the most visible manifestation of urban black political power.

Table 6.2 Black-White Composition of the Parties

2009	All Adults	Republican	Democrat	Independent
	%	%	%	%
White, non-Hispanic	68	88	56	72
Black, non-Hispanic	12	2	22	7
Hispanic	14	6	15	12
Other, non-Hispanic	6	4	6	7
2000				
White, non-Hispanic	73	88	64	79
Black, non-Hispanic	11	2	21	8
Hispanic	11	7	11	9
Other, non-Hispanic	5	2	4	4
Change in % White NH	−5	0	−8	−7

Source: Pew Research Center, 2009, http://people-press.org/report/?pageid=1516

The concentration of blacks in urban areas has also been beneficial to national Democratic Party politics. In order to win presidential elections, Democratic candidates typically need to win the battleground states of Illinois, Ohio, and Pennsylvania. To do so, the candidates must win decisive victories in the states' large cities, which in turn requires overwhelming support from blacks. For example, wins by Barack Obama in the above three states in the 2008 presidential race were vital to his ultimate defeat of John McCain. Overwhelming black turnout in support of Obama in Chicago, Cleveland, and Philadelphia was one of the most important determining factors for his win in these states respectively. In each state, blacks overvoted their share of the black voting age population, and Obama received a higher percentage of the black vote than did John Kerry in 2004 (Bositis 2008). In Illinois the black vote for Obama was 7 percentage points higher than it was for Kerry; in Ohio it was 13 points higher; and in Pennsylvania it was 12 points higher (Bositis 2008). The black vote was also instrumental in Obama victories in the battleground state of Florida, and also in North Carolina and Virginia, two states that have been reliable Republican states in presidential elections for more than thirty years.

The importance of the black vote to Democratic Party victories is also apparent in statewide elections with national implications. For example, black voters were crucial to the 2008 election of U.S. senators Kay Hagan (D-NC) and Mary Landrieu (D-LA). It is important to note that the significance of the black vote to Democrat successes is neither a recent development nor a phenomenon that is necessarily associated with having a black Democratic candidate for president. The margin of victory in Jimmy Carter's 1976 win in thirteen states was provided by the black vote (Gurin et al. 1989). In 1998, high black turnout was responsible for the election of Democratic governors in Alabama, Georgia, and South Carolina, and a U.S. senator in North Carolina (Sack 1998). Given these very salient examples, there is widespread recognition by Democratic Party elites and rank and file party members alike of the importance of the overwhelming support from blacks for the party's success.

The Democratic Party has not been the only benefactor of black support. There have been a number of direct positive political developments for blacks as well. Three of the most significant of these developments has been a dramatic growth in the number of black elected officials at all levels of government; increased responsiveness to black interests; and greater inclusion of blacks in party affairs.

The growth in the number of black elected officials over the past forty years is among the most noticeable developments in American politics. According to the Joint Center for Political and Economic Studies, in 1970 there were 1,469 black elected officials nationwide (Joint Center for Political and Economic Studies 2001). By 2008, that number had grown to over 10,000. The growth has been at all levels of government. And we know from several studies that the election of blacks to public office leads to more black interest issues being added to policymaking agendas and enacted into law (Bratton and Haynie 1999; Bratton, Haynie, and Reingold 2006; Browning, Marshall, and Tabb 1984; Haynie 2001, 2005). Thus similar to their experience with the Republican Party in the late nineteenth century, blacks' strong affiliation with the Democratic Party since the midtwentieth century has had important, tangible benefits.

The growth in the number of black elected officials together with blacks' influence in determining election outcomes have resulted in a second benefit for blacks, and greater responsiveness to their social, political, and economic interests. Beginning with the 1964 party platform, 1964 Civil Rights Act, and the 1965 Voting Rights Act, the Democratic Party has increasingly sought to respond to the needs and interests of black Americans. Although the party's motivations for doing so have not always been altruistic, it nevertheless has long been the party considered by most blacks to be the one most responsive to their concerns.

In their seminal study of ten Californian cities, Browning, Marshall, and Tabb (1984) show that the support of liberal white Democrats is instrumental in the formation of successful biracial governing coalitions that resulted in the incorporation of blacks and other minorities into the political system. Political incorporation is the extent to which a group is represented and influential within authoritative policymaking bodies. A direct consequence of political incorporation is increased policy responsiveness, which has material benefits for minority communities. In the California cities in the Browning et al. study, for instance, "When liberal coalitions composed of minorities and whites (typically Democrats) gained control of councils, city employment of minorities increased, police review boards were created, more minorities were appointed to commissions, more minority contractors were utilized by the cities, and minority-oriented programs were established."[12] Similarly, in several multistate studies of blacks in state legislatures, scholars have found that the incorporation of black representatives in legislative institutions is responsible for increased state government responsiveness to black interests. The presence of blacks has caused state governments to devote more attention to issues of particular concern to blacks, such as greater access to quality education and healthcare, and ending racial discrimination in education, employment, and housing. These studies also show that party affiliation is a significant variable in the advocacy of such issues. White Democrats are more likely to advocate and support black interests than are their white Republican counterparts (Bratton and Haynie 1999; Bratton et al. 2006; Haynie 2001).

Another visible benefit for blacks, which is related to their strong ties to the Democratic Party, is their greater inclusion in party affairs. One indication of this inclusion is the growth over time in the number of black delegates to national party conventions. In 1968, blacks were 12 percent of the party's membership, but represented less than 6 percent of the delegates to that year's national convention (Tate 1993, 58). At the 2000 convention, blacks were 20 percent of the delegates, which was nearly proportionate to their 21 percent representation in the party at large.[13] By 2008, blacks' representation among Democratic Party national convention delegates exceeded their representation in the party as a whole. They comprised 22 percent of the party in 2008, and they made up 24.5 percent of the delegates at the convention.[14]

Blacks' have also ascended to influential and visible Democratic Party leadership positions. For example, in 1988 Ronald H. Brown was selected as national chairman of the party, becoming the first black to lead a major U.S. political party on a full-time basis.[15] In 2000, Democratic presidential candidate Albert Gore, Jr. named Donna Brazile, an African American woman, as his campaign manager. Brazile was the first, and to date, the only black to manage a general election presidential campaign. The ultimate exemplar of blacks' visibility in party leadership positions is Barack Obama, the Democratic Party's 2008 nominee for president. Obama is the first person of African descent to be a major party's nominee for president. Upon winning the general election, Obama not only became the most powerful individual in government, he also assumed the position of de facto leader of the Democratic Party. His election is a clear sign of blacks' rise to the highest plateau of party politics.

The Other Side of the Coin

The above beneficial outcomes notwithstanding, the severely unbalanced black identification with the Democratic Party has had some equally important negative political consequences for blacks, the Democrats, and the political system. Barker and Jones (1994) warn that black politics runs the risk of becoming too "routinized' or normalized as a consequence of the growing political influence blacks are achieving as a result of their almost undivided allegiance to one party. Routinized or normalized black politics is a politics that is similar to that practiced by the mainstream. They contend that, as blacks become more integrated and incorporated into political institutions, they tend to place less emphasis and importance on race and the advocacy of black interests. This "routinization," they argue, leads to black elected officials' becoming conventional politicians, in "more of a *system supporting than a system challenging fashion*" (322, emphasis in the original). They summarize this dilemma in the following way: "Seeking to retain a viable political force, the national Democratic Party has followed its erstwhile white supporters to the political right and, in order to remain within the mainstream of the Democratic Party, black political operatives have also moved toward the conservative center, de-emphasizing in the process race-specific interests" (323). Over time routinization leads to a state of affairs in which there are few if any advocates for the specific and sometimes distinctive concerns of blacks.

Related to problems associated with the routinization of blacks in politics, another negative consequence for blacks stemming from their overconcentration in the Democratic Party is the increased propensity of white party elites to take the black vote for granted, and to ignore blacks and their interests whenever it is politically expedient to do so. That is, although the Democratic Party, over the past forty-five years, has clearly been more responsive to mainstream black interests than the Republican Party, it may not have been as responsive as it might otherwise be if it had to seriously compete for black votes and support. An important finding from the research on race and representation in state legislatures illustrates this point. In his study of five legislatures, Haynie (2001) notes that before blacks were elected to these bodies, few black interests issues were placed on legislative agendas, notwithstanding the fact that for years white Democrats who had been elected with significant black support had dominated many of these legislatures.[16]

Bill Clinton's 1992 and 1996 presidential campaigns are other examples of the Democrats taking black support for granted.[17] Regarding the 1992 campaign, Walton and Smith (2003) write, "While Clinton in his 1992 campaign did make a number of pledges to deal with issues important to the black community…, in general the campaign involved a strategically calculated effort to distance the candidate and the Democratic Party from blacks while appealing to the concerns of disaffected "Reagan Democrats" and the white middle class generally."[18] Similarly, Clinton's successful 1996 reelection campaign, by design, largely ignored race-related matters and issues of direct concern to the black community. Nevertheless, he received an overwhelming majority of the black vote in both elections, 82 percent in 1992 and 84 percent in 1996.

Because of the country's history of racial tensions and racial polarization, the coalition of blacks, white liberals, and conservative Southerners that came into existence in the mid-1960s has at times proven to be unstable and difficult to hold together, especially in the South and in national elections. The coalition has often come undone at the most critical times—during elections. The behavior of white Democrats has been an important source of this instability. There is a historical pattern of many middle and working class whites leaving the party as a result of the party undertaking visible efforts to solicit black support and incorporate black interests onto the party's agenda (Huckfeldt and Kohfeld 1989). In their influential study on this topic Huckfeldt and Kohfeld (1989) conclude, "The extent to which whites are willing to support the Democratic Party is directly related to the reliance of the party on black voters. As the Democratic coalition becomes blacker, whites become less willing to participate" (184). A result of this dynamic is the South, the region of the country where most blacks live, which has been transformed from an area of Democratic dominance to one of the regions where, the Republican Party is strongest. And because blacks are overwhelmingly tied to the Democratic Party, Republicans have few incentives to advocate for black interests. In fact, Republican candidates have often used race-related issues as wedges in attempts to exploit racial divisions in the electorate and within the Democratic Party.[19]

Another consequence of whites leaving the Democratic Party as blacks become more prominent participants in party affairs is that the Republican Party has become whiter. Whites now make up 88 percent of the Republican Party. At the same time, racial and ethnic minorities are becoming a larger proportion of the Democratic Party (see Table 6.2). While the partisanship of the rapidly growing Latino population is beyond the scope of this study, it is an important factor in American party politics. At present, Latinos are trending toward the Democrats in terms of party identification. If this continues, in the not so distant future the Democratic Party will become a party in which racial and ethnic minorities are a majority of its members. This would leave us with one party that is overwhelmingly white and one that is mostly made up of racial and ethnic minorities. This dynamic could lead to more racial divisions and more conflictual politics all across the country. If, on the other hand, both parties became more racially and ethnically balanced, the likelihood of widespread race-related political volatility in the political system would be lessened (Huckfeldt and Kohfeld 1989).

Can the Republican Party Attract More Blacks?

Is the near monolithic identification of blacks with the Democrats likely to change in the foreseeable future? This has been a question that has interested political scientists for a number of years. Thirty years ago some researchers predicted that by now a larger percent of blacks would be Republican than is currently the case. This prediction was based on the belief that the growing black middle and upper classes would result in significantly more blacks identifying with Republican economic ideologies and policies.[20] Yet, although the black middle class has more than quadrupled, and the number of blacks among the upper class has grown dramatically since the 1970s, the percentage of blacks who identify as Republican hasn't changed that much; this despite occasional aggressive recruitment efforts by the party.

Public opinion polls have detected what may be cracks in the black support for the Democrats, however. For example, their present overwhelming identification with the Democratic Party notwithstanding, since 1964 the percentage of blacks who are Democrats has fallen by 10 percent (see Table 6.1).[21] When we look at the data on gender differences in party identification among blacks (Figure 6.1 above), blacks look less monolithic. Black men are less likely than black women to identify as Democrats. Moreover, the black men who do identify as Democrats tend to have less intense attachments to the party than black women Democrats. We find similar gender differences among blacks on some public policy issues. A 2001 Pew Research Center Poll shows, for example, that black women are much more opposed to decriminalizing marijuana use than are black men.[22] In a 2003 Pew Poll, 57 percent of black men agreed that the decision to invade Iraq was the right decision, while only 33 percent of black women held this view.[23] The black monolith is also called into question when we look at black party identification by age (Figure 6.4). A much smaller proportion of blacks between 18 and 29 years of age identify as Democrats when compared to blacks 49 years old and older. Because younger blacks have come of age in the post-civil rights era and in a society that is much more racially integrated, has far less overt racism, and provides them with many more social, political, and economic opportunities than the society in which older blacks matured, race consciousness and racial group identity may wane over time as driving forces relative to partisan identification. This suggests that the advantage the Democratic Party receives from overwhelming black support today could be in jeopardy sometime in the future.

It is possible that the gradual decline in the percentage of blacks who identify as Democrats and the gender and generational differences observed in opinion polls will lead to more black support for the Republican Party. To date, however, there are very few indications that the Republicans will benefit from these trends. The Democratic and Republican parties have distinct reputations that are related to past legacies and current policy positions. Since at least the mid-1960s, when it took a firm pro-civil rights position, the Democratic Party has had the reputation of being more favorably disposed toward blacks and their interests. Conversely, the Republican Party's opposition to the 1964 Civil Rights Act saddled it with an antiblack reputation. These reputations in part explain the inability of the Republican Party to attract more blacks to its ranks.

Several specific actions and occurrences over the past forty-five years have reinforced the Republicans' negative reputation. For example, in the 1980s Republican administrations resisted pressure to impose sanctions on the racist apartheid regime in South Africa, and the Republican Party openly opposed affirmative action and many of the social welfare programs that had provided some material benefits to poor and middle class blacks. Also during the 1980s, David Duke, a former leader of a faction of the Ku Klux Klan, ran for governor and the U.S. Senate in Louisiana as a Republican. Even though Republican Party elites and most rank and file members of the party opposed Duke's candidacies, his campaigns reinforced the image that the party is antiblack.

Public opinion surveys confirm the existence and persistence of the negative views blacks hold about the Republican Party. According to a 1986 ABC News/Washington Post Poll, 56 percent of black respondents believed that then-Republican president Ronald Regan was a racist. Seventy-two percent of the same respondents thought Republican Party leaders did not care about their problems.[24] A 2008 Gallup Poll similarly reveals clear party differences regarding views about the extent to which racism against blacks exists in the United States. Sixty-seven percent of Democrats in the poll agreed this problem is widespread, while only 39 percent of Republicans held this view.[25]

Race consciousness and racial group identification are two important factors that determine blacks' partisanship (Dawson 1994; Gurin et al. 1989; Tate 1993). As Dawson (1994) put it, "...within the realm of mainstream American politics, African-American political behavior remains powerfully influenced by African Americans' perceptions of group interests. What is perceived as good for the group still plays a dominant role in shaping African-American partisanship, political choice, and public opinion" (204). The widespread and persistent perception among blacks that the Republican Party is unsympathetic to, uninterested in, or even hostile toward their collective concerns, makes it unlikely that large numbers of blacks will join the ranks of the Republicans anytime soon.

In order for there to be significant growth in the number of black Republicans, the Republican Party must radically change its reputation among the black electorate. In 2009, Republicans selected Michael S. Steele, an African American, as its national party chairman. Steele's selection is widely viewed as an attempt to improve the party's image among blacks and other racial and ethnic minorities. Steele's selection is also recognition on the part of some members of the party elite that the party has to make concerted and continuous efforts to attract minority group supporters in order to challenge the Democrats' dominance in terms of minority group support. While Steele's selection is important both substantively and symbolically, it should be viewed as only an early step. Many blacks will not see the Republican Party as an alternative to the Democrats unless the party transforms its national policy agenda. In order for the Republican Party to become a viable option for blacks it must advocate for (or at least refrain from attacking) policies and programs that are compatible with the civil rights era policies widely credited with reducing racial discrimination and generating black social and economic mobility.

The fact that race remains a salient cleavage in American politics makes this task a difficult one. As it attempts to recruit more blacks and other minorities into the party, Republicans are very likely to face the same racial volatility that the Democrats have experienced. That is, the more the Republican Party attempts to incorporate and accommodate racial and ethnic minorities and their policy interests, the more white supporters they are likely to lose. Given U.S. Census projections that nonwhites will be a majority of the U.S. population by the middle of this century, this is a risk the Republican Party must take if it is to remain competitive in elections at all levels of government.

Notes

1. The authors intentionally use the more racially comprehensive term *blacks* to reflect the fact that the group under study is not limited to African Americans.
2. American National Election Studies, 1956–2008.
3. http://www.cnn.com/ELECTION/2004/pages/results/states/US/P/00/epolls.0.html
4. http://www.cnn.com/ELECTION/2008/results/polls/#USP00p1
5. On the local level, black Republicans experienced some successes and maintained some influence in party affairs. In general, and especially in terms of national politics, the situation for them in the party was decidedly negative.
6. There is significant disagreement among scholars about the extent to which the New Deal should be credited with bringing blacks to the Democratic Party. Some scholars (e.g., Sitkoff 1978) argue that Roosevelt offered positive incentives that attracted blacks, while others (e.g., Weiss 1983) suggest blacks moved to the party despite the fact that they received few direct benefits from the New Deal.
7. The inclusion of a civil rights plank in the 1948 Democratic Party platform resulted in white Southern Democrats walking out of the convention, and led to the eventual formation of the Dixiecrats, a breakaway states' rights and prosegregation faction. In 1952, many blacks, especially those living in the South, supported Republican Dwight D. Eisenhower for president to protest the influence the Dixiecrats had in party affairs.
8. http://pewresearch.org/pubs/773/fewer-voters-identify-as-republicans.
9. See McClain and Stewart (2010, 83–85) for a good discussion of gender and black partisanship.
10. http://people-press.org/report/?pageid=1516.
11. Ibid.
12. Browning, Marshall, and Tabb (1984, 250).
13. http://people-press.org/report/?pageid=1516; http://www.jointcenter.org/index.php/news_room/press_releases/joint_center_releases_new_report_on_blacks_and_the_2000_democratic_national_convention
14. http://www.cbsnews.com/htdocs/pdf/DEMDELS_Who_they_are.pdf
15. In 1884, John R. Lynch, a state legislator from Mississippi, served as temporary chairman of the 1884 Republican national convention. In 2009, Michael S. Steele, an African American, was chosen to be chairman of the Republican National Committee.
16. See also Bratton and Haynie (1999).
17. See for example, Barker, Jones, and Tate (1999, 351–55); Philpott (2007); and Walton and Smith (2003)
18. Walton and Smith (2003, 157).
19. See Huckfeldt and Kohfeld (1989, chapters 1–2). It is important to note that some Democratic candidates and elected officials also exploit racial fears and divisions when they have perceived it to be in their interest to do so.

20. See for example Dawson (1994); and Gurin et al. (1989).
21. The rise in the percentage of blacks identifying as Democrat in 2008 is a very Barack Obama effect. It remains to be seen if this increase will hold.
22. http://people-press.org/report/16/interdiction-and-incarceration-still-top-remedies
23. http://people-press.org/report/179/war-concerns-grow-but-support-remains-steadfast
24. ABC News/Washington Post Poll, March 1986.
25. http://www.gallup.com/poll/109258/Majority-Americans-Say-Racism-Against-Blacks-Widespread.aspx

Chapter 7

Class in American Politics

Jeffery M. Stonecash

The role of class in American politics eludes and puzzles us. There is no agreement on what class means, how to measure it, or whether it matters in politics. The only area of agreement seems to be that the extent of class political divisions should be measured by how much individuals of different classes vary in their partisan opinions or behavior. But there is little agreement on how to define class and classify individuals. The differing definitions and measures of class result in disagreements about whether class is a significant source of political divisions. Some use self-definition and find class divisions declining. Others use some combination of income, education, and occupation and reach mixed conclusions, with many finding class of declining relevance. Some use relative position in income distribution and find class divisions growing. Others use absolute levels of income and argue class is of diminishing relevance. To complicate matters more, some argue that Americans have moved beyond class concerns and that the real issues are racial and cultural. The diversity of approaches and claims about the political relevance of class divisions is confusing.

The puzzle of conflicting claims is compounded by the strong claims of others who argue that class is central to our society, our politics, and the policy decisions made. To some it appears that class issues are present in many public policy debates. Inequality in the distribution of income has steadily increased for decades and studies are presented arguing that mobility among income strata has declined (Shapiro et al. 2001). Proposals to cut taxes are followed by arguments about which income groups get how much and what is fair. Increases in grants to attend college are proposed in Congress to increase access to college for low income students, and are contested by others as unnecessary. Access to health care and pensions varies by income level and health care legislation is debated with a clear undertone of whether to use taxes to expand access to health care for those with lower incomes. Bankers make bad loans, are bailed out with federal funds, collect bonuses, and there is an outcry about the rich being protected while average workers lose jobs (Frank 2008). It appears that class is relevant, especially at a time when income inequality is increasing. But agreement about just how relevant is difficult to find among academics, think tank publications, or politicians. The essence of the puzzle is that many think class does or should matter, but the empirical evidence that it does matter is mixed, and depends on how class is defined. The uncertainty affects politicians and how they talk about policy. Should they focus on issues of class, speak and make appeals about such issues, or will they be making appeals with a focus that does not resonate with the public?

This chapter is an attempt to clarify the issue of the role of class in American politics. Does it matter? The first issues to assess are the individual level situations. What are the changes in American society that make many think that class matters? Then we move to efforts to measure class and review how the approach used affects what we find. Then we shift focus and examine two other means by which class issues are injected into American political debates. One is through the growing role of ideology and the debate between liberals and conservatives about the issue of class. The other is through the distribution of the population across legislative districts. If districts vary considerably in their composition and concerns and representatives respond to these varying concerns and make arguments involving class differences then it may be that class emerges as relevant through the representation process. Both of these sources of class discussions raise the issue of whether we have been mistakenly looking for the emergence of class issues just through individual variations in partisan behavior, while it may emerge through diverse means.

Social Conditions and the Relevance of Class

The role of class remains a matter of concern because conditions within American society prompt many to think that class must matter somehow. From the late 1940s through the 1960s inequality in the distribution of income declined. It declined because those in the bottom of the distribution did better than those at the top. Everyone experienced income growth, but the greater growth at the bottom reduced inequality (Danizger and Gottschalk 1985). Since the early 1970s the trend has reversed, with the more affluent making significant gains and those at the bottom gaining very little. Table 7.1 indicates what has happened since 1979. It indicates how much inequality exists and how much it has changed since 1979. Since the 1970s those in the upper income groups have made significant gains while others have improved very little.

In addition to current income, inequalities in the distribution of wealth are even greater and becoming more unequal (Keister 2000). People vary enormously in the resources and opportunities they have and these differences are likely to be a basis of political conflicts (Bartels 2008; Kelly 2009; McCarty, Poole, and Rosenthal 2006). There is also evidence that mobility—movement among income strata—has declined slightly over time (Bradbury and Katz 2002). Local schools vary tremendously in their tax bases, in their resources

Table 7.1 Pre-Tax Average Household Income by Income Groups (2004 dollars), 1979–2004

Income quintile	1979	2004	% Change 1979–2004	Dollar Change 1979–2004
Lowest fifth	15,100	15,400	2.0	$300
Second fifth	32,700	36,300	11.0	$3,600
Middle fifth	49,000	56,200	14.7	$7,200
Fourth fifth	66,300	81,700	23.2	$15,400
Top fifth	127,100	207,200	63.0	$80,100
Top 10 %	165,600	297,800	79.8	$132,200
Top 5 %	225,400	443,400	96.7	$218,000
Top 1 %	498,200	1,259,700	152.9	$761,500

Source: Congressional Budget Office, *Effective Federal Tax Rates, 1979 to 2004*, Table 4C, December 2006. Data from: http://www.cbo.gov/publications/bysubject.cfm?cat=33

and their physical quality, and in the preparation their students receive (Wong 1999). The greater the level of education the higher is the subsequent income, and there is persistent evidence that those from more affluent families are more likely to be able to complete college (Bowen, Chingos, and McPherson 2009). Those who are more affluent are more likely to have better health, have health care insurance, and have a pension plan. It appears that income, or something related to resources, matters for individuals (Bowles, Gintis, and Groves 2005; Massey 2007).

It is also hard not to see the issue of class in the policy battles that dominate Washington. In the 1980s and 1990s Republicans sought to reduce welfare benefits while most Democrats opposed change. There are persistent battles over tax cuts and who will get the benefit of proposed tax cuts. Democrats do not want to repeal the tax on estates when the money is received by others, while Republicans call it a "death tax" and seek to eliminate it (Gaertz and Shapiro 2004). When the economy collapsed in 2008, Washington bailed out banks and bankers who had made the bad loans. Then the bankers who caused the collapse received bonuses, and many were angry because they saw those at the top being protected. When the Obama administration proposed health care reform that would expand coverage, large insurance firms sought to undermine the efforts. Many of the major battles in Washington appear to involve class issues. It seems that class matters in American politics.

Defining Class and Generating Conclusions

The sense that class somehow matters has prompted a considerable volume of research to assess how much it matters. The pursuit of this issue first requires that we decide how to group individuals by class and settle on an approach to analysis. For much of the last forty years the focus has been on whites only. That is because the black population has been so overwhelmingly Democratic since the mid-1960s that there is little variation to consider. Since they vote Democratic at all class levels, including them obscures class divisions to some extent. However, with the emergence of Hispanics as a significant part of American society and multiple racial identities now being allowed in census reports, studying only whites makes less sense in understanding the relevance of class.

Then there is the central issue of how to measure class divisions and how to define class. With regard to the first matter, most have defined class divisions as the extent to which opinions and political behavior vary by class. If lower and higher class individuals do not differ much in their partisan attachments and voting, then it is difficult to argue that class matters very much. While that logic seems simple, the next issue of defining class so we can conduct an analysis has not been simple. What traits do we focus on to classify someone as lower or working class, or middle, or higher class? The definition we use has proved to be crucial because it affects whether we conclude that class matters. For some, the best way to define it is to ask individuals how they see themselves. Rather than impose a class status or assume a political perspective, one approach is to ask someone if she regards herself as working or middle class. When that definition is used, the evidence indicates that partisan differences have been steadily declining over time (Abramson, Aldrich, and Rohde 1995; Alford 1963). Others have defined it as some combination of relative income, education, and occupational status and found that class divisions are declining (E. C. Ladd 1975, 226–72). To simplify the issue some use just education levels and find that Democratic support among those with lower levels of education has steadily declined (Kenworthy, Barringer, Durr, and Schneider 2008). In sum, if we measure class using self-identification or some combination of education, occupation, and income, class is of diminishing relevance in American politics.

Further, it may be that the whole issue is of declining relevance. Some argue that with education and income steadily increasing in American society, the percentage of the public in the working class (people with limited education and low income levels) is steadily declining and it may be that this issue is no longer of great relevance (Abramowitz and Teixeira 2008). In this view class is not a relative position, but an absolute trait. With most people experiencing absolute increases in income and education, the issue of lower class political differences is less relevant because there are fewer in the category.

But this consensus of the declining relevance of class is disrupted by other evidence. Class can also be defined by income—the resources that individuals have access to—and the evidence using differences in relative income position indicates that the difference in identification with or voting for the Democratic Party between those in the bottom and top third of the income distribution has steadily increased in recent decades (Bartels 2008; Ortiz and

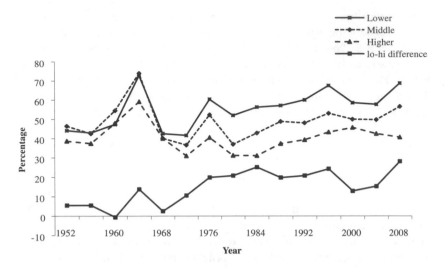

Figure 7.1   Democratic Presidential Voting by Income Groups, 1952–2008.

Stonecash 2009; Stonecash 2000). Figure 7.1 indicates the percentage of voters in the bottom, middle, and top third of the income distribution in each year that have voted for Democratic presidential candidates since 1952. The bottom line indicates the difference in Democratic voting between the bottom and top thirds, and indicates that the difference has increased.

All in all, there are grounds for disagreeing about how to define class and whether it is of relevance in politics. At issue is a fundamental question about what defines class and that is an issue which cannot be easily resolved. The reality is that class is not clearly defined because it involves multiple dimensions. It includes self-identity because how a person sees herself is often very important for what she thinks she is capable of and what she aspires to. It involves income, either absolute or relative levels, because that reflects resources and access to opportunities in society. It includes education because it involves status, cognitive abilities, and the credentials to move into certain occupations. It includes occupation because societies do attribute greater status to some jobs than others. While many will simply define class as one attribute over another, that will not resolve the issue. It involves the general notion that some people have more of something than others, but the devil is in the details.

The consequence of ambiguity in the meaning of class means that politicians in America often are reduced to their instincts about what class is, the feedback they get from constituents and others, and their sense of whether it matters. Their own experiences often affect their sense of the nature of class (Reeher 1996). They study the expressed concerns and language of politics and must decide whether an appeal to some notion of class is appropriate. They look at where their party appeal succeeds and where it fares poorly. That gives them a sense of whether their appeal is resonating or not. Needless to say, that creates considerable variation in interpretations of the relevance of class.

Explaining Declining Relevance

With some studies indicating that class is of declining relevance, several arguments have been presented as to why class is not a source of political divisions. To some, the finding that class, however defined, does not divide Americans politically is not surprising. America was founded as a nation without rigid social classes and where opportunity was prevalent. From the beginning of the nation the belief that individuals can and should succeed based on their own efforts has been a fundamental ideal (Jillson, 2004). When people are asked in surveys "Do you think what you achieve in life depends largely on your family background or on your abilities and hard work?" a majority say the latter. Over 80 percent agree that "While people may begin with different opportunities, hard work and perseverance can usually overcome those disadvantages" (Stonecash 2007). Given these responses, it is plausible that class divisions would not be significant within American society.

Others begin with an assumption that class might matter, but argue other factors have displaced whatever class political divisions there were in American politics. The essence of these arguments is that the issues of importance to voters have changed and they now care more about matters other than class. First there was the argument that ideology (presumably involving class issues) was of declining relevance (Bell 1962). This was followed by the argument that as affluence increased in American society, voters were less and less concerned with materialistic matters. We were presumably entering into an era of post-materialism in which the quality of life was more important. The argument was backed up with survey responses which presumed to tap into materialistic concerns (Inglehart 1971, 1977, 1990).

There are also those who argue that in the 1960s and after, issues revolving around race changed American politics. Blacks had made a moral case that segregation and discrimination were persistent. Democrats responded to this position more than did Republicans, making the issue one that divided the parties. Working class whites saw affirmative action as a program that was creating reverse discrimination against them, for conditions they did not create. Troubled by urban riots, their voting became shaped more by race issues than class inequities. They began to vote more on their resentments about race than their class positions (Carmines and Stimson 1989; Edsall and Edsall 1991; Huckfeldt and Kohfeld 1989).

Then, as Laura Olson reviews in chapter 9, the cultural wars emerged (Hunter 1991; Layman 2001). Conservative voters were upset about what they saw as a decline in morals. Abortion was declared legal; the number of births to unwed mothers increased; welfare loads and crime increased; and divorce increased (Brewer and Stonecash 2007). Much of this division was connected to religion, with secularists more tolerant of these changes than those strongly attached to religion. Republicans have recognized these differences and emphasized cultural issues as a way to draw the working class away from the Democratic Party (Frank 2004; Hillygus and Shields 2008). Since those with less education were less likely to be tolerant of changed mores, they were more motivated to vote for Republicans. Since education and income are associated, to the extent that the less affluent were motivated more by cultural issues, differences in partisan voting by class would decline.

The cumulative effect of these interpretations is that political divisions revolving around class issues might have become significant, but they were displaced by other issues. At the same time ideological conflict was declining and affluence made materialistic concerns less salient. Then resentments about first race and then cultural issues, more prevalent among the less affluent, pushed many in this stratum to desert class voting, reducing the extent to which class issues were a part of political debates.

The Roles of Income and Cultural Issues

Sorting out the effects of these competing issues is important. While there are many assertions that the displacement of class issues is occurring, the evidence is often less compelling than the assertions. Two examples will be reviewed here. It is common to assert that the dominant issue in the transition of the South has been race (Black and Black 2002, 244–50). That is, the divisions that emerged in the South beginning in the late 1950s and since have largely involved issues of blacks versus whites. The difficulty is that the evidence involving the South indicates that beginning in the 1950s a significant class difference in partisan voting emerged among whites and opinions about race issues did not suppress the growth of that division (Brewer and Stonecash 2001; Shafer and Johnston 2006).

The evidence about the impact of cultural issues also presents problems. Presumably those who are less affluent but conservative on a social issue like abortion are moving to the Republican Party, resulting in less class voting. Figure 7.2 provides an effort to sort out this issue. Assume that we can measure class by relative income position (but remember there is considerable disagreement about this). We can classify people by relative income position, so we can place voters in the bottom or top third of the income distribution. We can also classify voters by whether they define themselves as pro-choice or pro-life. This allows us to track the voting behavior of those who are in the lower third and who are pro-choice or pro-life, and those in the top third who are pro-choice or pro-life.

In the 1970s, before cultural issues emerged, those in the lower third, regardless of abortion opinions, voted more Democratic and those in the top third of the income distribution voted less Democratic by about 20 percentage points. Over time as the abortion issue increased in saliency, opinions about

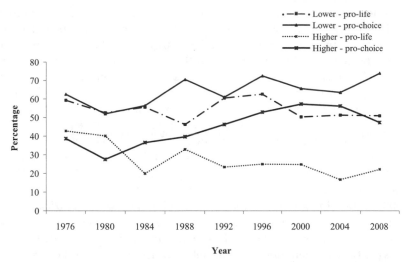

Figure 7.2   Abortion Views, Class, and Democratic Presidential Voting, 1976–2008.

this issue have come to play a greater role in affecting votes. Among those in the lower third, those pro-choice moved more Democratic and those pro-life moved less Democratic. A cultural issue mattered, but its effect among those less affluent and pro-life has been to reduce their Democratic voting by only about five percentage points. As indicated in Figure 7.1, however, *overall* those in the bottom third are now voting *more* Democratic now than they did in 1980.

Equally interesting is what has happened among the more affluent. Opinions about abortion have had a significant effect within this group. Those pro-life have moved away from the Democratic Party while those pro choice have moved more Democratic. The more affluent generally have more education and are more inclined to be pro-choice. The *net effect* is that since 1980 the more affluent have moved more Democratic. In short, the relationship is just the opposite of the argument that the less affluent are moving Republican. It is the more affluent who are moving more Democratic (Liscio, Stonecash, and Brewer 2010). This, of course, will not settle the matter, as some will not accept the definition of class used here. But there are grounds for doubting the assertions that other issues are displacing class issues and moving the working class more Republican.

Latent Divisions: Trust, Ignorance, and the Activism of the Lower Class

While this debate goes on, others have been unwilling to accept that class political divisions cannot matter. Rather, accepting some of the evidence that class divisions are not as great as we might expect them to be, they regard class divisions as latent, or as having the potential to exist if some basic hurdles could be overcome. This argument takes different forms. Some argue that surveys indicate there is a consensus that inequality is a problem and something should be done about it. The problem is that Americans do not trust government to be a means to address the problem, so less gets done than might be the case (Page and Jacobs 2009). Others argue that the reason that class matters less than it might is because lower income voters have less education and are less likely to be aware of the implications of public policy debates for themselves. The essential matter is that they lead lives in which gathering information is less common than among those with higher education and many working class people simply are uninformed (Bageant 2007; Bartels 2008).[1] It is also the case that those with less education and income vote less (Stonecash 2000) so their impact on politics is less than it might be. Either because they do not trust government or know less or vote less, this view is that if effective programs were to be designed, or if awareness and mobilization were to occur, class political divisions might become relevant. The potential is there, just currently stymied.

The Enduring Presence of Class Issues: The Role of Ideology

While we struggle to find class divisions in the behavior and opinions of voters, it still appears that it matters in public policy debates. Efforts to enact legislation in Congress often have a distinct class focus: How will the legislation affect those in different strata? The issue then is how this focus emerges if voters are not that divided by class in their partisan voting. We have much to learn about this, but it appears that it emerges in two ways. One involves the interaction between partisan voting by income level and the variation in electoral bases across legislative districts. The other involves the growing role of ideology.

District Compositions and Electoral Bases

The search for the relevance of class generally involves examining differences in partisan voting among individuals. This neglects the fact that the expression of concerns about class may also emerge in the policy preferences of representatives in Congress, depending on the electoral base they represent. National surveys treat voters as one aggregated unit, without regard to their distribution across states and House districts. To take House districts as an example, there are enormous variations in the economic composition of House districts. Based on 2000 census data, the median family income in House districts during the 2000s ranged from $20,924 to $91,571. The populations being represented by members differ enormously. These differences are likely to make members vary in their concern for class issues.

Table 7.2 District Composition, National Voting, and Party Electoral Bases

Income	% D	District 1		District 2		District 3		District 4	
		Pop	D Votes	Pop	D votes	Pop	R Votes	Pop	R votes
Lower	60	80	48	60	36	10	4	0	0
Middle	50	20	10	30	15	30	15	20	10
Higher	40		0	10	4	60	36	80	48
Winner			D: 58		D: 55		R: 55		R: 58

Second, House Members are not elected by the entire constituency in a district. Democrats are more likely within each district to draw votes from lower income constituents and Republicans are likely to draw votes from higher income constituents. Table 7.2 provides an illustration of this. Let us assume that based on national surveys 60 percent of those in the bottom third (lower) vote Democratic, 50 percent of those in the middle do so, and 40 percent of those in the top third do so. Those percentages are in the second column. Then to the right of that are four House districts, with varying population compositions. In district 1 the population is 80 percent lower income and 20 percent middle. If each group votes follows the national pattern and there are 100 votes in the district, then the Democrat receives 48 votes from lower- and 10 from middle income voters. The Democrat wins with 58 of 100 votes. This Democrat has an electoral base that is heavily lower income. In contrast is district 4, which is 20 percent middle and 80 percent higher. If the national voting pattern prevails, then the winner is a Republican with a heavily higher income base. The result is that many Democrats are likely to be forceful in their representation of lower class concerns and more likely to vote for corresponding legislation. Republicans are more likely to oppose such legislation. These differences are a direct reflection of the distributions of populations across districts. While the national individual level survey results do not show major differences in partisanship by income, the distribution of populations across states and House districts and the differences in electoral bases of party members create significant differences in representation concerns. These differences are surely a source of much of the class content of debates in Congress.

Ideology

The other important factor involves ideology. The presumption of many individual level studies has been that the lower class will be liberal and concerned about inequality and the upper class will be conservative and less concerned. Those relationships have not developed. Again using income as an indicator of class, the differences by income in views about inequality are more muted than some expect. Table 7.3 presents results from one national survey in 2004 about inequality. Among those with a family income less than $50,000, 27.9 percent said just some have an opportunity to succeed in America. Among those making $100,000 or more the percentage was 15.4. The less affluent were almost twice as likely to hold this negative view about opportunity, but overall the differences by income are not large and the responses by income groups are somewhat similar. These limited differences suggest to many that class divisions about economic issues and opportunity are not of great importance in American politics. This is despite the growing differences in partisan voting shown in Figure 7.1.

Despite these limited variations in opinions about the presence of opportunity by income, issues of opportunity and fairness still emerge with considerable force and salience in American politics because of the role of ideology and its relationship to partisanship. Issues of fairness and opportunity are central to ideology. As Abramowitz documents in chapter 8, in recent decades ideology has become more important as a source of differences in American society. Liberals tend to think that opportunity should exist, but that that it is not as widespread as it should be. As shown in the table, 42.1 percent of liberals think that only some have an opportunity to succeed while only 11.1 percent

Table 7.3 The Existence of Opportunity: Variations by Income, Party, and Ideology, 2004

Percentages sum across to 100 for each category

Family Income	How Many have Opportunity to Succeed?		
	Everyone	Most	Just some
Under $50,000	26.4	44.3	27.9
$50 – 99,999	28.8	50.5	20.2
$100,000 plus	23.1	58.5	15.4
Political Ideology			
Liberal	14.0	43.9	42.1
Moderate	21.1	58.8	18.6
Conservative	43.1	44.2	11.1
Party Identification			
Democrat	17.9	49.0	33.2
Independent	18.3	56.5	23.5
Republican	42.8	47.3	8.5

Source: Maxwell School Survey on Inequality and Civic Engagement, the Campbell Institute, the Maxwell School, Syracuse University. The results are from a nationwide survey of 611 adults conducted in October, 2004. The specific question asked was: "Do you think everyone in American society has an opportunity to succeed, most do, or do only some have this opportunity?"

of conservatives see that situation. In contrast, 14.0 percent of liberals think everyone has an opportunity to succeed, while 43.1 percent of conservatives endorse that view.

These different evaluations of American society lead to very different policy positions of liberals and conservatives. Liberals believe that differences in resources and possibilities for success vary significantly by class, and that government should play a role in trying to equalize opportunity. Government should provide day care, distribute more state aid to poor school districts, provide cash public assistance to those who are struggling, provide medical care through Medicaid or Medicare, and maintain a Social Security system that makes sure no elderly people are without some minimum of money. They want a progressive tax system (the more you make the higher the percentage of income paid in taxes) because those who have benefited from the system are most capable of contributing revenues to address inequities.

Conservatives also support the importance of opportunity but are much more likely to think that it already exists. They place much more emphasis on individual initiative as being central to taking advantage of the opportunities that they see existing. They also stress individual responsibility and providing inducements such as lower taxes for those who succeed. They are much more likely to believe that individual effort can overcome a family background that was not helpful. They are uneasy about government stepping in to alter who wins and who loses and think such matters should be determined by individuals. They are much less supportive of the programs liberals support because they think a society that prizes opportunity and rewards achievements will work much better if government minimizes its intrusions. They see government programs as undermining individual initiative. They oppose a progressive tax system because it discourages initiative.

Those with these differing views of the world have increasingly aligned themselves with different parties. Liberals are increasingly likely to identify with and play a major role within the Democratic Party and conservatives are increasingly likely to identify with and play a major role within the Republican Party (Abramowitz 1998; Abramowitz 1994; Gerring 1998; Stonecash 2007; Taylor 1996). The result is that the liberal and conservative differences just discussed have now become central to the views expressed by each party. As shown in the bottom of the table, 43.0 percent of Republicans think that everyone has opportunity while only 17.9 percent of Democrats think so. The parties are not completely divergent or polarized, but their centers of opinion about inequality as a problem are growing farther apart. These differences, however, do not always line up with class. Those in the lower class are not invariably liberal and those in the higher class are not invariably conservative. The fact that class and ideology among individuals are not the same has been the source of considerable puzzlement to some, who assume they might be related.

Ideology, Party, and Policy Debates

With this ideological divide growing, it increasingly structures the debates about policy. Liberals and their various interest groups produce studies that support their arguments about the existence of inequality and lobby for their policy agenda to respond. Conservatives produce their opposing studies. The result is that the liberal–conservative divide, much of which (but not all) revolves around class and issues of opportunity and the role of government, organizes much of the debate that occurs in the political arena.

The result is that issues of class may not emerge because class strata differ significantly in their opinions, but because there are differences in legislators' electoral bases and ideological differences about class that are central to current party debates. As inequality increases, Democratic liberals argue for programs to increase equality of opportunity and conservatives argue there should be clear limits on the role of government in intruding on individual responsibility and initiative (McCarty et al. 2006). Politicians often find maneuvering in this context difficult because they cannot be certain just how many of the lower class favors liberal policies and just how many of the higher class favors conservative policies. They are bombarded by commentary expressing all the conflicting arguments discussed before—class is irrelevant, post-materialism defines us, race is most important, the cultural wars pull the working class to Republicans—all of which create some uncertainty about what is occurring in American politics. But ideology has become more important in defining the parties and central to policy debates about inequality. Three recent major policy conflicts illustrate how many policy debates have a focus on class and opportunity. They are changes in the welfare program in 1996, various changes to tax laws, and the efforts to change Social Security in 2005.

Welfare

The availability of public assistance or welfare has been a particularly contentious matter since the 1960s, when the number of people receiving assistance increased significantly. The debate about the desirability of welfare assistance has largely been between conservatives and liberals who see the program very differently. Conservatives have long seen welfare as destructive to individual responsibility. Their argument has been that welfare diminishes personal initiative to work and creates dependency on government (Murray 1984). Using that logic conservatives have continually sought to cut back the amount of welfare benefits and how long someone can stay on welfare. Liberals are convinced that the combination of low-income family background and bad neighborhoods and schools have the cumulative effect of leaving many people without the personal resources and skills to cope in a constantly changing environment. As a consequence they argue strongly that welfare is necessary to help those struggling with their lives. In the 1994 elections Republicans won control of Congress. They quickly pursued changes in welfare and 1996 welfare eligibility was changed from an allowance that an individual, meeting eligibility requirements, could stay on welfare for an unlimited time to two years at any one time and five years total in a lifetime (Stone 2007). The battle over welfare has largely been an ideological one, carried by actors on each side with strong convictions that their views accurately capture how society works (Teles 1998). Welfare is largely of benefit to those with limited incomes and this was a battle over a class issue. The lower class may have had little direct voice in these changes but their fortunes were carried by those committed to their cause.

Taxes

There have been several major changes in tax law in the last two decades. Three that are particularly important are the "marriage penalty," the estate or death tax, and the general income tax system. For years a married couple had to pay more in income tax if they filed as a couple than if they filed individually. In 2001 the Republicans were in the majority in both houses in Congress and they held the presidency so they set out to change this outcome. While many members of Congress agreed that the problem should be addressed, it quickly became an ideological and partisan issue. Republicans made proposals that directed most of the benefits to upper income filers while Democrats wanted most of the benefits to go to those in the middle of the income distribution or below (Kelly 2009, 51–78). Most voters were probably unaware of the ideological battle about who should receive the benefit of change, but it was primarily a battle driven by ideological advocates.

The estate tax was another major debate in Congress during the early 2000s. Republicans wanted to repeal the tax, imposed on those who receive an estate after someone dies. They framed the issue as involving the "death tax" and focused on the argument that those who achieved should be able to pass it along to whomever they wanted. Their emphasis was on the right to do what you wanted with your private property. Democrats equally quickly framed the issue as the wealthy passing along their income and as the children of the wealthy being able to receive income without having to pay taxes. To Democrats this was a case of the wealthy being able to evade taxation. Again, the argument quickly became an ideological one revolving around class and the replication of inequality. Both sides claimed that certain effects would follow, generally without definitive evidence. The emphasis was primarily on the ideological issue of class and fairness (Graetz and Shapiro 2004). Again, the issue was probably not well understood outside Washington, but the ideological opponents created a debate focused on the class issues involved.

Finally, in 2001 George W. Bush presented Congress with a proposal to significantly cut the federal income tax (Jacobson 2007). As with other tax issues, the support and opposition to the cuts became ideological with a primary focus on class effects. Conservatives claimed that the largest percentage cuts went to those with the lowest income while liberals argued that over-whelmingly the largest amounts of money went to the more affluent. Groups like The Tax Foundation and the Cato Institute, conservative groups, strongly supported the proposals. Liberal groups like Citizens for Tax Justice and the Center on Budget and Policy Priorities strongly opposed the proposals (Brewer and Stonecash 2007, 41–65). Again and again the focus was on the effects of tax cuts by class: how much went to income classes and what was fair. As with welfare, class impacts were ever present in the debates (Stonecash 2001). While voters may or may not have picked up on the class implications of proposals for these three tax changes, liberals and conservatives did and forcefully led the effort to affect the outcome.

Social Security

Conservatives have wanted to change the Social Security system for some time. Their concern is the principle that individuals should be encouraged to be more responsible for their financial future. Their argument is that the existence of a promise of government retirement benefits discourages indi-viduals from saving for the future and increases the burden on government and increases taxes. Following the 2004 presidential election President Bush chose to focus on this issue. He advocated taking a portion of the social secu-rity tax paid by each individual and allowing each to create an individual account. Each individual could make his or her own investment decisions for the account. The goal was to create more individual responsibility and more people who were focused on investing and the growth of the economy.

Liberals had a very different sense of what should be of concern in consid-ering the system. The reality is that the Social Security system is redistributive. The program provides greater benefits, relative to the amounts contributed over a lifetime, for those with lower incomes than for those with higher incomes. It is also the case that the importance of Social Security varies tremendously by income groups. Social Security is the primary source of income for lower-income seniors and reliance on it declines steadily as income increases (Brewer and Stonecash 2007, 61–65). The program is both redistributive and provides the bulk of support for low income seniors. As the Bush administration sought to change Social Security and fulfill a conservative agenda of having indi-viduals be responsible, liberals pushed back with an argument that the change would hurt those most dependent on the program. With trust in Bush declin-ing because of problems in Iraq, conservatives lost the debate.

In each of these debates the central issue was about class. Would welfare reform hurt the lower class? Would tax reform help the affluent more than others? Would changes in Social Security hurt those most reliant on it? In each case the battle was between liberals who saw themselves as protecting those not as well off and conservatives who saw themselves as advocating for principles and encouraging individual responsibility.

Summary

We have much to learn about how class issues play a role in American politics. Individuals of different classes (however defined) do not seem to differ as much in their partisan support as we many think they might. But because of the varying distribution of populations across states and House districts there are representatives who come from and represent very different economic circumstances. That leads to different concerns in policy discussions. Added to that is the role of ideological differences among representatives. Class issues appear to be central to many policy debates, but it emerges in ways we often do not expect.

Note

1. As an example, the results of the 2008 NES survey indicate that those with lower incomes are much less likely to place themselves when asked if they are liberal, moderate, or conservative. Forty-one percent of those in the bottom third of the income distribution place themselves; among those in the middle third 27 percent do not place themselves; while among those in the top third only 15 percent do not place themselves. Those with less education and less income do not follow politics as much and are not as familiar with the substance of many of the debates occurring in American politics.

Chapter 8

Ideological Realignment among Voters

Alan Abramowitz

Following his victory in the 1932 presidential election, Franklin Delano Roosevelt forged an electoral coalition that dominated American politics for the next thirty-six years. Between 1933 and 1969, the Democratic Party controlled the presidency for twenty-eight years and both chambers of Congress for thirty-two years. During these years Democrats also controlled a majority of the nation's governorships and state legislative chambers along with most other state and local elected offices (Congressional Quarterly 2005).

Democrats dominated American politics during these years because they enjoyed the support of a substantial majority of the electorate, as the authors of *The American Voter* discovered when they undertook their pioneering national surveys during the 1950s (A. Campbell, Converse, Miller, and Stokes 1960). In 1952, for example, even as Republican Dwight Eisenhower was winning a landslide victory in the presidential election, 56 percent of American voters identified with or leaned toward the Democratic Party compared with only 39 percent who identified with or leaned toward the Republican Party. While Republicans were able to hold onto some of their traditional state and local strongholds in the aftermath of the New Deal realignment, the GOP could only win national elections during these years when short-term forces in their favor were strong enough to overcome the Democrats' substantial lead in party identification within the American electorate (Stokes 1966).

The electoral coalition that Roosevelt forged during the 1930s was based primarily on group loyalties, some of whose origins could be traced back to events that took place long before the New Deal, and secondarily on the widespread association of the Democratic Party with prosperity and the Republican Party with economic hardship in the aftermath of the Great Depression. Ideology was a relatively minor component of party identification at the mass level during these years, as the authors of *The American Voter* documented. When Americans were asked in 1956 what they liked or disliked about the Democratic and Republican parties, only a small minority mentioned the parties' ideological stances. The large majority of positive and negative comments about the parties fell into two other categories: about 40 percent referred to group benefits while about 25 percent referred to the nature of the times (Campbell et al. 1960, chapter 10).

The major groups comprising Roosevelt's New Deal coalition were white voters in the South and white ethnic (largely Catholic) and working class voters in the North (Andersen 1979; Berelson, Lazarsveld, and McPhee 1954; Lazarsveld, Berelson, and Gaudet 1948; E. E. Robinson 1947). Black voters, who had been strong supporters of the Republican Party in the decades following the Civil War and Reconstruction, also began to shift their loyalties to the Democrats during the thirties, but they did not become a major component of the Democratic electoral coalition until the mid-1960s when the passage of the 1965 Voting Rights Act finally made it possible for large numbers of blacks in the South to register and vote (Keyssar 2000, chapter 8; Lusane 1996).

What brought these disparate groups of voters together under the Democratic umbrella was a common perception that the interests of each group were better served by the Democrats than by the Republicans. That was the gist of most of the answers to the questions about party likes and dislikes that fell into the "group benefits" category. More than two decades after the onset of the Great Depression and Franklin Roosevelt's ascension to the presidency, the authors of *The American Voter* found that the Democrats were still viewed by most Americans as the party of the common man, the working class, and the average citizen while the Republicans were still viewed by most Americans as the party of big business and the wealthy (Campbell et al. 1960, chapter 10).

Among white voters in the South and white ethnic voters in the North, the Great Depression and Roosevelt's New Deal reinforced longstanding ties to the Democratic Party. For most Southern whites during the 1950s, the Republican Party was viewed not only as the party responsible for the Great Depression, which hit the South harder than any other region of the country, but also as the party that imposed Reconstruction on the South and granted voting rights to blacks following the Civil War (Key 1949). And for most white ethnic voters in the North, the Democratic Party was viewed not only as the party that offered jobs and hope during the Depression, but as the party that welcomed immigrants from Ireland and from Southern and eastern Europe during the nineteenth and early twentieth centuries (Erie 1988; Glazer and Moynihan 1963).

The continuing loyalty of these groups to the Democratic Party is clearly evident in the data from the 1952 National Election Study survey, which was the first one to include the standard party identification questions. Among all voters in 1952, Democratic identifiers and leaners outnumbered Republican identifiers and leaners by 56 percent to 39 percent; among Southern whites, however, Democratic identifiers and leaners outnumbered Republican identifiers and leaners by 84 percent to 14 percent; among Northern white Catholics, Democratic identifiers and leaners outnumbered Republican identifiers and leaners by 68 percent to 26 percent; and among Northern white blue collar

voters, Democratic identifiers and leaners outnumbered Republican identifiers and leaners by 60 percent to 33 percent. The Republican Party did remain
dominant during this period among middle class white Protestants outside of
the South. Among these voters, Republican identifiers and leaners outnumbered Democratic identifiers and leaners by 66 percent to 30 percent. But this
group was simply too small to allow Republicans to win national elections or
even to win elections in most states.

The Decline of the New Deal Coalition

The New Deal coalition kept the Democrats in power in Washington and in
most of the states for the better part of four decades. But it was an inherently
unstable coalition made up of groups that not only varied in political outlook
but, in some cases, mistrusted and disliked each other, and cracks began to
form in it shortly after the death of Franklin D. Roosevelt in 1945. In 1948
South Carolina Governor J. Strom Thurmond led a walkout from the Democratic national convention over its adoption of a weak civil rights plank and
ran for the presidency as the candidate of the States Rights, or Dixiecrat Party.
Thurmond carried several states in the Deep South, but Democratic President
Harry S. Truman was reelected anyway (Frederickson 2001). Four years later,
however, Dwight Eisenhower broke the Democratic grip on the White House
and became the first Republican since 1928 to carry any of the states of the old
Confederacy by winning the electoral votes of Virginia, Tennessee, Florida,
and Texas. Eisenhower carried all of these states again, along with Louisiana,
in his successful bid for reelection in 1956.

The movement of Southern white voters away from the Democratic Party
accelerated during the sixties and seventies with the party's embrace of civil
rights and the Republicans' adoption of a "Southern strategy" that combined
opposition to busing and affirmative action with a get tough approach to antiwar protesters and urban rioters under Richard Nixon (Aistrup 1996; Black
and Black 2002; Phillips 1969). As the evidence presented in the first graph in
Figure 8.1 shows, even the election of a Democratic president from the Deep
South, Jimmy Carter of Georgia, in 1976, could not stop the erosion of support
for the Democratic Party among Southern white voters.

The Southern strategy was designed to win over the large bloc of voters in
the South who had supported the independent candidacy of former Alabama
Governor George Wallace in 1968. But the Republican Party's conservatism
on racial and cultural issues did not just appeal to Southern whites. It also
appealed to many white ethnic and working class voters in the North who
were becoming increasingly uncomfortable with the liberalism of the national
Democratic Party on these issues and its growing dependence on the support
of black voters (Edsall and Edsall 1991). Many of these traditional Democrats
voted for Richard Nixon over George McGovern in 1972, and many of them
also voted for Ronald Reagan in 1980 and 1984.

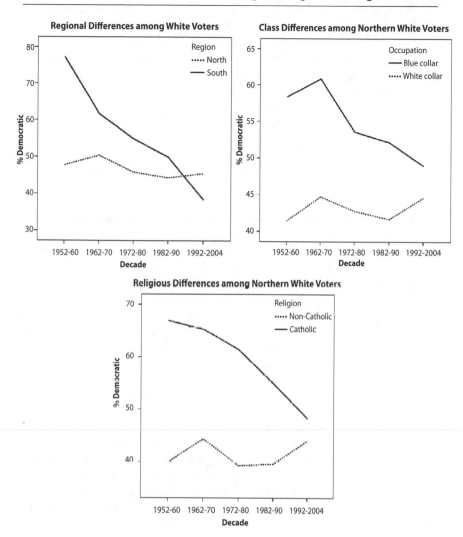

Figure 8.1   The Decline of the New Deal Coalition.

Reagan's ascension to the presidency in 1981 accelerated the process of ideological realignment that had begun under Richard Nixon. Reagan cemented the GOP's ties to socially conservative white evangelicals, a large voting bloc in the South, by attacking Supreme Court decisions legalizing abortion and banning school prayer. But he also appealed to many white voters in the North who were upset about welfare programs that they believed primarily benefited blacks who were unwilling to work and who applauded his efforts to strengthen the American military and stand up to the Soviet Union (Abramson, Aldrich, and Rohde 1986; Edsall and Edsall 1991; Germond and Witcover 1985; Tygiel 2004).

The graphs displayed in Figure 8.1 document the dramatic decline in support for the Democratic Party among the three groups that formed the core of Roosevelt's New Deal coalition: white voters in the South and white Catholics and working class voters in the North. The largest decline in Democratic identification occurred among the group with the longest-standing ties to the Democratic Party—white Southerners. Between the 1950s and the 1990s, Democratic identification among this group fell from close to 80 percent to less than 40 percent. During the same years, Democratic identification among white voters outside of the South declined only slightly. As a result, by the 1990s Democratic identification among white voters in the South was actually lower than Democratic identification among white voters outside of the South.

According to the data displayed in the second graph in Figure 8.1, the decline in Democratic identification among working class whites in the North began later than the decline among whites in the South. As late as the 1960s, over 60 percent of white blue collar voters in the North continued to identify with the Democratic Party. The data in this graph show that during the fifties and sixties, class differences in party identification were still quite evident among white voters in the North. During these years there was a difference of at least fifteen percentage points between blue collar voters and white collar voters in Democratic identification. Over the next three decades, however, this gap diminished dramatically as a result of a sharp decline in Democratic identification among white working class voters. By the 1990s, Democratic identification had fallen below 50 percent among white working class voters in the North. Meanwhile, Democratic identification among white middle class voters remained fairly stable at around 45 percent, only a few percentage points lower than among white working class voters. Although class differences in party identification did not completely disappear, they did become much smaller than in the years immediately following World War II.

The third major group that helped the Democrats dominate American politics from the 1930s through the 1960s was white ethnic voters in the North. The large majority of these white ethnic voters were Roman Catholics whose parents or grandparents had arrived in the United States during the massive waves of immigration of the late nineteenth and early twentieth centuries and had settled in the rapidly growing cities of the Northeast and Midwest where local governments were generally controlled by the Democratic Party.

As was the case for white voters in the South, the Great Depression and the New Deal served to reinforce the loyalty of white ethnic voters in the North to the Democratic Party. These voters gave massive majorities to Franklin D. Roosevelt in each of his four elections and in 1960 Catholic voters provided John F. Kennedy, the first Roman Catholic presidential candidate since Al Smith in 1928, with an overwhelming majority of their votes. According to the 1960 National Election Study, 82 percent of white Catholic voters supported Kennedy over his Republican opponent, Richard Nixon.

The data displayed in the third graph in Figure 8.2 show that between 1952 and 1960 almost two thirds of white Catholic voters in the North identified with the Democratic Party. By contrast, during those years only 40 percent of non-Catholic white voters in the North identified with the Democrats. These data underscore how crucial the Catholic vote was to the Democratic Party in the North during the postwar years. Over the next three decades, however, Democratic identification among Northern white Catholics declined steadily, falling below 50 percent during the 1990s. By that time, white Catholics were only slightly more supportive of the Democratic Party than non-Catholic whites, and another pillar of the New Deal coalition had crumbled.

Explaining the Demise of the New Deal Coalition: Ideological Realignment

Since the 1960s, political ideology has become a much more important influence on party identification as a result of growing ideological differences between the parties. The Democratic Party has become increasingly associated with a liberal philosophy that incorporates support for activist government, civil rights for women and minorities, and a preference for diplomatic over military solutions to international disputes. Meanwhile, the Republican Party has become increasingly associated with a conservative philosophy that emphasizes reliance on the free market, low marginal tax rates, and a strong military.

In the 1964 presidential election, conservative activists seized control of the Republican Party, nominating Arizona Senator Barry Goldwater for president and adopting a platform that opposed civil rights legislation and social welfare programs. Meanwhile, the Democratic Party under the leadership of President Lyndon Johnson embraced the cause of civil rights and activist government.[1] Johnson won a resounding victory, carrying all but five states in the Deep South and Goldwater's home state of Arizona. But the 1964 election and the Great Society legislation passed by the overwhelmingly Democratic 89th Congress (1965–67) accelerated the movement of conservative Democrats into the Republican camp.

The collapse of support for the Democratic Party among Southern whites, Northern white working class voters, and Northern white ethnic voters had a common cause: ideological realignment. This is clear from the data displayed in Figure 8.2. The three graphs in this figure show the trends in Democratic identification among liberals, moderates, and conservatives between the 1970s and the first decade of the twenty-first century. The first graph shows the trends for Southern white voters, the second graph shows the trends for Northern white working class voters, and the third graph shows the trends for Northern white Catholic voters.

The graphs show that in all three groups, Democratic identification declined only slightly among moderates and remained stable or increased among liber-

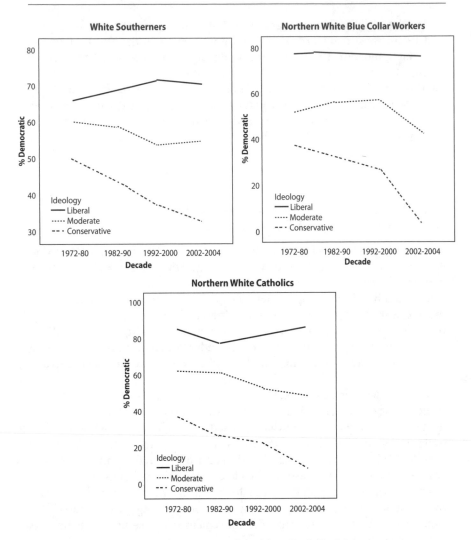

Figure 8.2 The Ideological Realignment of the New Deal Coalition.

als. In all three groups, the decline in Democratic identification between the 1970s and the first decade of the twenty-first century was concentrated almost entirely among conservatives. Among conservative Southern whites, identification with the Democratic Party fell from 40 percent during the 1970s to less than 10 percent in 2002 to 2004. However, among moderate Southern whites, Democratic identification only fell from 60 percent to 50 percent, and among liberal Southern whites, Democratic identification actually rose from 70 percent to 80 percent. The results were very similar for white working class and Catholic voters in the North. Among conservative white working class voters,

Democratic identification fell from close to 40 percent during the 1970s to less than 10 percent between 2002 and 2004; however, among moderate working class voters, Democratic identification only fell from 55 percent to 45 percent and among liberal working class voters, Democratic identification remained stable at close to 80 percent. Finally, among conservative white Catholics, Democratic identification fell from just under 40 percent during the 1970s to about 10 percent between 2002 and 2004. However, among moderate white Catholics, Democratic identification only fell from a little over 60 percent to about 50 percent; and among liberal white Catholics, Democratic identification rose just over 80 percent to close to 90 percent.

By the end of the twentieth century, the process of ideological realignment was almost complete among the politically engaged segment of the electorate, and the old New Deal coalition had largely disintegrated. There were almost no conservative Democrats left and the two parties were at near parity in party identification. In the elections of the first decade of the twenty-first century, a predominantly liberal Democratic Party supported by close to half of the electorate would oppose a predominantly conservative Republican Party supported by close to half of the electorate. Within this evenly divided electorate, however, new group divisions had emerged to replace the old divisions of region, class, and religion.

The Racial Divide

The most important divide within the contemporary electorate, because of its historical significance, its magnitude, and its influence on many other aspects of American politics, is the racial divide. And while party loyalties in the late twentieth and early twenty-first centuries have become increasingly based on ideology, the attachment of African Americans to the Democratic Party has defied this trend. It is an attachment that has remained rooted in group identity.

The Great Depression and Franklin Roosevelt's New Deal brought African Americans into the Democratic electoral coalition for the first time since the Civil War. But as recently as 1960, the Republican Party continued to enjoy significant support among African American voters. In that year's presidential election, according to the National Election Study survey, Richard Nixon received 26 percent of the black vote when he ran against John F. Kennedy. However, no Republican presidential candidate since then has approached that share of the black vote. Despite the increasing social and economic diversity of the black electorate, in the first decade of the twenty-first century, African Americans remain the most solidly Democratic voting bloc in the nation.

The data displayed in Figure 8.3 show that identification with the Democratic Party among African American voters increased from about 70 percent during the 1950s to close to 90 percent from the 1960s through the 1990s. Meanwhile, Democratic identification among white voters fell from just over

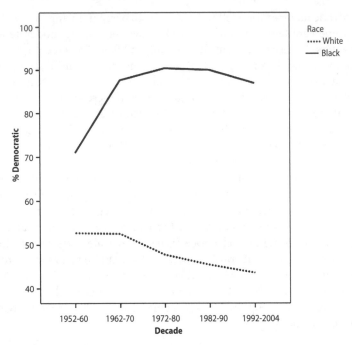

Figure 8.3   The Growing Racial Divide in Partisanship.

50 percent during the 1950s and 1960s to just over 40 percent during the 1990s. A twenty point racial divide in partisanship during the 1950s had grown into a fifty point racial divide in partisanship during the 1980s and 1990s.

The reason for the dramatic increase in the size of the racial divide in partisanship after 1960 was, of course, the emergence of a clear difference between the Democratic and Republican parties on civil rights and other racially charged issues such as busing, affirmative action, crime, and welfare (Brownstein 2007, chapter 4; Edsall and Edsall 1991). The same issues that drove many conservative white voters into the arms of the Republican Party during the sixties, seventies, and eighties caused the large majority of African American voters to view the GOP as unsympathetic to black people at best and racist at worst. As a result, no Republican presidential candidates, and very few Republican Senate and House candidates, have received much more than 10 percent of the black vote in any election since 1960.

The racial divide in partisanship is even deeper in the South, the region which continues to have by far the highest proportion of black voters, than in the rest of the country. In the period from 2002 to 2004, according to NES data, the Democratic Party was supported by 86 percent of black voters versus 44 percent of white voters in the North—a gap of forty-two percentage points. During the same period, the Democratic Party was supported by 89 percent of black voters versus only 33 percent of white voters in the South—a gap of fifty-six percentage points. In some parts of the South, especially in the Deep South where blacks make up a third or more of the electorate, the racial divide in partisanship is so great that the Republican Party has come to be viewed as the white political party and the Democratic Party has come to be viewed as the black political party.

As barriers to the social and economic advancement of African Americans have gradually come down over the past several decades, the black population of the United States has become increasingly diverse. Africans Americans are still an economically disadvantaged group, but a large black middle class has developed in the nation's major metropolitan areas and African Americans are increasingly found in professional and managerial occupations (Bowser 2007). In addition, in recent years an influx of immigrants from the African continent and the Caribbean has added to the diversity of America's black population (Shaw-Taylor and Tuch 2007).

Surprisingly, however, the growing diversity of the African American population has not led to growing diversity in the partisan orientations of African American voters. Despite recent efforts by the Republican Party to

Table 8.1   Democratic Identification among African-American Voters, 1992–2004

	Democratic %
AGE	
18–29	87
30–39	84
40–49	85
50–64	89
65+	89
GENDER	
Male	84
Female	89
EDUCATION	
High School	84
Some College	92
Graduated College	86
FAMILY INCOME	
Lower Third	86
Middle Third	88
Upper Third	87
IDEOLOGY	
Liberal	96
Moderate	85
Conservative	73

Source: NES Cumulative File

reach out to the black community and the presence of several African Americans in key leadership positions in the Bush Administration, black voters in the United States have remained steadfastly loyal to the Democratic Party. In 2004, according to national exit poll data, almost 90 percent of African Americans voted for Democrat John Kerry over President Bush. Moreover, the data displayed in Table 8.1 show that during the years 1992 to 2004, the Democratic Party remained dominant in every major subgroup within the African American community. Younger blacks were just as likely to be Democratic Party supporters as older blacks; black college graduates were just as likely to be Democratic Party supporters as blacks with only a high school education; and upper income blacks were just as likely to vote for the Democratic Party as lower income blacks. Black men were slightly less likely than black women to be Democratic Party supporters. Black conservatives were somewhat less likely to be Democratic Party supporters than black moderates and liberals, but even these differences were fairly minor. It is striking that almost three fourths of black conservatives, a group whose political outlook might have been expected to make them more sympathetic to the Republican Party's message, continued to identify with the Democratic Party during these years.

What these findings suggest is that the racial divide is different from every other social divide in the United States. For African Americans, in contrast to every other major social group in the United States, partisanship remains rooted in group identity rather than ideology. The large majority of African Americans continue to perceive the Republican Party as unsympathetic, if not hostile, to the needs and concerns of black people—a perception that was clearly reinforced by the Bush Administration's inept response to the devastation caused by Hurricane Katrina. As long as that perception remains, it is likely that black voters will continue to overwhelmingly identify with the Democratic Party and vote for Democratic candidates from the presidency down to the local level. The nomination and election of Barack Obama, the nation's first African American president, clearly has reinforced the loyalty of African American voters to the Democratic Party. According to the 2008 national exit poll, African Americans made up a record 13 percent of the national electorate and cast 95 percent of their votes for Obama. As long as Obama is in the White House the prospect of Republican inroads among African American voters would appear to be remote.

The New Divides among White Voters: Gender, Marriage, and Religious Commitment

Since the 1970s, as traditional group loyalties forged during the New Deal and earlier have faded in importance, several new divisions have developed among white voters in the United States. As we will see, however, the new divides are different from the older ones because they are largely by-products of ideology. Of these new divisions, the most significant are the gender gap, the marriage

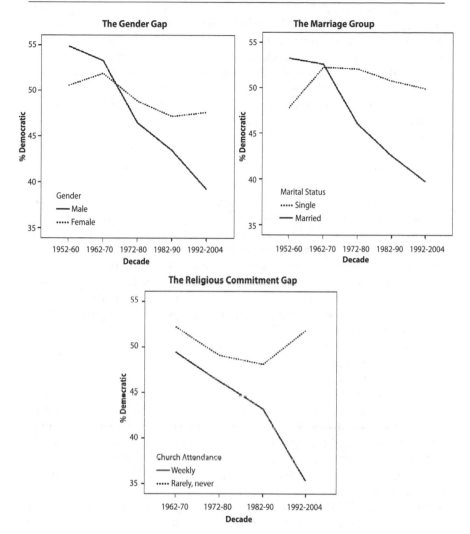

Figure 8.4 New Group Divisions among White Voters: Gender, Marriage, and Religious Commitment.

gap, and the religious commitment gap. The emergence of these divisions can be seen very clearly in the three graphs included in Figure 8.4. These graphs display the trends in Democratic identification over the past thirty to forty years among white male and female voters, white married and single voters, and white religious and nonreligious voters.

The gender gap has received perhaps the greatest attention from political scientists and journalists since its initial appearance in the 1970s. Over the past three decades, the fact that white women are more likely to identify with the Democratic Party and vote for Democratic candidates at all levels than white men has been frequently noted (Box-Steffensmeier, De Boef, and Tse-Min Lin 2004; Kaufman and Petrocik 1999). What the data displayed in the first graph in Figure 8.4 make clear, however, is that the gender gap was not a result of growing affection for the Democratic Party among white women. Instead, the gender gap developed because support for the Democratic Party declined less drastically among white women than among white men. It was for this reason that a gender gap of between five and ten percentage points in party identification was evident by the beginning of the twenty-first century.

A similar phenomenon is evident when we examine the development of the marriage gap among white voters (Plutzer and McBurnett 1991). The data displayed in the second graph in Figure 8.4 shows that before the 1970s there was little or no difference in party identification between single and married white voters. But since the 1970s, single white voters have consistently supported the Democratic Party to a greater extent than married white voters. As in the case of the gender gap, however, the marriage gap emerged not because of an increase in support for Democrats among single voters but because of the fact that support for Democrats declined less dramatically among single voters than among married voters. As a result, a marriage gap of over ten percentage points in party identification had developed by the beginning of the twenty-first century.

Perhaps the most politically significant division among white voters today, however, is the religious commitment gap. And once again, as the data displayed in the third graph in Figure 8.4 show, this gap is of relatively recent origin. Before the 1980s there was very little difference in party identification between religious and nonreligious white voters—religious voters were only slightly less likely to identify with the Democratic Party than nonreligious voters. Starting in the 1980s, however, something happened to increase the salience of religious commitments in the political arena and by the turn of the twenty-first century, the religious commitment gap among white voters was even larger than the gender gap or the marriage gap (D. E. Campbell 2007; Guth and Green 1991; Layman 2001). According to the data displayed in the third graph in Figure 8.4, in the most recent period, over half of nonreligious white voters identified with the Democratic Party compared with barely a third of religious white voters.

What happened during the eighties and nineties to create a religious commitment gap was that the Democratic and Republican parties became increasingly associated with opposing positions on issues such as abortion, school prayer, public subsidies for religious schools, and, later, gay rights—issues that tended to divide voters according to their religious beliefs and practices (White 2003). This process began during the 1980s with Ronald Reagan speaking out against Supreme Court decisions banning school prayer and legalizing abortion and culminated during the 2004 presidential election with George W. Bush's advocacy of a constitutional amendment to ban same sex marriage. By that time, however, the increasingly close relationship between the Republican

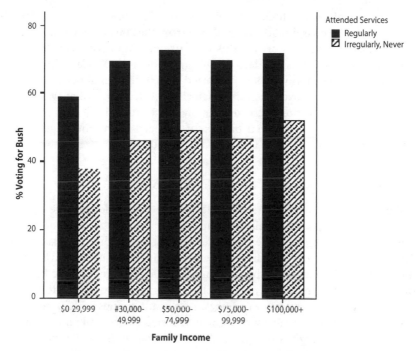

Figure 8.5   Religious Commitment vs. Class: Percentage of Whites Voting for Bush in 2004 by Family Income and Church Attendence. Source: 2004 Exit Poll.

Party and the Religious Right had begun to produce a backlash among more moderately religious and secular voters that is evident in the graph. Between the 1980s and the 1990s, Democratic identification fell by eight percentage points among religious whites but rose by five percentage points among non-religious whites.

In the 2004 presidential contest, religious commitment was a much stronger predictor of the vote among whites than social class. This can be seen in Figure 8.5 which displays the joint effects of family income and church attendance on the presidential vote among whites. The results indicate that among both frequent and infrequent churchgoers, support for President Bush was only slightly higher among upper income voters than among lower income voters. Within every income category, however, support for Bush was substantially greater among frequent churchgoers than infrequent churchgoers. The average difference in support for Bush within each income category was close to 20 percentage points. Support for George Bush was actually greater among frequent churchgoers with family incomes below $30,000 than among infrequent churchgoers with family incomes of $100,000 or more: a large majority of low income churchgoers voted for Bush while a majority of wealthy non-churchgoers voted for Kerry.

Among white voters today, the religious divide appears to be considerably deeper than the class divide. The evidence from the 2008 presidential election provides additional support for this conclusion. Despite the fact that many white evangelical voters had deep misgivings about John McCain's candidacy, and few members of this group supported him in the Republican primaries, McCain received the overwhelming majority of votes from white evangelicals in the November election. According to the 2008 national exit poll, 74 percent of white evangelicals cast their ballots for McCain, down only slightly from the 78 percent who voted for George Bush in 2004.

Explaining the Gaps: The Role of Ideology

All of these divides within the white electorate—the gender gap, the marriage gap, and the religious commitment gap—made their first appearance during the 1970s or 1980s and all reached their largest size within the past decade. That is because all of these divides are by-products of growing partisan-ideological polarization. Over the past three decades, the Democratic Party has moved to the left and the Republican Party has moved to the right on racial and cultural as well as economic issues. As a result, groups with more conservative views on these issues such as men, married voters, and religious voters have been increasingly attracted to the Republican Party while groups with more liberal views on these issues such as women, single voters, and nonreligious voters have found the Republican approach much less appealing.

The crucial role played by ideology in producing all of the new divides within the white electorate is evident in Table 8.2. This table displays the rela-

Table 8.2 Explaining the Gaps: Ideology and Democratic Identification among White Voters, 1992–2004

	Liberal	Moderate	Conservative
GENDER			
Male	78	52	21
Female	78	50	24
MARTIAL STATUS			
Married	76	50	21
Single	80	52	26
CHURCH ATENDANCE			
Weekly or More	78	52	24
Seldom or Never	80	48	22

Source: NES Cumulative File

Table 8.3 Political Engagement and Group Differences in Party
Identification among Whites, 1992–2004 (% Democratic – %
Republican)

	Low Engagement	High Engagement
Female	+ 17	+ 4
Male	+ 11	−16
Difference	+ 6	+ 20
Single	+ 20	+ 13
Married	+ 10	− 21
Difference	+ 10	+ 34
Non-Observant	+ 21	+ 15
Observant	+ 5	− 31
Difference	+ 16	+ 46

Source: NES Cumulative File

tionship between party identification and gender, marital status, and church attendance among white voters while controlling for ideology. The results indicate that all three gaps disappear after controlling for ideology. Liberal, moderate, and conservative men are just as likely to identify with the Democratic Party as liberal, moderate, and conservative women; liberal, moderate, and conservative married voters are just as likely to identify with the Democratic Party as liberal, moderate, and conservative single voters; and liberal, moderate, and conservative churchgoers are just as likely to identify with the Democratic Party as liberal, moderate, and conservative nonchurchgoers.

Because the gender, marriage, and religious commitment gaps are themselves by-products of more fundamental ideological divisions within the electorate, the size of these gaps should vary with the level of political engagement of citizens. The largest gaps should be found among the most politically engaged members of the public because, as we have seen, it is among the most politically engaged citizens that the link between ideology and party identification is strongest. And that is exactly what the evidence displayed in Table 8.3 shows: the gender, marriage, and religious commitment gaps were all considerably larger among the most politically engaged citizens than among the least politically engaged citizens. In the United States today, the deepest party divisions are found among the most interested, informed, and active citizens.

The impact of political engagement is particularly striking when it comes to religious commitment. In the low engagement group, the difference in party identification between frequent and infrequent churchgoers is relatively small: there is a twenty-one point Democratic advantage among infrequent churchgoers compared with a five point Democratic advantage among frequent churchgoers. In the high engagement group, however, the difference in party identification between frequent and infrequent churchgoers is much larger: there is a fifteen point Democratic advantage among infrequent churchgoers compared with a thirty point Republican advantage among frequent churchgoers. While Democrats slightly outnumbered Republicans among the least politically engaged religious whites, Republicans outnumbered Democrats by a two to one margin among the most politically engaged religious whites. This finding calls into question the claim that the Republican Party has made gains among religious white voters by duping the most politically naïve members of this group into voting against their own self-interest (Frank 2004). In fact, Republican gains among religious white voters have been concentrated among the most politically sophisticated members of this group.

The 2008 Election: Polarization Continues

While the results of the 2008 election reflected the special circumstances of that year, including a severe economic downturn and the extraordinary candidacy of Barack Obama, they also reflected the intense ideological polarization that has been evident in recent years in American politics. There was some hope that the departure of George W. Bush from the political scene would lead to moderation of the partisan divisions that marked his presidency. And there is no question that Mr. Bush was an extremely divisive figure (Jacobson 2007). But the results of an October 2008 Time Magazine Poll demonstrate that partisan polarization is alive and well in post-Bush America. In fact the evidence from this poll suggest that divisions between Democratic and Republican voters, divisions that make it very difficult for Democratic and Republican politicians to compromise, may be deeper than ever.

The Time Magazine Poll involved telephone interviews with 1,053 likely voters from October 3 to 6, 2008, just one month before the presidential election. Barack Obama led John McCain in the poll by a margin of five points, 48 percent to 43 percent, with 9 percent undecided. This was very close to Obama's margin of just over seven points in the actual election results. What makes this poll especially useful, however, is that in addition to the usual questions about party and ideological identification, the survey included a series of questions on ten specific policy issues—abortion, gay marriage, the war in Iraq, health insurance, regulation of financial institutions, global warming, offshore oil drilling, home mortgage assistance, business tax cuts, and the federal bailout of banks and financial institutions.

On each issue, respondents were asked to place themselves on a scale ranging from zero for "strongly disagree" to ten for "strongly agree." These questions allow us to determine not only which side of an issue voters came down on but also the intensity of their preference on that issue. In addition, the survey included five political information questions in which respondents were asked to name the Vice President, Secretary of the Treasury, Speaker of the House, Chief Justice of the Supreme Court, and home state of Barack

Obama. Answers to these questions can be combined to measure respondents' overall level of political information, which is a key indicator of political engagement.

A number of scholars have argued that the American people, in contrast to the nation's political leaders, are fundamentally moderate in their political views (Fiorina, Abrams, and Pope 2006). In a similar vein, some conservative commentators have recently suggested that despite Democratic victories in the 2008 presidential and congressional elections, the United States remains a center-right country. An important piece of evidence for these claims is the fact that when Americans are asked to place themselves on a liberal–conservative scale, the middle position is invariably the most popular and the conservative label is generally preferred to the liberal label. This was also the case for respondents in the Time Magazine Poll. Given a five-point liberal–conservative scale, 9 percent of respondents described themselves as "very liberal," 20 percent as "somewhat liberal," 29 percent as "moderate," 26 percent as "somewhat conservative," and 16 percent as "very conservative."

Despite the popularity of the middle position and the preference for the conservative label over the liberal label, however, responses to the ten policy questions in the Time Poll portray the American electorate in a very different light. These responses revealed an electorate that was often deeply divided and that tilted to the left on some major policy issues. Table 8.4 shows the percentage of respondents who placed themselves on the far right (0–1) or far left (9–10) on each issue compared with the percentage who placed themselves near the center (4–6). On six of the ten issues, including abortion, health care,

Table 8.4 The Electoral Divide: Public Opinion on 10 Policy Issues in 2008

Issue	Extreme Liberals (9-10)	Moderates (4-6)	Extreme Conservatives (0-1)
Gay Marriage	31%	14%	41%
Abortion	43%	16%	27%
Iraq War	30%	19%	22%
Health Care	30%	22%	20%
Financial Regulation	36%	25%	11%
Offshore Drilling	10%	19%	48%
Global Warming	30%	28%	12%
Wall Street Bailout	9%	27%	28%
Business Tax Cuts	·12%	37%	23%
Mortgage Help	18%	38%	16%

Note: All issues are coded so that 0 is most conservative response and 10 is most liberal response.
Source: Time Magazine Poll, Oct. 3-6, 2008

financial regulation, global warming, and the war in Iraq, more respondents placed themselves on the liberal end of the scale than on the conservative end. Moreover, there was a high level of polarization on several issues with a much larger proportion of respondents placing themselves at the left or right extremes than at the center.

The deepest divisions were on the issues of abortion and gay marriage with more than two thirds of respondents placing themselves on the far left or far right and less than one fifth placing themselves near the center. However, high levels of polarization were also evident on the war in Iraq and health care. In fact, the only two issues on which more respondents were found at the center than at the extremes were business tax cuts and government assistance to homeowners threatened by foreclosure.

When it comes to polarization, though, the overall distribution of opinion on an issue may be less important than the intensity of partisan divisions. That's because when Democratic and Republican voters hold divergent views on an issue, those differences are much more likely to be reflected by Democratic and Republican candidates and office-holders. Table 8.5 shows that there were, in fact, large differences between Obama and McCain voters on many of the issues in the Time Poll. On average, Obama voters came down on the liberal side on eight of the ten issues while McCain voters came down on the conservative side on nine of the ten issues. On several issues, the gap between Obama and McCain voters was enormous: on the war in Iraq, health care, and abortion, the average Obama voter was well to the left of center while the average McCain voter was well to the right of center. The only issue on which

Table 8.5 The Partisan Divide: Average Liberalism of Obama and McCain Voters on 10 Policy Issues

Issue	Obama Voters	McCain Voters	Difference
Iraq War	7.5	2.3	5.2
Health Care	8.1	3.1	5.0
Gay Marriage	6.7	2.2	4.5
Abortion	7.7	3.7	4.0
Offshore Drilling	4.6	1.0	3.6
Global Warming	7.8	4.5	3.3
Financial Regulation	7.8	5.2	2.6
Business Tax Cuts	5.4	2.8	2.6
Mortgage Help	6.3	4.2	2.1
Wall Street Bailout	4.1	3.6	0.5

Note: All issues are coded so that 0 is most conservative response and 10 is most liberal response.
Source: Time Magazine Poll, Oct. 3-6, 2008

there was not a significant difference between Obama and McCain voters was the Wall Street bailout, which is not surprising given the complexity of the issue and the conflicting views expressed by both Democratic and Republican leaders.

Another important feature of public opinion in the United States today is that polarization is generally greatest among the most attentive, informed, and active members of the public—the sorts of citizens who vote in primary elections, contribute to political campaigns, and contact elected officials to express their opinions. The evidence displayed in Table 8.6 shows that this was very clearly the case in the Time Poll. When we divide respondents into those who had scores of zero through two on the political information test (36% of respondents) and those who had scores of three through five (64% of respondents), we find that on every issue policy differences between Obama and McCain voter were larger among the better informed respondents than among less informed respondents. On several issues, including health care, abortion, gay marriage, and global warming, party differences were substantially larger among the better informed respondents.

Another characteristic of politically engaged citizens is that they tend to have more consistent opinions across issues than less engaged citizens and this was also the case for respondents in the Time Poll. Among those who scored three or higher on the political information test, the average product-moment correlation among the ten issue questions was .41; among those who scored below three, however, the average correlation was only .25. The consequences of this for ideological polarization can be seen very clearly in Figure 8.6 which

Table 8.6 Partisan Differences on 10 Policy Issues by Political Information

Issue	Low Information	Moderate to High Information
Iraq War	4.5	5.6
Health Care	3.7	5.8
Gay Marriage	3.0	5.3
Abortion	2.1	4.9
Offshore Drilling	2.3	4.2
Global Warming	1.7	4.2
Financial Regulation	1.8	3.2
Business Tax Cuts	1.5	3.1
Mortgage Help	1.9	2.1
Wall Street Bailout	− 0.3	0.7

Note: Difference score represents average liberalism of Obama voters minus average liberalism of McCain voters.
Source: Time Magazine Poll, Oct. 3-6, 2008

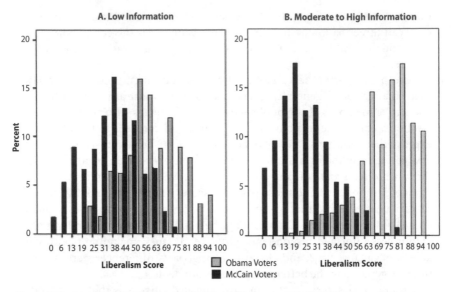

Figure 8.6   Ideological Differences between Obama and McCain Voters by Political Information. Source: Time Magazine Poll, Oct. 3–6, 2008.

compares the scores of less informed and more informed voters on an eight-item ideology scale. This scale combines seven of the policy issues (abortion, gay marriage, health care, regulation of financial institutions, global warming, Iraq, and business tax breaks) with the liberal-conservative identification question. This eight-item scale has a reliability coefficient (Cronbach's alpha) of .85 which is well above the accepted cutoff of .7 for a satisfactory scale.

The two distributions look very different. Among less informed voters the differences between McCain and Obama supporters were muted and moderates predominated. Among better informed voters, however, the differences between McCain and Obama supporters were much sharper: Obama supporters were concentrated on the liberal side of the scale while McCain supporters were concentrated on the conservative side of the scale. Among these politically engaged voters, just as among members of Congress, the center of the ideological spectrum was largely empty.

Summary and Conclusions

The electoral coalitions supporting the Democratic and Republican parties have undergone a dramatic transformation over the past half century. By the beginning of the twenty-first century, the three major pillars of the coalition forged by Franklin Roosevelt during the Depression years—white Southerners and white working class and ethnic voters in the North—had largely collapsed. As a result of defections by self-identified conservatives, Democratic identification within each of these groups fell steadily from the 1960s through the 1990s until by the end of the century there were almost no conservative Democrats left.

The disintegration of the New Deal coalition was accompanied by the emergence of new divisions within the electorate—divisions based on race, gender, marital status, and religious commitment. During the 1960s and 1970s, as the national Democratic Party embraced the cause of civil rights and the Republican Party began aggressively courting racially and culturally conservative whites in the South and elsewhere, African Americans went from being a solidly Democratic voting bloc to being an overwhelmingly Democratic voting bloc. Meanwhile, within the white electorate, groups with conservative views on racial and cultural issues, such as men, married voters, and frequent churchgoers, shifted their loyalties to the Republicans while groups with more liberal views on these issues, such as women, single voters, and infrequent churchgoers, continued to support the Democrats.

The end result of all of these changes has been the emergence of a new American party system—one in which party loyalties are based primarily on voters' ideological beliefs rather than their membership in social groups. This transformation of the party system has had profound consequences for almost every aspect of the electoral process in the United States and its results were clearly evident in the 2008 presidential election.

Note

1. See chapter 3 for a discussion of the electoral strategies that motivated party leaders to adopt these positions.

Chapter 9

Religion, Moralism, and the Cultural Wars

Competing Moral Visions

Laura R. Olson

For generations, observers and analysts of American politics presumed that the most significant political divisions among American voters arose primarily from differences in race, class, and ideology. In recent decades, however, religion has emerged as an equally important partisan dividing line. The competing visions of moral order, rules, and authority that flow from different religious traditions' teachings have given rise to deep—and by now enduring—political cleavages. Most significantly, individuals who participate frequently in organized religion display markedly more conservative political views than more secular citizens. The emergence of these political differences has prompted debates about what role government should play in supporting competing moral visions, especially when they are tied closely to particular religious perspectives. After all, the U.S. Constitution forbids any "establishment of religion," meaning government cannot advantage any one faith over others.

This chapter will review the political divisions that have developed in recent times around the competing moral visions concomitant with religious pluralism in the United States. As recently as the late 1970s, most analysts of American politics thought religion's political relevance was a straightforward matter of affiliation: white Protestants were Republicans, while Catholics and Jews were Democrats. Some even thought religion's significance in American society was dying away altogether. Over the past three decades, however, God has not died, and variation in religious attachment has taken on new political significance. How and why has religion emerged as such a politically salient social construct? What do political scientists mean by "religion," and exactly how does religion affect American voters' partisan attachments and voting behavior?

The Culture Wars Thesis

In the post-World War II era, social scientists agreed that the political relevance of religion was anchored primarily in religious *affiliation*. In short, white Protestants were Republicans, while African American Protestants,

Catholics, and Jews were Democrats (Herberg 1955; Lenski 1961). While today this assumption might seem overly simplistic, particularly in light of the great diversity that has always characterized American Protestantism (Glock and Stark 1965; Marty 1970), it was for the most part accurate. White Protestants represented the establishment, while Catholics and Jews still were viewed—and to an extent viewed themselves—as "outsider" immigrant groups (Forman 2001; Green 2007; Leege, Wald, Krueger, and Mueller 2002; Reichley 2002; Wuthnow 1988). For their part, African American Protestants largely turned away from the party of Lincoln to join the New Deal Coalition because of the Democrats' greater commitment to social justice (Harris 1999; Savage 2008). By the postwar era, the Republican Party's alliance with business interests was well established, and the Democrats continued to be seen as the party of the "little guy" (Key 1942). As "outsider" ethno-religious groups, Catholics and Jews were especially compelled by the egalitarian policies of the New Deal era—and dismayed by perceived biases against them on the part of white Protestants and the Republican Party (Forman 2001; Leege et al. 2002). Thus they retained strong and rather homogeneous ties to the Democratic Party well into the twentieth century. Other than Southern evangelicals, who were almost all Democrats for historic regional reasons (Key 1949), white Protestants threw the vast bulk of their support to Republicans. White Protestants' allegiance to the Republican Party in the postwar era was not the result of sociomoral conservatism; instead, it was mainly a matter of appreciation for the GOP's fiscal conservatism.

Drawing on classical sociological theory, especially the observations of Karl Marx, Max Weber, and Emile Durkheim, some scholars began asserting that the political and social significance of religion was in decline (e.g., Berger 1967). They argued that the 1960s had put the United States on a path to secularization; religion was in a sense being ushered out of the public square (Neuhaus 1984). Increasingly, Americans were opting out of religious life altogether, so proponents of secularization theory naturally hypothesized that religion's relevance was shrinking rapidly. In particular, scholars thought secularization was the logical end result of some key social changes of the twentieth century. The growth in government's responsibility for less fortunate Americans chipped away at the social-welfare function of churches and synagogues. The spread of science and technology provided explanations for naturally occurring phenomena that had nothing to do with the divine. To borrow from Friedrich Nietzsche, God was presumed dead.

However, just as social scientists were concluding that religion's influence on partisanship and voting was either a straightforward matter of Protestants on one side versus Catholics and Jews on the other—or that religion was irrelevant in American electoral politics—another hypothesis entered the scholarly discourse. Sociologist Robert Wuthnow (1988) was the first to propose that American religion had not vanished, but instead had undergone a substantial and complex transformation since World War II. Religion's social and political significance had not dwindled, it had changed: no longer could it be understood on the basis of religious affiliation only. The assimilation of ethno-religious groups (which for decades had been viewed as outsiders) into mainstream American society had the effect of weakening the ties many felt to the churches of their nations of origin. Wuthnow astutely noticed a significant rift emerging *within* religious families "between self-styled religious 'conservatives' and self-styled religious 'liberals'... [rooted in] deep differences in theological, moral, social, and political orientations" (1988, 133). For instance, conservative Methodists now had more in common with conservative Baptists than they did with liberal Methodists. And in part because ideology and religion were growing increasingly connected in the minds of American voters, religion was becoming more politically salient, not less so—in direct repudiation of secularization theory.

A few years later, sociologist James Davison Hunter (1991) extended Wuthnow's argument beyond the strict context of organized religion in his landmark book *Culture Wars*. Hunter portrays American society in general and its elites in particular as falling into two mutually antagonistic camps: the orthodox, who take unyieldingly traditional stands on sociomoral issues, and the progressives, who are unwilling to accept unbending notions of right and wrong. These two camps, argues Hunter, are locked in "culture wars" in which neither side is willing to compromise. The primary battlefields in the culture wars are sensitive moral issues arising from human sexuality, including abortion, pornography, and gay rights.

Moral issues such as these are, of course, the natural province of religious congregations and their leaders (Green, Guth, Smidt, and Kellstedt 1996; Guth, Green, Smidt, Kellstedt, and Poloma 1997; Leege et al. 2002). The cultural upheaval of the post-World War II era transformed American religion itself, creating deep cleavages within religious families that had not been especially relevant before. At the same time, the broader American culture could not decide whether or not to acquiesce to the changes wrought by the 1960s. Thus the division between liberals, who embraced change, and conservatives, who resisted it, became all the more relevant—and painful—both inside and outside of organized religion. Suddenly the most politically relevant aspect of religion was not whether one was Protestant or Catholic, but rather whether one was a religious conservative or a religious liberal—and by the 1970s both groups were in ample supply within both Protestantism and Catholicism.

Like any social scientific theory, however, the culture wars thesis is not a perfect representation of human behavior. Accordingly, both political scientists (Fiorina et al. 2006; Leege and Wald 1998; Olson 2002; Wolfe 1998) and sociologists of religion (DiMaggio, Evans, and Bryson 1996; J. H. Evans 2003; Greeley and Hout 2006; Williams 1997) have called elements of the culture wars thesis into question. In particular, scholars contend that most ordinary American citizens do not perceive themselves as combatants in the culture wars. Elites may be quite well aware that these divisions exist—and many use the divisions for political gain (Domke and Coe 2008; Kuo 2006; Leege et al. 2002)—but by no means do all rank-and-file voters cleave neatly into one of the two culture wars camps. A classic observation about the American voter is that only 2.5 percent of citizens display perfect ideological constraint, or consistency, across issue positions (Converse 1964); it makes sense, then, that relatively few Americans would be perfectly consistent culture warriors either. Nevertheless, it is entirely true that various dimensions of religion have become much more salient for American voters since roughly 1980—and that these religious differences have contributed to the increased polarization of the American electorate.

Measuring "Religion"

Social scientists have noted that three key dimensions of religion have political relevance: "belonging," "behaving," and "believing" (J. C. Green 2007; J. C. Green et al. 1996; Layman 2001; Leege and Kellstedt 1993). Religious *affiliation* ("belonging") refers to the specific religious tradition with which an individual identifies (the Roman Catholic Church, the Southern Baptist Convention, Reform Judaism, etc.). Different religious families take distinctive approaches to politics that are rooted in their particular religious traditions and teachings. For example, Catholic theology places heavy emphasis on the infinite value of all human life; as a result, the political agenda of Catholic leaders focuses on protecting life in all its forms, which means opposing abortion, euthanasia, and the death penalty, and supporting government policies designed to help less fortunate members of society (Cochran and Cochran 2003). Evangelical Protestants (such as Southern Baptists) focus on saving individual souls one-by-one through acceptance of Jesus Christ as personal savior. Once saved, believers are encouraged to live in accordance with traditional moral standards to guard against temptations of the flesh that might lead to "backsliding." Thus evangelicals are strong supporters of social policies designed to preserve and defend traditional family structures and social mores (Smith 1998; Wilcox and Larson 2006).

Religious *commitment* ("behaving") refers to the extent to which an individual prioritizes and spends time in the practice of religion (e.g., praying, worshiping, reading holy scriptures)—regardless of religious affiliation. Some people simply prioritize religious practice more than others. It stands to reason that individuals who are deeply involved in religious activities would be exposed to a systematically different set of experiences and information than those who do not prioritize religious participation. For example, people who attend worship services on a regular basis are exposed continually to information from clergy and fellow worshipers; individuals who do not attend services are not exposed to such information. This information often is politically relevant, both because it reflects the teachings of the religious tradition to which one belongs, but also because being involved in religious activities simply sets one apart—both psychologically and socially—from people who do not participate (Djupe and Gilbert 2006; Djupe and Grant 2001; Verba, Schlozman, and Brady 1995; Wald, Owen, and Hill 1988, 1990). Politicians have learned that it is fruitful to appeal to voters who perceive themselves as religious—in a generic but socially definitive sense of the word (Domke and Coe 2008).

Religious *belief* ("believing") refers to the relative strictness with which an individual interprets and understands the teachings of his or her particular faith tradition. For example, many American Catholics do not rigorously follow all of the teachings of the Church, but a minority—typically termed "traditional" or "conservative" Catholics—interpret and adhere to Church doctrine much more strictly (Cochran and Cochran 2003). By the same token, some Protestants (known as fundamentalists) believe that every word of the Bible is literally true, while other Protestants (more liberal individuals within the broader mainline Protestant tradition) believe that the Bible is primarily a set of parables and is thus open to multiple interpretations.

"Old" Religious Cleavages

Until the 1980s, scholars were correct in asserting that religion's influence on partisanship and voting behavior arose primarily from religious affiliation. Most Protestants (outside of the South) were Republicans, while most Catholics and Jews were loyal members of the New Deal Coalition. As an illustration, consider Table 9.1, which displays the relationship between religious "belonging" and the 1944 presidential vote. The first thing to notice in the table is the fact that white mainline Protestants (that is, members of large, socially dominant denominations such as the Episcopal Church) comprised nearly half of the American electorate in 1944. Despite the tremendous popularity of Franklin D. Roosevelt at the height of World War II, white mainline Protestants voted decisively for Roosevelt's Republican challenger, Thomas Dewey. Meanwhile, African American Protestants, Catholics, and (especially) Jews lent the vast majority of their support to Roosevelt. In what might now seem like an ironic twist, the support of white evangelical Protestants—a majority of whom lived in the solidly Democratic South—helped put Roosevelt over the top. In 1944, white Southerners voted for Roosevelt, as they did for most other Democratic candidates, principally because he was not a Republican (Key 1949). To them, the Republican Party was still the party of Lincoln, and thus of "Northern aggression." On the basis of mainline Protestants' numeric dominance in the American electorate of 1944, however, it is entirely fair to say that white Protestants as a group were overwhelmingly Republican, while African American Protestants, Catholics, and Jews were overwhelmingly Democratic. This pattern was common during the first half of the twentieth century.

In the last several decades, however, this old "belonging" cleavage has been blurred rather substantially. Several demographic and theological factors account for the change, including the expansion of religious pluralism, the

Table 9.1 Presidential Vote by Religious Tradition, 1944

	Population Share (%)	% Vote for Roosevelt (D)	% Vote for Dewey (R)
White Evangelical Protestants	17.5	55.9	44.1
White Mainline Protestants	44.4	42.1	57.9
African American Protestants	8.3	69.8	30.2
Catholics	17.5	68.4	31.6
Jews	4.0	92.7	7.3
All	—	**53.8**	**46.2**

Source: Adapted from Green (2007): 38–39. Population share percentages do not sum to 100 because not all religious traditions are included.

dramatic growth of evangelical Protestantism, the assimilation of Catholics into American society, and the growing social acceptability of eschewing religious life altogether.

Religious pluralism is a basic fact of American life. Even colonial America was religiously diverse (Ahlstrom 1972; Finke and Stark 2005; Reichley 2002), with members of small Protestant sects, Catholics (particularly in Maryland), and Jews settling alongside the dominant Congregational Church (Puritans) and the Church of England (Anglicans, who became today's Episcopalians). The ratification of the Bill of Rights ensured that the federal government could not advantage one religious tradition over others, nor could it prohibit Americans from practicing the religion of their choice. Under the protective cover of the First Amendment's guarantee of religious freedom, organized religion thrived and diversified in nineteenth-century America, creating a vibrant religious marketplace complete with dramatic innovation and the founding of entirely new religious traditions, most notably the Church of Jesus Christ of Latter-day Saints (Ahlstrom 1972; Finke and Stark 2005). The second half of the twentieth century witnessed the emergence of even greater religious pluralism in the United States. The "market share" of mainline Protestantism slipped as evangelical Protestantism grew (Finke and Stark 2005). Meanwhile, new immigrants (especially Catholics from Latin America and Muslims from Asia and Africa) brought their own religious traditions to American shores. As American religion grows ever more variegated, no single religious tradition can stake a claim to dominance. Today, even the broad Protestant tradition, encompassing all of its diverse mainline, evangelical, and African American denominations, can barely claim a majority (51.3 percent) of the American population as adherents (Pew Forum 2008). Thus the political significance of religious "belonging" in the old sense is no longer as straightforward or transparent as it was as recently as the mid-twentieth century.

One reason why the old "Protestant-Catholic-Jewish" dividing lines lack political meaning today is the remarkable growth enjoyed in recent decades by

evangelical Protestantism. Evangelical Protestants, who adhere to strict interpretations of Christian scripture and doctrine, once were painted as mainline
Protestants' "poor relations" (C. Smith 1998). Their reluctance to accommodate to modernity in the early twentieth century (as illustrated by their insistence that Charles Darwin's theory of evolution was heretical, made famous in
the Scopes "monkey trial" of 1925), as well as their piqued skepticism of secular society, led them to be stereotyped as uneducated and backward. However,
by midcentury evangelical leaders such as Rev. Billy Graham were arguing for
an "engaged evangelicalism" that encouraged evangelicals to become more
involved in the worldly spheres of business, education, and the professions
(Ahlstrom 1972; Marty 1970; Smith 1998). Evangelical Protestantism thus
began to prosper. Its growth was spurred even more when many Americans,
alienated by the rapid social changes of the 1960s, began seeking refuge—
and strict moral teachings—in evangelical churches (Fowler 1989; Iannaccone
1994; Kelley 1972). As evangelical Protestantism thrived, the large and once-
dominant denominations of mainline Protestantism fell into numeric decline
(Finke and Stark 2005; Kelley 1972; Roozen and Nieman 2005). Some analysts argue that mainline churches simply failed to stay relevant in a rapidly
changing religious marketplace, while others point to the dissatisfaction some
parishioners felt with the progressive political activism undertaken by their
clergy in the civil rights and antiwar movements of the 1960s and 1970s (Finke
and Stark 2005; Hadden 1969; Wuthnow and Evans 2002).

Change was afoot among American Catholics during the second half of
the twentieth century as well. Long seen as "outsider" immigrant groups and
defined by ethno-religious identities (Polish Catholics, Irish Catholics, Italian Catholics, etc.), by the postwar era the stigma of being Catholic in the
United States was lessening (Leege et al. 2002). The 1960 election of John
F. Kennedy to the presidency showed that a Catholic American could rise
to the highest political office in the land. While some Protestants retained
anti-Catholic biases, animosity directed toward American Catholics was on
the wane. Meanwhile, the Roman Catholic Church itself was undergoing
momentous change. The Second Vatican Council, a meeting of top Church
officials that spanned the period 1962 to 1965, dramatically modernized
Catholic doctrine and practice (Wilde 2007). This modernization ultimately
had the unintended effect of making it easier for American Catholics to
retain their religious identity while ignoring many of the Church's teachings
(for example, virtually no American Catholics today adhere to the Church's
official prohibition of artificial birth control). Thus in the second half of the
twentieth century, American Catholics became extremely diverse in every
possible way, including politically (Cochran and Cochran 2003; Leege et al.
2002). No longer was it reasonable to equate Catholic religious affiliation with
Democratic partisanship.

Finally, in the wake of the 1960s it became increasingly acceptable to opt
out of religious life altogether. Americans spent much of the 1960s question-

ing authority and rejecting the social institutions and cultural constructions of previous generations. Consistent with this questioning, many chose to leave traditional religious faith behind and embrace alternative religions—or pure secularism—instead. In terms of religion, in the words of Bob Dylan, "the times they were a-changin'." And the change took hold and spread: the 1990s alone witnessed a doubling of the number of Americans claiming no religious affiliation, from 7 percent in 1991 to 14 percent in 1998 (Hout and Fischer 2002).

Partisanship, Voting Behavior, and Religious "Belonging" in Contemporary American Politics

Since roughly 1980, the old "Protestant-Catholic-Jewish" rubric for understanding how religion affects American partisanship and voting behavior slowly has been rendered obsolete. This is not to say that religious "belonging" does not still affect partisan leanings or vote choice; to the contrary, religious affiliation is an important determinant of American voters' orientations to politics. However, as will be discussed below, religious "belonging" is only one piece of the puzzle; today differences in religious "behaving" and "believing" play just as important a role as affiliation in structuring partisanship and voting behavior.

The most striking—and electorally important—recent change in the relationship between religious affiliation and political orientation has transpired among *evangelical Protestants*. As mentioned above, the size of the white[1] evangelical Protestant population has grown rapidly; 26 percent of Americans today are evangelical (Pew Forum 2008). Undoubtedly this growth would have increased evangelicals' political clout in any event. An even more momentous change, however, has been the thoroughgoing partisan realignment that began within the evangelical community in the 1980s. Until that time, evangelicals leaned Democratic, especially in the South. However, a myriad of factors converged to make evangelicals ripe for realignment by the time Ronald Reagan became the 1980 Republican nominee for the presidency. Reagan sensed the growing frustration of evangelicals, many of whom felt overwhelmed by the social and political changes of the previous two decades. Accordingly, Reagan undertook a substantial outreach effort to evangelicals, promising a return to more traditional social policy around the issues that concerned them the most, such as legal abortion and the removal of prayer from public schools. By 1980 evangelicals (and white Southerners in general) were thoroughly disgusted with the Democratic Party, which had moved in an increasingly progressive direction without the assent of Southern Democrats (Poole and Rosenthal 1997). Reagan worked hard to convince evangelicals that they might be better served by supporting the more conservative of the major parties—and in doing so began a movement of evangelicals into the GOP column that continued apace through the 1990s.

The vast majority of evangelical Protestants today are conservative Republicans in some part out of continuing affection for Reagan, but in larger part because moral and political conservatism is profoundly consistent with the theological teachings of their religious tradition. Evangelical Protestants are primarily concerned with the individual salvation of souls; in fact, for many decades evangelicals avoided politics altogether because they felt it was unproductive—indeed, destructive—to focus much energy on anything of "this world." Evangelical theology is uncompromisingly black and white; the Bible is to be taken at its word, and there are clear standards of right and wrong. As social change gripped the nation in the 1960s and 1970s, evangelicals increasingly became convinced that the lines between right and wrong were blurring. Everywhere they saw signs that America's moral standards were in decline (Murphy 2009; Wilcox and Larson 2006): prayer in school was ruled unconstitutional; no-fault divorce was introduced; abortion was legalized; traditional gender roles were being challenged; gay and lesbian people were demanding equal rights. Reagan's assertion that the Republican Party could be the party of traditional moral values was appealing, and soon evangelical Americans were rallying not only around Reagan and the GOP but also a nascent social movement that became known as the Religious Right. The Religious Right (led in its early days by Rev. Jerry Falwell's Moral Majority and brought to its apex in the 1990s by Rev. Pat Robertson's Christian Coalition) reinforced the message that evangelicals should be social conservatives—and that government should take their views seriously. As Table 9.2 reveals, evangelicals today display solidly conservative attitudes on sociomoral issues: they are 10 percent more likely than the population at large to say "government should do more to protect morality in society," and they are on average 20 percent more likely to oppose homosexuality and abortion. Table 9.3 shows that evangelicals are also much more Republican than the average American, which helps to explain the

Table 9.2 Socio-Moral Issue Positions by Religious Tradition, 2008

	% Agreeing: "Government should do more to protect morality in society"	% Agreeing: "Homosexuality should be discouraged"	% Agreeing: "Abortion should be illegal in most/ all cases"
Evangelical Protestants	50.0	64.0	61.0
Mainline Protestants	33.0	34.0	32.0
African American Protestants	48.0	46.0	46.0
Catholics	43.0	30.0	45.0
Jews	22.0	15.0	14.0
All	**40.0**	**40.0**	**43.0**

Source: Pew Forum (2008). N=35,556.

Table 9.3 Partisanship and Presidential Vote by Religious Tradition, 2008

	Population Share (%)	% Identifying as or Leaning Republican	% Vote for McCain (R)
Evangelical Protestants	26.3	50.0	57.8
Mainline Protestants	18.1	41.0	50.6
African American Protestants	6.9	10.0	0.3
Catholics	23.9	33.0	33.0
Jews	1.7	23.0	15.8
All	—	**36.0**	**32.9**

Sources: Population share and partisanship data: Pew Forum (2008). N=35,556. Vote choice data: American National Election Studies, 2008 Time Series Study, available at <http://www.electionstudies.org>. N=2,102. Protestants are categorized using the technique presented in Steensland et al. (2000). Population share percentages do not sum to 100 because not all religious traditions are included.

substantial degree of support they lent to John McCain in the 2008 presidential election.

Mainline Protestants have not only lost members in recent decades, but they too have been experiencing what might be termed political evolution. Their political transformation has been neither as uniform nor as rapid as the changes that have occurred among their evangelical counterparts, but they are significant nonetheless. Mainline Protestants, who now account for 18 percent of the U.S. population (Pew Forum 2008), include members of eight large and relatively hierarchical denominations[2] known for interpreting scripture in a more liberal manner than evangelicals. There is a long tradition within mainline Protestantism of being involved in the affairs of "this world," particularly around issues of social justice. Mainline Protestants understand the person of Jesus Christ more as a moral example and a champion of the disadvantaged, while evangelicals see Christ primarily as the savior of individual souls.

Historically, mainline Protestants were Republicans in large part because they were socioeconomic elites. In recent times, however, mainline Protestants have become an important swing constituency. As Table 9.3 illustrates, mainline Protestants split their vote almost exactly equally between Barack Obama and John McCain in 2008, although fewer than half claim Republican partisanship.

At least two significant factors have led to this transformation. First, a majority of mainline Protestants take issue with the Religious Right's emphasis on traditional moral values. On the whole, they are somewhat more liberal than other Americans on sociomoral issues such as homosexuality and abortion, and substantially more liberal than evangelical Protestants (see Table 9.2). Moreover, the leaders of mainline denominations have long been even more socially and politically progressive than the people in their pews, and recent times have brought no break from that tradition. The same mainline denominations that stood strongly against racist Jim Crow policies in the South during the civil rights movement (Campbell and Pettigrew 1959; Findlay 1993; Friedland 1998) now are moving to embrace gay men and lesbians in their ranks, not just as congregation members but also as clergy (Cadge, Olson, and Wildeman 2008; Olson, Cadge, and Harrison 2006). While not all congregation members agree with mainline leaders on church policy around sociomoral issues, it is nevertheless politically significant that the denominations themselves are as progressive as they are.

Second, mainline Protestantism's numeric decline might mean that those who choose to remain in mainline churches are especially aware of the longstanding connections between mainline theology and progressive political views. The recent trend has been for the most conservative mainline Protestants to depart when they perceive their denomination to be too liberal (Kraft and Goodstein 2008). It is reasonable to hypothesize that today's smaller mainline denominations are not only leaner but also that they are home to more political liberals than would have been the case as recently as the 1980s. Some conservatives do remain within mainline Protestantism, to be sure, but evidently there are now enough liberal mainline adherents as well so that in the aggregate, the tradition acts as a swing constituency.

A similar political transformation has occurred among American *Catholics*, but for different reasons. As established above, Catholics traditionally were Democrats, in large part because of their "outsider" status. However, like mainline Protestants, Catholics have become a swing constituency since the 1980s. Because of their seamless assimilation into American society, Catholics today face much less social stigmatization due to their religious affiliation. Thus most Catholics no longer perceive themselves as disadvantaged, which has dramatically reduced their political cohesion. Today there is no clear answer to the question of what it means politically to be a Catholic in the United States, because Catholics have diversified so thoroughly since the midtwentieth century. As Table 9.2 shows, Catholics' views on sociomoral issues are both divided and rather closely reflective of the overall views of the American population. It is especially noteworthy that only 45 percent of Catholics agree that abortion should be illegal in most or all cases; this is prime evidence of the growing tendency of American Catholics to reject some of the Church's key teachings while remaining Catholic in their religious identity.

To an extent, what might appear on the surface to be a lack of unified political vision ironically is a reflection of the consistency of Catholic social teaching. As mentioned above, the Roman Catholic Church places great emphasis on the sanctity of human life in all its forms. At the elite level, this provides political opportunities aplenty for Catholic leaders and activists to work in coalition with both conservatives (on abortion) and liberals (on a range of issues focused primarily around social justice and poverty). At the mass level, it plays out as a somewhat bewildering mixture of conservative and liberal attitudes. Consequently we see a mixture of Republican and Democratic allegiances among Catholics, as Table 9.3 illustrates.

Another dynamic that has affected the overall political profile of American Catholics in recent years has been the influx of Catholic immigrants from Latin America. Were it not for the arrival of these new Catholics on American shores, the Catholic Church might be facing a similar decline in membership as the one that currently afflicts mainline Protestantism. The influx of Hispanic Catholics, however, has kept the overall Catholic share of the U.S. population rather steady at just under one-quarter (24 percent; Pew Forum 2008). And the influx of Catholics is significant for political reasons as well: Hispanic Catholics are overwhelmingly Democratic, which has offset gains made by the Republican Party among white Catholics since the late 1990s (Kelly and Kelly 2005). Not all Hispanic Americans are Catholic, of course; approximately one-third of them are evangelical Protestants (Pew Forum 2008). However, as long as the Catholic Church retains its majority status within this growing sector of the American population, the Church's overall market share should stay stable for at least a generation—and its political diversity should be expected to persist.

Meanwhile, the relationship between religious affiliation and political orientation has not changed much for two other significant American religious groups: African American Protestants and Jews. As Table 9.3 reveals, members of both traditions remain quite uniformly loyal to the Democratic Party. In the case of African Americans, however, Democratic identification is more a result of the continuing social significance of race in the United States than it is a measure of liberalism on sociomoral policy. Table 9.2 shows that African American Protestants, who comprise 7 percent of the U.S. population (Pew Forum 2008), take markedly conservative positions on sociomoral issues. This conservatism is consistent with the theological conservatism of African American Protestantism, which resembles evangelical theology more than mainline theology. Yet African Americans remain Democratic despite their sociomoral conservatism. In essence, race still trumps religion at this point in American history.

Likewise, Jews have retained their historic ties to the Democratic Party, although they now display a bit less uniform cohesion than African Americans (Table 9.3). Jews' numbers are small—they account for less than 2 percent of Americans (Pew Forum 2008)—but they are politically consequential because of their high levels of civic engagement as well as their relatively homogeneous political views (Djupe 2007; Greenberg and Wald 2001). Table 9.2 shows that a large majority of Jews espouse liberal attitudes on sociomoral issues, which makes the Democratic Party a natural home for them. Moreover, there is a long tradition of concern about social justice and civil liberties within American Judaism that has given rise to political progressivism and thus identification with the Democratic Party that continues to this day (Forman 2001; Greenberg and Wald 2001).

Two additional American religious groups merit mention in any discussion of the relationship between religious "belonging" and political orientations: Mormons and Muslims. Adherents of the Church of Jesus Christ of Latter-day Saints (Mormons) comprise slightly less than 2 percent of the U.S. population, and their numbers are growing (Pew Forum 2008). Significantly, no religious tradition is more uniformly Republican than are Mormons (Campbell and Monson 2007). The number of American Muslims is small—currently Muslims account for less than 1 percent of Americans (Pew Forum 2008)—but growing. Many Muslims share evangelical Protestants' conservative attitudes on sociomoral issues, and for a time it appeared that Muslim Americans were developing an identity as Republicans. A plurality of Muslims voted for George W. Bush in 2000—in part because they appreciated clear statements he made on the campaign trail against racial, ethnic, and religious profiling (Djupe and Green 2007). However, the events and aftermath of September 11, 2001 seem to have undone any progress the GOP may have been making among Muslim Americans.

Why do we observe the relationships discussed above between religious affiliation and political attitudes, partisanship, and voting behavior? In short, the answer to this question lies in the pluralism of American religion. Because such a vast array of religions has been able to thrive in the United States, we should expect nothing less than a widely divergent range of religious views on moral order, authority, rules, and traditionalism. These differences among religious traditions are rooted in both theology and history. Alexis de Tocqueville observed about religion and politics in the United States: "Every religion has some political opinion linked to it by affinity. The spirit of man, left to follow its bend, will regulate political society and the City of God in a uniform fashion; it will, if I dare put it so, seek to harmonize earth with heaven" (1840/1988, 287). Religious teachings affect the way individuals perceive the entirety of the human experience, so it should come as no surprise that different religious traditions would have their own unique visions—grounded in their holy scriptures—of the "good" society and the "good" polity. Indeed, political scientists have argued that different religious traditions espouse identifiable *social* theologies: organized understandings of how religious beliefs should inform attitudes on matters of public policy, and even more broadly, the issues of the day (Guth et al. 1997). Over centuries (or in the case of Catholicism and Judaism, millennia), religious traditions have evolved as a result of their historical experience and the reinterpretation of their beliefs and teachings by generations of believers. Part of this natural evolutionary process is the development of consistent—and culturally bound—modes of applying religious belief to political outlook. Thus we cannot understand the political orientations of Americans—or those of citizens of any other country, for that matter—without appreciating the influence of distinct theological beliefs upon normative definitions of the "good" society and the "good" polity.

Partisanship, Voting Behavior, and Religious "Behaving and Believing" in Contemporary American Politics

Although religious affiliation plays a significant role in structuring Americans' partisanship and voting behavior, it is by no means the only politically relevant aspect of religion in American politics today. The late twentieth and early twenty-first centuries witnessed the emergence of a sizable "worship attendance gap" separating religiously observant Americans from their more secular counterparts (Olson and Green 2007). The existence of the worship attendance gap caught scholars' attention because of its magnitude; this discovery led them to a broader and deeper understanding of how and why being rooted in organized religion has political consequences.

The "worship attendance gap" reflects the fact that differences within religious "belonging" groups are now at least as politically significant as differences between and among religious groups (Green 2007; Olson and Green 2007). Regardless of whether one identifies as a Catholic, Baptist, Lutheran, Presbyterian, or something else, the more involved one is in religious life in general, the more conservative and Republican one will be. Frequent attendance at worship services is a good proxy measure of one's level of religious commitment, but other measures would work just as well, such as frequency of prayer, scripture reading, or self-reported levels of religion's importance in one's life. No matter how it is measured, greater involvement in religious life is strongly related to greater conservatism and Republican identification (Green 2007).

The worship attendance gap has its roots in the emergence of the Religious Right and the related culture wars. The political mobilization and Republican realignment of evangelical Protestants led the GOP to expand their strategic appeals beyond evangelicals to committed people of faith across religious groups. By the dawn of the twenty-first century, a majority of Americans perceived the Republican Party as substantially "friendlier to religion" than the Democratic Party (Pew Forum 2006). Republican candidates succeeded in portraying themselves as in touch with the values and priorities of people of faith—and in painting Democrats as effete coastal elites (Campbell 2007; Domke and Coe 2008).

The culture wars simply fanned the flames. Americans increasingly were becoming aware of, and concerned with, the clash between traditional and progressive conceptions of morality and the good society. Because culture wars issues connect so closely to religious teachings, the Republican Party had a slightly easier time creating a viable political strategy of reaching out to people of faith. At root the message Republicans sought to convey to people of faith was that their candidates would stand for "traditional family values," which became code for opposition to political liberalism and unchecked social change. They knew this message would appeal to Americans who embrace a religio-cultural worldview that rejects nontraditional interpretations of gender roles, family structure, and sexual morality.

Table 9.4 displays support for the Republican presidential candidate among five groups: the entire U.S. population, all voters who report attending worship services on a weekly basis, all *evangelical* voters who attend weekly, all *mainline* voters who attend weekly, and all *Catholic* voters who attend weekly. A clear "worship attendance gap" has existed since 1980 among evangelical Protestants. The high point came in 1996, when Bob Dole earned nearly 80 percent of weekly-attending evangelicals' votes despite being defeated soundly by Bill Clinton. The overall worship attendance gap, however, did not emerge until 1992, when George H. W. Bush received substantially more votes across the board from weekly-attending Americans across religious traditions. Although Ronald Reagan was enormously popular among evangelical Protestants, the Republicans did not succeed until the decade after his presidency in conveying their broader appeal to all committed people of faith.

Two subthemes emerge from Table 9.4. First, notice that the worship attendance gap has grown substantially in recent years among weekly attending mainline Protestants. It was larger than ever (a difference of nearly 30 per-

Table 9.4   The Worship Attendance Gap, 1980–2008

	% for GOP Candidate, Total	% for GOP Candidate, All Weekly Attendees	% for GOP Candidate, Evangelical Weekly Attendees	% for GOP Candidate, Mainline Weekly Attendees	% for GOP Candidate, Catholic Weekly Attendees
1980 (Reagan)	51.5	57.6 (+6.1)	68.4 (+16.9)	55.9 (+4.4)	58.5 (+7.0)
1984 (Reagan)	58.0	60.0 (+2.0)	85.7 (+27.7)	59.3 (+1.3)	51.7 (−6.3)
1988 (Bush)	53.3	54.2 (+0.9)	72.7 (+19.4)	62.9 (+9.6)	44.4 (−8.9)
1992 (Bush)	33.7	46.5 (+12.8)	70.3 (+36.6)	47.9 (+14.2)	36.1 (+2.4)
1996 (Dole)	39.0	58.2 (+19.2)	79.3 (+40.3)	54.0 (+15.0)	53.6 (+14.6)
2000 (Bush)	46.3	58.9 (+12.6)	74.8 (+28.5)	69.6 (+23.3)	51.4 (+5.1)
2004 (Bush)	49.3	58.9 (+9.6)	80.3 (+31.0)	61.3 (+12.0)	56.5 (+7.2)
2008 (McCain)	32.9	42.4 (+9.5)	71.5 (+38.6)	62.5 (+29.6)	39.4 (+6.5)

Source: American National Election Studies, 1952-2008, available at <http://www.electionstudies.org>. Protestants are categorized using the technique presented in Steensland et al. (2000).

centage points) in 2008. This growth likely reflects a tendency for the most committed mainline Protestants (as measured by worship attendance) also to be among the most conservative in their religious *beliefs*. Conservative interpretation of religious doctrine goes hand-in-glove with conservative political orientations. While mainline denominations themselves appear quite progressive from the outside, it is by no means the case that all mainline people in the pews share in denominational leaders' progressivism.

Second, note the fact that the worship attendance gap has been relatively small—but steadily *positive*—among Catholics since 1996. In 1984 and 1988, weekly attending Catholics were more likely to support the *Democratic* presidential candidate. The Republican Party has made significant inroads among the most committed Catholics since the 1980s because it has worked to broaden its appeal beyond evangelicals to all people of faith, but also because it has been quite intentional about reaching out to Catholics who oppose abortion. George W. Bush's 2004 reelection strategy focused on mobilizing evangelicals through their churches—but also on courting conservative Catholics in their parishes (Campbell 2007). A majority of the "values voters" who played such an important role in reelecting Bush to his second term were evangelicals, but they were joined quite eagerly by a significant number of Catholics. In fact, recently the Religious Right has been making successful overtures to the most observant— and doctrinally conservative—American Catholics (C. Robinson 2008).

The worship attendance gap is primarily a reflection of the broadest possible political significance of religious commitment. The more committed one is to religious life (of which weekly worship attendance is just one measure), the more exposed one will be to special forms of information, such as sermon messages, bulletin inserts that deal with sociomoral issues, or political conversations with fellow attendees (Djupe and Gilbert 2009). Weekly worship attendees are the most likely of all to be exposed to this special information. However, the specific content and tone of the information will vary by religious tradition and even by congregation. Thus the worship attendance gap is especially large and historically stable among evangelical Protestants, who for decades have been taught that their religious doctrine is consistent with sociomoral conservatism, while it is somewhat more tenuous among Catholics, who since Vatican II have asserted their prerogative to pick and choose what they like most about Catholic doctrine.

Conclusion

The primary contention of this book is that Americans have become more polarized in their partisan orientations and at the ballot box. This increased political polarization is rooted in the differences between what we might term *churched* and *unchurched* Americans. By and large, the Americans who are most deeply invested in religious life seem most compelled by the conservative flank of the ongoing culture wars. They continue to lend overwhelming support to the Republican Party and its candidates, even in electoral lost causes like John McCain's 2008 presidential candidacy. Loyalty to the GOP among the most religious Americans also persists despite meaningful dissatisfaction with the number and quality of policy outcomes delivered by the GOP to its "churched" base, and in the face of accusations that Republican mobilization of "values voters" in their places of worship is shallow and disingenuous (Domke and Coe 2008; Kuo 2006). However, as we look to the future, there are several signs suggesting that the present-day relationship between religion and politics might shift yet again in the years to come.

First we must consider evangelicals themselves. While they lent almost as much support to McCain in 2008 as they did to his Republican predecessors, an important change might be afoot that could weaken the GOP's hold on this valuable and growing constituency. Social movements never last forever, at least not in the same form, and the Religious Right is now in the process of evolving. Once a nationally powerful political force, especially in the 1990s, the movement today has diversified and adapted itself to different state- and local-level political contexts (Wilcox and Larson 2006). As a result, the Religious Right today lacks the unified national leadership—and vision—it once enjoyed. Moreover, a new generation of evangelical leaders is emphasizing a broader swath of issues than Jerry Falwell and Pat Robertson ever did. For example, Rev. Rick Warren, pastor of Saddleback Church in Orange County, California (where weekly attendance is roughly 20,000), combines traditional opposition to homosexuality and abortion with a more progressive emphasis on issues of poverty and justice, such as fighting the HIV/AIDS epidemic in Africa. The more evangelical Protestantism grows and diversifies, the more difficult it will be for the Republican Party to retain the remarkably high levels of support they have enjoyed among evangelicals in recent decades.

Separately, two traditions that already are swing constituencies—mainline Protestantism and Catholicism—should be expected to continue their sociological and political evolution. Painful divisions over sociomoral issues abound within mainline Protestantism. If the mainline is to continue thriving into the next century, it will need to adapt to the changes that the present-day divisions will create. It is likely that mainline denominations will be even smaller in the decades to come, but this does not mean they might not become more politically unified. If liberal mainline Protestants remain and conservatives exit, these proud and historically significant denominations might well reestablish themselves as progressive champions of social justice. Meanwhile, there are continuing questions within the Catholic Church about whether abortion should be Catholics' first and only policy priority or whether attention should be spread across the full range of issue positions consistent with Catholic social teaching. Because the Church's emphasis on affirming life in all its forms does not match up well with the policy priorities of either major party in the United States, Catholics are likely to remain a swing constituency for generations to come.

The Democratic Party realized that they had a "religion problem" after the 2004 election (when the evangelical Bush was able to draw significant numbers of Catholic voters away from the candidacy of their fellow Catholic John Kerry) and Democratic candidates are working hard to correct it. Both Barack Obama and Hillary Clinton had staff members charged with religious outreach in place throughout their battle for the 2008 Democratic presidential nomination. In his successful general election campaign, Obama and his campaign staff worked hard to reach out to younger people of faith, even in evangelical contexts. And many Democrats beyond Obama are touting their religious beliefs in successful runs for high office: for example, Sen. Sherrod Brown (D-Ohio) and Sen. Robert Casey, Jr. (D-Pennsylvania) were elected to the Senate from "purple" states in 2006 in large part because they presented themselves as individuals of substantial religious faith. In 2009, former Virginia Governor Tim Kaine became the chair of the Democratic National Committee; Kaine is well known for being a deeply committed Catholic. Undoubtedly Kaine would be pleased to see the Democrats find ways of reaching out to Americans of faith without being perceived as disingenuous.

In the future, religion's relevance to American political polarization likely will be even more complex than it is at present. Will the culture wars ever be resolved, or will they become more entrenched? Will African Americans remain as solidly Democratic as they are today as the ugly legacy of slavery and Jim Crow fades more distantly into the past? American religious pluralism will only increase as the Protestant "market share" declines. The Mormon and Muslim components of the U.S. population are small but growing rapidly. Will Mormons remain loyal Republicans? What political identity will American Muslims—who tend to be conservative on sociomoral issues but progressive on social justice issues—forge for themselves? The number of Americans who opt out of religious life will likely increase as well, but it is difficult to imagine a good political strategy for mobilizing secular voters without offending religious voters. Thanks to the First Amendment's guarantee of religious freedom, the relationship between religion and politics in the United States is both complex and dynamic, and we should expect it to remain so for many decades to come.

Notes

1. Throughout this discussion of evangelical Protestants, I am speaking specifically about *white* evangelical Protestants.
2. These denominations include the American Baptist Churches USA; the Christian Church (Disciples of Christ); the Episcopal Church; the (awkwardly named) Evangelical Lutheran Church in America; the Presbyterian Church (U.S.A.); the Reformed Church in America; the United Church of Christ; and the United Methodist Church. Only Protestants who belong to one of these denominations are considered mainline Protestants.

Chapter 10

Immigrants and Political Parties

Marika Dunn and Jane Junn

Introduction

In the United States today more than one in ten Americans are immigrants. When the children of immigrants are included, both documented and undocumented, that proportion increases to 20 percent foreign-born or second-generation Americans. Tens of millions of immigrants have arrived in the United States over the last decade, and scholars estimate that since 1995 alone, more than twenty million people have become potential voters (Fix, Passel, and Suche 2003). These numbers include those who are already naturalized U.S. citizens and those who will soon become eligible to become citizens.

While the United States has always been a nation of immigrants, the most recent wave of new Americans is unique in three ways. In contrast to the immigrants of the late nineteenth and early twentieth centuries, who came from European countries, the highest proportion of immigrants in the early twenty-first century arrive from Mexico and other countries in Latin America, as well as a large share from Asia and the Caribbean. Not only do today's immigrants bring with them distinctive languages and cultures, but they also add diversity to the nation's population in terms of ethnic and racial background. Second, and in contrast to a hundred years ago when there were few federal laws governing immigration other than those explicitly barring Asians, laws today regulate both entry and rights once immigrants are in the United States (Gyory 1998; Phaelzer 2008; Tichenor 2002).

Immigrants are important to political parties not only because of their potential as new voters and voting coalitions, but also because they systematically affect the distribution of the U.S. population in terms of racial and ethnic composition. Because they are not distributed evenly across the United States, their immediate and eventual impact on partisanship and voting will also vary by location. Parties represent an important avenue through which new members of the American polity can be incorporated into the political fold. However, they can also be used to organize interests that oppose the extent to which such incorporation occurs. Additionally, as in other types of public policies, individual party members' sentiments on immigration may not overlap neatly with their parties' public stances on the issue and create conflicts within each party.

In this chapter, we analyze the impact of immigration on political parties and representation in the United States. We start with an examination of the demographic changes the nation has experienced as a result of immigration; the impact that change has had on political representation in the U.S. House of Representatives; and move on to examine current trends in immigration and apportionment. Next we consider the potential implications of these population shifts in terms of the two major political parties by reviewing scholarship about the political orientations of immigrants. Do they support the Republicans or the Democrats? Which party will benefit from more immigrants and which types of new Americans? Finally, we summarize the current positions of the Democratic and Republican parties on proposed immigration legislation and draw several conclusions about the landscape for political parties in a nation of immigrants.

Immigration and the U.S. House of Representatives

The steady increase in immigration coupled with the wide array of countries from which new immigrants originate has created the most racially and ethnically diverse population in U.S. history. According to the 2005 American Community Survey (ACS), more than a quarter of the population self-identifies as a race other than white, and 20 percent of Americans today are either immigrants or the children of immigrants. While this degree of racial and ethnic diversity is unprecedented, the nation has actually undergone similar population transformations through a large wave of immigrants from Southern and Eastern Europe at the turn of the twentieth century. During that time, immigrants made up an even greater proportion of the population than they do today. These observations underscore the dynamic nature of the U.S. population at present and the possibilities for change it portends.

As the size and composition of the population has changed, it has significantly affected the House of Representatives. Throughout the nation's history, the distribution of members within the House from various states has shifted due to the westward push toward settlement and the growth of large immigration destinations in different regions of the country. Similarly, the composition of the House in terms of the racial and ethnic backgrounds of the members themselves has been influenced tremendously by immigration waves. Also, as we now know, nearly a hundred years ago new immigrant stock and their children helped to transform the American political party system (Andersen 1979; Dahl 1961; Reichley 1992), and with that, helped to alter the composition of the membership within the House.

We begin by examining the effects that past waves of immigration have had on the House as a political institution. Understanding immigration's role in these changes will help us in determining to what extent future population growth and shifts as a result of immigration may affect the distribution and composition of the House of Representatives. Additionally, to better understand the nature of political representation, we will also examine research on the political behavior of House members when confronted with population changes in their districts. This research will help us understand more clearly how both political parties and representatives within these parties adapt to population shifts and growth as a result of immigration.

Political Representation and Changing Demographics

In the 1788 *Federalist* 55 through *58*, James Madison discussed the rationale behind representation in the lower house of the federal legislative body as framed in the proposed constitution. He asserted that a reasonable number of representatives is one that "seems necessary to secure the benefits of free consultation and discussion, and to guard against too easy a combination for improper purposes; as, on the other hand, the number ought at most to be kept within a certain limit, in order to avoid the confusion and intemperance of a multitude." In *Federalist 57*, Madison stated that the diversity of the electorate in terms of class and social status, as well as the lack of any class or social status requirement to hold federal elected office were just two of the reasons why the House's size would not succumb to the hands and for the benefit of the privileged few.

But how might representatives respond to an increase in their numbers of constituents, and the growing diversity of their constituents due to transnational migration, both of which were present from the earliest days of the country's founding? In her seminal work on theories of representation, Hannah Pitkin writes, "The history of representative government and the expansion of the suffrage is one long record of changing demands for representation based on *changing concepts* of what are *relevant features* to be represented" (1967, emphasis added). This underscores the concept of *responsiveness* as the linchpin to effective representation. Not only must constituents within a population demand that their interests be represented by their elected legislator, but the legislator must also recognize and accept these interests as *worthy* of being "presented again" to the entire legislative body.

The literature on legislators' responsiveness to changes within their constituencies strikes at the core of the ability and desire of legislators to recognize and accept new interests. To what degree do legislators perceive and respond to these demographic changes within their constituencies, and if they are responsive, what tools do they utilize to take such changes into account in their behavior? Richard Fenno (1978) describes what he calls *constituency careers*, although the term itself is a bit of a misnomer for the chapter in that it is not so much a description of the ebbs and flows of a constituency as it is a description of the relationship of a legislator to his or her constituency (1978). However, Fenno does give some description of changes within a district, namely the effects of redistricting and the issues surrounding a "transient" segment of the population within a district.[1] Fenno notes that a member may try to maintain old constituents as well as expand to get new people on board. Such is also the case with changing constituencies in a district due to redistricting or migration. However, he also states that House members may be somewhat disinclined to introduce themselves to new populations once they have settled into a protectionist mode.

One of the problems with changing constituencies within a House member's district, Fenno surmises, is that House members lose reference points that make them feel comfortable and electorally "safe" (195). House members, through Fenno's findings, are not very adaptable to different needs of new constituents—especially when those constituencies possess policy priorities and demographics that are increasingly different from those of the members' core constituencies; that is, the ones which have helped these members to obtain and maintain their elected positions. Due to immigration and other population shifts throughout the country's history, members of the House have had to hold a delicate balance between maintaining personal power and tenure in the institution and representing the political interests of their increasingly diverse constituencies.

Previous research on the matter involving more recent population shifts has revealed varying results by legislators in their responsiveness to population changes within their districts. Glazer and Robbins (1985) were some of the first researchers to measure changes in legislative behavior as a response to population changes within a constituency. The authors found that Democratic members on average became more liberal in their roll call votes as their constituency became more liberal, while Republican members on average followed the increasingly conservative ideology of their constituency. LeVeaux and Garand (2003) found that while Democratic support for legislation that would appeal to African Americans increased following redistricting, Republican support for the same legislation actually decreased in some respects. This finding supported their hypothesis that legislators may respond favorably to an increase in the strength of their core constituency and unfavorably to increases in strengths of constituencies not common to their voting base. We may conclude from these studies that legislators are sensitive to core constituencies.

Indeed, such observations also apply well to the connection between immigration concerns and political parties in the United States. Immigration continuously reshapes the demographics of a country's population, causing political officials to respond to these demographic shifts and the political concerns of their core constituencies. Many times, public officials and the parties to which they belong take one of two main stances: either they protect their core constituencies from these demographic changes, or they incorporate these changing demographics into their political fold. We have seen this occur throughout the country's history, even from its infancy. For instance

Daniel Tichenor (2002) has noted that the country's first two political parties, the Federalists and the Democratic-Republicans, were at odds over the issue of naturalization in the early republic (53). The Federalists, led by Alexander Hamilton, tended to distrust Irish immigrants due to their perception of the Irish as an uncivilized people. They also distrusted French immigrants because of the ties to ideals promoted by the French Revolution, which was taking place during the early years of America's government. The Democratic-Republicans, led by Thomas Jefferson, supported less restrictive naturalization policies for European immigrants. As a result of this policy, the party would benefit from the support of Irish and French immigrants in the decade to come: many enfranchised immigrants would vote for presidential candidate Jefferson and fellow party candidates in the election of 1800, leading the party to victory.

As Kristi Andersen (1979) illustrates, throughout the 1920s and 1930s, the Democratic Party actively recruited many Eastern and Southern European immigrants in major urban areas such as Chicago and New York who had come to the United States during the second wave of immigration at the turn of the twentieth century. The party assisted many immigrants with the naturalization process in exchange for political service, and such a system of patronage between the Democratic Party and immigrants in the urban centers of the Northeast and Midwest gave the party a clear advantage in the electoral politics in the decades to come. Although immigration restriction laws of the 1920s severely limited the number of new immigrants in the United States, and thus the number of potential voters the party was able to recruit, the party machines in place within these urban centers fostered loyal Democratic supporters that allowed the party to be the dominant legislative force from the New Deal era until the political realignment of the late 1960s.

The following sections will examine some of the ways in which public officials and the political parties to which they belong have acted in response to significant demographic shifts due to immigration. Political parties and their members have been, and continue to be, active in both restricting immigration and in organizing immigrants who were and are already present within the country's borders. We will see that these motivations are sometimes nefarious, sometimes commendable, but yet consistently strategic in furthering the political or economic interests of the public officials and parties involved.

Effects of the First Wave of Immigration

A number of significant population increases and shifts have occurred during the country's history, which have had an important impact on changes in congressional representation in the U.S. House of Representatives since Madison's writings on the subject in the 1780s. One of the first shifts in population was the country's westward expansion from the thirteen original states. The Louisiana Purchase in 1803 alone doubled the size of the United States, extend-

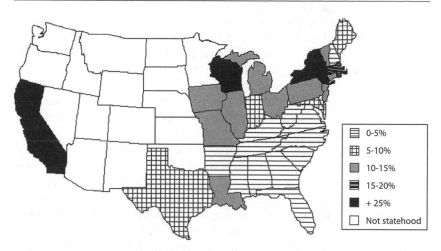

Figure 10.1 Proportion of Foreign Born Population by State, 1850.

ing its territory past the Mississippi River. Direct descendents of settlers in the American states and immigrants alike heeded the nineteenth century call of "Manifest Destiny." During the first major wave of immigration from the 1820s to the 1840s, thousands of immigrants—from Ireland and Germany, as well as Scandinavia and other areas of Western Europe—settled predominantly in the Northeast and Midwest regions of the United States. This distribution of foreign-born populations throughout the country is evident in Figure 10.1, which depicts the proportion of residents in each state who were foreign born as of 1850.

However, the steady influx of immigrants, particularly from Ireland and Germany, caused some uneasiness amongst those in political power, and over the course of the next two decades, a strong nativist sentiment swept local, state, and national politics, which led to placing a number of supporters of immigration restriction in the halls of Congress. At the same time that the Democratic Party was incorporating new immigrants into its ranks, smaller parties, such as the Anti-Masonic Party, were organized during this wave to further an anti-immigrant and anti-Catholic agenda in the political sphere. The Whig Party also launched itself into the mainstream during this period and embraced some of this nativist rhetoric. However, many nativists grew disappointed in the party for the lower priority that Whig leaders gave to immigration issues on the national stage. It was in this era that the American Party—whose members were more popularly known as "Know Nothings" for their sometimes secret, fraternal order-like operations—gained some success in local, state, and federal government. The American Party was the vehicle for anti-Catholic, anti-immigrant policy agendas to take a more prominent position in national politics. From the 29th to the 36th Congresses (1845–

60), the American Party succeeded in electing sixty members to the House, including Rep. Nathaniel Prentice Banks, who served as Speaker of the House in the 34th Congress. At its peak, the party had 49 members in the 34th Congress (1855–56), accounting for roughly 20 percent of the 237 total seats in the House at that time. Those from the American Party who served in the House came from numerous states, including eleven from Massachusetts, seven from New York, and six from Kentucky. Despite the efforts of the American Party to severely restrict immigration to the United States and naturalization within the country, immigration and naturalization were not significantly curtailed. However, the country did experience a slight decline in immigration levels in the decade following the surge of the American Party in the House. Nevertheless, individuals from abroad continued to seek opportunities in the young nation. For example, the Homestead Act of 1862 assisted settlers as well as new immigrants from such areas as Scandinavia, Ireland, and Germany in gaining property rights in these western territories and new states of the Union (Jacobson 1998; Keyssar 2000; Tichenor 2002).

In the first ninety years after the Constitution was ratified, the number of states in the Union doubled, and the size of the House grew to 293 seats from its original 65. As Figure 10.2 shows, 1870 census data reveal that states in the Northeast and upper Midwest, along with California and Nevada in the Far West, had the highest proportion of foreign-born residents living within their borders. As of 1870, states in the Northeast and Midwest alone accounted for more than 87 percent of the country's foreign-born population. By this time, these two regions also accounted for 65 percent of the seats in the House of Representatives. However, while the next wave of immigration also brought with it more westward expansion of the foreign-born population, it also

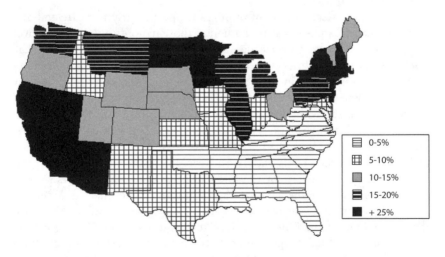

| 0-5% |
| 5-10% |
| 10-15% |
| 15-20% |
| + 25% |

Figure 10.2 Proportion of Foreign Born Population by State, 1920.

morphed immigration into an urban versus rural issue at the national level that both parties and legislators within these parties confronted with much difficulty.

Effects of the Second Wave of Immigration

The next wave of immigration was from Southern and Eastern Europe (Jacobson 1998; Tichenor 2002). Many if not most of these new immigrants during this period settled within the urban areas of the Northeast and Midwest, as opposed to earlier immigrants who had settled in urban and rural areas alike. The disproportionate settlement of the new immigrants in these urban areas not only increased the population of Northeastern and Midwestern states, but also upset the balance between urban and rural areas within states themselves and the nation as a whole (see Figure 10.2). Indeed, at the same time that African Americans were migrating from the South to Northern cities for economic opportunities, Southern leaders attempted to recruit new European immigrants to settle in their states (Tichenor 2002).

Historian Charles Eagles (1990) has painted a detailed portrait of the political landscape during this period, in which the distinguishing political, social, and economic characteristics of the urban and rural areas were established. A climate of religious fundamentalism, nativism, and racism fostered a perfect storm of events that included the ratification of the Prohibition amendment in 1920 and the Scopes "monkey" trial regarding the teaching of evolution in 1925. The fractured party climate of the early twentieth century depleted some strength from the Democratic and Republican parties in both local and national arenas while allowing political groups outside the party process to be influential on certain policies, not least of which included immigration restriction (Tichenor 2002, 116). Two key examples in which the fractured political climate and immigration debates of this era were intertwined were the federal reapportionment impasse of the 1920s and the passage of the National Origins Act of 1924, which severely restricted immigration from countries outside Western Europe.

Following the 1920 Census, many members of Congress from rural areas cited some discrepancies in the way that the Census was conducted that would potentially place them at a disadvantage in the upcoming reapportionment process in comparison to urban areas that were flush with new immigrant populations. Due to these concerns, members of both parties within the House of Representatives were unable to resolve this reapportionment issue for nearly a decade. The House throughout the 1920s proceeded with the same apportionment from the 1910 Census even though major population changes, largely due to immigration, had taken place after that time.

Arguments from rural Members of Congress regarding apportionment addressed what they considered the threat to the country's values, particularly in urban areas, as a result of the current wave of immigration and of what they saw as immorality. For instance, Representative Edward C. Little, Republican from Kansas, advocated against increasing the size of the House and warned that to do so would be "to turn this government over to the cities where ignorance, poverty, vice, and crime are staring you in the face…. It is not best for America that her councils be dominated by semicivilized foreign colonies in Boston, New York, Chicago" (quoted in Eagles 1990, 38). Even in the Senate, which had largely taken itself out of heated debates regarding apportionment during the decade, members did show their colors on this topic. In debating the long-awaited 1929 apportionment bill that had just recently been passed by the House, some senators proposed an amendment that would exclude noncitizens from apportionment. Senator James Thomas Heflin, Democrat from Alabama, supported the measure, and Eagles notes that the senator "referred to aliens as crooks, criminals, kidnappers, bandits, terrorists, racketeers and 'refuse of foreign countries' and claimed that most came to the United States illegally" (Eagles 1990, 77). Such rhetoric from public officials in both major parties highlighted the perceived threat that Eastern and Southern European immigrants posed not only for the political strength of rural communities, but also to American society and culture.

This rhetoric was even more apparent with regard to the immigration restriction legislation of the 1920s, most notably the National Origins Act of 1924. However, groundwork for the bill had been laid in the legislature more than a decade before by the findings of the U.S. Immigration Commission, headed by Senator William Dillingham, Republican of Vermont. The joint House-Senate Committee, containing members from both the Republican and Democratic parties, was formed in 1907 to study the consequences of Eastern and Southern European immigration for American society. Through immigration statistics and eugenics studies, the latter of which allegedly proved the inferiority of certain races and ethnicities, the Commission concluded in 1911 that this newer wave of immigrants posed a threat to American culture and society, and suggested that their numbers should be drastically reduced. However, the defeat of both Progressives and Republicans at the hands of Democrat Woodrow Wilson in the 1912 presidential election placed efforts to implement the Commission's suggestions on hold. With the election of Warren Harding in 1920 on a nationalist platform, Congress set out to implement the suggestions of Dillingham's commission, which had been waiting for nearly a decade.

Along with the 1921 Emergency Quota Act, the National Origins Act of 1924 emanated from the suggestions of Dillingham's commission and the nativist sentiments it embodied. The 1924 bill's two main sponsors were Congressman Albert Johnson of Washington and Senator David Reed of Pennsylvania. Both sponsors were Republicans, but the bill had bipartisan support, though not without strong opposition from a handful of legislators and their political allies. Two of the restrictionist movement's most vociferous opponents were Democratic members of the House of Representatives, Fiorello La Guardia and Emanuel Celler, both of New York, who railed against the racist bases of the movement and warned of the serious consequences of such policies for the United States. They were joined in their efforts by social activists like Jane Addams as well as ethnically oriented groups such as the American Jewish Committee and the German-American Alliance. To some extent, the National Association of Manufacturers was also resistant to restrictionists' efforts, although its stance was motivated by fears of immigrant labor shortages, which it anticipated would hurt its members' industries.

The National Origins Act barred nearly all immigration from Asian countries and imposed small yearly quotas on immigrants from Eastern and Southern European countries, which were based on percentages of immigrants from these countries as reported in censuses at the beginning of immigration's second wave. Thus, the act favored Northern European sending countries, which prior to the second wave, produced the greatest numbers of immigrants to America. As a result, immigration as a whole significantly declined to low levels never seen before in the nation's history. For instance, in 1910 immigrants comprised nearly 15 percent of the nation's population. By 1960, however, that figure had dropped to 5 percent.

The success of immigration restriction proposals also came from the strong efforts from such extraparty groups as the Immigration Restriction League (IRL) and the American Federation of Labor (AFL). The IRL had been active since the turn of the century, exerting influence on legislators with regard to immigration restriction policies for both new European immigrants in the Eastern part of the country as well as those Asian immigrants in the West who were not already barred from entering. (The passage of the 1882 Chinese Exclusion Act, which had the backing of Western Republicans, all but eliminated the prospect of Chinese immigration to the United States for decades to come.) The AFL was commonly found on the side of the Democratic Party, which had been for years accumulating a broad base of immigrant supporters. However, by the 1920s, the labor organization separated itself from the base of the Democratic Party on this issue. AFL's leader, Samuel Gompers, saw immigration in this second wave as a threat to organized labor, for a large number of immigrants in this period held semiskilled positions that were not unionized. Additionally, using the purported findings of eugenics research, the AFL's leadership reasoned that Eastern and Southern European immigrants were intellectually inferior and were ill-suited to higher-skilled union jobs. Severe immigration restrictions, therefore, were a way to control the flow of laborers into the United States and also the number of workers seeking craft union positions.

Since the Progressive era, organized labor's relationship with immigration reform has complicated its relationship with the Democratic Party. It should be noted that although the language of scientific racism was toned down and eventually eliminated from the rhetoric of organized labor's support for immigration restriction, the rhetoric of immigration as a threat to native born workers remained for decades. For instance, although the United States severely restricted immigration for those who sought permanent residency, it maintained Mexican temporary worker programs from the 1920s to the 1960s, workers who were not subject to National Origins Act quotas (Fine and Tichenor 2009; Tichenor 2002). However, the AFL's opposition to these guest worker programs was largely unsuccessful due to a coalition of immigration defenders and Southern and Western agribusiness. Fine and Tichenor (2009) have noted aptly that "labor's struggle has turned fundamentally on whether it views new waves fundamentally as a threat, which elicits a strategy of restriction, or an opportunity, which elicits a strategy of solidarity" (85).

Current Trends in Immigration, Parties, and Political Power

Civil rights legislation in the 1960s accelerated the Southern shift of the Republican Party that was long in coming. Along with this legislation came significant immigration reform that eliminated the country-based quota system of the 1920s. Instead, the Immigration and Nationality Act of 1965 established hemisphere-based yearly limits for immigrants and placed an emphasis on family reunification (with more recent limits on family sponsorship). In a turnaround that had been in the making for several years, the AFL-CIO (representing AFL's merge with the Congress of Industrial Organizations) actively lobbied President Lyndon Johnson's administration to dismantle the quotas of the 1920s (Fine and Tichenor 2009). These changes have been the major contributors to the relationship that U.S. parties have had with both immigrants and immigration reform well into the twenty-first century.

Despite the enormous numbers of immigrants in recent decades, as Janelle Wong (2006) and other scholars have demonstrated, the two parties have failed to take advantage of the potential political power within these communities, and have not mobilized voters within immigrant communities as much as we might expect. In order to better understand the current relationship that the Republican and Democratic parties have with foreign-born constituents, and to visualize the types of relationships these parties may have with immigrants in the future, it will help to discuss the current stances the parties have taken toward immigration policies and immigrants themselves. Following both this discussion and one of population changes and immigrants' political behavior, we will be able to visualize how U.S. political institutions may be affected by this third wave of immigration.

Population Shifts and Demographic Changes in Immigration's Third Wave

Immigration to the United States since the 1960s' reforms has grown exponentially, both in sheer numbers and in the diversity of countries and ethnicities represented in this newest wave. The majority of immigrants in this third wave are from Latin America, Asia, the Caribbean, and Africa; that is, regions that were underrepresented for the bulk of the twentieth century. The Census Bureau indicates that nearly one third of the current population growth is caused by net immigration (U.S. Census Bureau 1993). Furthermore, projections indicate that roughly 86 percent of the population growth by the year 2050 may be due to the effects of post-1992 net immigration (U.S. Census Bureau 1993). Since individuals from Asian and Latin American countries will continue to comprise an overwhelming majority of immigrants to the United States, it is no coincidence that Asian and Hispanic populations will experience double to triple net increases.

Additionally, this third wave of immigration has exacerbated existing population shifts within the United States that place the bulk of the nation's population increasingly in the South and West. Since the latter half of the twentieth century, the population of the Midwest and Northeast, which were once stable, has been on the decline in comparison to other regions of the country. The clearest indication of this is in apportionment in the U.S. House of Representatives. Because apportionment has officially been a zero sum game since the 1920s, the states that lose seats are those whose rates of population growth are relatively low. As the population has shifted away from the Midwest and the Northeast, so too have seats and power in the U.S. House of Representatives. Northeastern and Midwestern states have seen their industries move to the South or West (or overseas in many instances), and their residents have followed this trend to some extent through internal migration. Additionally, a more recent trend among new immigrants is a primary or secondary migration not to traditional immigration gateways such as larger cities, but to smaller communities in the rural areas of nontraditional immigrant receiving states. North Carolina, Virginia, and Georgia are just a few of the states whose agribusinesses and other industries have attracted new immigrants.

One way of demonstrating this change in population and its effect on regional political power is through the change in proportion of apportioned seats by region between 1790 and 2010. In the post-World War II era, the South has obtained the greatest proportion of seats in the House of Representatives. Following the 2000 census, the West surpassed the Midwest in having the second largest proportion of seats in the House. The trajectories of population growth in the South and the West are in an upward direction, which indicates that barring any congressional or constitutional provisions to the contrary, the South and West will continue to hold a majority of the U.S. population, and will therefore hold the majority of seats in the House (Figure 10.3).

The implications of these shifts for congressional representation are significant. The five largest states (California, Texas, Florida, New York, and Illinois), which comprise 10 percent of states in the union, will account for nearly 40 percent of all representatives in the U.S. House of Representatives. What this means is that power in Congress will become even more concentrated in the most populous states (Woodrow-Lafield 2001). Overall projections by the

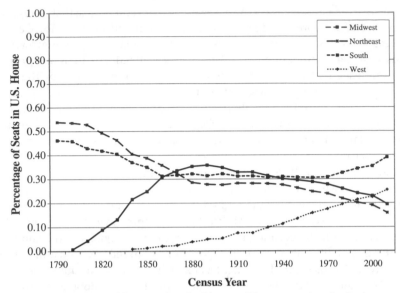

Figure 10.3 Percentage of Seats within the House of Representatives by Region, 1790–2004.

Census Bureau from 2000 to 2030 indicate that 88 percent of the nation's population growth between 2000 and 2030 will occur in the South and West, home to the ten fastest-growing states over the period (U.S. Census Bureau 2004). Additionally, the share of the population living in the South and West will increase from 58 percent in 2000 to 65 percent in 2030, while the share in the Northeast and Midwest will decline from 42 percent to 35 percent (U.S. Census Bureau 2004). Specifically, Nevada, Arizona, Florida, Texas, and Utah—states in the West and South—will experience the highest rates of population increase. Not coincidentally, the states with the largest projected gains are those with some of the largest projected growth of foreign-born populations.

As we have demonstrated, patterns of international migration are regionally specific. Therefore, we can expect that different areas of the country will experience distinctive changes in their populations in terms of race and ethnicity. Census Bureau projections for 1995 to 2025 document this phenomenon.[2] Population increases are not uniform either for race or region. Blacks in the West and Asians in the South will experience much slower growth rates than Hispanics or whites in these areas. Whites in the Northeast will experience a negative growth rate, while other racial and ethnic groups will experience modest gains in population. Hispanics will account for more than half of the population growth in the West and the Northeast (Figure 10.4).

Based on the regional population projections by race, between 1995 and 2025, the West and South will experience the largest growths of population (P. R. Campbell 1996). Florida and Texas will gain the most, amounting to a more diverse constituency state wide within the next twenty years. However

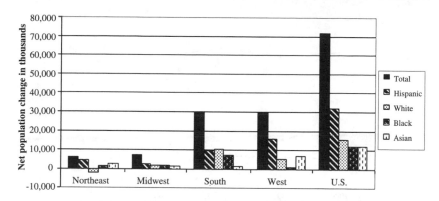

Figure 10.4 Rate of Changes in Racial and Ethnic Populations by Region, 1995 to 2025. Source: Campbell, "Population Projections for States by Age, Sex, Race, and Hispanic Origin, 1995–2025." U.S. Census Bureau, 1996.

California will continue to experience large rates of increase in Asian and Hispanic populations, and will account for 41 percent of the entire U.S. Asian population and 36 percent of the U.S. Hispanic population. New York will also see substantial increases in Asian and Hispanic populations by 2025.

The impact of immigration on these population projections can be clearly seen in these data. Figure 10.5 displays projected immigration to the United States by race and ethnicity through the twenty-first century.[3] As expected, Asian and Latin American immigration will account for the largest net increases in population due to immigration. What is interesting to note is a shift midcentury whereby Asian immigration will surpass Latin American immigration. Moreover, Latin American immigration is projected to experience a decline throughout the twenty-first century. European immigration will peak at midcentury and then decrease; immigration from Africa and the Caribbean will experience a moderate but consistent increase throughout the twenty-first century. Ultimately, the Census Bureau projects that by 2050, the proportion of the U.S. population that is foreign born will have grown to 13 percent (2000), something that has not been seen since the 1920s.

The significance of changes in both regional shifts and racial and ethnic composition within the U.S. population paints a picture of the diverse constituencies to whom political parties must speak in the decades ahead. However, which of these states will remain "red" or "blue"—either solidly Republican or Democratic—over the next several decades? Similarly, which of the "purple" states that remain in play as swing states will lean Democratic or Republican? Answers to these questions lie in a closer examination of the composition of the populations that will live in these states, yet it is difficult to draw inferences at this stage because of the relative dearth of knowledge we have about the partisan leanings and attachments of new immigrant groups. Systematic research into the partisan hearts and minds of Latinos and Asian Americans

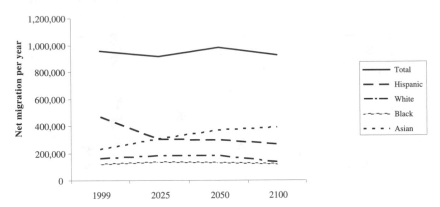

Figure 10.5 Yearly Migration to the U.S., 1999–2100. Source: U.S. Census Bureau, Population Division Working Paper No. 38, January 2000.

is growing, but remains a new area of research among political scientists (de la Garza 1992; Hajnal and Lee 2005; Lien, Conway, and Wong 2004; Ramakrishnan 2005; R. R. Rogers 2006). Party organizations at the local level may or may not recognize the electoral significance of an estimated 22 million new voters, many of whom are clustered in the most populous and powerful states in the American South and West (Jones-Correa 1998; Wong 2006).

Immigrants' Political Orientations

Partisanship among Latinos and Asian Americans remains a moving target not only because the population continues to change as a result of continuing migration from Latin America and Asia, but also because the partisan identifications and political orientations of immigrants are in flux. "Democrat" and "Republican" take on political meaning in the American landscape only after immigrants arrive in the country. Large proportions of voters who are Latino and Asian American are foreign-born naturalized citizens, many of whom have yet to acquire experience in American politics. In addition, complicating any analysis of immigrant political orientation is the absence of reliable data sources about party identification among Latinos and Asian Americans.

Several things are known about immigrants' political orientations Eight in ten Asian American adults are foreign born, while approximately six out of ten Latino adults are foreign born. However, looking specifically at the characteristics of Latinos and Asian Americans as voters, Latino voters are more likely to be native born, while Asian American voters are as likely to be Americans by birth as well as naturalized citizens. This is due in large part to the fact that Asian Americans are faster to naturalize to citizenship than any other racial or ethnic immigrant group. It remains to be seen if there are unique patterns of voting registration and partisanship among Asian Americans due to these circumstances. Asian Americans constitute a highly diverse group, with the six largest national origin groups being Chinese, Asian Indian, Filipino, Vietnamese, Korean, and Japanese. With the exception of a small proportion of Asian Americans of Chinese and Japanese ancestry—many of whom have family histories in the United States dating back five or six generations—Asian Americans are new to the U.S. political system. Early research on Asian American partisanship showed differences between national origin groups (Lien et al. 2004). Recent work based on the 2008 National Asian American Survey shows that Vietnamese Americans are the only national origin group that leans to the Republican Party, while Japanese Americans and Asian Indian Americans lean toward the Democratic Party (Ramakrishnan, Wong, Lee, and Jun 2009).

What characterizes Asian Americans most distinctly, however, is their lack of affiliation with political parties in the United States. More than a third of Asian Americans who are eligible to vote say they are either independent or do not think in terms of political parties. It remains to be seen the extent to which the Republicans and the Democrats attempt to bring Asian American voters into their parties. While most of the evidence suggests modest efforts at the national level to reach out to Asian American voters, parties and candidates for office in states with large Asian American populations such as California, New York, and New Jersey have made greater attempts to woo this group of voters. Asian Americans constitute over 4 percent of the population nationally, but are nearly 15 percent of the population in California, and 8 percent in both New York and New Jersey. Potential swing voters because of their status as undeclared partisans, Asian Americans are also increasingly likely to be targeted for mobilization by political parties because of their relatively high levels of education and income resources. As with all Americans, those with higher levels of social and economic resources are most likely to be active in politics.

Latinos, on the other hand, are less likely than Asian Americans to be foreign born, and 55 percent of Latino adults in the United States are immigrants. Latinos are a highly diverse group, which includes Americans with ancestors from locations and nations as diverse as Mexico, Puerto Rico, and Cuba in addition to a number of Latin American countries. The main distinction between national origin groups among Latinos is the strong Republican Party support among Cubans. In contrast, Puerto Ricans—mostly located in states in the Northeast and Midwest—have a strong affiliation with the Democratic Party. The raw numbers of Cuban Americans in the United States is much smaller than those of the other groups, with Mexican Americans being the largest group by far, accounting for more than half the population of Latinos in the United States.

In terms of partisanship overall, Latinos have traditionally leaned toward the Democratic Party (Alvarez and Garcia Bedolla 2003; de la Garza 1992; DeSipio 1996; Garcia and Uhlaner 2005; Welch and Sigelman 1993). At the same time, exit poll data from the 2004 national election found that a surprisingly large proportion of Latino voters supported the Republican Party, particularly George W. Bush in his bid for reelection. Additional data and subsequent analyses indicate, however, that issue positions may have been behind this vote rather than an abrupt change in partisan identification (Abrajano and Alvarez forthcoming; Abrajano, Alvarez, and Nagler 2008; Leal, Bareto, Lee, de la Garza 2005). Indeed, the 2008 national election saw strong support among Latinos for Democratic presidential candidate Barack Obama.

Parties' Positions on Immigration Reform

The extent to which both the Republican and Democratic parties, and their leaders, can adapt to the country's changing demographics will be integral to their success in the coming years. Although the parties, their supporters, and their platforms have changed significantly since the second wave of immigration at the turn of the twentieth century, we encourage the reader to think broadly of parallels that may exist between the current rhetoric and the debates of the past.

The Republican National Committee's (RNC) 2008 platform on immigration issues is one based on three main principles: rule of law (enforcement), an industrious work ethic, and assimilation with regard to core American values. The platform of the RNC characterizes immigration as a national security issue, and therefore couches this issue within its commitment to upholding the rule of law. In essence, the Republican Party sees illegal immigration in the United States as a breakdown of this commitment, and therefore the first step to countering the illegal immigration issue is through enforcement: at the workplace, in neighborhoods, and at the border. The RNC strongly opposes amnesty, using again the "rule of law" argument to hold that amnesty discourages illegal immigrants from honoring the important commitment to U.S. laws. However, its platform also describes the value that immigrant communities bring to the lives of Americans, whose ancestors were themselves immigrants.

In addition to fostering a commitment to the rule of law, the RNC also sees a commitment to core American values as a sine qua non for immigrants who seek to become citizens. Another essential component for immigrants to be incorporated into the fabric of America is the adoption of English, which the RNC notes is "essential as a unifying cultural force" (RNC 2008). The RNC acknowledges that refugees seeking political asylum are a part of the nation's tradition, but opposes granting refugee status for lifestyle choices or nonpolitical factors. The Party notes that noncitizens are often intertwined with America's national security through their participation in the armed forces, and states that their commitment to U.S. values should inspire other immigrants to strive for full citizenship and "help their communities avoid patterns of isolation" (RNC 2008).

The Democratic Party's platform also centers on commitment to the rule of law and enforcement, the importance of family reunification policies, and pathways to citizenship for illegal immigrants. The most recent platform of the Democratic National Committeee (DNC) notes the innate disrespect for the rule of law in the current state of immigration. The DNC underscores the need for comprehensive immigration reform that is "tough, practical, and humane" (DNC 2008). The DNC suggests stronger border patrols with more sophisticated intelligence as a method for developing greater enforcement of current laws.

Whereas the Republican Party couches immigration as an *individual* act driven by economic decisions, the Democratic Party also acknowledges the importance of *family reunification* as a goal, one which not only has positive community benefits, but also economic ones as well. However, the Democratic Party notes that any economic benefits the country's employers obtain through immigrant workers must be as a result of humane and nondiscriminatory workplace environments. Its platform also includes a commitment to bring immigrants living illegally in the United States out from the shadows, proposing a pathway to citizenship for persons in otherwise good standing, noting that "[t]hey are our neighbors, and we can help them become full tax-paying, law-abiding, productive members of society" (DNC 2008).

Both parties acknowledge that a climate of disrespect for the rule of law and lack of enforcement have burdened U.S. immigration. Furthermore, both parties understand that comprehensive immigration reform is necessary, and that enforcement of current laws is key to this. However, for the Republican Party, enforcement appears to be an action that the government must take at all levels and in all sectors of civil society. For the Democratic Party, however, it appears that such enforcement should be a federal responsibility with border control as a priority. The Republican Party prioritizes assimilation as a condition for citizenship to a greater degree than does the Democratic Party. However, the only concrete language regarding assimilation the Democratic Party uses is when stating that the pathway includes a requirement to learn English. All other requirements use language more akin to a commitment to the rule of law.

Efforts for Immigration Reform in the Twenty-First Century

In Republican President George Bush's second term, Congress and the Executive Branch attempted unsuccessfully to reform federal immigration laws. In 2005 and 2006, the political climate among the public and the federal government was fraught with impatience over immigration reform. Although socially and economically conservative, President Bush departed from the sentiments of other conservative Republicans and supported a temporary guest worker program for immigrant laborers; however his administration ultimately could not foster a compromise with the Congress on this component. At the end of 2005, the Republican Party, led by James Sensenbrenner of Wisconsin, proposed a bill that would criminalize unauthorized immigrants or those who assist them, and would authorize, among other provisions, a fence to be built along the border between the United States and Mexico (Border Protection, Antiterrorism, and Illegal Immigration Control Act 2005). The bill passed in the House but was not pursued widely in the Senate. In response, thousands of immigrants and their supporters convened in marches in Los Angeles, New York, and other major cities in the spring of 2006.

Also during this time, members of the Senate entertained three bills in hopes of reaching a compromise on key components of immigration reform. One bill cosponsored by Republicans John Cornyn of Texas and Jon Kyle of Arizona emphasized border and worksite immigration enforcement and would have expanded a guest worker program for foreign workers (Comprehensive Enforcement and Immigration Reform Act 2005). A bipartisan bill put forth by Republican John McCain of Arizona and Democrat Edward Kennedy of Massachusetts would have expanded a guest worker program while providing more avenues for citizenship (Secure America and Orderly Immigration Act 2005). A third bill, which emanated from the Senate's Judiciary Committee also included many of the same provisions as the Kennedy/McCain bill (Comprehensive Immigration Reform Act 2006). Like the House's bill months before, none of the Senate's proposals became law. The immigration reform efforts of 2005 and 2006 thus illustrate two vastly different approaches taken by the Republican-controlled House and Senate. The House's punitive approach toward immigration reform contrasted sharply with the Senate's guest worker and amnesty provisions, underscoring the differences in doing business between the chambers (Baker 2001). Following the 2006 midterm elections, the Democratic Party reclaimed a majority of seats in the House and Senate. However, the Party was unsuccessful in garnering widespread support for immigration reform through the end of President Bush's second term.

Currently, it appears that the Republican Party may have the more daunting task of incorporating immigrant voters into their ranks. The 2008 election led to the party's large losses in both the House and Senate and portrayed the party as a largely Southern party with a homogenous member base. The Democratic Party, however, saw a rise in its voter turnout among diverse populations and increases in House and Senate seats, due in large part to the lengthy coattails of the first African American elected president.

Conclusion

Political parties have been inextricably linked with immigration policy throughout the course of American history. Parties have used methods of inclusion and exclusion to address the concerns of public officials, interest groups, and constituents alike. Each major wave of immigration to the

United States brings with it new Americans of various ethnicities and shifts in regional demographics. However, despite these changes within its borders, many of the responses that American political parties and their members have had to these waves revolve along the same questions of whom to exclude and whom to incorporate into the political fold, and what should the costs and benefits be to native-born Americans and immigrants alike.

This latest wave of immigration to the United States brings with it not only new Americans from the greatest diversity of nationalities in the country's history, but coincides with high levels of internal migration. Not only are new people joining the polity at high rates, but Americans already within the country's borders (native and foreign born alike) are relocating to other states, adding to their already large populations. Changes in partisanship at the individual level, dominance of one political party at the expense of another within states, and the relationship between large and small states within the federal legislative body are all consequences of these population shifts. And yet, even considering many historical factors and patterns of participation among the newest Americans, it may still be too soon to make definitive conclusions as to what role political parties will play in this immigration wave.

Many questions remain regarding these demographic and political uncertainties with regard to the current state of immigration in this country. Can legislators step up to the challenge of representing the interests of an increasingly diverse and steadily growing constituency? How will political parties incorporate or exclude new Americans from their ranks? What will be the nature of the relationships which new Americans form with political parties? What is at stake in the questions we raise lies at the very heart of the theory and practice of representative democracy in America, and political parties play an integral role in this process. Through the historical, demographic, and political context provided throughout this chapter, we hope to have given the reader a framework through which to understand the political system's responses to past, current, and future immigration shifts in America.

Notes

1. This type of situation can be compared to a "core constituency"—a more stable group of individuals or interests on which a member relies for reelection and support.
2. The last time the Census Bureau estimated race and ethnicity projections for regions and states was in 1995 when it generated interim projections to 2025 (P. R. Campbell 1996).
3. This projection includes a projection of legal residents, temporary workers, and undocumented immigrants. Persons from Puerto Rico are treated as international migrants.

Chapter 11

Partisan Trends in the South and Northeast

Political Ping-Pong

Howard L. Reiter

Sectionalism has always played a key role in American politics. With the Electoral College and both houses of Congress based on state and substate constituencies, the enormous regional variation in the nation has produced widely varying electoral effects, with each party having exceptional strength in particular parts of the nation. When change occurs, as when one major party's fortunes rise while the other's sink, the effects are usually felt differently in different parts of the country. Sometimes the parties have even traded places geographically.

Such has been the case in the past half-century. In the 1950s, the most Democratic part of the country was the "Solid South," the region where presidential nominee Adlai Stevenson won most of his electoral votes, the party claimed all governors and U.S. Senators, and more than 90 percent of House members were Democrats. At the same time, the Republican stronghold was the Northeast, where President Dwight D. Eisenhower racked up his highest vote totals, and Republicans usually won the lion's share of other elective offices. By the turn of the twenty-first century, the parties had traded places in those regions. The South is now the Republican heartland, its strongest region in presidential and congressional elections, and the Northeast has become the Democrats' base. In this chapter, I will review how this extraordinary transformation occurred.

Because of the South's racial and cultural distinctiveness, because it was more monolithic in the past, and because its march toward Republicanism spearheaded that of the rest of the nation, much of the attention of scholars, journalists, political activists, and the general public has been focused on changes in that region (e.g., Black and Black 1987, 1992; Edsall and Edsall 1991; Lublin 2004; Shafer and Johnston 2006). Less commented on has been the major countertrend in the Northeast (but see Mellow 2008; Speel 1998). Indeed, had it not been for changes in the Northeast, Republicans would have dominated national politics, winning presidential and congressional elections by wide margins. Specifically, if the Northeast were still voting as it was in the middle of the twentieth century:[1]

- George W. Bush would have won in 2000 and 2004 with comfortable margins in the Electoral College, obviating the controversies in Florida and Ohio;
- John McCain would have fallen only nine electoral votes short of winning the 2008 presidential election; and
- Republicans would have controlled both houses of Congress by comfortable margins throughout Bush's presidency, and narrowly won the Senate in the 111th Congress.

This chapter will present the evidence for the changes just summarized, and why they occurred. In it, I will show that changes in the South and the Northeast have to a great extent had a reciprocal relationship: Change in one region, and the parties' attempts to court that part of the country, have to a great extent led to changes in the other region.

Indeed, throughout American history the South and the Northeast have frequently been on opposite sides of the political fence, engaging in a giant game of ping-pong with each other, in which every move by one side leads to a countermove by the other. In the early years of the republic, the South was the heartland of Jeffersonian Republicanism, while the Northeast was where the Federalist Party ran best. As the Civil War approached, the Northeast became the home of much of the abolitionist movement that sought an end to Southern slavery. After the war, the South allied itself with the Democratic Party, the Northeast with the young Republican Party. Today, they are again on opposite sides, aligning themselves with the party that used to dominate the other section.

The South Breaks with the Democrats

Because so much has been written about the South, I will review developments there briefly. From the Civil War to the Great Depression, the Democrats dominated the South, which was its most loyal section. As a result of the Depression, Franklin Delano Roosevelt was elected president of the United States in 1932 and promulgated the reform program that he called the New Deal. Much of that program was aimed at helping the poorer and more rural regions of the country, which meant that the South benefited from the New Deal as much as any other area. However, the domination of Roosevelt's administration by Northern reformers laid the seeds for Southern discontentment. Among the New Dealers' highest values were egalitarianism, the desire for equal treatment of all social groups, which made them look with skepticism on the treatment of black people in the segregated South; and strong support for the growing labor movement, some of whose unions wanted to organize both white and black workers in the South and raise wages in that low-paid part of the country. White Southern conservatives began to see with apprehension that New Dealers would be challenging the status quo in the South.

Along with this concern about the ideological thrust of the New Deal was the uncomfortable fact that the South was no longer vital to Democratic Party fortunes. Winning his first two terms in popular and electoral vote landslides, Roosevelt became the first Democrat elected president since the Civil War who would have won even without the South. Adding to segregationist concerns was the fact that 1936 was the first presidential election in which most African American voters opted for the Democrat. The South was becoming an expendable part of the Democratic coalition, while Northern blacks, concentrated in states with large numbers of electoral votes, were becoming an essential part of it.

As early as the 1930s, southern Democratic fears began to take the form of congressional votes against the New Deal and the northern wing of their party. In the 1940s, tensions mounted over issues like a proposed federal fair employment practices commission, nondiscriminatory hiring by defense contractors, the poll tax, allowing blacks to vote in Southern Democratic primaries, and enabling blacks in the military to vote in federal elections. By 1948, when President Harry Truman, Roosevelt's successor, initiated civil rights policies such as a civil rights committee and desegregation of the military, arch-conservative Southerners had had enough. When Governor Strom Thurmond of South Carolina ran for president on a "States' Rights" third-party ticket, he carried four states, and Southern white allegiance to the Democratic Party cracked (on these trends, see Freidel 1965; Frymer 1999; Garson 1974; Katznelson, Geiger, and Kreiger 1993; McKee 2010; J. T. Patterson 1967; Reiter 2001).

Much of Thurmond's appeal was to segregationists, but a different kind of defection came in the next three presidential elections, when Republicans Dwight D. Eisenhower and Richard M. Nixon each carried several Southern states by appealing to moderate and middle-class voters. The biggest shift came in 1964, when conservative activists won the presidential nomination for Arizona Senator Barry Goldwater, who ran on a strong states' rights platform and voted against the landmark Civil Rights Act of 1964. The only states that Goldwater carried besides his home state were in the deep South, and his campaign not only gave a shot in the arm to Republicans in that subregion; it also inaugurated an era when most Republican presidential candidates—notably Richard Nixon in 1968 and 1972 and Ronald Reagan in 1980 and 1984—made a strong play for Southern votes. In their reelection bids, Nixon and Reagan swept the entire region and attained their highest vote totals there.

It is important to keep in mind the sources of Republican strength in the South. As I will argue later, part of it was racial because Goldwater and his successors promised not to pursue desegregation aggressively, and committed themselves to states' rights. Part of it was general conservatism, as white Southerners are more conservative on many domestic and foreign policy issues than people in other parts of the nation. And beginning with the Reagan campaign in 1980, part of it has been religious, as Reagan began an alliance between his party and Christian fundamentalists, who are so numerous in the South. Issues such as abortion, homosexuality, and prayer in schools gave the Southern Republican cause a new cultural dimension (Martin 1996).

All in all, then, the white South's transition from the Democratic to the Republican party was in large part a consequence of the national Democratic Party's move to the left in the New Deal period and after, and the Republicans' shift to the right in order to woo white Southerners and build a national base.

The Northeast Breaks with the Republicans

These events in Dixie did not go unnoticed in the Northeast. As the Eisenhower and 1960 Nixon campaigns presented a moderately conservative image, Northern Republicans had little reason to reconsider their party allegiance. However, starting with the Goldwater campaign, with its air of opposition to civil rights and defense of ideological extremism, many moderate Republicans in the Northeast began to feel as though they might be in the wrong party. This was a feeling that only increased as the Republican leadership continued to pursue white Southerners and other staunchly conservative voters. As a result, Democrats began to win more and more elections in the Northeast.

The evidence of Democratic gains in the Northeast over time is strong. The data are in Figures 11.1 to 11.4; the lines represent the percentage of popular votes for President and congressional seats won by the Democrats. Figure 11.1 shows that in national politics, there was an upsurge in Democratic strength in the 1930s, during the New Deal, a dropping off until the 1960s, and a gradual rise in Democratic voting since the 1960s.

Figure 11.2 shows the results for state-level elections [2] The lines show the percentage of governorships and state legislative seats held by the Democrats.

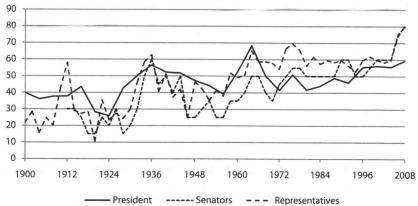

Figure 11.1 Democratic Percentage of Presidential Popular Votes, U.S. Senators and Representatives, Northeast, 1900–2008.

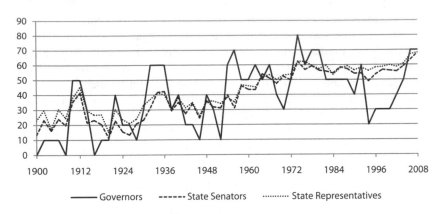

Figure 11.2 Democratic Percentage of Governors and Members of State Senates and Houses of Representatives, Northeast, 1900–2008.

The trends are similar to those of Figure 11.1, except that there are more fluctuations in the governorships. This probably reflects the fact that elections for governors are based on state issues and revolve around personalities, and therefore do not necessarily reflect national trends (Carsey and Wright 1998; Hinckley, Hofstetter, and Kessel 1974; Squire and Fastnow 1994).

Figure 11.3 shows how Northeasterners have identified with, or leaned toward, the Democrats and Republicans. The data are based on responses to the question, "Generally speaking, do you usually think of yourself as a Democrat, a Republican, an Independent, or what?" Respondents who said that they were Independent were then asked if they felt closer to one of the major parties. Because researchers have shown that even leaning toward a party is associated with voting for that party (Keith et al. 1992), I have combined those who identified with a party with those who said they were Independent but

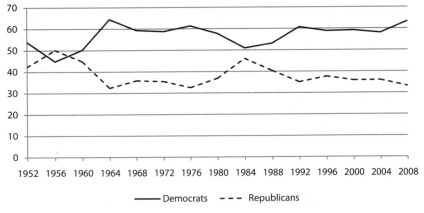

Figure 11.3 Party that Northeasterners Identified with or Leaned Toward, 1952–2008.
Source: American National Election Studies.

leaned toward that party. According to the graph, which shows the percentage of respondents who identified with or leaned toward each party, Democrats have outnumbered Republicans in the Northeast since the early 1960s, and by fairly constant margins. Starting in the 1980s, however, the proportion of Democrats has slowly risen while that of Republicans has declined. All in all, these three graphs give us a picture of an electorate in the Northeast that, while not dramatically increasing its identification with the Democrats for the past half-century, has been voting more and more Democratic. That has resulted, for example, in the fact that after the 2008 election, there were no Republicans from any New England state in the U. S. House of Representatives, and only four Northeastern Republican senators (one of whom, Pennsylvania's Arlen Specter, defected to the Democrats a few months later).

One final question is how these trends in the Northeast compared with those in the rest of the country. Figure 11.4 shows the comparison, by subtracting from the Northeast's Democratic percentage the percentage of Democrats from the rest of the country. If the resulting number is positive, Democrats were more successful in the Northeast than elsewhere; if it is negative, the Democrats were less successful in the Northeast than elsewhere. The solid line in the graph represents the mean of the six elected offices presented in Figures 11.1 and 11.2, and the dotted line shows party identification (Figure 11.3). In all cases, there was a dramatic upward trend since the middle of the 20th century, and by the 1990s the Northeast, which had once been far more Republican than other regions, had become more Democratic.

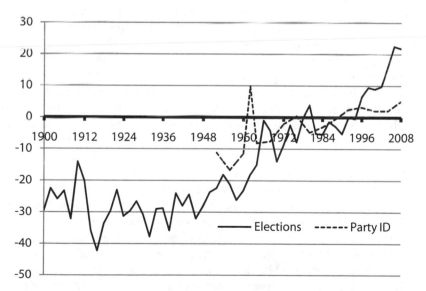

Figure 11.4 Difference between Democratic Percentage in the Northeast and Democratic Percentage in Other States, Mean of Six Electoral Measures, and Party Identification, 1900–2008. Source: NES files.

The Shrinking Republican Base

What was the mechanism by which Republicans began to lose elections in the Northeast? It is not because those who identified as Republican deserted the party and began to vote for Democrats. There was a slight drop in their voting for their party's presidential nominees, of about 8 percent from 1952 to 2008, but it was not much different from the drop among Republicans elsewhere (6 percent). Northeastern Republicans remained loyal to their party; the problem was that there were fewer of them.

In the middle of the nineteenth century, Republicans inherited from the Whig party an affluent, Protestant base. In other words, from their earliest days as a party they have represented the American Establishment, including Wall Street and the broader business community, as well as small-town business owners. The Republican appeal to such groups was based on several economic and cultural factors (Gerring 1998). One was a consistently probusiness platform, including sound money, trade protectionism until the midtwentieth century and free trade thereafter, and general opposition to the regulation of business by the government. Another factor was the alliance of the party with the Protestant clergy, including at times fundamentalists; this has made the party more resistant than the Democrats to the immigration of non-Protestants and more willing to use the government to promote moral behavior. Partly in response, Roman Catholic voters have always largely identified with the Democrats, as have most Jewish voters since the 1930s, and other non-Christians in recent years (Gienapp 1987, 434–39; Rossiter 1960, 101–02; Viorst 1968, 37). Republicans have also been a predominantly white party. Ever since black voters, who had identified with the Republicans since that party was founded as an antislavery party in the 1850s, swung to the Democrats in the 1930s, the Republicans have drawn few members of racial minority groups to their coalition (Frymer 1999).

The Republicans' natural base has long been upper income (defined as above the median in family income) white Protestants. We can examine the extent to which this group has identified with or leaned toward the party in every decade for which we have reliable survey data.[3] Figure 11.5 shows the results for the Northeast, for the Southeast which have been so distinctive, and for the rest of the country, the Middle West and Far West combined. The dark bars in the graph show that the proportion of Northeastern upper-income white Protestants who chose the Republican party plummeted over the decades, from over 70 percent in the 1950s and 1960s to less than 45 percent in the first decade of the new century. At the same time, the proportion of such people in the South who chose Republicanism (the gray bars) has skyrocketed; that of Westerners (the white bars) has increased only slightly over time.[4]

Compounding this problem for Northeastern Republicans is that the proportion of people who are upper-income white Protestants has been declining, both in the Northeast and in the nation as a whole. This is partly because of

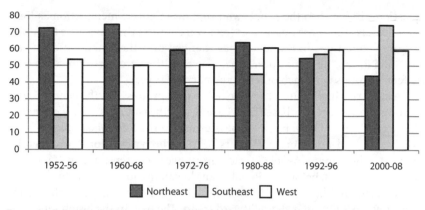

Figure 11.5 Percent of Upper-Income White Protestants Identifying with or Leaning Republican, by Section, 1950s to 2000s. Source: NES files.

immigration and high birth rates among nonwhites, but more importantly due to declining proportions of people identifying themselves as Protestants. This latter trend is partly due to the immigration of people from Latin America and Asia, and partly due to the rising proportion of Americans who do not identify with any religion at all. One recent survey found that the proportion of nonidentifiers in the Northeast rose from 7 percent in 1990 to 17 percent in 2008, a higher increase than in any other region (Kosmin and Keysar 2009).

These findings beg the question, why has the tendency of what should presumably be the Republican base in the Northeast to choose the party been declining so much? One possibility is that they are becoming more liberal than they used to be. We can first look at whether they have been less likely to call themselves conservative than they used to. Over a twenty-year period, there was a 6 percent increase in the tendency of upper-income white Protestants in the Northeast to call themselves conservatives, but it was exceeded by the 12 percent increase in the self-declared conservatism of such voters elsewhere. Relatively speaking, then, the potential Republican base was not keeping pace with the rightward drift of similar voters elsewhere.

However, data on the ideological labels that people apply to themselves are suspect, because different people mean different things by the terms *conservative* and *liberal*, and may take stands on issues that seem to contradict those labels (Free and Cantril 1967). A better way to gauge people's political opinions is to look at specific issues. Identifying such issues is challenging because they change over time, as does the wording of questions about them asked in the American National Election Studies surveys. Nevertheless, I have identified four issues that have been asked about fairly consistently from 1956 through 2008: whether the federal government should (1) guarantee jobs and living standards; (2) provide health insurance; (3) aid blacks (or minority groups); and (4) aid education. For each year, I divided the survey respondents into two groups, as equal in size as possible, based on their answers to the issue questions. I identified the people who supported government action as (relative) liberals, and those opposed as (relative) conservatives. Because the wording of the questions in the survey has changed over the years, these data are not valid in tracing trends over time. However, they are useful in comparing different groups with each other in any particular year.

In constructing Figure 11.6, I looked at four groups: Northeasterners who were in the Republican base ("NE Base"), Northeasterners who were not in that base ("NE Other"), non-Northeasterners in the Republican base ("Non-NE Base"), and non-Northeasterners outside the base ("Non-NE Other"). I calculated how many people in each group were conservative in the period from 1956 to 1968, before the Republicans began to move sharply to the right. I also calculated how many in each group were conservative in the period from 1996 to 2008, after the rightward trend. The bars in the graph represent, for each group on each issue, whether the people in it had moved in a more conservative direction (above the dark horizontal line) or in a more liberal direction (below that line).

The figure shows that over forty years, Northeasterners in the Republican base (the leftmost and darkest bar in each cluster) moved the farthest away from the conservative side of any of the four groups, either becoming more liberal (medical care and education), or growing more conservative at a slower pace than the others (job guarantee and aid to blacks).

As suggestive as these trends are, they can only explain part of the reason why the Northeast has been so inhospitable to Republicans in recent decades. For one thing, the bars in Figure 11.6 that represent the Republican base in the Northeast are not that different from those representing the Republican base in other parts of the country. Much of the trends we are observing are trends among all potential Republicans, not just those in the Northeast. Another factor can be ruled out: Northeastern upper income white Protestants increased their churchgoing over the period, and frequency of church attendance is associated with greater support for the Republican Party.

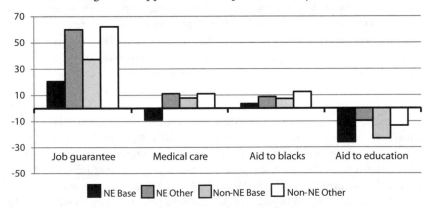

Figure 11.6 Change in Percent Conservative, 1956–1968 to 1996–2008, on Four Issues, by Membership in Republican Base and Section. Source: NES files.

Another way to approach the question of why Northeastern Republicans have been unable to mobilize their natural base is to look at the timing of Democratic gains. Perhaps this will suggest factors leading to Republican decline. Careful scrutiny of the solid line in Figure 11.4 shows that there were two periods of sharp Democratic gains in Northeastern elections: 1958–1966, and 1990–2006. In both these periods, the Democratic share of elections rose by about 27 percent. The first period saw the presidential nomination of John F. Kennedy, the first Roman Catholic President of the United States. Kennedy, a New Englander, drew strong support in the Northeast, carrying all states in the region except for the three in northern New England. He also appealed to fellow Catholics, who are more numerous in the Northeast than elsewhere, and his election helped spur Democratic gains in the region.

Kennedy's election, however, was a one-time event. More useful for explanatory purposes is the fact that the two periods under examination had one important feature in common: a marked shift in the national Republican Party, geographically to the South and West and politically to the right. As I argued earlier, the early 1960s saw the growth of the Southern and Western-based conservative movement, which attacked the Northeastern leadership of the Republican Party that had been responsible for the nomination of liberal and moderate presidential nominees from 1940 through 1960. Nearly all those nominees resided in the Northeast. The conservative uprising resulted in the nomination in 1964 of Arizona's Senator Barry Goldwater, who had suggested that the Eastern seaboard be sawed off and left to float into the ocean (Barnes 1998; Perlstein 2001). Despite Goldwater's crushing defeat in November, his nomination began an era when conservatives dominated the presidential party; after 1976, all the nominees were clearly from that wing of the party, and none lived in the Northeast. All but one were from the Sun Belt states of California, Texas, or Arizona. Years later, Goldwater told his biographer, "We knew that the only thing we could accomplish would be moving the Republican headquarters from New York to the West Coast, and we did that. We got it away from the money" (Goldberg 1995, 208).

Not only was the party increasingly dominated by conservatives, but the conservatives represented a new breed that focused less on small government and balanced budgets, and more on social issues such as race, abortion, pornography, crime, prayer in schools, and homosexuality, as well as national security. A substantial part of the new tone of the Republican Party resulted from its alliance with the Religious Right, primarily evangelical Protestants, that began with Ronald Reagan's campaign in 1980 (Martin 1996). The Northeast was especially resistant to those appeals, largely because it has a lower proportion of Protestants than any other region, and even fewer evangelical Protestants. On issues like abortion, Northeasterners are consistently more liberal than people in other parts of the country.

For these reasons, Northeasterners found themselves less in the mainstream of the Republican Party, although they were still open to attractive

Republican presidential nominees. Ronald Reagan carried all but one North-eastern state in 1980 and all of them in 1984, and George H. W. Bush won all but three in 1988. Starting with Bill Clinton in 1992, however, the Northeast became a Democratic stronghold. This raises the question of why there was a second spurt in Democratic fortunes from 1990 to 2006. The period saw a major solidification of Southern dominance of the congressional party, with the Republican takeover of Congress in the 1994 elections. In the House, all three top positions were held by Southerners: Speaker Newt Gingrich (Georgia), Majority Leader Richard Armey (Texas), and Majority Whip Tom DeLay (Texas). Senators were led by Kansan Bob Dole, but when he resigned in 1996, he was succeeded by Trent Lott of Mississippi, who would in turn be succeeded in 2003 by Bill Frist of Tennessee and in 2007 by Mitch McConnell of Kentucky. And of course the President from 2001 to 2009 was George W. Bush of Texas.

In 1964, when asked if there was anything they liked about Goldwater, and anything they did not like about him, Northeastern Republicans were significantly more negative about him than were Republicans from outside the Northeast. On thermometer scales, in which respondents were asked to rate public figures from 0 to 100, there was also a tendency for Northeastern Republicans to rate Gingrich in 1996 and Bush in 2004 a little lower than their counterparts elsewhere. By 2008, that gap regarding Bush had widened to more than 10 percent. It is striking that the gap between Northeastern Republicans and other Republicans was greater than the gap between Northeastern Democrats and other Democrats, and between Northeastern Independents and other Independents. This reflects the growing alienation of Northeastern Republicans from the rest of their party.

Trends in Congress

It should not be surprising that, just as ordinary voters in the Northeast are more liberal than those elsewhere, especially the Republicans, the members of Congress who represent them reflect these differences. I can illustrate this with roll-call votes in Congress over the past century on economic issues, arguably the most important and most persistent of the concerns that face the national legislature. As James Madison wrote in the Tenth *Federalist*,

> A landed interest, a manufacturing interest, a mercantile interest, a moneyed interest, with many lesser interests, grow up of necessity in civilized nations, and divide them into different classes, actuated by different sentiments and views. The regulation of these various and interfering interests forms *the principal task of modern legislation*, and involves the spirit of party and faction in the necessary and ordinary operations of the government. (Hamilton, Madison, and Jay 1787/1961, 79; emphasis added)

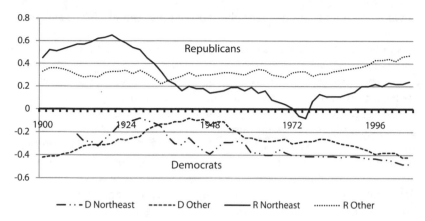

Figure 11.7 Degree of Conservatism of Senators on Economic Issues, by Party and Section, 1901–2008.

Keith Poole and Howard Rosenthal have given each member of Congress a score based on that person's votes on a dimension "that represents conflict over the role of government in the economy," the central political issue throughout so much of American history (Poole and Rosenthal 1997, 35). It is these scores that I am using to compare the voting records of Northeastern members of Congress with members from other parts of the nation. In Figure 11.7, the higher the point on the graph, the more conservative was the average senator from each group.

The graph shows that early in the twentieth century, in both parties, Northeastern senators were more conservative than their counterparts elsewhere. The same was true in the House of Representatives. Northeasterners were more conservative because they were associated with the business sector centered on Wall Street, and the Populist movement that represented poorer farmers and workers had its home in the South and West. In the 1920s and 1930s, however, the two sections began to trade places. Just as Franklin D. Roosevelt's New Deal, with its programs to help the urban working class, improved the Democratic showing in elections, it inspired members of Congress from both parties in the Northeast to move to the left. Meanwhile the growing conservative movement in the South and West pushed those regions to the right. Figure 11.7 also shows that a narrowing gap between Northeastern Democrats and those from other regions in recent years. This is because Democrats outside the Northeast became more moderate, due in large part to the movement of Southern white conservatives into the Republican Party and the growing black vote as a key component of the Democratic Party in the South. On the other hand, in the Republican Party, Northeastern liberalism has maintained a fairly wide gap between legislators from the Northeast and those from elsewhere. Indeed, in both houses of Congress, the sectional gap among Republicans has been about three times the size of the gap among Democrats.

Similar results occurred when I analyzed votes on racial issues, using the "key votes" selected by *Congressional Quarterly*. Each year the publication chooses between ten and twenty votes in each house of Congress that it deems the most important, and I selected from those lists those votes on issues that involved race. These issues include the landmark civil rights laws of the 1950s and 1960s, and later votes on busing and school desegregation. There were thirty-seven votes on racial issues in the Senate (1945–2007) and thirty-two in the House (1945–2006). In both houses of Congress, Northeasterners in both parties were more liberal than members from elsewhere, but as the gap among Democrats narrowed over time, that among Republicans grew wider—just like the trends on economic issues.

National Conventions

Another way to place the Northeast within the context of national politics is to examine voting at national party conventions. Unlike legislative bodies, conventions are created by their parties, and their votes include representatives of all state parties. Finally, the primary business of the national convention, to select the presidential and vice-presidential ticket, to adopt the platform, and to decide on the rules, includes the most important activities of the national party. Because different conventions have had different numbers of roll-call votes, it would be misleading and unwieldy to examine every such vote. Instead, I have selected from each convention a "key vote," usually the decisive vote for the presidential nominee, which indicates the most important division within the convention (Reiter 2004). Because the Republicans had their most recent divided roll-call vote in 1976, and the Democrats in 1992, I have used media reports of how the states were prepared to vote on Ronald Reagan's nomination at the 1980 Republican national convention, and delegate counts of both parties' conventions in 2008.[5]

Figure 11.8 shows, for each of the conventions since 1896, the absolute value of the difference between how the average Northeastern delegation voted, and how the average state in the rest of the nation voted.[6] For the Democrats, the Northeast diverged from the rest of the country more before the 1930s than since then, especially in the 1896 convention when William Jennings Bryan's populist appeal fell on deaf ears in the Northeast, in 1908 when the Pennsylvania delegation was the subject of the key vote, and in the 1920s when the ethnocultural split between Northeastern pro-immigrant and anti-Prohibition attitudes clashed with the opposite views of Southerners and Westerners. For the Republicans, Northeastern exceptionalism began in earnest in the 1940s, and reached its peak with the Goldwater and Reagan candidacies of the 1960s and 1970s. The net effect is that ever since 1952, Northeasterners have been far

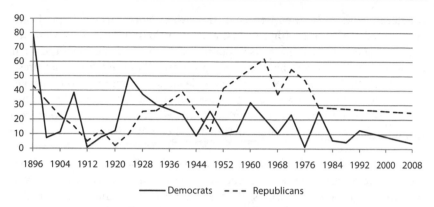

Figure 11.8 Differences between Votes of Northeastern Delegations, and Those from Other Parts of the Nation, Key Votes at National Party Conventions, 1896–2008.

more exceptional among Republicans than among Democrats—a pattern that we have seen in Congress as well.

The South, the Northeast, and American Party Politics

In this chapter, I have shown that in the past fifty years, the Republicans have come to dominate the South, and Democrats have established themselves as the reigning party in the Northeast. I have also provided evidence that Republican gains in the South were in response to the leftward shift of the national Democratic party in the 1930s and 1940s, and that Democratic gains in the Northeast have been primarily due to the fact that the national Republican Party, in order to shore up its support in the South, has moved to the right and shifted its geographic base. The result has been that Northeastern Republicans have been the "odd men out" in their party, a moderate-to-liberal remnant of a once dominant faction, while Northeastern Democrats staked out a liberal position to which the rest of their party has gravitated. These trends have been apparent in votes in Congress and at national conventions.

These developments have affected the broader political system, not least in providing within each party a relatively liberal bastion. Another way in which the Northeast has affected our national politics is that the region has been a counterweight to the growing trend of polarization between the parties (Hetherington 2001; Stonecash 2002). Democrats and Republicans in the Northeast are closer together ideologically than their counterparts in the rest of the nation, and as a consequence they slightly reduce the degree of polarization between the national parties.

These conclusions point to a complex relationship between Republican advances in the South and Democratic gains in the Northeast. In the nineteenth and early twentieth centuries, when Northeastern Republicans represented Wall Street, high tariffs, and the gold standard, they were the natural leaders of their party (see Bensel 2000). Northeasterners and their conservative allies in neighboring Ohio provided all of the Republican presidents from 1877 through 1929, and many leaders of Congress from Speaker Thomas "Czar" Reed of Maine to Senator Henry Cabot Lodge of Massachusetts to Speaker Nicholas Longworth of Ohio. However, when the New Deal inspired a leftward shift among Northeastern Republicans, they began to lose their dominance.

Just as the liberalism of the New Deal made the Democratic Party more attractive to Northeasterners, it made white conservatives in the South reevaluate their traditional moorings. By the late 1950s, it became apparent that many were ripe for realignment, and the Republican Party began to develop a "Southern strategy" by moving to the right on racial issues (Klinkner 1994). The success of that strategy had its costs, however, as moderate-to-liberal Republicans began to feel ignored and unwanted, and conservative presidential nominees began to have difficulty winning the region. In 1964, Barry Goldwater's candidacy suffered a 17 percent drop from Richard Nixon's showing four years earlier in the average Northeastern state. According to the American National Election Studies, the biggest drop was among Northeastern Republicans (35 percent). As we have seen, that campaign precipitated a hemorrhaging of Republicanism in the Northeast that leveled off in the Reagan era but accelerated again with the advent of Newt Gingrich and George W. Bush. All in all, then, the phenomenal success of the conservative movement in colonizing the Republican party and making it as monolithic as any major party in American history has resulted in severe disadvantages in the more liberal parts of the nation, notably the Northeast.

As of this writing, Republicans are in a lamentable position in the Northeast. They have won only one Northeastern state in the past five presidential elections, and that one only once. They control only three Northeastern governorships, four Senate seats, fewer than a fifth of the seats in the U.S. House of Representatives, and only one state legislative house. What is worse, the national Republican Party shows no sign of moving significantly in a more moderate direction, one that would gain support in the Northeast. The best that Northeastern Republicans can hope for is that Democrats will make so many mistakes that they cause a backlash that will benefit the Republican Party, and Northeastern Republicans will be carried along in the tide as they were in the 1980s. In the meantime, there is little that Northeastern Republicans can do.

More broadly, this analysis suggests that American politics is dynamic, always changing and often in dramatic ways. It also reveals that party gains can contain the seeds of future problems. The Democrats' attainment of a national majority in the 1930s led ultimately to the disaffection of their Southern white wing, and the Republicans' path to parity with the Democrats late in the twentieth century alienated their Northeastern supporters. We conclude, like physicists, that political actions often contain equal and opposite reactions, in different parts of the country. Any party that seeks a national majority will ignore this lesson at its peril.

Notes

1. The presidential election of 1948 and the congressional election of 1950 were relatively close, and I used those elections as a baseline for the "would haves" in the text. For more on these trends, see Reiter and Stonecash (2010). Here, and in the forthcoming volume, the Northeast is defined as the six New England states, as well as Delaware, New Jersey, New York, and Pennsylvania.
2. I am indebted to Jeffrey M. Stonecash for the state legislative data.
3. Because of small sample sizes for some of the years, in several of the following tables I have grouped all the years in the same decade.
4. The reader may wonder how the Democrats' natural base behaved. If we define them as lower-income non-Protestants, there was virtually no difference between people who live in the Northeast and those who live elsewhere in their tendency to identify with or lean toward the Democrats in any of the decades since 1952.
5. For 1980, see *Congressional Quarterly Weekly Report*, June 28, 1980, p. 1801; and July 12, 1980, p. 1936. For 2008, see http://politics.nytimes.com/election-guide/2008/results/delegates/index.html; http://politics.nytimes.com/election-guide/2008/results/gopdelegates/index.html (both accessed August 16, 2008).
6. For conventions that had no roll-call votes, I simply connected the line between adjacent points on the graph.

Part IV

Party Actions, Institutions, and Impacts

Chapter 12

The President as a Partisan Actor

Sidney M. Milkis

The President and the Development of the American Party System

The relationship between the president and the parties has never been easy, though its dynamics have varied over the course of American political history. The architects of the Constitution established a nonpartisan president who, with the support of the judiciary and Senate, was intended to play the leading institutional role in checking and controlling "the violence of faction" that the framers feared would rend the fabric of representative government. Even after the presidency became a more partisan office, its authority continued to depend on an ability to remain independent of party politics, especially during national emergencies such as the Civil War and the Spanish-American War (Ketcham 1984). Indeed, the institutional imperatives of the executive appear at first glance to be inherently at odds with the character of political parties. Party organization seems better suited to legislative bodies, which have a collective action problem, than to an executive dedicated to vigorous and expeditious administration. Presidents can best display their personal qualities "above party," Wilson Carey McWilliams observed. By contrast, "Congress cannot be effective, let alone powerful, without the institution of party.... A legislature can rival the executive's claim to public confidence only to the extent that it is accountable, which presumes a principle of *collective responsibility*" (McWilliams 1989, 35, emphasis in original).

Nonetheless, presidents and parties need each other. The early history of the republic showed that the original constitutional presidency was too elevated and aloof to have a vital connection with the country. Even George Washington, who was by temperament and background uniquely suited to stand above the partisan fray, was attacked for fostering "consolidation" that would create an unacceptable divide between the executive and the people. By the 1790s, Thomas Jefferson and his political allies charged that Washington, spurred on by his Secretary of the Treasury Alexander Hamilton, was claiming domestic and international responsibilities for the executive branch that would undermine popular sovereignty and start the United States down the path toward a

British-style monarchy. Jefferson and James Madison took the lead in forming the Republican Party to mobilize popular support against the original constitutional presidency, which Alexander Hamilton and the Federalist Party championed. The Republicans' decisive triumph over the Federalists in the 1800 election—the "Revolution of 1800," as Jefferson called it—initiated an important constitutional development that tied executive authority to a party program that was sanctioned by "the decisions of the majority" in presidential elections (Ceaser 1979, chapter 2). Jefferson was the first president to serve simultaneously as party leader; and the Republican Party was indispensable to his election and the enactment of his policies.

Jefferson and the Republicans were committed to defeating the Federalists, not to establishing partisanship as a permanent fixture in presidential politics and governance. But their successors—the Jacksonian Democrats—believed that political parties played a critical role in holding presidents accountable to public opinion. By the 1840s, the presidency was enmeshed in a highly decentralized and fiercely competitive party system that relentlessly organized and mobilized the American voter (Milkis 1999, chapter 2).

Presidents thus became dependent on parties, both in campaigning and governing, to shore up their electoral fortunes in a political culture highly resistant to centralized administration. Even presidential quests for independence have required the support of party. Throughout American history, but especially in the twentieth and twenty-first centuries, presidents have needed the support of their partisan brethren in Congress to establish institutions and programs that secured authority to exercise executive power autonomously. At the same time, parties have relied on presidential candidates and presidents to convey a coherent message and to infuse their organizations with energy. From the 1830s to the 1890s, the highly localized parties found their strength principally in the political combat of presidential elections—a battleground that encouraged Democrats and Whigs in the antebellum period and Democrats and Republicans after the Civil War to overlook their differences in the interest of victory. Parties became more dependent on presidents in the twentieth century as campaigns became more focused on national candidates. Even so, presidents continued to represent their parties' ideals and principles to the nation.

Although a combination of principle and strategy has created a degree of symbiosis between presidents and parties, the relationship has frequently been tense. Before the New Deal, presidents who sought to exercise executive power expansively, especially in the service of centralized administration, were thwarted "by the tenacity of [a] highly mobilized, highly competitive, and locally oriented democracy" (Skowronek 1982, 40). With the consolidation of executive power during the 1930s and 1940s, the president, rather than the Congress or the party organizations, became the leading instrument of popular rule—in Theodore Roosevelt's capacious phrase, "the steward of the public welfare." The rise of the modern presidency in the wake of the Great

Depression and Second World War thus appeared to signal the end of an old institutional order based on decentralized political control and the beginning of a permanent ascendance of national, nonpartisan executive administration (Schlesinger 1949). The birth of the modern presidency and the decline of traditional localized parties better equipped the federal government to carry out vital tasks at home and abroad; at the same time, this development appeared to portend an era of chronically low public engagement and voter turnout and an increasingly fractious national politics (Lowi 1985; Milkis 1993; Shea 1999).

The erosion of old style partisan politics, however, allowed for a more national and issue-based party system to develop, forging new links between presidents and parties. Republican presidents, like Ronald Reagan and George W. Bush, dedicated themselves to building a national party organization that might mobilize popular support for, and devote governing institutions to, a new conservative political order. Allied to an assault on the liberal administrative state, the formation of an executive-centered national Republican party seemed to promise a new presidential leadership synthesis and a "new" party system (Milkis and Rhodes 2007a). Although Bush's party leadership ultimately became an albatross for the Republican Party in the 2008 election, the experience suggests that vigorous presidential leadership in the present configuration of executive and party has the defects of its virtues. In the hands of an overweening executive, the party may simply become a means to the president's end, sapping the organization of both its autonomy and its ability to adapt to changing political circumstances.

The emergence of an executive-centered party system thus might represent an important change in the relationship between the presidency and the party system. The traditional decentralized parties, nourished by the patronage system, acted as a gravitational pull on presidential ambition. The new national parties, sustained not only by the national party committees, but also by advocacy groups, think tanks, the mass media, and use of the Internet to raise funds, recruit volunteers, and mobilize voters, encourage presidents to advance bold programs and policies. The "new party system" is prone to rancorous conflict, but partisan clashes over domestic and foreign policy have aroused the interest and increased the participation of the American people in elections. Without question, the rise of more national and programmatic parties deprives partisanship in the United States of some of the tolerance that hitherto has made party loyalty so compatible with the pluralistic traditions in American politics. It may be, however, "that a politics more clearly tied to principles and ideals is more appropriate to the current stage of our national life" (Reichley 1985, 199).

The rest of this chapter traces the evolution of the relationship between the presidency and political parties. It highlights key developments in the nineteenth century that tied executive power to party leadership. These developments made presidential politics and governance more popular but at the cost of subjecting executive power to highly decentralized organizations that often relegated presidents to brokering sectional interests and mediating patronage appointments. By the same token, the emancipation of the executive from the constrictive grip of parties during the Progressive and New Deal eras gave rise to a more active and better-equipped national government. But in the absence of strong parties, that more powerful government lacks sufficient means of common deliberation and public judgment, the pillar of a vital civic culture. The discussion of the Reagan and Bush presidencies details how they benefited from and helped advance the new executive-centered party system. Although Democrats renounced the fierce partisanship that the White House and Republican Congress practiced during the first six years of the Bush presidency, there is reason to suspect that the national structure of the party system—and a politics that privileges national issues and conflicts—will endure. Many liberal public officials and strategists have expressed more than grudging admiration for the effective party building that has buttressed partisan rancor in the nation's capital. The 2008 election made clear that Barack Obama and the Democrats learned a great deal from the political tactics employed by the Republicans; indeed, the Obama campaign exceeded the fundraising and grassroots successes that Republicans had experienced in recent campaigns. More to the point, given the way national parties have served executive ambition, earnest presidential party leadership is likely to be an important feature of American politics for the foreseeable future.

Presidential Leadership and the Rise of the Mass Party System

The critical and uneasy relationship between the American presidency and political parties sheds light on the central question of the American constitutional experiment: whether it is possible to realize self-government on a grand scale. This was the question that divided the Federalists and Anti-Federalists; and it was revisited in the constitutional struggles between the Jeffersonian Republicans and the Hamiltonian Federalists. As formed during the first three decades of the nineteenth century, political parties reflected the concern first expressed by Anti-Federalists, and later revised by Jefferson, that the Constitution provided inadequately for the cultivation of an active and competent citizenry. The Anti-Federalists were not fond of partisanship, but like their Jeffersonian descendants, they viewed political parties as the most practical remedy for the erosion of confidence between rulers and ruled, Localized political associations could provide a vital link between constitutional offices, especially the executive, and the citizenry, thereby balancing local self-government—the bedrock of the American democratic tradition—and the national government, strengthened by the Constitution of 1787 (Borowiak 2007; Storing 1981).

Significantly, Madison, the principal architect of the "Constitution-against-Parties," became a defender of parties and local self-government during the critical battles between the Republicans and Federalists (Hofstadter 1969, 40–121). Alexander Hamilton's success as Washington's Secretary of the Treasury in strengthening the executive led Madison to recognize that the Anti-Federalists might have been more correct in their criticisms of the Constitution than he previously had thought. By the early 1790s, he joined Jefferson in opposition to the Federalists, in the formulation of a party program of government decentralization, and, consequently, gave birth to the American party system (Edling 2003; Ferling 2005; Freeman 2001; Ketcham 1984).

"Out of this original clash [between the Federalists and the Republicans] there developed in America the tension between party politics, on the one hand, and governmental centralization and bureaucracy, on the other" (Piereson 1982, 51). This tension contributed significantly to the fracturing of the Jeffersonian Republican party and, eventually, to the welding of a formal two-party system to the Constitution. In the wake of the War of 1812, which dramatically exposed the limitations of Jeffersonian Republican principles, Madison recommended several measures to solidify the national resolve, including the chartering of the Second Bank of the United States. In fact, to facilitate the development of the domestic economy, the so-called National Republicans, led by the powerful Speaker of the House, Henry Clay, advanced an ambitious program later known as the "American System," that included a protective tariff, government supervision of public land distribution, and the construction of public works (Jensen 2003; Larson 2000). With the selection of the ardent nationalist John Quincy Adams to the presidency in the controversial election of 1824, an incipient administrative state began to take shape, a development which appeared to restore the nonpartisan character of the executive branch. For these proto-state builders, "the founders' bold experiment in republican government was open-ended, and the central government a progressive, developmental force" (John 2003, 56).

The task of fending off the National Republicans' administrative ambitions fell after the 1824 election to more traditional Republicans, such as Martin Van Buren of New York and Thomas Ritchie of Virginia. The outcome of this election, in which Adams was selected by the House of Representatives, even though Andrew Jackson had more popular and electoral votes, persuaded Jacksonian reformers that the Constitution's vulnerability to centralized administration had not been corrected by Jeffersonian democracy. Adams's selection of Clay, who orchestrated his victory in the House, as secretary of state, and the president's first state of the union address, which proposed an active role for the federal government in the economy and society, further aroused the controversy. With the weakening of the national party structure, Van Buren lamented, a system of personal and local factions displaced the "common sentiment" that had upheld republican principles, thus favoring the champions of "consolidation" (Van Buren 1867, 4–6).

The Jacksonian ambition to revitalize partisanship gave rise to the Democratic Party. Styling themselves as "old Republicans," Democratic party leaders, as Van Buren put it, sought "to redraw anew and...reestablish the old party lines" (Van Buren 1827). The Federalists and National Republicans, dedicated to strengthening national power and limiting popular rule, did not need a mass based party rooted in the states and localities to advance their program. They sought to center government responsibility in the executive, which would cultivate and maintain the support of commercial interests through the disbursement of bounties, licenses, and tariffs. In this way, the executive would wed commercial interests to state power—and develop, in turn, a stable commercial republic. In contrast, Van Buren argued, the ortho-dox Republicans, and their heirs, the Democrats, stood in need of "an extrane-ous force to secure harmony in its ranks." The Jacksonian Democrats intended to organize public opinion in support of government decentralization. Dedi-cated to the tradition of local self-government, and to the provincial liberties that supported it, the Republicans would be successful, Van Buren counseled, as long as they had the prudence to "employ the [party] caucus system...and to use in good faith the influence it is capable of imparting to the popular cause" (Van Buren 1867, 4–6).

Jefferson and his supporters established a wall between the national gov-ernment and states. Their commitment to majority rule was tempered by an understanding that the role of the national government had to be limited in a political order dedicated to inalienable—natural—individual rights. It was critical, Jeffersonian Republicans believed, that the president, as party leader, spearhead the campaign to defeat initiatives to enhance the power of the national government, regardless of how benign the purposes of those initia-tives appeared to be.

In the face of the National Republicans' attempt to revitalize the Federal-ists' centralizing ambitions, Jacksonian Democrats fortified the Jeffersonian barrier against national administration. The Jacksonian ambition to make partisanship part of the "living Constitution" was embodied by the Demo-cratic Party, which organized voters on the basis of principles that were mili-tantly decentralizing, as was the very process of party politics they established. The Jeffersonian emphasis on legislative supremacy comported with national parties, which rested on the nomination of presidential tickets by the con-gressional caucus. The caucus, which gave Republicans in the House and Sen-ate the power to nominate presidential and vice presidential candidates and to formulate party policy, lost considerable influence by 1824; moreover, the legislative maneuvers that led to Adams's selection over the popular Andrew Jackson, discredited Congress's intrusion on the presidential selection pro-cess. Although the charge that Adams and Clay had made a "corrupt bargain" to violate the will of the people probably was unfounded, the controversial election ensured the final demise of what critics had come to call "King Cau-cus." Presidential tickets were soon nominated by national conventions, which were dominated by state party organizations. Moreover, although patronage appointments were not uncommon during the Jeffersonian era, the Jacksonians exalted the practice of "rotation in office" into a political creed, and exploited positions in the widely scattered post offices and custom houses to recruit party foot soldiers and to raise campaign funds (McCormick 1986; Summers 1988).

Ostensibly, the national party organization gave presidents a source of political authority that was independent of the Congress. Indeed, scandalized by the way the legislative caucus and Congress rebuffed the popular Jackson in the notorious 1824 election, Democrats sought to make the president the "tribune of the people" (Korzi 2004; Laracey 2002). President Jackson is often credited with anticipating the modern presidency by establishing a direct relationship with the American people and by declaring, in his nullification proclamation, that secession was treason and the Union perpetual (Remini 1967; Stampp 1980, 33–35). Nonetheless, Jackson's powers were inextricably linked to a party dedicated to a program that "significantly weakened the organizational capacities of the central government" (John 2003, 65). After his election in 1828, Jackson withdrew the federal government from the realm of internal improvements, reduced the size of the military, held down government expenditures, dismantled the hated Bank of the United States and reinvested its deposits in state banks. In effect, the strengthening of the presidency during Jackson's stay in the White House "mobilized the powers of the government for what was essentially a dismantling operation" (Meyers 1957, 29).

By 1840, the Whigs, the heirs to the National Republicans who were committed to expanding the economic and social responsibilities of the national government, embraced the decentralizing practices of nomination by convention and the "spoils system" first championed by the Jacksonians. Although the Whigs' adoption of Jacksonian principles was in part a strategic effort to avoid the fate of the Federalists, they also had an appreciation for the critical role parties had come to play in maintaining the local democratic liberties of the nation's citizens. Indeed, Whigs claimed that as the party that championed legislative supremacy they, not the Democrats, were the true heirs of Jefferson.

Even the rise of the Republican Party during the 1850s, as a result of the slavery controversy, and the subsequent demise of the Whigs, did not alter the essential characteristics of the party system in the United States, and these characteristics—decentralized organization and hostility to administrative centralization—restrained rather than facilitated executive power. The failure of Reconstruction was attributable in no small part to the Republicans' diffidence in the task of "state-building," so much so that the self-styled modern reformers who emerged at the end of the nineteenth century overwhelmingly viewed party politics as an obstacle to their ambition to construct a modern state on American soil.

Progressive Democracy and the Decline of Localized Party Politics

The decentralized party system did not always constrain presidential ambition. Indeed, Washington apart, all of America's "reconstructive leaders"—those presidents who have presided over major partisan realignments—have used parties to remake American politics in their own image, to "reset the very terms of constitutional government" (Skowronek 1997, 38–39). But political parties kept these presidents faithful to broader interests, even as they gave executives the political strength to embark on ambitious projects of national reform. Moreover, prior to the New Deal, none of the programs to which the electorate had subscribed during a partisan realignment had called for a substantial exercise of executive power.

The late nineteenth century represented a way station between traditional partisan politics and the executive-centered polity of the twentieth century. Starting in the late 1880s, reforms in the states had resulted in the advance of the secret or official ballot;[1] the adoption of registration requirements; the growth of civil service reforms; and the introduction of the direct primary in state, local, and congressional elections. These measures, combined with the emergence of mass-circulation newspapers and magazines, independent of the traditional party press, had begun to weaken the grip of party organizations on candidates, government institutions, and the loyalties of voters (Reynolds 2006). Furthermore, beginning with the unsuccessful campaign of Samuel Tilden in 1876 and intensifying with William McKinley's successful effort in 1896, presidential candidates began to experiment with more candidate-centered, media-driven campaigns that downplayed traditional party labels and practices (Klinghard 2005; McGerr 1986, 70; Troy 1996, 82–107).

During the first two decades of the twentieth century, Progressive reformers elaborated the innovations that had begun to transform the relationship between the presidency and parties into a comprehensive program of political and constitutional reform. Progressives perceived that the concentration of wealth brought on by industrialization—symbolized by the giant "Trusts"—threatened American democracy by undermining the right of individuals to earn a living. To Progressives, local party leaders, corrupted by big business, were complicit in this development. Reformers thus saw little possibility of converting the existing party machinery into an instrument for the realization of their national program. Like the National Republicans of the early nineteenth century, their goal was to restore the national character of the Constitution, to emancipate national administration from the constraints and corruption of localized parties. Many Progressives championed strengthening the federal bureaucracy to rein in the "Trusts" and advocated social welfare measures that would protect Americans from the tyranny of unbridled capitalism. But unlike the Federalists and National Republicans, reformers at the dawn of the twentieth century celebrated a "New Nationalism," which promised to hitch national administration to mass democracy. Progressives advocated "direct democracy" in the form of women's suffrage and direct election of senators, as well as measures such as the direct primary, initiative, referendum, and recall that would forge direct ties between the government and public opinion. This commitment to national administration and direct democracy became the centerpiece of Theodore Roosevelt's Progressive Party campaign of 1912, which was sanctified as a "covenant of the people," as a deep and abiding pledge to make the people "masters of their Constitution."

The brief, but significant, experience of the Progressive Party underscores the powerful centrifugal force of progressive democracy. With the celebrated TR as its candidate, the Bull Moose Party won 27.4 percent of the national popular vote and eighty-eight electoral votes from six states in 1912. This was extraordinary for a third party, the largest percentage of the popular vote ever achieved by a third party candidate for the presidency. Despite its remarkable showing in 1912, the Progressive Party was dead four years later its fate inseparable from the charismatic leader who embodied its cause. Still, the Progressive Party lies at the very heart of fundamental changes in the relationship between the president and the parties. The personal quality of Roosevelt's campaign was part and parcel of these changes, but they went much deeper than his desire to regain past political mastery. The Progressive Party, with its leader-centered organization, accommodated and embodied an array of reformers—insurgent Republican office holders, disaffected Democrats, crusading journalists, academics and social workers, and other activists— who hoped that the new party coalition would realize their common goal of expanding the responsibilities of the federal government and making it more responsive to popular, economic, social, and political demands. Public opinion, Progressives argued, would reach its fulfillment with the formation of an independent executive power, freed from the provincial and corrupt influence of political parties (see Milkis 2009; Milkis and Tichenor 1994).

Many contemporary scholars point to the apparent contradiction between Progressives' celebration of direct democracy and their hope to achieve a more powerful, executive-oriented government (Rogers 1982; Wiebe 1995, chapter 7). But Progressives hoped to recast the constitutional presidency into an agent of social and economic reform. As Roosevelt described this concept of executive power, the president was "a steward of the people bound actively and affirmatively to do all he could for the people, and not content himself with the negative merit of keeping his talents undamaged in a napkin" (T. Roosevelt 1926, 20: 347). During his tenure as president, Roosevelt had made important efforts to fulfill this new understanding of executive power (see Arnold 2003). TR used his authority under the Pendleton legislation, enacted in 1883, to extend merit protection to approximately 60 percent of the civil service and thus establish a bulwark of administrative competence within the executive. Roosevelt also persuaded Congress to pass such measures as the Hepburn Act of 1906, which strengthened the Interstate Commerce Committee's authority to regulate the railroads in the public interest and set a major precedent for subsequent national state-building. These policy ends were pursued through direct presidential appeals to public opinion and the mass media that heralded the emergence of the "rhetorical presidency" (Tulis 1987).

Woodrow Wilson, the victor of the 1912 election, would further extend Roosevelt's legacy. As the Democratic candidate in 1912, Wilson adhered to his party's commitment to decentralized administration, attacking the Progressive Party for proposing to create a bureaucratic agency to regulate unfair business practices. But in the aftermath of TR's celebrated insurgency, Wilson embraced many features of New Nationalism. His first term, the *New Republic* celebrated, "waxed increasingly paternalistic, centralizing, and bureaucratic" (*New Republic* 1916, 103). Wilson accepted the idea of a regulatory commission with broad responsibilities for overseeing business practices, resulting in the creation of the Federal Trade Commission (FTC) in 1915. Wilson also persuaded the Democratic Congress to enact the Federal Reserve Act in 1913, which established a board to oversee the national banking and currency system. In each case, Wilson overcame the Democratic Party's traditional antipathy to national administrative power, suggesting that with the growing prominence of presidential candidates, party leaders in Congress were willing to sacrifice programmatic principles to win the White House (James 2000; Ware 2006).

Wilson also sought to further emancipate the presidency from party politics by strengthening the rhetorical presidency, most notably, reviving the practice, abandoned by Thomas Jefferson, of appearing before Congress to deliver important messages, including the State of the Union Address. With the rise of the mass media, Wilson believed, such occasions would help concentrate public attention on the actions of the president and Congress. He recognized, that the president now "stood at the intersection of party organization and national popular opinion and, if he was willing to assume the charge, could harness each to great national effect" (James 2005, 19).

To militant reformers, Wilson's full conversion to Progressive principles appeared to mark the triumph of a new political order. In his prosecution of World War I, however, Wilson revealed that the promise of modern executive leadership also portended dangerous possibilities. Most Progressives believed that "the righteous use of superior force" in world affairs was even more critical than were battles for reform at home. Wilson's war message to Congress clearly linked the country's entry into the European fray as the fulfillment of progressive democracy. "The world must be made safe for democracy," the president stated in a famous phrase. Only total war would advance the cause of self-government, "achieve the ultimate peace for the world and for the liberation of its peoples, including the German peoples," who were suffering under the Prussian autocracy (Link 1984, 41: 519–27). Unmoored from the moderating effects of party, however, Wilson's idealistic rhetoric was joined to a plebiscitary politics that ultimately undermined civil liberties.

To convey his war aim—"to make the world safe for democracy"—to the American people, Wilson formed the Committee on Public Information (CPI), which enlisted 75,000 speakers to "persuade" the American public that the war was a crusade for democracy against Germans, a barbarian people bent on world domination. The CPI and a number of self-styled patriotic groups sought to discourage and sometimes repress dissent. People who refused to buy war bonds were often ridiculed, and some were even assaulted. Those with German names, scorned as "hyphenate Americans," were persecuted indiscriminately. Wilson championed repressive legislation such as the Espionage Act of 1917, which imposed fines and jail sentences for persons convicted of aiding the enemy or obstructing military recruitment, and the Sedition Act of 1918, which made "saying anything" to discourage the purchase of war bonds, or "utter[ing] print[ing], writ[ing], or publish[ing] any disloyal, profane, scurrilous, or abusive language" about the government, the Constitution, or the uniforms worn by soldiers and sailors, crimes (Capozzola 2008). Socialist leader Eugene Debs, who received 6 percent of the popular vote in 1912, was sentenced to ten years in jail for making an antiwar speech. Ironically, a socialist, dedicated to nationalizing the means of production, became the champion of natural rights. In his statement to the court, Debs scorned the Sedition Act, which he charged was in "flagrant conflict with democratic principles and the spirit of free institutions" (Debs 1918).

The overreaching of the Progressives—the dire threat new nationalism posed to sacred freedoms eventually led to a strong backlash against reformism, first in the defeat of the Wilson's League of Nations Treaty, and then in the 1920 election. Republican Warren Harding was elected calling for a "return to normalcy." Riding the wave of his landslide victory, which in important respects marked a referendum on the modern presidency, the Republicans resumed power in March 1921, militantly determined to rehabilitate constitutional sobriety, rugged individualism, and party organization to their former stature. The twenties did, in fact, revive certain features of the old order. But the Great Depression and World War II gave Franklin D. Roosevelt and a revamped Democratic Party the opportunity to resurrect Progressive democracy in a new, more familiar suit of clothes.

The Flowering of the Modern Presidency and Administrative Partisanship

The decisive break with the decentralized party system came with Franklin D. Roosevelt in the 1930s and his deft reinterpretation of the "liberal tradition" in the United States (Hartz 1955). Liberalism had always been associated with Jeffersonian principles and the natural rights tradition of limited government drawn from John Locke's *Second Treatise of Government* and the Declaration of Independence. Roosevelt pronounced a new liberalism in which constitutional government and the natural rights tradition were not abandoned but were linked to programmatic expansion and an activist federal government. This new liberalism presupposed a fundamental change in the relationship between the presidency and political parties, albeit one that seemed more consonant with traditional American values and institutions than had New Nationalism.

Roosevelt first spoke about the need to modernize elements of the old faith in his Commonwealth Club address, delivered during the 1932 campaign and appropriately understood as the New Deal manifesto. The theme was that the time had come—indeed, had come three decades earlier—to recognize the "new terms of the old social contract." It was necessary to rewrite the social contract to take account of the national economy and the concentration of economic power. With the adoption of a new compact, the American people would establish a countervailing power—a stronger national state—lest the United States steer a "steady course toward economic oligarchy." Protection of the national welfare must shift from private citizens to the government; the guarantee of equal opportunity required that individual initiative be restrained and directed by national administration. As Roosevelt put it in a well considered phrase, "The day of enlightened administration has come" (Roosevelt 1938–50, 1: 751–52).

Yet the task of modern government, FDR announced, was to enhance, rather than abandon the natural rights tradition—"to assist the development of an economic constitutional declaration of rights, an economic constitutional order." The traditional emphasis in American politics on individual self-reliance should therefore give way to a new understanding of individualism, in which the government acted as a regulating and unifying agency, guaranteeing individual men and women protection from the uncertainties of the marketplace. These new rights were never formally ratified as part of the Constitution, but Roosevelt's effective, well-timed use of the rhetorical presidency ensured they became the foundation of political dialogue. In the wake of the Roosevelt revolution, nearly every public policy was propounded as a right, attempting to confer constitutional status on programs like Social Security, Medicare, welfare, and food stamps. Consequently, with the advent of the New Deal political order, an understanding of rights dedicated to limiting government gradually gave way to a more expansive understanding of rights, a transformation in the governing philosophy of the United States that required major changes in American political institutions.

The modern presidency thus became part of the living constitution, not as the steward of the people, but, rather, as the guardian of new rights. As became all too clear during Wilson's tempestuous second term, the Progressive dream of national responsibility portended an unvarnished majoritarianism that threatened the Constitution's promise to protect individual freedom from the vagaries of mass opinion. The New Deal understanding of reform, however, appealed more directly to the American constitutional tradition by asserting a connection between nationalism and "programmatic rights." Roosevelt gave legitimacy to Progressive principles by embedding them in the language of constitutionalism and interpreting them as an expansion of the natural rights tradition (Melnick 1989).

No less than the Progressive creed, however, the new understanding of the Declaration of Independence required an assault on the established party system, which had long been allied with constitutional arrangements that favored a decentralization of power. This effort to weaken traditional party organization, begun during the Progressive era, became an enduring part of American politics with the consolidation of the New Deal political order. Nonetheless, Roosevelt's attack on partisanship was more ambivalent than that of his Progressive predecessors. Indeed, Roosevelt and his New Deal political allies, many of whom experienced first-hand the short-lived Progressive Party, recognized that the Democratic Party was a critical means to the creation of the administrative constitution they envisioned.

In part, Roosevelt hoped to overcome the state and local orientation of the party system, which was suited to congressional primacy and was poorly organized for progressive action by the national government, and establish an executive-centered party, more suitably organized for the expansion of national purposes. Roosevelt's administration modified traditional partisan practices in an effort to make the Democratic Party, as FDR put it, one of "militant liberalism" (Roosevelt 1938–50, 7: 31) This, in turn, would bring about a structural transformation of the party system, pitting a reformed Democratic party against a conservative Republican party.

The most dramatic moment in Roosevelt's challenge to traditional party practices was the so-called purge campaign of 1938. This campaign involved FDR directly in one gubernatorial and several congressional primary campaigns in a bold effort to replace conservative Democrats, particularly conservative Southerners, with candidates who were "100 percent New Dealers" (T. Stokes 1940, 503). FDR's extraordinary effort to remake his party was anticipated and attended by other important initiatives. For example, Roosevelt and his New Deal political allies won a hard fought battle to eliminate the "two-thirds" rule, championed by Southern Democrats, which required a candidate to receive two thirds of the convention delegate votes in order to win the party's nomination. After 1936, Roosevelt used political patronage to reward New Dealers rather than Democrats associated with the traditional party machinery, thus deploying an "ideological patronage" that further abetted the party's national, programmatic character (Van Riper 1958, 327). The administration also worked to expand the Democratic coalition to incorporate new groups and social movements, especially labor, African Americans, and women (Milkis 1993, chapter 3).

The Roosevelt administration's challenge to traditional partisan practices initiated a process whereby the party system evolved from predominantly local to national and programmatic organizations. And yet by recasting and giving political effect to progressive principles, the New Deal also made partisanship less important. Roosevelt's partisan leadership, although it brought about important changes in the Democratic Party, envisioned a personal link with the public that would enable the president to govern from the position as leader of the nation, not just the party that governed the nation (Frisch 1975, 79). Following the example TR set at the Progressive party convention, FDR accepted the 1932 Democratic nomination of his party in person setting a precedent within the two-party system and signaling the emergence of presidential campaigns conducted less by parties than by individual candidates. In the past, out of respect for collective responsibility, major party nominees had stayed away from the convention, waiting to be notified officially of their nomination. But FDR meant to show his party and the nation that he would not hesitate to break revered traditions that obstructed energetic presidential leadership. Moreover, like Wilson, Roosevelt rejected the Jeffersonian tradition that prohibited presidents from delivering important messages before Congress. With Roosevelt's 1933 State of the Union address this practice became an enduring routine—an annual ritual that, with the rise of the mass media, encouraged presidents to make direct appeals to public opinion. Indeed, exploiting the growing importance of radio broadcasting, FDR used his famous "fireside chats" to speak more directly and frequently to the people than any previous occupant of the White House. Finally, as the "purge" campaign exemplified, Roosevelt's often chose to make a direct appeal to public opinion rather than attempt to work through or to reform the regular party apparatus.

The "benign dictatorship" Roosevelt sought to impose on the Democratic Party was more conducive to corroding the American party system than reforming it. The emphasis FDR placed on forging a direct link between himself and the public echoed the Progressives' lack of faith in party politics and a deliberate attempt to supplant collective responsibility (based on the give and take between the president and Congress) with executive responsibility. The immense failure of the purge campaign reinforced this view (Milkis 1993, chapter 4).[2] More to the point, Roosevelt and his political allies did not view the welfare state as a partisan issue. The reform program of the 1930s was conceived as an "economic constitutional order" that should be established as much as possible in permanent programs, like Social Security, beyond the uncertainties of public opinion and elections. Unlike the Progressives who sought to weaken the judiciary's institutional power, FDR's controversial court-"packing" plan and judicial appointments presumed to transform the way the federal courts interpreted the Constitution, to codify the development of an executive-centered administrative state (McMahon 2003).

Similarly, the most significant institutional reform of the New Deal did not promote party government but fostered a program that would establish the president as the guardian of an expanding national state. This program, as embodied in the 1937 executive reorganization bill, would have greatly extended presidential authority over the executive branch, including the independent regulatory commissions. The president and executive agencies would also be delegated extensive authority to govern, making unnecessary the constant cooperation of party members in Congress.

Ironically, the administrative reform bill became, at Roosevelt's urging, a party government-style "vote of confidence" for the administration. Roosevelt initially lost this vote in 1938, when the reorganization bill was defeated in the House of Representatives, but he did manage to keep administrative reform sufficiently prominent in the party councils so that a compromise version passed in 1939.

With the 1939 Executive Reorganization Act, Roosevelt's extraordinary crisis leadership was, in effect, institutionalized. This statute ratified a process whereby public expectations and institutional arrangements established the president, rather than Congress or political parties, as the center of government activity. The reorganization act represents the genesis of the "administrative presidency," supported by an elaborate network of presidential aides, which was equipped to govern independently of the constraints imposed by the regular political process (Nathan 1983). The Roosevelt administration's civil service reform solidified this program to replace partisan politics with executive administration. Through executive order and legislation, Roosevelt extended merit protection to thousands of New Deal loyalists, most of whom had been brought into government outside of merit channels (Milkis 1993, chapter 6). Since the Progressive era, the choice was poised as one between politics and spoils, on the one hand, and nonpartisan, nonpolitical administration, on the other. As the administrative historian Paul Van Riper has noted, the New Deal celebrated a new form of administrative politics, "a sort of intellectual and ideological patronage rather than the more traditional partisan type" (Van Riper 1958, 327).

The modern presidency's independence from party politics was greatly augmented by World War II and the cold war. With the Great Depression giving way to war, another expansion of presidential power took place, as part of the national security state, further weakening the executive's ties with the party system. As the New Deal prepared for war, Roosevelt spoke not only of government's obligation to guarantee "freedom from want" but also of its responsibility to provide "freedom from fear"—to protect the American people, and the world, against foreign aggression. This obligation to uphold "human rights" became a new guarantee of security, which presupposed a further expansion of national administrative power (Roosevelt 1938–50, 9: 671–72). The forces of internationalism allowed Roosevelt's successor, Harry Truman, to persuade Congress to carry out additional administrative reform in 1947, which increased the powers of, and centralized control over, the National Security State. Dubbed the National Security Act, it created the National Security Council, the Central Intelligence Agency, and the Department of Defense (Shefter 2002, 123).

The Administrative State and the Fracturing of Liberalism

The consolidation of the modern presidency during the 1930s and 1940s transformed the executive office dramatically, with profound consequences for American democracy. Before FDR, the presidency was a simple office; the White House Office—the "West Wing"—did not exist. But in the wake of the "Roosevelt revolution, people in that wing of the White House came to form the nerve center of the Executive Office of the President (EOP). As the EOP, which also included important staff agencies such as the Bureau of the Budget[3] and the Council of Economic Advisors, developed into an elaborate institution, presidents no longer ran for office and governed as the head of a party; instead, they campaigned and sought to enact programs as the head of personal organizations they created in their own image. These institutions carried out tasks party leaders and organizations once performed, such as staffing the executive branch, connecting the president to interest groups, formulating public policy, and directing campaigns. Perhaps most important, the presidential staff played a critical part in enabling the president to communicate with the people. Roosevelt was not only the first president to make effective use of the radio, he also was the first to make extensive use of surveys and pollsters, thus giving the president information about what the people were thinking and how they were responding to his program (Eisinger and Brown 1998; Jacobs 2005; Milkis 2002).

The emancipation of the presidency from the traditional constitutional order anchored by localized parties gave rise to "potentialities and pathologies" (James 2005, 25). On one hand, the modern executive allowed for a more expansive national state that responded effectively to domestic and international crises. Absent an independent executive, it is difficult to imagine the federal government possessing the national resolve to tackle disruptive economic insecurity and forced segregation at home or fascism and communism abroad. On the other hand, the rise of the modern presidency and the administrative state risked the recrudescence of the political diseases that reared their ugly head during the Progressive era: a plebiscitary politics in which effective and responsible leadership was dependent on the accident of personality; a tendency for presidents to rely extensively on unilateral executive action that denigrated Congress and encouraged corrosive interbranch conflict; and a serious decline in public interest, trust, and participation in government and politics. Indeed, the flowering of the modern presidency raised the fundamental question of whether a distant president, no matter how perspicacious, can forge meaningful links with the public.

The promise and the limitations of the modern presidency came into full relief when Lyndon Johnson assumed the office. Roosevelt's pronouncement of two new freedoms—Freedom from Want and Freedom from Fear—proclaimed and began the task of establishing the executive as the guardian of an administrative constitution, but it fell to Johnson to "codify the New Deal vision of a good society" (Rovere 1965, 118). This program entailed expanding the economic constitutional order with such policy innovations as Medicare, Medicaid, and, even more important, extending those benefits to African Americans. It also required upholding liberal internationalism's "containment" policy as the cold war metastasized into a protracted struggle to control the development of third world countries in Southeast Asia.

Johnson's attempt to fulfill the promise of the modern presidency accelerated the effort to transcend partisan politics. LBJ took Roosevelt's experience to be the best example of the generally ephemeral nature of party government in the United States, and he fully expected the cohesive Democratic support he received in Congress after the 1964 election to be temporary. Moreover, Johnson's greatest programmatic achievement, the enactment of the 1964 and 1965 Civil Rights bills, created considerable friction between the White House and local party organizations, especially in the South. Thus Johnson, like Roosevelt, looked beyond the party system toward the politics of "enlightened administration."

The early years of the Johnson presidency marked the historic height of presidential government. Equally important, the civil rights acts enlisted the president and several executive agencies in an ongoing effort to ban racial discrimination. These laws empowered the federal bureaucracy—especially the Department of Justice, the Department of Health, Education, and Welfare, and the newly formed Equal Employment Opportunity Commission—to assist the courts in successfully creating enforcement mechanisms for civil rights (see Milkis 1993, chapters 7 and 8; Milkis 2008). These proved effective, greatly accelerating the desegregation of Southern schools and the registration of black voters below the Mason-Dixon Line. No sooner had liberalism crested, however, than it fractured. Since the 1930s, Democratic presidents had emphasized administrative politics that had reduced their dependence on traditional party organizations and practices. By the end of the 1960s, executive aggrandizement was giving way to a battle over how to use the national administrative power forged on the New Deal and the Great Society. With the enactment of the Voting Rights Act of 1965, Johnson ensured the transformation of Southern Democracy that had eluded FDR. Civil Rights reform freed the Democratic Party from its most conservative wing. But this gain in doctrinal consistency came at the price of weakening the Democratic coalition, ultimately driving a majority of Southern white voters into the Republican Party and sharply reducing the size of the southern Democratic congressional delegation. Moreover, the Voting Rights Act substantially increased the number of black voters in the South, thus assuring that those seats that remained in Democratic hands would tend to be much more liberal than those representatives who balked at Roosevelt's "court-packing" and executive reorganization plans.

The transformation of Southern politics, fueled by deep division over race, was reinforced by the Johnson administration's decision to expand the American troop commitment in Vietnam. Not only did this action accentuate the isolation of the White House from Congress and the public, but it also further fractured the liberal coalition. The Vietnam War drove many younger middle class liberals to oppose executive prerogative in foreign affairs. Meanwhile Southern whites, as well as other formerly strong Democratic constituencies such as Northern Catholics, supported Republican presidents who were inclined to use U.S. military power (Shefter 2002, 124–25). These developments dramatically changed the New Deal party system, preparing the ground for the rise of more national and programmatic parties. With the rise of a "new" party system, moreover, the modern executive became complicit in heated partisan conflicts that both renewed and dramatically transformed the relationship between presidents and parties.

Ronald Reagan and the Stirrings of National Partisanship

Ronald Reagan was the first modern president to pose fundamental challenges to received government arrangements, a stance that required the support of a national, programmatic Republican Party. Swept into office on principled opposition to the New Deal and Great Society, it was thus fitting that he would also initiate important changes to the relationship between the presidency and the political parties. In addition to reinvigorating the Republican Party's hostility to the liberal administrative state, Reagan would invest in the GOP's organizational and fundraising capacity, suggesting that modern presidential leadership was not inconsistent with party-building. Nonetheless, Reagan's party leadership was shaped, and in important respects overshadowed by the modern presidency. Conceiving of the modern presidency as a two-edged sword that could cut in a conservative as well as a liberal direction, the Reagan White House emphasized popular appeals and administrative politics that ultimately undermined collective responsibility.[4]

Reagan's basic message was that centrally administered government demoralized and enervated its citizenry (Berman 1990; Heclo 2003; McAlister 2003; Muir 1988). In the context of the late 1970s and early 1980s Reagan's rhetorical assaults on the liberal administrative state and his paeans to individual responsibility were powerful party-building maneuvers. The president's forceful oratory altered the national political agenda, placing Republican issues such as tax and budget cuts, defense spending, and traditional morality at the center of American politics, and consolidated linkages between the Republican Party and constituencies such as Southern whites, suburbanites, union workers, and Catholics (Beck 1988; Busch 2001, chapter 5; Ginsberg and Shefter 1990). These developments permitted Republicans to dominate presidential politics during the 1980s and early 1990s and forced the Democrats to accept fundamental departures from liberal orthodoxy. Bill Clinton, the Democrats' presidential standard-bearer during the 1990s, repeatedly sought the center during his presidency; his "third way" approach to leadership championed welfare reform, free trade, government "reinvention,"[5] and accountability in education (Skowronek 1997, postscript).

Reagan's rhetoric was coupled with unusual attention to the exigencies of party leadership. Building on efforts by Republican Party leaders in the 1960s and 1970s, Reagan encouraged the further improvement of the party's organizational and fundraising capacity (Klinkner 1994, 133–54). His efforts to ensconce allies in the RNC—particularly his pick of Richard Richards for the RNC chairmanship—proved to be a boon for the party, strengthening its fundraising and improving coordination of campaign efforts and policy development between the RNC and the White House. The president's frequent speeches and fundraising appearances on behalf of the party's congressional candidates served to fortify the party's organizational base. These efforts contributed to the GOP's widening organizational advantage over the Democrats during the 1980s (Galvin 2009 ; Mason 2008; Milkis and Rhodes 2007a).

Still, Reagan's efforts to square the institution of the modern presidency with the demands of party leadership were only partially successful. While Reagan waged a rhetorical assault on modern liberalism, he failed at key moments to present his programs in the strongly partisan terms that would give voters a compelling reason to endorse enduring Republican leadership or a fundamental reshaping of liberal programs. Most important, his reelection campaign of 1984—celebrating the ostentatiously nonpartisan theme of "Morning in America"—was a personalistic, media-driven campaign that did not attempt to make a strong case for conservative programs (Mason 2008; Troy 2007). This executive-centered campaign drained the election of the broad political meaning that might have boosted the fortunes of Republican congressional candidates. Moreover, flagging Republican strength in Congress denied Reagan the support necessary to pose a fundamental challenge to the institutional foundation of the New Deal–Great Society order. When the Republicans did finally gain control of the House and Senate in the highly charged partisan contests of 1994, they did so in the middle of Clinton's first term. Moreover, Clinton skillfully foiled the aggressive partisan maneuvers of Speaker of the House Newt Gingrich in an eyeball-to-eyeball confrontation over the future of Medicare that strengthened the Democratic president's hold on the political center and launched his successful 1996 reelection campaign.

Without a strong Republican congressional presence to reinforce and advance his reconstructive ambitions, Reagan was increasingly forced to retreat to administrative politics to achieve his policy objectives. Indeed, his campaign to master the bureaucracy was "more self-conscious in design and execution, and more comprehensive in scope, than that of any other administration in the modern era" (Benda and Levine 1988). The Reagan White House made extensive use of staffing authority, regulatory review, and executive orders to achieve its policy goals (Aberbach 2005; Stehr 1997). These moves were often supported by the president's congressional allies; at the same time, the emphasis on executive administration undermined collective responsibility for policy and threatened the stability of the Republican coalition. The scope of the administration's efforts to impose its will through the bureaucracy suggested that Reagan's ambitions substantially outstripped congressional support. The Reagan administration's political isolation was confirmed when the White House's most ambitious administrative maneuvers—its efforts to cut Social Security benefits and support Contra insurgents in Nicaragua—produced political embarrassment for the president and his party (Derthick and Teles 2003; Ehrman 2005, chapter 4).

Reagan's ambiguous legacy of presidential party leadership illustrated the difficulty of reconciling partisanship with modern presidential power. There is a real sense in which Reagan's emphasis on presidential politics was a logical response to the liberal administrative state. The New Deal, like its successor the Great Society, was less a partisan program than an exercise in expanding the president's rhetorical and administrative powers. It is not surprising, then, that the challenge to liberal policies that culminated in the elevation of Reagan to the White House produced an effort to deploy the modern executive for conservative objectives. For a time, at least, this development retarded the revival of partisanship.

George W. Bush and the "New" American Party System

The promise and pitfalls of executive-centered partisanship would be cast in further relief during the presidency of George W. Bush. During his first six years in office, Bush elaborated on the partisan practices embraced by Ronald Reagan, prompting the further evolution of the "new" American Party System. Indeed, Bush surpassed Reagan with his dramatic and unprecedented efforts to build his party at the congressional, grassroots, and organizational levels. Bush's presidency also revealed that the modern administrative state, so often anathema to party-building, could be wielded to advance partisan objectives. Indeed, the Bush administration's party-building efforts were allied to an attempt to redefine Republican conservatism that envisioned exploiting rather than rolling back national administrative power. These efforts helped produce a remarkable string of electoral victories for Republicans at all levels of government. Until the 2006 elections, in fact, the party was as strong as at any point since the 1920s. Nonetheless, in the final analysis, Bush's presidency, which ended with record-low approval ratings and Republican defeats in 2006 and 2008, demonstrates the enduring tension between the modern presidency and a vigorous party system.

Brought to the White House in the remarkably close and highly controversial 2000 election, Bush's sustained attention to party leadership stemmed from his realization that his ambitious domestic and foreign policy agendas would founder without vigorous popular and partisan support. His administration thus sought to reconcile presidential and party leadership with a comprehensive effort to form an executive-centered Republican organization. At the rhetorical level, Bush believed that building an enduring Republican majority would require redressing Reagan's "blind spot" to the important role government had come to play in people's lives (Heclo 2003; Milkis and Rhodes 2007a). Rather than curtail New Deal and Great Society entitlements, as the Reagan administration and Gingrich-led 104th Congress attempted, the president and his Republican congressional allies, sought to recast them in a more conservative image. Bush proposed to change federal and state regulations to permit private "faith-based" charitable organizations to play a larger role in providing government services to disadvantaged members of society. Instead of eliminating the Department of Education, as Reagan had proposed, Bush championed No Child Left Behind, which requires all states to set educational standards and hold schools accountable for results. To signal his concern for the elderly, he fought for a costly expansion of Medicare that would add coverage for prescription drugs, albeit with provisions that might set the program on the road to privatization (Beland and Waddan 2007; Fortier and Ornstein 2003; Mucciaroni and Quirk 2004). Even Bush's ill-fated proposal to permit Americans to invest portions of their Social Security savings presumed that the government would continue to require Americans to save for their retirements and control their investment strategies. Although Bush fought successfully for issues that appealed to the Republican base—most notably, massive tax cuts, punitive welfare reforms, class-action lawsuit reforms, and a ban on "partial birth" abortions—his domestic agenda was crafted to redirect, rather than retrench, national administrative power, and thereby appeal to a broader swath of the American public (Milkis and Rhodes 2007a, 2007b).

Bush's unprecedented efforts to strengthen the national Republican organization demonstrated the impressive potential of the modern presidency as an instrument of party building. In 2002, 2004, and 2006, Bush proved himself a committed party leader, raising funds for campaigns and stumping for candidates (Bass 2004; Beachler 2004; Busch 2005; G. C. Jacobson 2003; Milkis and Rhodes 2007a). Moreover, attempting to meld executive prerogative and party strategy, the Bush White House sought to make the president's personal leadership of the war on terrorism a partisan issue, trumpeting Republicans' superiority over Democrats in matters of national and homeland security. This sharply partisan approach to foreign affairs reaped dividends in 2002 and 2004, with the Republicans consolidating their hold on both houses of Congress. Indeed, Bush became the first modern president since Franklin Roosevelt to win a second term while his party was gaining seats in the House and Senate.

The most innovative, and potentially consequential, component of Bush's party leadership was the administration's cultivation of a "national party machine." The "machine," which emerged from Bush-Cheney and GOP strategists' disappointment with Republican turnout in the 2000 presidential election, was an effort to systematically organize and mobilize the party's grassroots supporters. Relying on a combination of centralized hierarchy and decentralized volunteer effort, the GOP's grassroots campaign sought to develop personal lines of communication between the Bush campaign and local activists. Campaign volunteers, recruited by professional staff on the ground as well as through e-mail and the Internet, were charged with responsibilities for reaching specific goals developed by the Bush-Cheney headquarters: recruiting additional volunteers, organizing rallies and campaign events, writing letters to the editor, registering voters, or canvassing particular neighborhoods. Campaign officials in the states oversaw grassroots activity with tough love, holding volunteers accountable for meeting performance targets set by higher local officials.[6] The campaign was highly successful in mobilizing supporters and voters: campaign officials estimate that between 1.2 and 1.4 million individuals volunteered for the campaign nationwide. Significantly, the grassroots machine was calibrated not only to bolster the president's reelection bid but to advance GOP prospects across the board. The Bush organization, coordinating with the Republican National Committee, emphasized reaching and turning out "lazy Republicans" who were predisposed to vote for Republicans at all levels but who were unreliable in their voting habits (Milkis and Rhodes 2007a).

Energized by the Bush-Cheney mobilization, the 2004 election appeared to mark an important advance of a nationalized party system. The Republicans and, in a more defensive posture, the Democrats, had made efforts since the 1970s to strengthen their discipline in Congress and to become a valuable source of campaign funds and other services for candidates. But the halting development of national, programmatic parties, overshadowed in important ways by Republican presidents' infatuation with the modern presidency, had failed to stir the passions and allegiances of the American people, as attested by the declining voter turnout from the 1970s to 2000. In contrast, the 2004 election was passionate, polarized, and participatory, redressing the long secular decline of voting turnout (Abramowitz and Stone 2006; McDonald 2004, 2005). Beyond its immediate effectiveness in securing Bush's reelection, then, the Republicans' White House-inspired mobilization effort in 2004 provided a plausible blueprint for revitalized party politics that draws more people into the political process and renews the linkages between citizens and their elected officials.

At the same time, Bush's administrative presidency threatened to undermine the party's forward march. Reagan made extensive use of executive administration at a time when Congress was usually in the hands of Democrats. That Bush also made considerable use of the administrative mechanisms to achieve his goals, even when his party controlled both houses of Congress, suggests that the administrative presidency might impede the emergence of a more collaborative, party-centered policy process under the most favorable circumstances. Indeed, subscribing to the "unitary executive" prescribed by Vice President Cheney, Bush became a more zealous defender of presidential prerogatives than his Republican predecessor (Jones 2007; Pfiffner 2008; Rudalevige 2005).[7] The president's staffing practices and aggressive use of the Office of Management and Budget's powers of regulatory review were gauged to maximize presidential control over the civil service. In domestic and foreign policy Bush made extensive use of executive orders, signing statements, and regulatory rule-making to achieve significant departures from past policy. The president also used executive orders to make headway on controversial social issues, launching "faith-based" initiatives, limiting funding for stem-cell research, and denying funds to family-planning organizations overseas that offered abortion counseling (Aberbach 2008; Rudalevige 2005). Although these efforts often had the support of congressional Republicans, they also suggested that the Bush administration preferred to transcend institutions of collective responsibility rather than work through them to achieve compromise or consensus. Even when the administration sought to work with Congressional Republicans, it tended to do so in a heavy handed manner as when Vice President Cheney, sometimes with Bush's top political strategist, Karl Rove in tow, intruded on senate Republicans' weekly strategy sessions to press the administration's views on its GOP leaders (Mahler 2008).

Bush's administrative strategy not only impeded the emergence of a more collaborative, party-centered policy process, it also contributed directly to the party's declining fortunes after 2004. The administration's ineffectual response to the Hurricane Katrina disaster undermined the claim to administrative competence that had previously bolstered the Republican Party. The negative consequences of Bush's administrative overreaching for the GOP were most evident in the fallout from the White House's imperious and insulated management of the war in Iraq and the broader war on terrorism. Determined to wage war on its own terms, the Bush administration made a series of unilateral decisions that departed from historic and legal convention: it would deny habeas corpus rights to "enemy combatants" captured in the war on terrorism; abrogate the Geneva Conventions, and sanction torture of detainees during interrogations; and engage in warrantless surveillance of American citizens suspected of communicating with alleged terrorists abroad (Pfiffner 2008). When these controversial decisions were revealed, they provoked widespread public condemnation and damaged the GOP's public support. The administration's insistence on a free hand to manage the war in Iraq resulted in the erosion of public confidence in the Republican Party as it became clear that the administration had badly botched reconstruction efforts (M. Jacobson 2008; Schier 2009, chapter 5). As the 2006 elections revealed, well before the 2008 economic crisis overwhelmed all other issues, the administration's and the party's prestige had been severely wounded.

Reagan might have erred on the side of insufficient attention to party-building; Bush's experience illustrated the risks posed by overweening presidential partisanship. Ironically, the very vigorousness of the Bush administration's party leadership—and the evident dependence of the GOP on Bush's stewardship—endangered the integrity of the Republican Party. Between 2001 and 2005, the GOP relied heavily on Bush's personal charisma and prestige as a wartime leader for its political sustenance (Abramson, Rickershauer, and Rhode 2007; G. C. Jacobson 2003; Milkis and Rhodes 2007a). Both the 2002 and the 2004 elections celebrated executive power, turning on the issues of international and domestic security that emphasized the modern presidency as the center of government. The White House also played a dominant role in organizing the massive grassroots efforts that characterized the 2004 election cycle and stimulating public participation in these efforts (Milkis and Rhodes 2007a). Although this approach reaped political dividends for GOP candidates in the short run, it threatened to make the party subservient to presidential authority and to enervate its capacity to hold the president accountable to broader principles. The modern GOP thus appeared to signal a political future where the party would "in effect [becomes] whatever the president needs it to be, and whatever capacity it had to hold its leaders to account would accordingly be lost" (Skowronek 2005, 829). The ironic denouement of this development was revealed following the 2008 presidential election, in which many Republicans blamed Bush, whom they had previously followed with alacrity, for casting them into the political wilderness.

Barack Obama, the 2008 Presidential Election, and the Future of the "New" American Party System

Democratic Senator Barack Obama of Illinois offered the voters "Change We Can Believe In" during the 2008 presidential campaign. But his extraordinary two-year quest for the White House left unclear what kind of change he proposed. Calling on the people to trust in the "audacity of hope," Senator Obama ran an idealistic campaign that sought to reprise the modern presidency's role as "steward of the public welfare." He pledged to bring Americans together and to overcome the raw partisanship that had polarized the Washington community for nearly two decades and that had begun to divide the country during George W. Bush's eight years in office. "In the face of despair, you believe there can be hope," he told the large, enthusiastic audience that gathered in Springfield, Illinois, in February 2007, to hear him announce his candidacy for the presidency. "In the face of politics that's shut you out, that's told you to settle, that's divided us for too long, you believe we can be one people, reaching for what's possible, building that more perfect union" (Obama 2007). As the child of a white mother from Kansas and a black father from Kenya, a man of color raised in Hawaii and Indonesia, and a reformer schooled in Chicago politics as a member of the post-civil rights generation, Obama seemed to embody the aspirations of the entire nation—to transcend, as no previous modern president could, the racial, ethnic, religious, and economic differences that long had divided the country.

To be sure, Obama aroused considerable opposition among conservatives, who dismissed him as a doctrinaire liberal posing as a statesman who could lift the nation out of the muck of partisan rancor. His candidacy was also heavily criticized by his chief rival for the Democratic nomination, Senator Hillary Clinton of New York, the former first lady who, as the first strong woman candidate for president, also had a legitimate claim to inherit the progressive mantle. To a remarkable degree, however, Obama overshadowed Clinton in inspiring the admiration of the country: he was cast perfectly it seemed to play the role chartered by the architects of the modern presidency.

Yet Obama and his leading advisers also saw enormous potential in the national party politics that George W. Bush had practiced. His organizational efforts, in fact, were modeled on the techniques that Republicans had pioneered in 2004. Eschewing the Democrats' traditional reliance on organized labor and other auxiliary organizations to mobilize the party faithful, Obama vowed to wage a "fifty-state campaign" (a policy developed by DNC Chair Howard Dean) that would "build grassroots organizations" in every state, help "elect Democrats down the ballot," and register millions of new voters who would support his cause. Obama's organizational strategy, combining Internet-based recruiting of volunteers, the use of data files to carefully target potential loyalists, and old-fashioned door-to-door canvassing, elaborated on Bush tactics that had worked successfully in 2004 (Rutenberg 2008b). The remarkable effectiveness of Obama's fundraising operation, which drew heavily on small, Internet-solicited donations, further reflected lessons learned from the Bush campaign. The Obama campaign developed an unprecedented capacity to raise funds, so much so that the Illinois Senator became the first presidential candidate to refuse public funds for the general election.

Like the formidable Bush-Cheney machine of 2004, the Obama-Biden organization relied in part on the regular party apparatus. Democratic National Committee DNC chairman Howard Dean's decision to extend the reach of his party's campaign efforts beyond the battleground states laid a foundation that state and local party leaders credited with contributing significantly to the party's impressive victories in 2006 and 2008. Just as the Bush-Cheney machine of 2004 resulted in a Republican victory, so the Obama-Biden campaign of 2008 resulted not only in a decisive triumph at the presidential level but also substantial gains in House and Senate races. This success was in large measure the result of voters' unhappiness with Bush, who had mired the country in an unpopular war and a severe financial crisis. But Obama's sophisticated grassroots campaign linked a vast network of volunteers, elicited enormous enthusiasm among potential supporters, and mobilized the highest voter turnout since 1968. Coming on the heels of the substantial increase in voter participation in the 2004 election, the 2008 campaign appeared to confirm the emergence of a national party system that was ameliorating the chronic voter apathy that had afflicted the presidency-centered administrative state.

Nevertheless, the further development of an executive-centered party system has not eliminated the tension between presidential and party leadership. Hoping to reap the benefits of their party-building efforts during the election, Obama campaign officials announced in January 2009 that the new administration intended to maintain the grassroots campaign in order to press the president's agenda and lay the groundwork for his reelection. "Organizing for America" was housed in the DNC, headed by Virginia governor Timothy Kaine, who had endorsed Obama's candidacy early in the primary fight and provided critical support for his general election campaign. Dubbed "Barack Obama 2.0" by insiders, the plan called for hiring full-time organizers to mobilize the Internet-based grassroots network forged during the presidential campaign, which had generated a database of 13 million e-mail addresses and tens of thousands of phone bank volunteers and neighborhood coordinators. During the first year of Obama's presidency, Organizing for America engaged in Internet-based grassroots mobilization for important policies such as the administration's stimulus package, its budget bill, and health care reform. Grassroots mobilization became particularly important during the summer and fall of 2009, as the president and his Democratic allies struggled to get a health reform plan through Congress in the face of concerted Republican opposition and growing voter unease about the potential regulatory burdens and costs of reform (Eggen 2009). Although most Democrats and liberal groups welcomed these campaign style events, the DNC strategy aroused tensions with moderate—"Blue Dog"—Democrats, who did not welcome the idea that Obama's political network might target them from within their own states and districts. Moreover, although some state-level Democratic officials were enthusiastic about imbedding Obama's machine in the DNC because they viewed Organizing for America as an extension of Dean's fifty-state strategy, others expressed concern that it could become a competing political force that revolved around the president's ambitions while diminishing the needs of other Democrats (Wallstein 2008).

Obama's aides, including his highly regarded campaign manager, David Plouffe, denied that Obama 2.0 was merely a permanent campaign to advance the president's fortunes. They insisted that the grassroots network's purpose was to deliver on the reform that Obama and his party had promised during the 2008 election. Moreover, the president's political aides assured their partisan brethren that Obama 2.0 would be a force in mobilizing support for Democratic candidates in the 2010 congressional and state races (Taddeo 2009). Congressional Republicans' near-unanimous resistance to the president's overtures for bipartisan support of his emergency economic stimulus bill in February 2009 appeared to confirm the need to sustain a strong Democratic organization.

It remains to be seen, however, whether the vaunted Obama machine can be transformed into a durable organization that simultaneously strengthens the administration and bolsters the Democratic Party. Like the Bush-Cheney machine, the Obama-Biden campaign organization benefited other Democratic candidates. At the same time, just as the 2004 Republican campaign was directed by Bush-Cheney strategists, so was the 2008 Democratic grassroots effort run out of the Obama-Biden headquarters. The architects of the Obama campaign praised Dean's fifty-state strategy, but they relied almost completely on their own staff, money, and organization, not only to compete in battleground states but also to make incursions into traditional Republican territory. And just as the Bush-Cheney machine relied on volunteers whose principal loyalty was to the president, so did the Obama-Biden grassroots organization rest in the volunteers' deep admiration for the Democratic standard-bearer (Nagourney 2008). As one liberal blogger fretted toward the end of the 2008 election, "Power and money in the Democratic Party is being centralized around a key iconic figure. [Obama] is consolidating power within the party." Embedding the Obama campaign organization in the DNC only served to reinforce this concern, arousing fears that Obama was building an "Obama party" (Goldstein and Klein 2008).

Beyond the 2008 election, then, the Democrats will be challenged to sustain a collective commitment independent of their devotion to Obama. The Bush administration was split between presidential loyalists and those who wanted to meld the campaign organization with the GOP. The Obama administration, following a campaign that promised to bring about a "postpartisan age," is likely to be even more divided between advisors who want to integrate the campaign into the party structure and those who view the vast network of activists, neighborhood organizers, and volunteers as a force that should remain "an independent entity—organized around the 'Obama brand'" (Wallstein and Hamburger 2008; Saslow 2009).

The question remains, therefore, whether the profound revival of the modern executive's governing authority in the wake of 9/11 has brought a national party system to fruition or continued the long-term development of a modern presidency that renders collective partisanship impractical. Indeed, there is a real sense that the "new" party system may be a creature of, and dependent on, the modern presidency. When asked how his initial appointments to administrative positions, many of whom were old Washington hands, would carry out the campaign's promise to transform national politics, President-elect Obama replied, "What we are going to do is combine experience with fresh thinking. But understand where vision for change comes from first and foremost. It comes from me" (Corn 2008). This assertion of presidential prerogative dovetailed with Obama's plan to concentrate more power in the West Wing than any president since Nixon. In organizing the White House Office, he assembled a group of policy "czars" who would have broad programmatic authority to "cut through—or leapfrog—the traditional bureaucracy" in matters of national security, climate change, economic policy, health care, housing, and education (King 2009; Sheer and Connolly 2009). Similarly, President Obama's early days in the White House saw him reverse a number of important domestic and foreign policies with the stroke of the pen, including an executive order that banned the use of controversial CIA interrogation tactics (Eggen and Sheer 2009). Finally, although the president changed course on the War on Terror, proscribing the use of torture against foreign detainees and setting a timetable for withdrawal from Iraq, he vowed to continue, indeed expand, the struggle against radical Islam in Pakistan and Afghanistan. This policy, which makes impractical any retreat from the strong claims of presidential prerogative that marked the Bush presidency, had stronger support from Republicans than it did from Democrats (Wilson and Partloe 2009).

Recent developments thus suggest that executive aggrandizement will likely continue to complicate efforts to achieve greater collective responsibility for policymaking. More significantly, the very vigor of strong party leaders such as George W. Bush and Barack Obama threatens the integrity of political parties as collective organizations with a past and a future. During the Progressive era, at the dawn of the modern presidency, the militant reformer Herbert Croly noted that Woodrow Wilson's effort to put his stamp on the Democratic Party suggested that aggressive executive partisanship might erode the integrity of collective responsibility, even as it strengthens party organization in the short term: "At the final test, the responsibility is his [the president's] rather than the party's. The party which submits to such a dictatorship, however benevolent, cannot play its own proper part in the system of government. It will either cease to have any independent life or its independence will eventually assume the form of revolt" (Croly 1914, 346). Croly's observation about the inherently antagonistic relationship between collective responsibility and executive dominion was made in a context when localized, decentralized parties prevailed. Yet it still may provide guidance for analyzing the dynamics of the relationship between the president and parties in an era of modern administration and nationalized, programmatic parties.

Notes

1. The secret ballot made voting decisions, which were made in public until the end of the nineteenth century, confidential, thus forestalling efforts by party organizations to intimidate voters.
2. All but two of the incumbent Democrats whom Roosevelt opposed were renominated. Widely condemned as an assault on the constitutional system of checks and balances, Roosevelt's actions galvanized the political opposition, likely contributing to the heavy losses the Democrats sustained in the 1938 general elections.
3. Richard Nixon issued an executive order on July 1, 1970 that transformed the Bureau of the Budget into the Office of Management and Budget, with a new

supervisory layer of presidentially appointed assistant directors for policy inserted between the OMB directors and the office's senior civil servants. Consequently, the budget office, already part of a burgeoning presidential institution, not only assumed more responsibility for administrative management but also became even more responsive to the president.

4. Reagan's administrative partisanship was not created out of whole cloth; it resorted to some of the same tactics that Richard Nixon and his staff had first deployed. Like Nixon, Reagan centralized power in the White House, thus preempting the Republican Party organization's political responsibilities; like Nixon, too, Reagan pursued his programs with acts of administrative discretion that weakened efforts to carry out broad-based policy programs. Reagan's rhetoric and executive administration were more purposeful than Nixon's, and tended to please conservative stalwarts. Still, the centrality of presidential politics and policymaking highlighted the White House's failure to make a compelling public case for a *Republican* realignment or a fundamental reshaping of liberal programs. Reagan thus left an ambivalent legacy of presidential party leadership that would prefigure George W. Bush's subsequent experience.

5. "Reinventing Government" built on the ideas of journalist David Osborne and former city manager Ted Gabler, who argued that the failure of traditional bureaucracies to solve basic social and economic problems demonstrated the need for an alternative standard, centralized administration. Although the Clinton program, chaired by Vice President Al Gore, did not so reorient the federal bureaucracy, it did accomplish more than its critics anticipated. As one prominent scholar of the American bureaucracy has written, "It energized employees…attracted citizens…drew media attention to government management,… and made the point that management matters" (Kettl 1994, ix).

6. Matthew Dowd, political strategist for the Bush-Cheney 2004 campaign, insisted that a *centralized* grassroots campaign was not an oxymoron. The "ground war" was built with community volunteers, but "once they volunteered, we ask them to do certain things. A national organization had to have a consistent message and mechanics. If the message is not consistent, if task are not systematically assigned, the campaign will implode. This was the message of the [failed Howard] Dean campaign: letting people loose can get the candidate in trouble. The message and organization must be relatively disciplined" (Personal Interview with Matthew Dowd, July 6, 2004).

7. Like progressivism, the theory of the unitary executive claims considerable discretionary power for the president. Unlike the architects of the modern presidency, however, advocates of the unitary executive proscribe innovative institution building. Invoking Hamilton, it rests the case for presidential aggrandizement "squarely on the Constitution as it was originally conceived and ratified" (Skowronek 2009).

Chapter 13

Consequences of Electoral and Institutional Change

The Evolution of Conditional Party Government in the U.S. House of Representatives[1]

David Rohde and John Aldrich

The U.S. Congress has changed in many ways over the last fifty years, but perhaps the most dramatic has been the changing role of the political parties. David Mayhew's study of the Congress (published in 1974) argued that political parties were weak institutions in the Congress, and that they were weak because the members wanted it that way.[2] Virtually as he was writing, the Democratic Party (in the midst of its forty-year reign as majority party), began revising its own rules to strengthen its party organization and its leadership in the House. These changing electoral and legislative circumstances resulted, in time, in the passage of more partisan legislation. That is, many of the most important pieces of legislation, after these changes were fully in place, passed with a greater degree of party-line voting and with policy content that was closer to the views of a now more consensual majority in the Democratic Party than was true in the House Mayhew examined (see chapter 1 for a discussion of changes in party unity). This trend continued, indeed even expanded, when the Republican Party won majority control in the 1994 elections, and has persisted with the return of Democrats to power.

Why these changes? Their immediate cause was that the members increasingly came to favor stronger over weaker parties—they wanted it this new way rather than the way they had devised in the era Mayhew studied. That, in turn, raises the question of why they wanted to increase the strength of the political party in the House and, thus, why they revised the party's and even the chamber's rules to achieve a more partisan-focused set of ends. The primary answer to that question is that electoral circumstances changed greatly in the 1960s and 1970s and even into the 1980s. In particular, the Democratic Party had long been divided between Northern and Southern wings, and thus between more liberal and more conservative members. The South, through the 1960s, remained an essentially one-party region, with Republicans finding it very difficult to compete effectively in all but a handful of districts. As civil rights and related issues became a more prominent part of the agenda of congressional politics in the 1960s, the Democratic Party was split increasingly deeply between liberal Northerners and conservative Southerners, all the while nonetheless retaining majority status.[3] Thus, while the Democratic Party controlled the House, it was a deeply divided majority, one that could find agreement on fewer major issues than many majority parties had historically. Therefore, there was little that the majority party leadership could do that both wings wanted to achieve and, as a result, the party gave that leadership little power to work with.

Change came through elections. In 1953, for example, the Republicans held only 6 percent of the seats in the South but 65 percent of those in the East. By the 1970s, the Republicans carried about a quarter of the Southern House districts, but dipped under a half of those in the East. In 1981, they held over a third of the Southern House seats, and, by 2009, the GOP held a majority of the seats from the South (by now their strongest region) and under a fifth of the seats in the East.[4] The coming of a competitive Republican Party to Southern elections and compensating changes in other regions meant that there were fewer Southern Democrats in total and that those who remained (particularly those newly elected) had relatively more liberal voters supporting them. The Democratic constituencies were more liberal because of the incorporation of African Americans and poorer whites into the electorate, and because Republican candidates were taking many more votes from the most conservative end of the spectrum. These electoral changes meant that, in the House as a whole, Southern Democrats were no longer as distinctive from their Northern peers, and thus greater party consensus was able to be achieved on what kinds of legislation would be desirable, both for their own concerns and in their run for reelection in the next election. Moreover, there was greater differentiation between Democrats and Republicans on policy (chapter 1 provides evidence of this growing differentiation). Thus, elections induced more polarized parties in the Congress, with greater consensus within each party, and with increased distinctiveness of views between the two parties. The final step, then, was the organizational one. For at this point, the majority party had more policy agreement, and with that they had greater reason to give their leadership (and thus the House's leadership) more powerful tools by which they could translate that increased consensus into actual legislation.

This broad-brush view, then, is that electoral conditions had changed from the days Mayhew was describing, leading the House members to want more powerful parties so as to achieve more consensual partisan ends. Thus we call this explanation of changes in the strength of political parties "conditional party government" (CPG). When, as Mayhew described about the 1950s and 1960s, conditions were not favorable for relatively stronger parties in the chamber, then Members favored weaker party leaders and preferred power allocated via committees and seniority. When conditions were different— when, that is, voters elected members who had greater consensus among their fellow partisans in the Congress and greater division between the two parties (as has been the case for the last quarter century)—then they strengthened their party in the House. This is the general statement of the explanation, and the rest of this paper develops this more carefully and discusses the Congress in light of this theory of conditional party government.

In chapter 1 there are data about the effects of these changes on increasing policy polarization in the Congress and on increasing party unity (voting along party lines on the floor). We can see this in a slightly different way in Figure 13.1. Central to our argument is the combination of separation between the two parties on important policy considerations, that is, of polarization, and the increasing homogeneity of policy preferences among members of the same party, especially within the majority party—this is the "condition" in conditional party government. In Figure 13.1, we show a measure that combines these features, with the higher the value, the more intraparty homogeneity and the greater the interparty heterogeneity.[5] We report these data from the time Mayhew was studying (his book was published during the 93rd Congress) up to the 107th Congress (2001–02). As you can see there, Mayhew was writing in the early 1970s, a time in which the parties were showing decreasing internal agreement and this internal divisiveness was also reflected in lesser distinctiveness of the two parties from each other. That decline continued until about 1980 when it reversed and began to climb. By the time of the "Republican Revolution" of the 104th Congress (1995), the measure had increased considerably and it continued to increase consistently if now more slowly through the 105th Congress. In our view that increase is due primarily to changes in the electoral arena, and those changes have meant that the

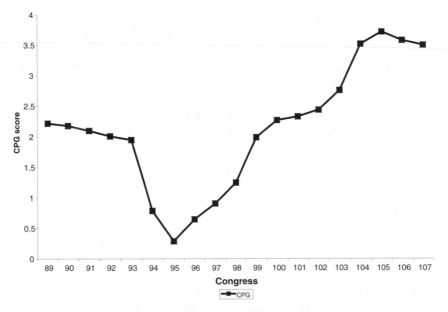

Figure 13.1 Conditional Party Government: 89–107th Congresses, 1965–2002.

"condition" in conditional party government has increased in strength so that the Members in Congress increasingly have desired stronger parties within the Congress so that they can achieve their more consensual partisan goals. It is this account we develop below.

Why Strong Parties?

The institutional structure of each House of Congress is designed by its members. The analytical challenge with regard to the enormous changes in the role of parties in Congress in recent decades involves explaining why members would opt to create strong parties. We conceive of members as goal-oriented individuals who make strategic choices to accomplish those goals. Thus an explanation must focus on what members want, and how various strategies lead to their desired ends.

Members' Goals

In the period leading up to the era of congressional reform in the 1970s, the most influential perspective on members' goals was offered by Mayhew (1974). He argued that members were motivated solely by the desire for individual reelection, and that they designed congressional rules to foster that goal. While we certainly agree that reelection is an important interest for legislators, and we will return to it below, our view is that it is only a part of the story. Other influential factors must be taken into account to explain the transformation of the Congress and its move to strong parties.[6]

Another goal of members is to enact policies that match their own preferences as closely as possible. We do not argue that legislators care more about policy than their own electoral fate, nor even that all members have strong policy motivations. We do contend, however, that a large portion of the membership has policy goals. Indeed this was a major factor in the reforms of the 1970s. Liberal Democrats faced an institution in which committees dominated the legislative process. Conservative Southern Democrats had disproportionate influence over those committees, influence that was protected by the seniority system. At the same time, party leaders were granted only limited power, and so they had few means of influencing the chairs and their committees. These circumstances prevented the liberals from moving policy in the direction they wanted, and that stimulated them to seek to alter the institution's arrangements. We will discuss some details of how they did so later, but it is sufficient to note here that policy goals were the driving force behind the effort (Aldrich 1995; Rohde 1991).

Policy was also central in the "Republican Revolution" of 1994, when the GOP gained fifty-two seats in the elections and won majority control of the House for the first time in forty years. Because of the desire for significant policy change among a great preponderance of newly elected Republicans, they supported major alterations in the operation of the House and further strengthened the powers of the majority leadership (Aldrich and Rohde, 1997–98, 2000a, 2000b). Members with policy goals will favor strong parties if they believe that will permit them to achieve the policies they want. Thus the more similar are the policy preferences of the party's members, the more attractive they will find strong party leaders.

A third motivation for legislators is the desire to achieve or maintain majority status, not so much for its own sake, but because that status has major implications for members' ability to achieve other goals. Members of the majority party will usually be more able to influence the institution than a corresponding minority member. For example, the Speaker (the top leader of the majority party) has more power than the minority leader, her counterpart. Similarly, the chair of a committee or subcommittee will usually have more influence than the ranking minority member of the same panel. Majority status has always been important, even in the era when parties were weak. This factor was not, however, prominent in our early development of conditional party government because, in that period, there was little doubt about which party would be in control. Between 1930 (when the Democrats won the House during the Depression) through the 1970s (and the end of the Democratic reform era), the Republicans controlled the House for only four years (1947–49 and 1953–55). As the initial strengthening of parties took hold, this factor did not affect members' calculations very much because they did not think it likely that their choices would affect the very high subjective probability that Democratic control would continue.

Indeed Democratic dominance continued until the surprising landslide of 1994, when the GOP ended forty unbroken years of Democratic rule. From that time through the 2006 elections, the majority party held only a small majority, meaning that retaining majority status was uncertain at every election. Moreover, representatives have recognized that how their party is perceived (often termed the party reputation or "brand") has become increasingly important to voters, thus tying, at least in part, their own electoral fate to the chances that their party will attain or continue to hold a House majority. In this context, there is a strong incentive to delegate power to party leaders so that they may take actions that will protect that reputation (Cox and McCubbins 1993). Legislators would not generally act to protect their party's collective reputation if they were left to pursue their own individual interests without constraint. Party leaders have the strongest interest in holding majority status, so they are less likely to use the powers they were granted to further their own goals at the expense of the party and its membership. Moreover, as parties were strengthened, majority status became even more important for members with policy goals because they were more likely to enact legislation to achieve them. If a party lost its majority, the other party would then be increasingly likely to pass policies the original majority opposed. All of this means that the desire to attain or maintain majority status was reinforcing itself over time.

A final goal of legislators is to have increasing influence within the chamber. Most members want to secure a position within the body that will give them the ability to influence the process in some significant way. This might be a place in the party leadership, in an informal caucus like the Republican Study Committee (the group of conservative Republicans in the House) or in committee or subcommittee leadership. For those in the formal or informal party leadership, strong parties are obviously advantageous. For committee and subcommittee leaders, the implications of strong parties are more uncertain. Every committee leader wants to exercise independent influence, so a strong party leadership is potentially problematic. How much so depends in large part on how compatible are the interests of the party and committee leaders. Here too, then, the more similar the policy goals of party members are, the more favorable committee leaders will be toward strong leaders.

This returns us, finally, to where we began: to individual reelection, which is intertwined with the other goals. Mayhew (1974), as we argued above, wrote that the primary goal of members was winning reelection. It was primary because it came first. No matter what else the member might like to achieve by being in office, she or he could not achieve those goals without being elected and reelected to office. With biennial elections, members of the House are always rapidly approaching their next election. It is for this reason that Mayhew titled his book *Congress: The Electoral Connection* rather than, say, *Congress: The Policy Connection*. Policy, in this view, is thus something at least in part induced by the wishes of the electorate.

A second major feature of the era in which Mayhew's observations were set was that members were increasingly able to take control of their own reelection fortunes. As a result, they, individually, were responsive to their constituencies' interests and concerns. The constituency, in turn, was increasingly likely to hold them responsible for what they had done. This made members focus on where they stood and how they voted on policy—"position taking" in Mayhew's parlance—instead of what policies actually passed or failed in Congress. This was particularly so when both parties were internally divided.

Once each party became more internally homogenous, it became easier to expect that consensus, at least within the majority party, should actually get translated into law. Members could expect that voters would want them not just to *stand for* the correct thing, but for them and their partisan peers (especially in the majority party) actually to *pass* those bills into law. Hence, as the condition for party government is increasingly strong, members should expect to be judged for where they stood *and* for what they enacted.

Of course, a constituency is not all like-minded. Indeed, there is a general tension for all candidates who seek election or reelection to any political office. In many states, congressional candidates need to win majority support in two constituencies, the primary electorate and general electorate, and those are rarely identical. Indeed, the primary electorate is nearly always more ideologically extreme than the general electorate, with Democratic primary voters more liberal and Republican primary voters more conservative than the full electorate. Each member must therefore appeal to a more extreme constituency for nomination and then a more moderate one for election. This dual pull—to the center for reelection and away from the center for nomination—is a common and repeated tension. Even in the general election, the candidate is often pulled one way to appeal to her party's "base" (which is often even more extreme than the primary electorate) and the other way to appeal to the swing voters more in the center. The centrifugal pressure arises not only from seeking votes in the primary election, but also for seeking support from activists to help staff the campaign, for fund raising, and from interest groups (at least on issues key to them) for resources, endorsements, and other sources of support. Merely seeking reelection, therefore, can generate countervailing pressures, even on a single policy.

As we noted above, the coming of full suffrage and of a competitive Republican Party in the South meant that the electoral forces Southern Democrats faced became more like their Northern counterparts. To be sure, newly enfranchised liberal, Southern constituencies might be only moderate compared to their Northern counterparts, but there were certainly fewer and fewer truly conservative Southern Democratic constituencies. At the same time, Republicans were losing their moderate Northern constituencies, while gaining the conservative vote in the South. The result is that, in both parties, the constituencies have increasingly become more similar across the country, both in terms of the primary and of the general electorate. It is not that every partisan constituency is alike, far from it, but the degree of similarity has increased substantially, especially as compared to that in the 1950s and 1960s. Thus, members of the same party have more opportunity to find common ground than they did, and they were less likely to find bitter opposition within their own party.

While these changes led to a general increase in the homogeneity within each party on what policies its members would like to see enacted, this is only an increasing similarity. There remain considerable differences of opinion within both parties. Thus, for example, there is only a subset of policies that divide the two parties. To be sure that subset has increased over time (adding first civil rights, then abortion, and so on to the cleavages between the two parties), but many issues and thus many policies on which members vote do not cleave the two parties.[7] Only on those party-cleaving issues—those that typically figure prominently in public debate between the two parties and in the public's voting choices between the two candidates—do the party members want their party to take action. For example many distributive policies are valued by members of both parties, as are many, albeit not all, defense programs, and there is no need for party leaders to use scarce resources to secure potentially wavering members' votes on bipartisan issues. Still other issues (immigration in recent years) divide one or both parties. Thus, only on those central issues that define the differences between the two would even the most partisan members want the party to employ its powers.

This combination of homogeneity on some issues and heterogeneity on others leads us to expect limitations on what issues members want their party to act on and thus limits on the scope of party leadership activity even during times of strong parties. A strong party leadership will not threaten the reelection chances of any member who generally shares the dominant policy preferences of the party. Indeed, strong leaders can provide many benefits that are electorally valuable. These include the ability to raise and distribute large amounts of campaign funds, to offer opportunities to visibly participate in the passage of important legislation, or to shelter members from politically risky legislative situations.[8] For members with preferences that diverge from their party, however, the electoral risks of powerful leaders, just like the risk to policy goals, would be greater. This is why the degree of preference homogeneity within parties is so central to our theory.

Goals, Parties, and Delegation

We have outlined what we see as the major goals of members of Congress and how each is related to the strength of parties. The set of legislators within each party must decide, in light of the mix of goals and preferences among them, how much authority (and which specific powers) to delegate to their leadership. Principal-agent theory is a theoretical tool that deals with decisions of delegating powers such as from party members to party leaders, in which a person or group (the principal) chooses someone (the agent) to act for them and secure benefits for them.[9] The perfect agent would be someone with identical preferences as the principal. It is rare or, in many cases, even impossible to find potential agents with identical preferences. The key question is: how different are they? The more similar are the preferences of principals and agents, the more certain the principals are that the agent will act faithfully to achieve their goals and, therefore, the more comfortable the former can be with delegating decision powers to the latter. This factor dictates the importance of the main condition in CPG: the more similar are the preferences of the members of the majority party, the more willing they will be to delegate strong powers to their leadership. With a high degree of preference homogeneity, there is less danger of the leaders, as agents, pursuing strategies that would endanger the interests of the principals (i.e., the rank-and-file members).

Thus when members choose party leaders, especially as part of an empowered leadership, they will likely seek agents who well reflect the preferences of the dominant faction of the party. Figure 13.2 illustrates this effect. While in the 111th Congress House Democrats retained their leadership from the 110th, the Republicans changed several leaders. Figure 13.2 shows how con-

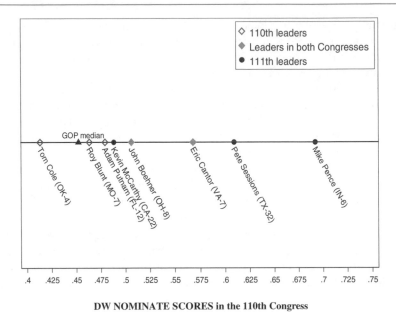

Figure 13.2 Conservatism of House Republican Leaders in the 110th and 111th Congresses.

servative the voting records of the GOP leaders in the both congresses were (based on roll call scores from the 110th).[10] The Republican membership in the 111th Congress was more cohesively conservative because of the departure of a substantial portion of the party's more moderate members. The new Republican leadership is now even more conservative than it was in the 110th and every leader is more conservative than the House Republican delegation was on average. Republicans, that is, consistently chose to select even more conservative members as their leaders.

Agents will usually have better information than their principals, especially about the agents' own preferences. Because there is always some divergence of preferences, agents will always have some incentive to "shirk" and pursue their own goals to the potential detriment of the principals. Thus it will be in the principals' interest to monitor the actions of the agents and take remedial measures if the agents stray. The greater the preference homogeneity, however, the less time and effort the principals need to invest in monitoring the actions of their agents. Thus, the CPG theory emphasizes the "bottom up" nature of the leader–member relationship in Congress, including the mechanisms by which members can monitor leaders, and pressure or even remove them if the members perceive their behavior to be unacceptable. Thus, the party leadership exerts its granted powers only when it has to. If a policy the majority party favors is going to pass anyway (or, rarely, fail miserably), there is no point in its using its powers. Most often, the party leadership uses its power to organize for collective action, making sure that the legislation that its majority actually favors comes to fruition. It uses its powers to get its members to vote as they would not otherwise vote only for those few roll calls needed to secure passage on the most closely fought issues.

Mayhew's basic point, that individual members want to win reelection, has not changed. What has changed is that partisan composition of constituencies is more similar across the country now than it was four decades ago, yielding a more consensual party in the House. Even so, there remains considerable diversity across districts (and within districts). As a result, when there is no consensus within the party or when their votes are not needed to make the difference between winning and losing, members are typically free to vote as they choose for their own reasons. In short, while party polarization has led to greater consensus within each party, which has led members to grant their party in the chamber greater resources and powers, the result is a considerable increase in party unity; that is, in party members voting alike and in opposition to the other party. But there remains—and should remain—considerable opportunity for individual members to defect from their party's position when they feel they have to represent their constituents, and on many other issues when there is no party position from which to defect because there is no agreement among its members to make it a partisan issue. We have written at length about the preferences of members and conditions under which they will want to grant leadership powers to achieve those preferences. Let us look now at how those powers have actually been employed.

Institutional Change and the Instruments of Partisan Advantage

Assuming that we may have convinced the reader that members may want strong parties, the question remains how the party (particularly the majority party) might go about securing some advantage for its members. What instruments can confer advantage, and how are they used? This is a big subject with many facets, and we will not be able to cover all of it in the available space. We will focus here mainly on the most important source of the majority's advantage: the ability to exert disproportionate control over the legislative agenda.

Agenda Control and the Rules Committee

There are many different aspects of the agenda that the majority party might want to influence. Cox and McCubbins (2005) talk about *positive agenda power* (the ability to bring desired proposals to the floor for a vote) and *negative agenda power* (the ability to prevent undesired proposals from getting to the floor). In the period leading up to the Democratic reforms of the 1970s, liberal Democrats' main complaint was that important committees that were controlled by conservative Southerners, supported by Republicans, served as a roadblock to liberal legislation. That is, the Southerners were exerting negative agenda power. Many of the reforms of the 1970s were designed to alter the distribution of both kinds of agenda power, decreasing the amount held by committees and increasing the power of the majority party leadership. Specific actions were aimed at both the substantive legislative committees (like Armed Services and Ways and Means) and at the Rules Committee, which controlled the terms of debate for most major bills that came to the floor. Subsequent developments during the period of Republican rule from 1995 to 2007, as well as the restoration of Democratic control after the 2006 elections related to these two main avenues. We will focus on the control of substantive committees in the next section, and deal first with the Rules Committee.

One thing that the two avenues of agenda control had in common before the 1970s reforms was the independence of committee leaders. Committee chairs were chosen via the seniority norm: the chair was the most senior member of the majority party in terms of continuous service on the committee. It did not matter whether the person in line to be chair was highly loyal to the party, or almost never voted with it; there was no practical way for the majority to bypass the most senior member or later to remove her or him. Thus committee chairs had little or no external incentive to support the majority party or its leaders.

The Rules Committee was a particular problem in this regard. Usually, for a major bill to come to the floor after it had been approved by the substantive committee of jurisdiction, a resolution from the Rules Committee (called a "special rule") was necessary. This resolution could specify how much time would be available for debate, and whether amendments would be permitted on the floor, as well as other considerations.[11] From 1945 through 1960, the committee had eight Democratic and four Republican members. Thus when the Democrats were in the majority, given that there always were two or more conservative Southern Democrats on Rules, those Southerners could join with the committee's Republicans and block a special rule from being granted to a bill they did not like, preventing its passage.[12] To mitigate this blocking power, in 1961 reformers secured the expansion of Rules to fifteen members. This eliminated the possibility of a six-six deadlock, but the committee and its leader still were independent of the majority party and able to interfere with Democratic priorities. This situation continued until 1974, when House Democrats adopted a party rule that vested the appointment (and potential removal) of the Democratic members of Rules and its chair in the Speaker of the House. From this point on, Rules was no longer independent. It became, in Oppenheimer's (1977) words, an "arm of the leadership."

Now that the committee was an agent of the majority leadership, rather than a potential adversary, the Democrats began to devise ways of using special rules to give them a legislative advantage. Most efforts revolved around controlling the amendment process, protecting the policy, reelection, and majority maintenance goals of the majority. It was in the interests of the leadership to block Republican amendments that could pass, and thereby move the legislation in question away from the Democrats' favored position. They also would want to prevent votes on amendments that would fail, but that would be politically embarrassing to members of the majority. This strategy would protect Democrats who had liberal personal preferences, but who came from relatively conservative constituencies, from having to choose between their policy and reelection goals. Over time the Democrats also developed more complex ways of using rules to advantage their bills, such as having certain amendments automatically adopted when the special rule passed, rather than having members vote separately on the amendments (Rohde 1991).

This transformation of institutional control and strategy put voting on special rules, which had long been routine and noncontroversial, at the center of the legislative process in the House. From the 83rd through the 91st congresses (1953–71), there was an average of only eighteen special rules roll calls per congress.[13] This was because there was rarely conflict about the special rules, and most were adopted by voice votes or unanimous consent. Over time the frequency of conflict increased, with roll calls on rules becoming more frequent and more partisan (see Figure 13.3). In the 1980s, with Reagan in the presidency, there were large numbers of rules votes, and on more than half of them a majority of Republicans disagreed with a majority of Democrats. Republican members recognized that the majority was using special rules to gain a legislative advantage, and they complained frequently and vociferously, contending that such manipulations of the agenda were unfair.

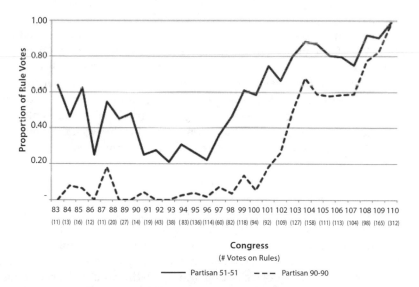

Figure 13.3 Roll Call Votes on Special Rules, 1953–2008. Note: Partisan 51–51 is the proportion of roll calls on which majorities of each party voted on opposite sides. Partisan 90–90 is the proportion of which at least 90 percent of each party were opposed.

Then in the 1990s, partisan conflict on special rules votes grew even sharper. As the data in Figure 13.3 indicate, in each congress during that decade, 80 percent or more of the rules votes saw party majorities on opposite sides. Even more illustrative is the second line in the figure, which uses a higher standard of party conflict: whether 90 percent or more of both parties are on opposite sides of a vote. Such a level of disagreement was very rare up until the 1980s. By the 1990s, however, a majority of votes on special rules surpassed that standard.

This further increase in party conflict reflected both the growing homogeneity of preferences in the parties that we discussed above, as well as the more extensive efforts by Republicans to use special rules to gain advantages after they took over the majority in the 104th Congress (1995–97). Having been in the minority for forty continuous years, the GOP came to power with great ambitions to change a wide range of public policies. In this effort, however, they perceived some significant challenges. The activists in the Republican Conference, led by the new leadership team of Speaker Newt Gingrich of Georgia, were concerned that their party's senior members on committees might balk at major changes in policies under their jurisdiction because they had built up a vested interest in the status quo.

To overcome this problem, the majority leadership decided on an imaginative solution: for a substantial number of policy changes they would bypass the substantive committees of jurisdiction and channel the shifts through the Appropriations process. But there was a difficulty with this solution. The task of the Appropriations Committee was deciding how much money should be allocated to programs that were authorized by other committees, and the rules of the House prohibited the inclusion of legislative language in appropriations bills. Fortunately for the GOP leaders, however, their control of the Rules Committee gave them a way around the problem: the special rule for each appropriations bill could waive the restrictions of the House rules and permit legislative changes to be included. This controversial strategy outraged the Democratic minority and led to extensive conflict between the Congress and the Clinton administration over virtually every appropriations measure. The resulting delays caused parts of the federal government to shut down twice in 1995 and 1996 because the legislation that authorized and appropriated their funds were not completed.[14]

In the end few of the House GOP's major changes became law due to resistance from the Senate and the president, but the fact that they came close was due to the GOP's aggressive use of the majority's agenda control powers. In subsequent congresses under Republican rule, party leaders employed these powers over a wider range of legislation. Indeed, in the words of Don Wolfensberger (2007, 293), who was the former Republican staff director of the Rules Committee, "[b]y the 107th Congress (2001–2002), their fourth consecutive Congress in power, the Republicans far exceeded the Democrats' worst excesses in restricting floor amendments."

Neither the efforts to use agenda control strategically, nor the partisan conflicts over them, ceased when the Democrats regained the majority in the 2006 elections. Nancy Pelosi employed her control of the Rules Committee to advantage right from the beginning of her tenure as Speaker, directing that a set of six top priority bills to be considered at the opening of the 110th Congress, all having special rules that restricted the minority's ability to offer amendments. Indeed, as Figure 13.3 shows, the conflict over special rules reached unprecedented levels in 2007–2008. The number of roll calls on those resolutions was nearly twice that in any previous congress (indicating a wider range of party conflict), and 98 percent of the votes were partisan by 90 percent of each party opposed criterion. The evidence is that in the last three decades, the majority party has expanded both the range and intensity of its efforts to extract partisan advantage from agenda control.

Controlling Party Subordinates

While the control of the Rules Committee by the leadership does, as we have seen, confer advantages, much of the legislative activity of the Congress is done in substantive committees pursuing their own priorities. Their decisions have major consequences for the goals of members. The interests of committee leaders will sometimes be the same as their party's and sometimes they will differ. In the latter case, the agents will have incentives to satisfy their own preferences unless their behavior is being monitored and there are countervailing incentives that induce the committee leaders to serve the interests of their principals.

During the Democratic reform era, many of the changes in the majority party's rules related to this problem. The reformers simultaneously followed two courses. One sought to place limits on the independent powers of committee chairs in order to mitigate the damage they could do to party interests. The other track was to adopt procedures that directly undermined the independence of chairs by permitting a party majority to remove them. The implications of the first set of changes, collectively known as the "subcommittee bill of rights" (Rohde 1991), are straightforward: powers that were formerly exercised by committee chairs came under the control of subcommittee chairs or the majority party caucus on a committee. The latter set of reforms affected the incentives of chairs regarding their use of the powers they retained. At the beginning of each congress the Democratic Caucus would take a secret-ballot vote on each chair from the previous congress, or each member next in line by seniority for a vacant position. If the Caucus voted against any nominee, an alternative chair would be chosen by the Caucus, potentially in a competitive election.

In 1974, the removal of chairs was shown not to be merely hypothetical, when three Southern chairs were removed and replaced by Northern Democrats. From that point on, committee chairs were no longer guaranteed their positions regardless of their behavior. Current or potential chairs, when making legislative decisions, now had to at least consider the preferences of their party colleagues. They might still choose to go their own way, but they recognized that they could be made to pay a heavy price. Committee leaders were less likely to try (and less likely to be able) to block legislation the party wanted, and they were more likely to seek to enact party priorities. Both the positive and the negative aspects of agenda control of the majority leadership were enhanced.

When the Republicans took over in 1995, they went even further in giving their leadership control over committee leaders. Shortly after the 1994 elections, speaker-designate Gingrich called a press conference and announced who would be the chairs of some major committees that would be important for the party agenda. With the exception of the chair of Rules, nothing in the party's rules gave the leader that power. Gingrich simply asserted it, and it was accepted by the majority of the party's members (Aldrich and Rohde 1997–98). At least as important, Gingrich made clear that he believed that he could engineer the removal of a chair who was not responsive to the party's wishes, and that view was widely accepted. The Republicans also adopted a six-year term limit for chairs.

In 2000, when the term limit was reached by many sitting chairs, the party (led by Speaker Dennis Hastert of Illinois) chose to vest the selection of their successors in the leadership-dominated Steering Committee, which conducted competitive elections among self-starting candidates from the committee in question. This process often chose someone other than the most senior candidate, and in many cases bypassed a more senior moderate to pick a more conservative but more junior member. Then in 2002, with the urging of Speaker Hastert, the GOP extended that selection mechanism to all subcommittee chairmanships on the powerful Appropriations Committee. In addition to influencing the initial selection of committee chairs, the Republican leadership demonstrated that they could penalize recalcitrant chairs. This happened in 2005, when Chris Smith of New Jersey was removed as chair of the Veterans Affairs Committee because his continuous efforts to increase spending on veterans programs conflicted with leadership priorities. Smith had been warned that he needed to be responsive to the leadership, and after he persisted in his efforts he was deprived of his position. Thus during the Republican era, the party leaders demonstrated that they could influence the selection (and even cause the removal) of committee leaders. Thus those committee leaders were forced to be responsive to the wishes of the leaders, who were themselves agents of the party membership.

When the Democrats regained the majority, they reverted to the mechanisms for control of committee leaders that had been in place before the GOP takeover in 1994. That is, instead of placing direct selection and removal power in the leader's hands, for most committees this capability was still vested in the full Caucus.[15] However, despite the procedural differences, the ultimate result was the same. In the 110th Congress, the Speaker demonstrated that she could induce committee chairs to shape their bills in accord with the preferences of the members of the Caucus. An example of this was when she summoned John Dingell of Michigan, the powerful chair of the Energy and Commerce Committee, to a meeting in her office to discuss the energy bill his committee was drafting. She demanded that he alter two provisions that Dingell had authored that conflicted with her priorities, and he complied (Aldrich and Rohde 2009).

Then after the election of Barack Obama in 2008, it was clear that Dingell's committee would be central to the new president's and the party's agenda due to its jurisdiction over energy, global warming, and health care, as well as other important matters. Based on their experiences in previous congresses, liberal Democrats distrusted Dingell's willingness to aggressively pursue party preferences on these central issues. As a result, Henry Waxman of California, the second-ranking Democrat on Energy, launched a challenge against Dingell for the chairmanship. Waxman held positions on the issues of concern that were more in accord with those of most rank-and-file Democrats (as well as being a strong ally of Pelosi), and the party Caucus voted to remove Dingell and replace him with Waxman. This made clear that House Democrats continued to see committee chairs as agents of the party Caucus, and that any chair who took positions that were too far from the Caucus's views on important matters risked a heavy penalty.

Conclusion

In this chapter we have sought to account for the increase in the strength of political parties in Congress over the last four decades through the application of the theory of conditional party government. The theory contends that observed increases in the homogeneity of policy preferences within congressional parties, and the increases in policy conflicts between the parties, are rooted in electoral changes. In turn, the increased intraparty homogeneity and interparty conflict led members of Congress to be willing to delegate strong powers to their party leaders, in order that those leaders as agents of the members could secure political advantages for their respective parties.

In offering evidence for our claims in the limited space available, we have focused on the central issues of agenda control, first with regard to the majority's need to shape the procedural environment on the House floor, and then with regard to efforts to influence the behavior of leaders of substantive committees.[16] Based on our theory, we expect that as long as the underlying condition continues to be met, strong centralized parties will continue to dominate the legislative process, and CPG will continue to offer a dependable explanation of congressional politics.

Notes

1. The authors are grateful for the able research assistance of Aaron King and Francis Orlando and Brittany Perry of the Political Institutions and Public Choice Program at Duke University.
2. In this chapter, we examine the House primarily. Due to space constraints, we consider the Senate only in passing. However, in our view the theory of conditional party government applies, with suitable attention to institutional differences, to the Senate as well (Aldrich and Rohde 2009). Indeed, there is mounting evidence regarding party effects in the Senate; see the essays in Monroe, Roberts, and Rohde (2008).
3. They held their majority at first in large part because the Republican Party—the party of Lincoln and the Union a century before—could not gain anything beyond a toehold in Southern congressional elections.
4. These data can be found in, for example, Abramson, Aldrich and Rohde (2009, Table 9-3).
5. The data in Figure 13.1 are taken from Aldrich, Rohde, and Tofias (2007).
6. Our perspective builds on the work of Richard Fenno (1973), who postulated multiple goals (reelection, influence in the House, and good public policy) for members in his analysis of congressional committees. Also see Sinclair (1995, 2006).
7. That is, while the issues that divide Democrats from Republicans tend to follow more or less along liberal–conservative lines, many other issues do not fit into that framework. Policy is a complicated, multidimensional aspect of governing.
8. We will offer more details on this later.
9. For an introduction to principal agent concepts see Shepsle and Bonchek (1997, 360–70), and for more extensive treatment see Epstein and O'Halloran (1999). In addition to the work on conditional party government, theoretical discussions of delegation in the congressional context are seen in Cox and McCubbins (1993) and Sinclair (1995, 2006).
10. The scores are first-dimension DW-NOMINATE scores. The scores, which measure positions on the aggregate of issues that most involve the parties, range from -1.00 (most liberal) to +1.00 (most conservative). See Poole and Rosenthal (2007) for a discussion of the scores, their computation, and their implications. We are grateful to Professor Michael C. Brady for drawing these developments to our attention and for creating the figure.
11. At this time a rule would be "open" (all germane amendments were allowed) or "closed" (no amendments allowed at all). As we will see, later things got a good deal more complicated.
12. Evidence also shows that the conservatives were sometimes able to push conservative legislation to the floor (Schickler and Pearson 2009).
13. The calculations reported here include both votes on passage of special rules and on the previous question on rules resolutions. For a more complete discussion of these votes and their implications see Finocchiaro and Rohde (2008).
14. For more details on the Republicans' use of the Appropriations Committee in the 104th and 105th Congresses, see Aldrich and Rohde (2000b) and Marshall, Prins, and Rohde (2000).
15. Speaker Pelosi was able to directly appoint five committee chairs, including that of the vital Rules Committee.
16. While we regard the aspects of agenda control we have considered to be the most important mechanisms of party influence, they are certainly not the only ones. Interested readers will find a fuller account in the various references we cite herein.

Chapter 14

Parties, Public Policy Differences, and Impact

Rebekah E. Liscio and Jeffrey M. Stonecash

Parties seek to respond to voters so they can attract a majority and control the presidency and Congress. In a two-party system, a party wishes for power presumably because it wants policies that differ from those of the other party. The final question in any analysis of parties, then, is just what do parties do with power when they acquire it? Does party control produce clear differences in policy? Do parties just make claims of what they will do or do they act on proposals? Further, has the developing polarization of recent decades altered how much control of government affects public policy?

We know less about this matter than might be expected. The impact of parties on public policy has received much less attention than have many other aspects of parties. During recent decades it was often difficult to explain this impact because for much of the 1980s and 1990s control of government was divided between Democrats and Republicans, limiting our ability to assess the impact of unified party control (Fiorina 1992). Given that situation, the concern was primarily whether divided control meant protracted policy stalemates, or whether parties could compromise over their differences and respond to pressing social problems. Then, while scholars considered that question, beginning in 2000 unified party control became more common than divided control. Now it seems possible to assess whether unified control of government by one party produces policy responses different from before. Does it produce policy likely to be more favorable to one set of interests in society?

The Importance of Conditional Party Government

To understand the relevance of parties, the first step is to consider variations in the composition and unity of parties. As Rohde and Aldrich argue in the previous chapter, parties are more likely to matter when their composition is homogeneous and party unity is high. When parties are diverse internally and do not differ much from each other, variations in party control do not mean as much and compromise between parties is more likely. Party control should affect public policy less. For much of the 1960s to 1980s the parties differed less, compromised more often, and passed significant legislation involving such issues as civil rights (1964), clean air (1970), and reform of the tax code (1986) (Mayhew 1991). These bills were a product of compromise, rarely satisfying both sides, but they were passed. On many other matters, parties stalemated (Binder, 1999).

Since that period there has been a gradual and steady realignment, with Republicans attracting fiscal and social conservatives, and Democrats attracting social and fiscal liberals (Brewer and Stonecash 2009; Polsby 2004). That process is by no means complete, but it has created greater polarization than prevailed in the past. The decade since the late 1990s provides an opportunity to assess the impact of party control in a situation in which the parties differ in their party bases and policy goals.

With that in mind, this chapter focuses on three questions. As polarization has increased, how has it affected the process of making decisions, the way we talk about and debate public policy, and the kinds of policies enacted? We first consider how the process within Congress has changed in the last several decades. Second, we examine the ways parties talk about issues, because if party differentiation affects how issues are approached, it should affect how parties present their concerns and criticize their opponents. Finally, we look at what parties have done when in power. In all three areas, we find significant effects of the recent increase in party differences.

Changes in Process

As Rohde and Aldrich discuss in some detail in chapter 13, the development of parties with different bases and different policy goals has changed how parties approach the process of making decisions. With parties developing less diversity, more agreement about what they want to achieve, and more internal unity, members in Congress have been willing to grant their leaders more power to get party members to go along with party goals (Rohde 1991). The commonplace assessment of the loyalty of party members before the leadership appoints committee chairs (Sinclair 2006) is a manifestation of these party developments.

This greater unity within each party has been used to exert more control over what is presented for votes and how much the minority party can change legislation through amendments once a bill is presented. The majority party is now more likely to put bills on the floor with closed rules, or rules that strictly limit how much anyone can use amendments to change the substance of a bill. When it comes to voting, party members are more likely to vote with fellow party members and against the other party. Figure 14.1 shows the percentage of Democrats and Republicans voting with a majority of their party in the Senate since 1952. In the 1960s about 75 percent of members voted with their party. Now it is up to 90 percent. The pattern in the House is very similar.

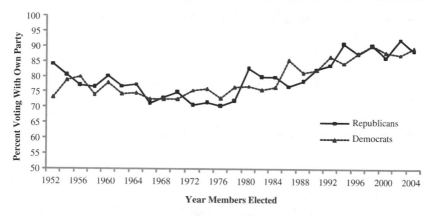

Figure 14.1 Average Party Unity Score by Party, Senate, 1952–2006.

The long-term process toward realignment has made considerable changes; partisan differences have become more central to policy debates, and interactions between the parties have been affected. To some observers the process has become nastier, with members less likely to socialize with each other and less likely to build relationships that transcend partisan differences. It appears that members of opposing sides are now more likely to distrust each other and more likely to seek advantage over the other party (Sinclair 2008). The increasing divisions between the parties over the last several decades have created a process in which there is greater focus on each party getting its way. It has made compromise more difficult and less likely.

Party Representation and Advocacy

As the formal legislative process unfolds in Washington, parties are also very concerned with presenting their arguments about desirable policy to the public. It is crucial to a party to get voters to understand the virtues of the party's approach and the flaws of the opposing party's approach. While many voters dislike these exchanges, regarding them as bickering, some have high hopes for the positive effects of this process. Parties are the vehicles for presenting differing sides of an issue. They provide alternative policies on issues of importance to the public. They critique each other, providing voters with arguments about the flaws in the opponent's proposals and thereby creating a dialogue. Parties are the groups that provide the debate between the "ins" and the "outs" on the record (Key 1949), and they are "mechanisms for comprising competing group demands" (Bibby and Schaffner 2008, 12). Ideally, when there are strong parties, differing concerns and groups are better represented, and the problems of citizen disengagement and of special interests biasing policy outcomes are ameliorated (Key 1949). In this view, political parties are central to democracy because they are the vehicles by which the disparate interests of the public are represented in public policy.

There has always been unease about how well parties play out this ideal role. Within the last two decades, with parties moving further apart, that unease has grown. The concern is that the development of greater party differences has gone beyond representation and has affected how we talk about and debate policy issues. The rhetoric seems to have become more ideological, emotional, and intense, with some arguing that the language has changed for the worse (Eilperin 2006).

In order to successfully gain office and to advance its policies, a party must communicate to the public that its issue positions are superior to those of the opposing party. Because policymaking is a contest over parties' different conceptions of realities, language—or rhetoric—"reflects, advances, and interprets" the alternative policy positions represented by parties (Rochefort and Cobb 1994, 9). The choice of language has become very important in the political communication process.

As party differences have increased, parties have become more concerned with "framing" issues to their advantage. A frame is a "central organizing idea or storyline that provides meaning" (Gamson and Modigliani 1989). Parties seek to present an interpretation of an issue using words laden with values and symbols that are designed to create favorable reactions by the public to parties' policy positions. Frames can embody broad, overarching principles, or they can involve narrower concepts. An example of a broad frame is the Republican Party's rhetoric on the economy. The party has continually emphasized jobs, economic growth, and supply-side economics. Former President Reagan regularly gave speeches on the economy in which he emphasized the effect of taxes and spending, claiming that "excessive taxation has robbed us of incentive" (Smith 2007). An example of a specific frame is former vice presidential candidate Sarah Palin's depiction of the Democratic Party's health care plan as opening the door to "death panels." With this language, Palin portrayed the health care plan as a policy that would deprive individuals of freedom over choices related to their health care.

Framing an issue is valuable for parties because it provides the public with an interpretation, a way to think about an issue in a way that connects with existing political battles (Callaghan and Schnell 2001). In 2009 Republicans wanted voters to see the health care proposal in a way favorable to their agenda of less government and more individual freedom. To make that connection they focused on the theme of restrictions in choice of doctors, framing the issue as involving a fundamental value, personal freedom. Parties use frames to present an issue to voters in a way that constructs a proposed policy's meaning and affects reactions among the public (Goffman 1974). Frames have such a powerful effect on citizens because many individuals do not have the time, energy, or resources to investigate policy implications. Numerous studies suggest that many Americans are "tuned out," showing that a large proportion of the citizenry lacks political knowledge and issue awareness (e.g., Converse 1964; Campbell, Converse, and Stokes 1960; Delli Carpini and Keeter 1996; Gilens 2000). Instead of becoming fully informed, voters—whether forming opinions, making judgments, or voting—often rely on cues provided by trusted members of their political party. For example, a person affiliated with the Democratic Party may support stem cell research because prominent members of the Democratic Party have framed the issue in terms of advancing our understanding of medicine and, more specifically, finding cures to diseases, rather than frame the issue in terms of moral and ethical concerns. In this case, if the individual trusts the opinions of members of his party, he is saved from researching the topic himself in order to determine whether he supports or opposes stem cell research. Following these types of cues facilitates decision making because it serves as a substitute for the costly process of obtaining full information.

All frames are not created equal. Parties are more successful in conveying policy platforms—most often via the media—when frames embody messages that are consistent, easily understood, and conducive to a narrative. For example, on the economy, the Republican Party has continually, and largely successfully, put forth messages of low taxes, no regulations, and a more efficient welfare state (Jones and Williams 2008; Smith 2007). The Democratic Party, on the other hand, has provided varying messages on the economy, which often have been difficult to explain to the public in clear terms (Smith 2007).

Polarization and Policy Rhetoric on Issues

While there are many studies demonstrating that political actors frame specific issues, there is a lack of systematic, longitudinal studies on whether parties have increasingly employed more polarized rhetoric. There is reason to suspect that the language on public policy issues has become more ideological. In recent decades parties have become more polarized (McCarty, Poole, and Rosenthal 2006; Stonecash et al. 2003), and voters of each party increasingly have different worldviews (Hetherington and Weiler 2009). Furthermore, as Hayes indicates in chapter 4, there are more news outlets and many of these sources—such as Fox News, MSNBC, right-leaning talk radio, and the left-leaning blogosphere—are more partisan than traditional news sources such as network television news. These more partisan venues are a form of party advocacy (Jamieson and Cappella 2008) and have enabled parties to amplify and to promote their messages, resulting in the recruitment and mobilization of their partisans.

While we need more studies of how language has changed, it appears that language is becoming more polarized. Two issues (healthcare and abortion) demonstrate the polarized nature of party language and suggest that party rhetoric has become increasingly ideological.

Health Care

In his first year as president, Barack Obama sought to overhaul the nation's health care system, an endeavor that was last attempted with former president Bill Clinton's failed reforms of the mid-1990s. The debate on health care reflects the polarized nature of parties' political communications, as well as the importance of constructing a clear and consistent narrative.

Republican opposition to the reform proposals has been vociferous and organized around the value of freedom. Republican members of Congress, activists, and citizens raise fears of government-controlled health care. At town hall meetings, throngs of people have chanted "tyranny" and "just say no." Many prominent politicians have claimed that "Obamacare" will result in "death panels" for the elderly, infirm, and disabled. Former vice presidential candidate Sarah Palin summarized the fear of government control: "The America I know and love is not one in which my parents or my baby with Down Syndrome will have to stand in front of Obama's 'death panel' so his bureaucrats can decide...whether they are worthy of health care. Such a system is downright evil" (Seelye 2009).

While the Republicans have consistently structured their opposition to the proposed health care reforms around the value of freedom, Democrats have neither clearly nor uniformly framed their arguments around an organizing principle. Messages from leading members of the Democratic Party range from reasoning that the provision of health care is a "moral obligation" to arguing that current health care costs are unsustainable. The Democrats' problems in winning the public relations campaign over health care is further complicated by the fact that citizens are typically more persuaded by arguments opposed to a policy initiative, as public opinion is biased toward the status quo (Cobb and Kuklinski 1997, 90–91).

Abortion

The rhetoric on abortion suggests just how much party language on some public policy issues has become polarized. The current discourse on abortion policy is structured around the two deeply held values of personal liberty and protection of life. Those who promote a woman's access to abortion seek to frame the issue in terms of a woman's right to maintain control over her body. Those who oppose the practice of abortion argue that human life begins at conception and conclude that an abortion is the taking of a life.

Polarized language on abortion took time to appear. While abortion was nationally legalized in 1973 with the Supreme Court's *Roe v. Wade* ruling, definite and unified party stances on the issue did not immediately surface. Layman (2001) notes that the parties did not adopt their current stances on abortion until party activists, beginning in earnest in 1979 with the creation of the Moral Majority, brought abortion to the parties' agendas. In the early

1980s, Ronald Reagan departed from previous Republican presidents Richard Nixon and Gerald Ford by formulating and promoting antiabortion rhetoric. When talking about abortion, Reagan used language that was "impassioned and moralistic," comparing the debate over abortion to that over slavery and equating abortion with taking the life of a person (Craig and O'Brien 1993, 170). Reagan's rhetoric brought a change to the Republican Party's doctrine by reinforcing "the hard-line antiabortion plank in his party's platforms" (Craig and O'Brien 1993, 170). The parties were becoming polarized on the issue and that was reflected in their language (Adams 1997). This framing continued with the issue of late-term abortion, or, as the Republicans framed it, partial-birth abortion. On the floor of the House Republicans tend to use the word baby rather than fetus more frequently than Democrats (Simon and Jerit 2007). These word choices affect public opinion. When individuals are exposed to news content reflecting the exclusive use of the word baby, they are more likely to support the ban, while those who are exposed to news content reflecting the exclusive use of fetus are more likely to oppose the ban. Parties seek these effects and devote considerable attention to framing issues.

This focus on framing an issue positively for one side and negatively for opponents has consequences. It appears that the language used to talk about issues of public policy has become more ideological and moral, and that debates have become more emotional and intense. With this ideologically and emotionally charged rhetoric, party elites seek not only to win the support of public opinion but also to mobilize their bases to make a clamor about issues of public policy. Increasingly polarized language over policy debates is not just an elite phenomenon. Today's voters are more partisan compared to those in the 1970s (Bartels 2000; Prior 2007; Stonecash 2005). Those voters who are more politically aware, are attentive to the cues provided by party elites (Zaller 1992) and seek out information consistent with their own political beliefs (Stroud 2008). When these voters encounter partisan messages—such as the Republican Party's communiqué that the Democrats' health care plan would curtail Americans' freedom in the domain of health—they may hold stronger opinions and engage in action, including boisterous behavior at town hall meetings, to oppose various policies and to help their party elites take control of the debate.

Parties, Polarization, and Policy Decisions

While language appears to have become more divisive, does this carry over into what parties actually do with power? Do they enact different policies? We know that they differ in the policies they propose. Republicans want lower taxes and fewer regulations. Democrats want to maintain taxes, have the more affluent pay more, and use the revenues to provide more social programs such as job training, health care, and aid to attend college. Republicans generally want legislation that will support traditional morals and Democrats generally want government to stay out of such matters (Brewer and Stonecash 2006). But do parties actually change policies when they have power? Further, has the increasing polarization between the parties affected this? Has polarization prompted parties to be more intense in their opposition to change, such that gridlock, or a lack of action occurs? Or, has polarization made parties more inclined to bond together in unity and enact policies over the opposition of the other party?

For much of the last fifty years it has been difficult to assess whether parties really make a difference in enacting policy because there were not that many years of unified party control, and when it did exist, party differences were muted. First, unified party control of government was not the norm from 1952 through 2000. That occurred only in the years from 1961 to 1968, 1977 to 1980, and 1993 to 1994. Those years might be used as tests of the impact of parties, but most of those years were also ones in which the parties were still diverse internally. During the first two sets of years, party diversity was high, differences between the parties were at their lowest, and party unity in voting was low. Parties differed, but each party had numerous moderates (Bond, Fleisher, and Stonecash 2009), and there was less consensus on what they wanted to achieve. Even in 1993–94 the polarization that we now see was only beginning to be evident. The result was that many policy proposals drew support from both parties, and the goals of parties were not so clearly different. The years 1965 to 1966 were the exception. During those years the large majorities that Democrats ran up in the 1964 election resulted in a major set of policy enactments called the Great Society program. That burst of legislation constitutes a clear case where a party pursued an agenda, won an election, interpreted it as a mandate, and acted (Brewer and Stonecash 2009, 81–103).

From the 1970s through 2000 the more common situation was divided control, but with growing differences between the parties. There were few situations of clear party control, and no situations of Republican control such that we could see what an alternation in party control might mean. The persistence of divided control prompted many to focus on whether anything was achieved. The general conclusion was that government still continued to enact major legislation (Mayhew 1991). Yet, while bills were enacted, the rise of party polarization had the effect of slowing down the rate of enactment. If the number of major bills proposed in each year is considered, over time a smaller percentage of those bills were enacted prior to 2000 (Binder 1999, 2003). Party polarization added to this stalemate: the greater the difference between the parties, the less likely major bills would be enacted (Binder 1999; Jones 2001).

We know that some bills were passed and that polarization appears to slow down passage rates, but we know much less about how divided control affected policy negotiations. Did gridlock merely create initial policy positions that were further apart as a bargaining strategy, but which were then compromised to produce moderate policies? Or, was the greater cohesiveness of Republicans a vehicle to mount a sustained attack on taxes and social programs? Smith

(2007) argues that the Republican Party developed a comprehensive program to criticize the value of programs (Murray 1984) and to recast policy debates within a conservative framework. That is, Republicans mobilized conservatives, systematically delineated problems associated with social programs, and successfully reduced these programs (Hacker 2008; Hacker and Pierson 2005). Bartels presents data indicating that under situations of divided control, when Republicans controlled the presidency inequality in the distribution of income consistently increased, compared to when a Democrat was president (Bartels 2008, 29–63). It appears that just partisan control mattered, at least of the presidency.

Did any of this affect the policies in existence? The link between partisan battles and policy is not as well researched as we might wish, but there is evidence that over the last two or three decades public policies have changed. Welfare was cut back; aid to attend college declined; taxes for the affluent were cut (Soss, Hacker, and Mettler 2007). What is less clear is how much this was due to shifts in public sentiment and how much it was due to party positioning and strategy. Stimson argues that there are mood swings in public sentiments that alter the degree of public support for various policies (Stimson 2004; Ellis and Stimson 2008). This suggests that the electorate vacillates between support for liberal and conservative policies and those fluctuations matter more than party control matters. At this point we need more analyses on how much parties shape broad shifts in public support, even while divided control exists, versus reacting to and taking advantage of changes over which parties have little control.

The years since 2000 provide a more interesting test of the joint impact of party control and party polarization. Party differences have been steadily increasing since the 1960s. Party unity is greater, with more Members of Congress willing to vote with their party. For the first time in many decades, Republicans gained control of the presidency and both houses of Congress. In an era when the party had a more clearly conservative base Republicans finally had power. In the 2006 election Democrats won control of the House and divided control prevailed for two years. Then in 2008 Democrats won control of both houses and Barack Obama won the presidency and unified control prevailed. Did these alternations of party control affect policy?

The unified control under George W. Bush appears to have had a significant impact. Bush quickly pursued a major tax cut, affirming Republicans' long-held view that existing tax levels served as a disincentive to entrepreneurs. The Republican controlled Congress agreed, with a party-line vote supporting his proposal. The estate tax was significantly cut back, fulfilling a long-standing Republican goal (Graetz and Shapiro 2004). The Bush administration was also able to cut back on many regulations affecting business and the environment (Hedge 2009). Regarding social issues, Bush pursued policy proposals that limited access to abortion. In response to the terrorist attacks of 9/11, Bush increased national security precautions by creating the Department of

Homeland Security and by reorganizing the national intelligence community with the creation of the Office of the Director of National Intelligence, as well as pursued a war with Iraq (Jacobson 2007, 69–74). The enactments of these policies were possible because the base of the Republican Party was more conservative and more cohesive than it had been in prior decades. The strategy of the Bush administration was to draw upon that greater party differentiation and unity to pursue a partisan agenda (Jacobson 2007, 75–94). As Rohde and Aldrich note in their analysis (chapter 13), party control mattered because the condition of an ideologically cohesive party existed.

By 2009, after two years of divided control and stalemate, Democrats gained unified control. Did that party control mean anything? That control had an impact through changed executive orders and legislation. Within the first two months of his presidency, Obama significantly changed the policy direction of many issues—including interrogation of enemy combatants, stem cell research, and abortion funding—by reversing Bush policies on these issues.

One of the first executive orders Obama signed was Ensuring Lawful Interrogation (EO 13491), which promotes "safe, lawful, and humane treatment of individuals in United States custody," and ensures compliance with the Geneva Conventions. This order revokes an executive order (EO 13444) issued by George W. Bush in 2007, which states that "members of al Qaeda, the Taliban, and associated forces are unlawful enemy combatants who are not entitled to the protections [of] the Third Geneva Convention," and that it is within the president's discretion "to interpret the meaning and application of the Geneva Conventions." In addition to the pledge to adhere to the Geneva Convention, that very same day, Obama also signed an executive order (EO 13492) that committed to closing the Guantanamo Bay detention facility within a year. Throughout the Bush presidency, this facility was used to detain individuals suspected of committing acts of terrorism. Supporters of the use of the facility under the Bush administration claimed operations there produced valuable information for winning the war on terror, while opponents cited allegations of mistreatment of Guantanamo detainees.

Also at the beginning of his presidency, Obama issued Removing Barriers to Responsible Scientific Research Involving Human Stem Cells (EO 13505), which, as the name suggests, removes limitations on government funding for scientific research involving human embryonic stem cells. This order revokes Bush's policy on stem cell research, which limited the use of stem cells to those obtained without "creating a human embryo" or "destroying, discarding, or subjecting to harm a human embryo or fetus" (EO 13435, issued in 2007).

During his first week as president, Obama issued a memorandum in which he reversed the Bush administration's ban on using federal money to fund international groups that perform abortions or provide abortion information and counseling. The policy on abortion funding for international groups was initially established in 1984 by former Republican president Ronald Reagan, and since then this policy has been reversed and reinstated by Democrat and

Republican presidents. In 1993, the first year of his presidency, Bill Clinton reversed the ban, and then, as one of his first acts in office in 2001, George W. Bush reinstated the ban.

Democratic control also meant the passage of legislation that reflected a more liberal agenda. Early in 2009 Congress passed legislation that increased the ability of women to sue a company for wage discrimination, even if they do not discover the practice until years after it began, reversing a Supreme Court decision (Stolberg 2009). Republicans had declined to pass such legislation. The Democratic Congress then passed an economic stimulus bill in an effort to boost the sagging economy. Republicans wanted extensive tax cuts, but Democrats put more emphasis and spending on "expanded unemployment benefits, food stamps, health care subsidies for those laid off and aid to states...[the bill also] includes spending for construction of highways and bridges, school renovations." The bill passed with almost no Republican support. Then during the summer of 2009 Democrats pursued expansion of health care coverage to those currently without coverage. It was again a policy initiative that Republicans had declined to pursue. Democratic Party control meant the enactment of policies and the pursuit of a policy agenda that Republicans would not have pursued, just as Republican control from 2001 to 2006 meant pursuit of an agenda Democrats would not have pursued.

The Consequences of Party Control: A Tentative Summary

These examples from 2000 to the present suggest two main points. First, policy is continually made, unmade, and remade. Increased polarization means that voters are presented with clearer senses of the differences between Democrats and Republicans. Increased party unity, at least under Republicans, allowed the president to act as if he had a greater mandate to change the direction of public policy than was the case in the past. The Democratic Party is now more diverse, and it remains to be seen just how much policy difference will occur under unified Democratic control. But if unified party control matters more now, it suggests that policy may be likely to fluctuate more as partisan control varies. As the examples above demonstrate, this results in stalemate for public policy outcomes. We may have entered a period in which policies are issued and enacted under one party, and then reversed when there is a change in party control.

A second and related point is that it appears that increased party polarization can lead to an executive with more policy impact. A president with a more clearly defined electoral base may be inclined to focus more on that base and to issue orders designed to respond to that base. When party control changes, policy directions change significantly with the use of executive orders. We do not know whether this occurred on a regular basis in the past, as we lack systematic analyses of this issue. But, by way of speculation, we presume that the greater clarity of presidential electoral bases has prompted executives to use their power more than in the past to respond to their electoral base. Polarization of parties is certainly not the sole cause of a more activist and forceful presidency. Indeed, scholars have long cited increased institutional power as an explanation for the bigger role that presidents now occupy in politics (e.g., Crenson and Ginsberg 2007; Lowi 1985). We attribute the increase in presidential power not only to institutional factors but also to the increasing polarization of the bases of parties. In the 1970s and 1980s, there was less party polarization accompanied by long periods of divided control. In the last decade, further polarized parties, along with increased institutional power, often means a unified government and a more powerful executive. From what we surmise, this has led to more occasions for policy stalemate, or, in other words, for policy to flip dramatically from one direction to another.

We have a great deal to learn about the impact of parties on public policy. Sorting this out has been difficult because the parties did not differ as much in prior decades and we had limited alternation of party power. Now we have parties that differ more and it appears that control means more. If polarization persists, we will have more and more cases for testing just how much party control matters.

Bibliography

Aberbach, Joel. "Transforming the Presidency: The Administration of Ronald Reagan." In *The Reagan Presidency: Assessing the Man and his Legacy*, edited by Paul Kengor and Peter Schweizer. Lanham, MD: Rowman & Littlefield, 2005, 191–207.

———. "Supplying the Defect of Better Motives? The Bush II Administration and the Constitutional System." In *The George W. Bush Legacy*, edited by Colin Campbell, Bert A. Rockman, and Andrew Rudalevige. Washington, DC: CQ Press, 2008, 112–34.

Abrajano, Marisa A., R. Michael Alvarez, and Jonathan Nagler. "The Hispanic Vote in the 2004 Election: Insecurity and Moral Concerns." *Journal of Politics* 70, no. 2 (2008): 368–82.

———, R. Michael Alvarez. *New Faces, New Voices: The Hispanic Electorate in America*. Princeton, NJ: Princeton University Press, 2010.

Abramowitz, Alan I. "Issue Evolution Reconsidered: Racial Attitudes and Partisanship in the U.S. Electorate." *American Journal of Political Science* 1 (February, 1994): 1–24.

Abramowitz, Alan I., and Kyle L. Saunders. "Ideological Realignments in the U.S. Electorate." *Journal of Politics* 60 (1998 August): 634–652.

Abramowitz, Alan, and Walter J. Stone. "The Bush Effect: Polarization, Turnout and Activism in the 2004 Presidential Election." *Presidential Studies Quarterly* 36, no. 2 (2006): 141–54.

———, Ruy Teixeira. "The Decline of the White Working Class and the Rise of the Mass Upper-Middle Class." In *Red, Blue and Purple America: The Future of Election Demographics*, edited by Ruy Teixeira. Washington, DC: Brookings Institution, 2008, 109–46.

Abramson, Paul R., John H. Aldrich, and David W. Rohde. *Change and Continuity in the 1984 Elections*. Washington, DC: CQ Press, 1986.

———. *Change and Continuity in the 1992 Elections*. Washington, DC: CQ Press, 1995.

———. *Change and Continuity in the 2008 Elections*. Washington, DC: CQ Press, 2010.

———. Jill Rickershauer, and David W. Rohde, "Fear in the Voting Booth: The 2004 Presidential Election." *Political Behavior* 29 (2007): 197–220.

Adams, Greg D. "Abortion: Evidence of an Issue Evolution." *American Journal of Political Science* 41, no.3 (1997): 718–37.

Agranoff, Robert. "Introduction: The New Style Campaigning." In *The New Style in Election Campaigning*, edited by Robert Agranoff. Boston: Holbrook, 1972, 3–50.

Ahlstrom, Sydney. *A Religious History of the American People*. New Haven, CT: Yale University Press, 1972.

Aistrup, Joseph A. *The Southern Strategy Revisited: Republican Top-Down Advancement in the South*. Lexington: University of Kentucky Press, 1996.

Aldrich, John H. *Why Parties? The Origin and Transformation of Political Parties in America*. Chicago: University of Chicago Press, 1995.

———, David W. Rohde. "The Transition to Republican Rule in the House: Implications for Theories of Congressional Politics." *Political Science Quarterly* 112 (1997–98): 541–67.

———. "The Consequences of Party Organization in the House: The Role of the Majority and Minority Parties in Conditional Party Government." In *Polarized Politics: Congress and the President in a Partisan Era*, edited by Jon Bond and Richard Fleisher, 31–72. Washington, DC: CQ Press, 2000a.

———. "The Republican Revolution and the House Appropriations Committee." *Journal of Politics* 62 (February 2000b): 1–33.

———. "Congressional Committees in a Continuing Partisan Era." In *Congress Reconsidered*. 9th ed., edited by Lawrence C. Dodd and Bruce Oppenheimer, 217–39. Washington, DC: CQ Press, 2009.

———, Michael Tofias. "One D Is Not Enough: Measuring Conditional Party Government, 1887–2002." In *Party, Process, and Political Change in Congress: Further New Perspectives on the History of Congress*, edited by David Brady and Mathew D. McCubbins. Stanford, CA: Stanford University Press, 2007.

Alford, Robert. *Party and Society*. New York: Rand McNally, 1963.

Alvarez, R. Michael, and Lisa Garcia Bedolla. "Similar Yet Different? Latino and Anglo Party Identification." *Journal of Politics* 63, no. 1 (2003): 123–41.

Allswang, John M. *The New Deal and American Politics: A Study in Political Change*. New York: John Wiley and Sons, 1978.

Andersen, Kristi. *The Creation of a Democratic Majority, 1928–1936*. Chicago: University of Chicago Press, 1979.

Ansolabehere, Stephen, and Shanto Iyengar. "Riding the Wave and Claiming Ownership over Issues: The Joint Effects of Advertising and News Coverage in Campaigns." *Public Opinion Quarterly* 58 (Autumn 1994): 334–57.

Arnold, Peri E. "Effecting a Progressive Presidency: Roosevelt, Taft, and the Pursuit of Strategic Resources." *Studies in American Political Development* (Spring 2003): 61–81.

Baer, Kenneth S. *Reinventing Democrats: The Politics of Liberalism from Reagan to Clinton*. Lawrence, KS: University Press of Kansas, 2000.

Bageant, Joe. *Deer Hunting with Jesus: Dispatches from America's Class War*. New York: Crown, 2007.

Baker, Peter. "Bipartisanship Isn't So Easy, Obama Sees," *New York Times*, February 13, 2009.

Baker, Ross K. *House and Senate*. 3rd ed. New York: WW Norton, 2001.

Barker, Lucius J., and Mack H. Jones. *Blacks and the American Political System*. 3rd ed. Upper Saddle River, NJ: Prentice Hall, 1994.

———, Katherine Tate. *Blacks and the American Political System*. 4th ed. Upper Saddle River, NJ: Prentice Hall, 1999.

Barnes, Bart. "Barry Goldwater, GOP Hero, Dies," *Washington Post*, May 30, 1998, A1.

Bartels, Larry M. "Messages Received: The Political Impact of Media Exposure." *American Political Science Review* 87 (1993): 267–85.

———. "Partisanship and Voting Behavior, 1952–1996." *American Journal of Political Science* 44 (January 2000): 35–49.

———. *Unequal Democracy: The Political Economy of a New Gilded Age*. Princeton, NJ: Princeton University Press, 2008.

Bass, Harold F. "George W. Bush, Presidential Party Leadership Extraordinaire?" *The Forum*, 2, no. 4 (2004): art. 6.

Beachler, Donald. "Ordinary Events and Extraordinary Times: The 2002 Congressional Elections." In *Transformed by Crisis: The Presidency of George W. Bush and American Politics*, edited by Jon Kraus, Kevin J. McMahon, and David M. Rankin. New York: Palgrave Macmillan, 2004, 29–50.

Beck, Paul A. "Incomplete Realignment: The Regan Legacy for Parties and Elections." In *The Reagan Legacy: Promise and Performance*, edited by Charles O. Jones. Chatham, NJ: Chatham House, 1988, 145–71.

Beland, Daniel, and Alex Waddan. "Conservative Ideas and Social Policies in the United States." *Social Policy and Administration* 41, no.7 (2007): 768–86.

Bell, Daniel. *The End of Ideology*. New York: Collier Books, 1962.

———. *The Coming of Post-Industrial Society*. New York: Basic Books, 1973.

Benda, Peter M., and Charles H. Levine. "Reagan and the Bureaucracy: The Bequest, the Promise, and the Legacy." In *The Reagan Legacy: Promise and Performance*, edited by Charles O. Jones, 102–42. Chatham, NJ: Chatham House, 1988.

Bendetto, Richard. "Bush Advocates Electronic Medical Record-Keeping," *USA Today*, May 27, 2004. http://ww.usatoday.com/news/politicselections/nation/president/2004 05 27-bush-medical-records_x.htm.

Bennett, W. Lance. *News: The Politics of Illusion*. 8th ed. New York: Longman, 2009.

Bensel, Richard Franklin. *The Political Economy of American Industrialization 1877–1900*. New York: Cambridge University Press, 2000.

Berelson, Bernard R., Paul F. Lazarsveld, and William N. McPhee. *Voting: A Study of Opinion Formation in a Presidential Campaign*. Chicago: University of Chicago Press, 1954.

Berger, Peter L. *The Sacred Canopy*. Garden City, NY: Doubleday, 1967.

Berlet, Chip, and Matthew N. Lyons. *Right-Wing Populism in America: Too Close for Comfort*. New York: Guilford Press, 2000.

Berman, Larry. "Looking Back on the Reagan Presidency." In *Looking Back on the Reagan Presidency*, edited by Larry Berman. Baltimore, MD: Johns Hopkins University Press, 1990, 3–17.

Bibby and Schaffner. *Politics, Parties, and Elections in America*. 6th ed. Boston, MA: Thomson Wadsworth, 2008.

Binder, Sarah A. "The Dynamics of Legislative Gridlock, 1947–1996." *American Political Science Review* 93 (September 1999): 519–33.

———. *Stalemate: Causes and Consequences of Legislative Gridlock*. Washington, DC: Brookings Institution Press, 2003.

———. "Consequence for the Courts: Polarized Politics and the Judicial Branch." In *Red and Blue Nation?* edited by Pietro S. Nivola and David W. Brady, 107–33. Washington, DC: Brookings Institution Press, 2008.

Bishop, Bill, and Robert Cushing. "The Big Sort: Migration, Community, and Politics in the United States of 'Those People.'" In *Red, Blue and Purple America: The Future of Election Demographics*, edited by Ruy Teixeira, 50–78. Washington: Brookings Institution Press, 2008.

Black, Earl, and Merle Black. *Politics and Society in the South*. Cambridge, MA: Harvard University Press, 1987.

———. *The Vital South*. Cambridge, MA: Harvard University Press, 1992.

———. *The Rise of Southern Republicans*. Cambridge, MA: Harvard University Press, 2002.

Bond, Jon R., and Richard Fleisher. *Polarized Politics: Congress and the President in a Partisan Era*. Washington, DC: CQ Press, 2000.

———, Jeffrey M. Stonecash. *"The Rise and Decline of Moderates in the House of Representatives,"* paper presented at the Going to Extremes Conference, Dartmouth College, June, 2008.

Boogers, Marcel, and Gerrit Voerman. "Surfing Citizens and Floating Voters: Results of an Online Survey of Visitors to Political Web Sites during the Dutch 2002 General Elections." *Information Polity* 8, nos. 1–2 (2003): 17–27.

Boorstin, Daniel J. *The Image: A Guide to Pseudo-Events in America*. New York: Vintage, 1961.

Borowiak, Craig. "Accountability Debates: The Federalists, the Anti-Federalists, and Democratic Deficits." *Journal of Politics* 43, no. 3 (2007): 640.

Bositis, David A. *Blacks and the 2008 Election: A Preliminary Analysis*. Washington, DC: Joint Center for Political and Economic Studies, 2008.

Bowen, William G., Matthew M. Chingos, and Michael S. McPherson. *Crossing the Finish Line: Completing College at America's Public Universities*. Princeton, NJ: Princeton University Press, 2009.

Bowles, Samuel, Herbert Gintis, and Melissa Osborne Groves. *Unequal Chances: Family Background and Economic Success*. New York: Russell Sage, 2005.

Bowser, Benjamin P. *The Black Middle Class: Social Mobility and Vulnerability*. Boulder, CO: Lynne Rienner, 2007.

Box-Steffensmeier, Janet M., Suzanna De Boef, and Tse-Min Lin. "The Dynamics of the Partisan Gender Gap." *American Political Science Review* 98 (2004): 515–28.

Bradbury, Katherine, and Jane Katz. "Are Lifetime Incomes Growing More Unequal?" *Regional Review Q4* (September 2002a). http://www.bos.frb.org/economic/nerr/rr2002/q4/issues.pdf.

———, Jane Katz. "Women's Labor Market Involvement and Family Income Mobility When Marriage Ends." *New England Economic Review* 4 (September 2002b). http://www.bos.frb.org/economic/neer/neer2002/neer402c.pdf.

Brady, David W., Ferejohn, John, and Laurel Harbridge. "Polarization and Public Policy: A General Assessment." In *Red and Blue Nation?* edited by Pietro S. Nivola and David W. Brady. Washington, DC: Brookings Institution, 2008, 107–33.

———, Craig Volden. *Revolving Gridlock*. 2nd ed. Boulder, CO: Westview, 2006.

Bratton, Kathleen A., and Kerry L. Haynie. "Agenda-Setting and Legislative Success in State Legislatures: The Effects of Gender and Race." *The Journal of Politics* 63, no. 3 (1999): 658–79.

———, Beth Reingold. "Agenda Setting and Black Women in State Legislatures." *Journal of Women Politics and Policy* 28, nos. 3–4 (2006): 71–96.

Brewer, Mark D. "The Rise of Partisanship and the Expansion of Partisan Conflict within the American Electorate." *Political Research Quarterly* 58 (June 2005): 219–29.

Brewer, Mark D., and Jeffrey M. Stonecash. "Class, Race Issues, Declining White Support for the Democratic Party in the South." *Political Behavior,* vol. 23, no. 2 (June 2001): 131–55.

———. *Split: Class and Cultural Divides in American Politics.* Washington, DC: CQ Press, 2007.

———. *The Dynamics of American Political Parties.* New York: Cambridge University Press, 2009.

Broder, David. *The Party's Over: The Failure of Politics in America.* New York: Harper and Row, 1972.

Broder, David. *Democracy Derailed: Initiative Campaigns and the Power of Money.* New York: Harcourt, 2000.

Browning, Rufus P., Dale Rogers Marshall, and David H. Tabb. *Protest Is Not Enough.* Berkeley: University of California Press, 1984.

Brownstein, Ronald. *The Second Civil War: How Extreme Partisanship Has Paralyzed Washington and Polarized America.* New York: Penguin, 2007.

Budge, Ian, and Dennis J. Farlie. *Explaining and Predicting Elections: Issue-Effects and Party Strategies in 23 Democracies.* London: Allen & Unwin, 1983.

Burner, David. *The Politics of Provincialism: The Democratic Party in Transition, 1918– 1932.* New York: Alfred A. Knopf, 1968.

Burns, James McGregor. *Deadlock of Democracy: Four-Party Politics in American.* Englewood Cliffs, NJ: Prentice-Hall, 1963.

Busch, Andrew E. *Ronald Reagan and the Politics of Freedom.* Lanham, MD: Rowman and Littlefield, 2001.

———. "National Security and the Midterm Elections of 2002." In *Transforming the American Polity: The Presidency of George W. Bush and the War on Terrorism,* edited by Richard S. Conley. Upper Saddle River, NJ: Pearson Prentice Hall, 2005, 40–61.

Cadge, Wendy, Laura R. Olson, and Christopher Wildeman. "How Denominational Resources Influence Debates about Homosexuality in Mainline Protestant Congregations." *Sociology of Religion* 69, no. 2 (Summer 2008): 187–207.

Callaghan, Karen, and Frauke Schnell. "Assessing the Democratic Debate: How the News Media Frame Elite Policy Discourse." *Political Communication* 18 (2001): 183–212.

Calmes, Jackie. "House Passes Stimulus Bill with No G.O.P. Votes." *The New York Times,* January 28, 2009. http://www.nytimes.com/2009/01/29/us/politics/29obama.html.

Campbell, Angus, Philip E. Converse, Warren E. Miller, and Donald E. Stokes. *The American Voter.* New York: Wiley, 1960.

Campbell, David E. *A Matter of Faith: Religion in the 2004 Presidential Election.* Washington, DC: Brookings Institution Press, 2007.

———, J. Quin Monson. "Dry Kindling: A Political Profile of American Mormons." In *From Pews to Polling Places: Faith and Politics in the American Religious Mosaic,* edited by J. Matthew Wilson, 105–29. Washington, DC: Georgetown University Press, 2007.

Campbell, Ernest Q., and Thomas F. Pettigrew. *Christians in Racial Crisis: A Study of Little Rock's Ministry.* Washington, DC: Public Affairs, 1959.

Campbell, Paul R. "Population Projections for States by Age, Sex, Race, and Hispanic Origin: 1995–2025." ed. Paul A. Djupe. Washington, DC: U.S. Census Bureau, 1996.

Capozzola, Christopher. *Uncle Sam Wants You: World War I and the Making of the Modern American Citizen.* Oxford, UK: Oxford University Press, 2008.

Carmines, Edward G., and James A. Stimson. *Issue Evolution: Race and the Transformation of American Politics.* Princeton, NJ: Princeton University Press, 1989.

Carpini, Michael X. Delli, and Scott Keeter. *What Americans Know about Politics and Why it Matters.* New Haven, CT: Yale University Press, 1996.

Carsey, Thomas M., and Gerald C. Wright. "State and National Factors in Gubernatorial and Senatorial Elections." *American Journal of Political Science* 42, no. 3 (July 1998): 994–1002.

Carter, Dan T. *The Politics of Rage: George Wallace, the Origins of the New Conservatism, and the Transformation of American Politics.* New York: Simon and Schuster, 1995.

———. *From George Wallace to Newt Gingrich: Race in the Conservative Counterrevolution.* Baton Rouge: Louisiana State University Press, 1996.

Ceaser, James. *Presidential Selection: Theory and Development.* Princeton, NJ: Princeton University Press, 1979.

Chiou, Fang-Yi, and Lawrence S. Rothenberg. "When Pivotal Politics Meets Partisan Politics." *American Journal of Political Science* 47 (July 2003): 503–22.

Chong, Dennis, and James N. Druckman. "Framing Public Opinion in Competitive Democracies." *American Political Science Review* 101, no. 4 (2007): 637–55.

Claibourn, Michele P. "Making a Connection: Repetition and Priming in Presidential Campaigns." *Journal of Politics* 70 (2008): 1142–59.

Clubb, Jerome M., and Howard W. Allen. "The Cities and the Election of 1928: Partisan Realignment?" *American Historical Review* 74 (1969 April): 1205–1220.

Cobb, Michael D., and James H. Kuklinski. "Changing Minds: Political Arguments and Political Persuasion." *American Journal of Political Science* 41, no.1 (1997): 88–121.

Cochran, Clarke E., and David Carroll Cochran. *Catholics, Politics, and Public Policy: Beyond Left and Right.* Maryknoll, NY: Orbis, 2003.

Coleman, John J. "Unified Government, Divided Government, and Party Responsiveness." *American Political Science Review* 93, no. 4 (1999): 821–35.

Congressional Quarterly. *Congressional Quarterly's Guide to U.S. Elections.* 5th ed. Washington, DC: CQ Press, 2005.

Converse, Philip E. "The Nature of Belief Systems in Mass Publics." In *Ideology and Discontent,* edited by David E. Apter. New York: Free Press, 1964.

Corn, David. "This Wasn't Quite the Change We Pictured,." *Washington Post,* December 7, 2008. http://www.washingtonpost.com/wp-dyn/content/article/2008/12/05/AR2008120502602.html.

Cox, Gary W., and Mathew D. McCubbins. *Legislative Leviathan.* Berkeley: University of California Press, 1993.

———. *Setting the Agenda.* New York: Cambridge University Press, 2005.

Craig, Barbara Hinkson, and David M. O'Brien. *Abortion and American Politics.* Chatham, NJ: Chatham House, 1993.

Crenson, Matthew, and Benjamin Ginsberg. *Downsizing Democracy: How America Sidelined Its Citizens and Privatized Its Politics.* Baltimore: Johns Hopkins University Press, 2002.

Crenson, Matthew, and Benjamin Ginsberg. *Presidential Power: Unchecked and Unbalanced*. New York: Norton, 2007.

Croly, Herbert. *Progressive Democracy*. New York: Macmillan, 1914.

Crotty, William. *American Political Parties in Decline*. 2nd ed. Boston: Little, Brown, 1984.

Dahl, Robert A. *Who Governs?* New Haven, CT: Yale University Press, 1961.

Dale, Allison, and Aaron Strauss. "Don't Forget to Vote: Text Message Reminders as a Mobilization Tool." *American Journal of Political Science* 53, no. 4 (2009): 787–804.

Dalton, Russell J., Paul Allen Beck, Robert Huckfeldt, and William Koetzle. "A Test of Media-Centered Agenda Setting: Newspaper Content and Public Interests in a Presidential Election." *Political Communication* 15 (1998): 463–81.

Daniel Galvin. *Presidential Party Building*. Princeton, NJ: Princeton University Press.

Danziger, Sheldon, and Peter Gottschalk. *America Unequal*. Cambridge, MA: Harvard University Press, 1995.

Dawson, Michael C. *Behind the Mule: Race and Class in Black Politics*. Princeton, NJ: Princeton University Press, 1994.

Debs, Eugene. "Statement to the Court Upon Being Convicted of the Sedition Act, September 18, 1918." http://www.wfu.edu/~zulick/341/Debs1918.html.

de la Garza, Rodolfo O. *Latino Voices: Mexican, Puerto Rican, and Cuban Perspectives on American Politics*. Boulder, CO: Westview, 1992.

Democratic National Committee (DNC). 2008. "2008 Democratic Party National Platform."

Derthick, Martha, and Steven Teles. "Riding the Third Rail: Social Security Reform." In *The Reagan Presidency: Pragmatic Conservatism and Its Legacies*, edited by W. Elliot Brownlee and Hugh Davis Graham. Lawrence: University Press of Kansas, 2003, 182–208.

DeSipio, Louis. *Counting on the Latino Vote: Latinos as a New Electorate*. Charlottesville, VA: University of Virginia Press, 1996.

de Tocqueville, Alexis. 1840. *Democracy in America*, edited by J. P. Mayer, translated by George Lawrence. New York: Harper and Row, 1988.

DiMaggio, Paul, John H. Evans, and Bethany Bryson. "Have Americans' Social Attitudes Become More Polarized?" *American Journal of Sociology* 102, no. 3 (November 1996): 690–755.

Dionne, E. J., Jr. *They Only Look Dead*. New York: Touchstone, 1997.

Djupe, Paul A. "The Evolution of Jewish Pluralism: The Public Opinion and Political Preferences of American Jews." In *From Pews to Polling Places: Faith and Politics in the American Religious Mosaic*, edited by J. Matthew Wilson, 185–212. Washington, DC: Georgetown University Press, 2007.

———, Christopher P. Gilbert. "The Resourceful Believer: Generating Civic Skills in Church." *Journal of Politics* 68, no. 1 (February 2006): 116–27.

———, Christopher P. Gilbert. *The Political Influence of Church*. New York: Cambridge University Press, 2009.

———, J. Tobin Grant. "Religious Institutions and Political Participation in America." *Journal for the Scientific Study of Religion* 40, no. 2 (June 2001): 303–14.

———, John C. Green. "The Politics of American Muslims." In *From Pews to Polling Places: Faith and Politics in the American Religious Mosaic*, edited by J. Matthew Wilson, 213–50. Washington, DC: Georgetown University Press, 2007.

Domke, David, and Kevin Coe. *The God Strategy: How Religion Became a Political Weapon in America*. New York: Oxford University Press, 2008.

Druckman, James N. "Priming the Vote." *Political Psychology* 25 (2004): 577–94.

———, Martin J. Kifer, and Michael Parkin. "The Technological Development of Congressional Candidate Web Sites." *Social Science Computer Review* 25, no. 4 (2007): 425–42.

———, Michael Parkin. "The Impact of Media Bias: How Editorial Slant Affects Voters." *Journal of Politics* 67, no. 4 (2005): 1030–49.

Dwyre, Diana. "Spinning Straw into Gold: Soft Money and U.S. House Elections." *Legislative Studies Quarterly* 21, no. 3 (August 1996): 409–24.

———, Victoria Farrar-Myers. *Legislative Labyrinth: Congress and Campaign Finance Reform*. Washington, DC: CQ Press, 2001.

———, Robin Kolodny. "The Parties' Congressional Campaign Committees in 2004." In *The Election after Reform*, edited by Michael J. Malbin. Lanham, MD: Rowman and Littlefield, 2006, 38–56.

Eagles, Charles W. *Democracy Delayed: Congressional Reapportionment and Urban-Rural Conflict in the 1920s*. Athens: University of Georgia Press, 1990.

Edling, Max. *A Revolution in Favor of Government: Origins of the U.S. Constitution and the Meaning of the American State*. Oxford: Oxford University Press, 2003.

Edsall, Thomas B., with Mary D. Edsall. *Chain Reaction: The Impact of Race, Rights, and Taxes on American Politics*. New York: Norton, 1991.

Eggen, Dan. "Health Care Reform, One Stop at a Time," *Washington Post*, August 31, 2009. http://www.washingtonpost.com/wp-dyn/content/article/2009/08/30/AR2009083002654.html.

———, Michael D. Shear. "The Effort to Roll Back Bush Policies Continues," *Washington Post*, January 27, 2009. http://www.washingtonpost.com/wp-dyn/content/article/2009/01/26/AR2009012602086.html.

Ehrenreich, Barbara. *Bait and Switch: The (Futile) Pursuit of the American Dream*. New York: Owl Book/Holt, 2005.

Ehrman, John. *The Eighties: America in the Age of Reagan*. New Haven, CT: Yale University Press, 2005.

Eilperin, Juliet. *Fight Club Politics: How Partisanship Is Poisoning the House of Representatives*. Lanham, MD: Rowman and Littlefield, 2006.

Eisenger, Robert, and Brown, Jeremy. "Polling as a Means toward Presidential Autonomy: Emil Hurja, Hadley Cantril, and the Roosevelt Administration." *International Journal of Public Opinion* 10 (1998): 239–56.

Eldersveld, Samuel J., and Hanes Walton, Jr. *Political Parties in American Society*. 2nd ed. Boston, MA: Bedford/St. Martin's, 2000.

Ellis, Christopher, and James A. Stimson. "On Symbolic Conservatism in America," paper presented at the 2007 Annual American Political Science Meetings, Chicago.

Epstein, David, and Sharyn O'Halloran. *Delegating Powers: A Transaction Cost Politics Approach to Policy Making under Separate Powers*. New York: Cambridge University Press, 1999.

Epstein, Leon D. *Political Parties in the American Mold*. Madison: University of Wisconsin Press, 1986.

Erie, Steven P. *Rainbow's End: Irish-Americans and the Dilemmas of Urban Machine Politics, 1840–1985*. Berkeley: University of California Press, 1988.

Evans, Geoff, ed. *The Political Significance of Class.* Oxford, UK: Oxford University Press, 1996.

Evans, John H. "Have Americans' Attitudes Become More Polarized? An Update." *Social Science Quarterly* 84, no.1 (March 2003): 71–90.

Farnsworth, Stephen J., and S. Robert Lichter. *The Nightly News Nightmare: Network Television's Coverage of U.S. Presidential Elections, 1988–2004.* 2nd ed. New York: Rowman and Littlefield, 2006.

Farrar-Myers, Victoria A. and Diana Dwyre. "Parties and Campaign Finance." In *American Political Parties: Decline or Resurgence?* edited by Jeffrey E. Cohen, Richard Fleisher, and Paul Kantpr. Washington, DC: CQ Press, 2001, 138–61.

Federal Election Commission. "FEC Reports Major Increase in Party Activity for 1995–96." Press release, March 19, 1997, http://www.fec.gov/press/press1997/ptyye1.htm.

———. "Party Committees Raise More Than $1 Billion in 2001–2002." Press release, March 20, 2003, http://www.fec.gov/press/press2003/20030320party/20030103party.html.

———. "Party Financial Activity Summarized for the 2008 Election Cycle: Party Support for Candidates Increases." Press release, May 28, 2009, http://www.fec.gov/press/press2009/05282009Party/20090528Party.shtml

Feinstein, Brian D., and Eric Schickler. "Platforms and Partners: The Civil Rights Realignment Reconsidered." *Studies in American Political Development* 22 (Spring 2008): 115–16.

Fenno, Richard F., Jr. *Congressmen in Committees.* Boston, MA: Little, Brown, 1973.

———. *Home Style: House Members in their Districts.* Boston, MA: Little, Brown, 1978.

Ferling, John. *Adams vs. Jefferson: The Tumultuous Election of 1800.* New York: Oxford University Press, 2004.

Festinger, Leon. *A Theory of Cognitive Dissonance.* Stanford, CA: Stanford University Press, 1957.

Findlay, James F. *Church People in the Struggle: The National Council of Churches and the Black Freedom Movement, 1950–1970.* New York. Oxford University Press, 1993.

Fine, Janice, and Daniel J. Tichenor. "A Movement Wrestling: American Labor's Enduring Struggle with Immigration, 1866–2007." *Studies in American Political Development* 23, no. 01 (2009): 84–113.

Finke, Roger, and Rodney Stark. *The Churching of America, 1776–2005: Winners and Losers in Our Religious Economy.* New Brunswick, NJ: Rutgers University Press, 2005.

Finocchiaro, Charles J., and David W. Rohde. "War for the Floor: Partisan Theory and Agenda Control in the U.S. House of Representatives." *Legislative Studies Quarterly* 33 (February 2008): 35–61.

Fiorina, Morris P. "The Decline of Collective Responsibility in American Politics." *Daedalus,* vol. 109, No. 3 (1980 Summer): 25–45.

———. *Divided Government.* Boston: Allyn and Bacon, 1992.

———, with Samuel J. Abrams and Jeremy C. Pope. *Culture War? The Myth of a Polarized America.* 2nd ed. New York: Pearson Longman, 2006.

Fix, Michael E., Jeffrey S. Passel, and Kenneth Suche. *Trends in Naturalization* (Policy Briefs/Immigrant Families and Workers). Washington, DC: Urban Institute, 2003.

Foner, Eric, ed. *Freedom's Lawmakers: A Directory of Black Officeholders During Reconstruction*. Rev. ed. Baton Rouge: Louisiana State University Press, 1996.

Foot, Kirsten A., and Stephen M. Schneider. *Web Campaigning*. Cambridge, MA: MIT Press, 2006.

Fordham, Benjamin O. "The Evolution of Republican and Democratic Positions on Cold War Military Spending: A Historical Puzzle." Manuscript, Binghamton University, n.d.

Forman, Ira N. "The Politics of Minority Consciousness: The Historical Voting Behavior of American Jews." In *Jews in American Politics*, edited by L. Sandy Maisel and Ira N. Forman, 141–60. Lanham, MD: Rowman and Littlefield, 2001.

Fortier, John C., and Norman J. Ornstein. "President Bush: Legislative Strategist." In *The George W. Bush Presidency: An Early Assessment*, edited by Fred I Greenstein. Baltimore, MD: Johns Hopkins University Press, 2003, 138–72.

Fowler, Robert Booth. *Unconventional Partners: Religion and Liberal Culture in the United States*. Grand Rapids, MI: Eerdmans, 1989.

Frank, Thomas. *What's the Matter with Kansas? How Conservatives Won the Heart of America*. New York: Metropolitan Books, 2004.

———. *The Wrecking Crew*. New York: Metropolitan Books, 2008.

Frederickson, Kari A. *The Dixiecrat Revolt and the End of the Solid South, 1932–1968*. Chapel Hill: University of North Carolina Press, 2001.

Free, Lloyd A., and Hadley Cantril. *The Political Beliefs of Americans: A Study of Public Opinion*. New Brunswick, NJ: Rutgers University Press, 1967.

Freeman, Joanne B. *Affairs of Honor: National Politics in the New Republic*. New Haven, CT: Yale University Press, 2001.

Freidel, Frank. *F.D.R. and the South*. Baton Rouge: Louisiana State University Press, 1965.

Friedland, Michael B. *Lift Up Your Voice Like a Trumpet: White Clergy and the Civil Rights and Antiwar Movements, 1954–1973*. Chapel Hill: University of North Carolina Press, 1998.

Frisch, Morton J. *Franklin D. Roosevelt: The Contribution to the New Deal to American Political Thought and Practice*. Boston, MA: St. Wayne, 1975.

Frymer, Paul. *Uneasy Alliances: Race and Party Competition in America*. Princeton, NJ: Princeton University Press, 1999.

Gamson, William A., and Andre Modigliani. "Media Discourse and Public Opinion on Nuclear Power: A Constructionist Approach." *American Journal of Sociology* 95, no. 1 (1989): 1–37.

Garson, Robert A. *The Democratic Party and the Politics of Sectionalism, 1941–1948*. Baton Rouge: Louisiana State University Press, 1974.

Germond, Jack W., and Jules Witcover. *Wake Us When It's Over: Presidential Politics of 1984*. New York: Macmillan, 1985.

Gerring, John. *Party Ideologies in America, 1828–1996*. New York: Cambridge University Press, 1998.

Gienapp, William E. *The Origins of the Republican Party 1852–1856*. New York: Oxford University Press, 1987.

Gilens, Martin. *Why Americans Hate Welfare*. Chicago: University of Chicago Press, 2000.

Ginsberg, Benjamin, and Shefter, Martin. "The Presidency, Interest Groups, and Social Forces: Creating a Republican Coalition." In *The Presidency and the Political System*. 3rd ed., edited by Michael Nelson, 335–52. Washington, DC: CQ Press, 1990.

Gitell, Seth. "The Democratic Party Suicide Bill." *Atlantic Monthly* (July/August 2003): 106–13.

Glazer, Amihai, and Marc Robbins. "Congressional Responsiveness to Constituency Change." *American Journal of Political Science* 29, no. 2 (1985): 259–73

Glazer, Nathan, and Daniel Patrick Moynihan. *Beyond the Melting Pot: The Negroes, Puerto Ricans, Jews, Italians, and Irish of New York City.* Cambridge, MA: MIT Press, 1963.

Glock, Charles Y., and Rodney Stark. *Religion and Society in Tension.* Chicago: Rand McNally, 1965.

Goffman, Erving. *Frame Analysis.* New York: Harper & Row, 1974.

Goldberg, Robert Alan. *Barry Goldwater.* New Haven, CT: Yale University Press, 1995.

Goldstein, Dana, and Klein, Ezra. "It's His Party." *The American Prospect,* August 18, 2008. http://www.prospect.org/cs/articles?article=its_his_party_08.

Graber, Doris. *Mass Media and American Politics.* 7th ed. Washington, DC: CQ Press, 2006.

Graetz, Michael J., and Ian Shapiro. *Death by a Thousand Cuts: The Fight Over Taxing Inherited Wealth.* Princeton, NJ: Princeton University Press, 2004.

Greeley, Andrew, and Michael Hout. *The Truth about Conservative Christians: What They Think and What They Believe.* Chicago: University of Chicago Press, 2006.

Green, Donald, Bradley Palmquist, and Eric Schickler. *Partisan Hearts and Minds.* New Haven, CT: Yale University Press, 2002.

Green, John C. *The Faith Factor: How Religion Influences American Elections.* Westport, CT: Praeger, 2007.

———, James L. Guth, Corwin E. Smidt, and Lyman A. Kellstedt, eds. *Religion and the Culture Wars: Dispatches from the Front.* Lanham, MD: Rowman and Littlefield, 1996.

Greenberg, Anna, and Kenneth D. Wald. "Still Liberal after All These Years? The Contemporary Political Behavior of American Jewry." In *Jews in American Politics,* edited by L. Sandy Maisel and Ira N. Forman, 161–93. Lanham, MD: Rowman and Littlefield, 2001.

Gurin, Patricia, Shirley Hatchett, and James S. Jackson. *Hope and Independence: Blacks' Response to Electoral and Party Politics.* New York: Russell Sage Foundation, 1989.

Guth, James, et al. "Faith and Foreign Policy: A View from the Pews." *The Review of Faith and International Affairs* 3, no. 2 (Fall 2005): 3–10.

———, John C. Green. *The Bible and the Ballot Box: Religion and Politics in the 1988 Election.* Boulder, CO: Westview Press, 1991.

———, Corwin E. Smidt, Lyman A. Kellstedt, and Margaret M. Poloma. *The Bully Pulpit: The Politics of Protestant Clergy.* Lawrence: University Press of Kansas, 1997.

Gyory, Andrew. *Closing the Gate: Race, Politics, and the Chinese Exclusion Act.* Durham, NC: University of North Carolina Press, 1998.

Hacker, Jacob S. *The Great Risk Shift: The New Economic Insecurity and the Decline of the American Dream.* New York: Oxford University Press, 2008.

———, Paul Pierson. *Off Center: The Republican Revolution and the Evolution of Democracy.* New Haven, CT: Yale University Press, 2005.

Hadden, Jeffrey K. *The Gathering Storm in the Churches.* Garden City, NY: Doubleday, 1969.

Hajnal, Zoltan, and Taeku Lee. "Out of Line: Immigration and Party Identification among Latinos and Asian Americans." In *Transforming Politics, Transforming*

America, edited by T. Lee, K. Ramakrishnan, and R. Ramierez, 129–50. Charlottesville, VA: University of Virginia Press, 2006.

Hamilton, Alexander, James Madison, and John Jay. *The Federalist Papers*. New York: New American Library, 1961.

Harris, Fredrick C. *Something Within: Religion in African-American Political Activism*. New York: Oxford University Press, 1999.

Hartz, Louis. *The Liberal Tradition in America*. New York: Harcourt Brace, 1955.

Hayes, Danny. "Does the Messenger Matter? Candidate-Media Agenda Convergence and Its Effects on Voter Issue Salience." *Political Research Quarterly* 61, no.1 (2008): 134–46.

———. "Party Communication in a Transformed Media Age." In *New Directions in Political Parties*, edited by Jeffrey M. Stonecash, 44–62. New York: Routledge, 2010.

———. "Agenda Convergence and the Paradox of Competitiveness in Presidential Campaigns." *Political Research Quarterly*. Forthcoming.

Haynie, Kerry L. "Representation and the First Black Members of Congress." Paper presented at the annual meeting of the American Political Science Association, Washington, DC, 1991.

———. *Black Legislators in the American States*. New York: Columbia University Press, 2001.

———. "Blacks and the New Politics of Inclusion: A Representational Dilemma?" In *Congress Reconsidered*. 8th ed., edited by Lawrence. C. Dodd and Bruce I. Oppenheimer. Washington, DC: CQ Press, 2005, 395–410.

Heclo, Hugh. "Ronald Reagan and the American Public Philosophy." In *The Reagan Presidency: Pragmatic Conservatism and its Legacies*, edited by W. Elliot Brownlee and Hugh Davis Graham. Lawrence: University Press of Kansas, 2003, 17–39.

Hedge, David M. "The George W. Bush Presidency and Control of the Bureaucracy." Paper presented at the American Political Science Association Meetings, Toronto, September 2009.

Herberg, Will. *Protestant, Catholic, Jew: An Essay in American Religious Sociology*. Garden City, NY: Doubleday, 1955.

Herrnson, Paul S. *Party Campaigning in the 1980s*. Cambridge: Harvard University Press, 1988.

———. "National Party Organizations at the Dawn of the Twenty-First Century." In *The Parties Respond: Changes in American Parties and Campaigns*, edited by L. Sandy Maisel. Boulder, CO: Westview Press, 2002, 47–78.

———, Diana Dwyre. "Party Issue Advocacy in Congressional Elections." In *The State of the Parties: The Changing Role of Contemporary American Parties*. 3rd ed., edited by John C. Green and Daniel M. Shea. Lanham, MD: Rowman & Littlefield, 1999, 86–104.

Hetherington, Marc J. "The Media's Role in Forming Voters' National Economic Evaluations in 1992." *American Journal of Political Science* 40 (1996): 372–95.

———. "Resurgent Mass Partisanship: The Role of Elite Polarization." *American Political Science Review* 95, no. 3 (September 2001): 619–31.

———, Jonathan Weiler. *Authoritarianism and Polarization in American Politics*. New York: Cambridge University Press, 2009.

Hillygus, D. Sunshine, and Todd G. Shields. *The Persuadable Voter: Wedge Issues in Presidential Campaigns*. Princeton, NJ: Princeton University Press, 2008.

Hinckley, Barbara, Richard Hofstetter, and John Kessel. "Information and the Vote: A Comparative Election Study." *American Politics Quarterly* 2, no. 2 (April 1974): 131–58.

Hindman, Matthew. "The Real Lessons of Howard Dean: Reflections on the First Digital Campaign." *Perspectives on Politics* 3, no. 1 (2005): 121–28.

Hofstadter, Richard. *The Idea of a Party System: The Rise of Legitimate Opposition in the United States, 1780–1840.* Berkeley: University of California Press, 1969.

Holbrook, Thomas M. "Economic Considerations and the 2008 Presidential Election." *PS: Political Science & Politics* 42, no. 3 (2009): 473–78.

Hout, Michael, and Claude S. Fischer. "Why More Americans Have No Religious Preference: Politics and Generations." *American Sociological Review* 67, no.2 (April 2002): 165–90.

Howard, Philip N. *New Media Campaigns and the Managed Citizen.* New York: Cambridge University Press, 2006.

Huckfedlt, Robert, and Carol Weitzel Kohfeld. *Race and the Decline of Class in American Politics.* Chicago: University of Illinois Press, 1989.

Hunter, James Davison. *Culture Wars: The Struggle to Define America.* New York: Basic Books, 1991.

———. *Culture Wars: The Struggle to Control the Family, Art, Education, Law, and Politics in America.* New York: Basic Books, 1992.

———. *Before the Shooting Begins: Searching for Democracy in America's Culture War.* New York: Free Press, 1994.

Iannaccone, Laurence R. "Why Strict Churches Are Strong." *American Journal of Sociology* 99, no. 5 (March 1994): 1180–1211.

Inglehart, Ronald. "The Silent Revolution in Europe." *American Political Science Review.* 65, no. 4 (December 1971): 991–1017.

———. *Silent Revolution.* Princeton, NJ: Princeton University Press, 1977.

———. *Culture Shift in Advanced Industrial Society.* Princeton, NJ: Princeton University Press, 1990.

Iyengar, Shanto, and Donald R. Kinder. *News That Matters.* Chicago: University of Chicago Press, 1987.

———, Mark D. Peters, and Donald R. Kinder. "Experimental Demonstrations of the 'Not-So-Minimal Consequences of Television News Programs." *American Political Science Review* 76 (1982): 848–58.

Jacobs, Lawrence R. "Communicating from the White House: Narrowcasting and the National Interest." In *The Executive Branch*, edited by Joel D. Aberbach and Mark A. Peterson. New York: Oxford University Press, 2005, 174–217.

Jacobson, Gary C. "Terror, Terrain, and Turnout: Explaining the 2002 Midterm Elections." *Political Science Quarterly* 118, no. 1 (2003): 1–22.

———. "The Public, the President, and the War in Iraq." Paper presented at the Midwest Political Science Association Meetings, 2005.

———. *A Divider, Not a Uniter: George W. Bush and the American People.* New York: Pearson Longman, 2007.

Jacobson, Matthew Frye. *Whiteness of a Different Color: European Immigrants and the Alchemy of Race.* Cambridge, MA: Harvard University Press, 1998.

James, Scott. *Presidents, Parties, and the State: A Party System Perspective on Democratic Regulatory Choice, 1884–1936.* New York: Cambridge University Press, 2000.

———. "The Evolution of the Presidency: Between the Promise and the Fear." In *The Executive Branch*, edited by Joel D. Aberbach and Mark A. Peterson. New York: Oxford University Press, 2005, 3–40.

Jamieson, Kathleen Hall. *Electing the President, 2004: The Insiders' View*. Philadelphia, PA: University of Pennsylvania Press, 2005.

———, Joseph N. Cappella. *Echo Chamber: Rush Limbaugh and the Conservative Media Establishment*. New York: Oxford University Press, 2008.

———, Paul Waldman. *The Press Effect*. New York: Oxford University Press, 2003.

Jensen, Laura. *Patriots, Settlers, and the Origins of American Social Policy*. Cambridge, UK: Cambridge University Press, 2003.

Jillson, Cal. *Pursuing the American Dream: Opportunity and Exclusion over Four Centuries*. Lawrence: University Press of Kansas, 2004.

John, Richard. "Affairs of Office: The Executive Departments, the Election of 1828, and the Making of the Democratic Party." In *The Democratic Experiment: New Directions in American Political History*, edited by Meg Jacobs, William J. Novak, and Julian Zelizer. Princeton, NJ: Princeton University Press, 2003, 50–84.

Johnston, Richard, Michael G. Hagen, and Kathleen Hall Jamieson. *The 2000 Presidential Election and the Foundation of Party Politics*. Cambridge, UK: Cambridge University Press, 2004.

Joint Center for Political and Economic Studies. *Black Elected Officials: A Statistical Summary 2000*. Washington, DC: Joint Center for Political and Economic Studies, 2001.

Jones, Bryan D., and Walter Williams. *The Politics of Good and Bad Ideas: The Great Tax Delusion and the Decline of Good Government in America*. Chicago: University of Chicago Press, 2008.

Jones, Charles O. "Governing Executively: Bush's Paradoxical Style." In *Second Term Blues: How George W. Bush Has Governed*, edited by John C. Fortier and Norman J. Ornstein. Washington, DC: American Enterprise Institute and Brookings Institution, 2007, 109–30.

Jones, David R. "Party Polarization and Legislative Gridlock." *Political Research Quarterly* 54 (March 2001): 125–41.

Jones-Correa, Michael. *Between New Nations: The Political Predicament of Latinos in New York City*. Ithaca, NY: Cornell University Press, 1998.

Judd, Dennis R., and Todd Swanstrom. *City Politics: The Political Economy of Urban America*. 6th ed. New York: Pearson/Longman, 2008.

Just, Marion, Ann N. Crigler, Dean E. Alger, Timothy E. Cook, Montague Kern, and Darrell M. West. *Crosstalk: Citizens, Candidates, and the Media in a Presidential Campaign*. Chicago: University of Chicago Press, 1996.

Kafka, Peter. "Has Matt Drudge Lost His Mojo?" *The Business Insider*, January 3, 2008. http://www.businessinsider.com/2008/1/has-matt-drudge-lost-his-mojo (accessed July 23, 2009).

Kahn, Kim Fridkin, and Patrick J. Kenney. "The Slant of the News: How Editorial Endorsements Influence Campaign Coverage and Citizens' Views of Candidates." *American Political Science Review* 96, no. 2 (2002): 381–94.

Karol, David. *Party Position Change in American Politics: Coalition Management*. New York: Cambridge University Press, 2009.

Katznelson, Ira, Kim Geiger, and Daniel Kryder. "Limiting Liberalism: The Southern Veto in Congress, 1933–1950." *Political Science Quarterly* 108 (Summer 1993): 283–306.

Kaufmann, Karen M., and John R. Petrocik. "The Changing Politics of American Men: Understanding the Sources of the Gender Gap." *American Journal of Political Science* 43 (1999): 864–87.

Keister, Lisa. *Wealth in America.* New York: Cambridge, 2000.

Keith, Bruce E., David B. Magleby, Candice J. Nelson, Elizabeth Orr, Mark C. Westlye, and Raymond E. Wolfinger. *The Myth of the Independent Voter.* Berkeley: University of California Press, 1992.

Kelley, Dean M. *Why Conservative Churches Are Growing: A Study in Sociology of Religion.* New York: Harper and Row, 1972.

Kelly, Nathan J. *The Politics of Income Inequality in the United States.* New York: Cambridge University Press, 2009.

———, Jana Morgan Kelly. "Religion and Latino Partisanship in the United States." *Political Research Quarterly* 58, no. 1 (March 2005.): 87–95.

Kenworthy, Lane, Sondra Barringer, Daniel Durr, and Garrett Andrew Schneider. "The Democrats and Working Class Whites." Unpublished manuscript, 2008.

Kernell, Samuel. "Facing an Opideal Point Congress: The President's Strategic Circumstance." In *The Politics of Divided Government,* edited by Gary W. Cox and Samuel Kernell, 87–112. Boulder, CO: Westview, 1991.

Ketcham, Ralph. *Presidents Above Parties.* Chapel Hill: University of North Carolina Press, 1984.

Keyssar, Alexander. *The Right to Vote: The Contested History of Democracy in the United States.* New York: Basic Books, 2000.

Key, V. O., Jr. *Politics, Parties, and Pressure Groups.* New York: Crowell, 1942.

———. *Southern Politics in State and Nation.* New York: Alfred A. Knopf, 1949.

———. "Secular Realignment and the Party System." *Journal of Politics* 21 (May 1959): 198–210.

———. 1949. *Southern Politics in State and Nation.* Knoxville: University of Tennessee Press, 1984.

Keyssar, Alexander. *The Right to Vote: The Contested History of Democracy in the United States.* New York: Basic Books, 2000.

King, Neil. "Role of White House Czars Sparks Battles," *Wall Street Journal,* September 11, 2009. http://online.wsj.com/article/SB125261851127501015.html.

Klapper, Joseph. *The Effects of Mass Communication.* New York: Free Press, 1960.

Klinghard, Daniel P. "Grover Cleveland, William McKinley, and the Emergence of the President as Party Leader." *Presidential Studies Quarterly* 35, no. 4 (December 2005): 736–60.

Klinkner, Philip A. *The Losing Parties: Out-Party National Committees, 1956–1993.* New Haven, CT: Yale University Press, 1994.

Kolodny, Robin. "The Several Elections of 1824." *Congress and the Presidency.* Vol. 23, no. 2 (Fall 1996): 139–164.

———. *Pursuing Majorities: Congressional Campaign Committees in American Politics.* Norman: University of Oklahoma Press, 1998.

———, Diana Dwyre. "Party-Orchestrated Activities for Legislative Party Goals: Campaigns for Majorities in the US House of Representatives in the 1990s." *Party Politics* 4, no. 3 (July 1998): 275–95.

———. *Pursuing Majorities: Congressional Campaign Committees in American Politics.* Norman: University of Oklahoma Press, 1998b.

Korzi, Michael. *A Seat of Popular Leadership: The Presidency, Political Parties, and Democratic Government.* Amherst: University of Massachusetts Press, 2004.

Kosmin, Barry A., and Ariela Keysar. *Religious Identification Survey* (ARIS 2008). http:www.americanreligionsurvey-aris.org/reports/ARIS_Report_2008.pdf (accessed June 16, 2009).

Kraft, Dina, and Laurie Goodstein. "Anglican Conservatives, Rebelling on Gays, Will Form New Power Bloc," *The New York Times*, June 30, 2008, A6.

Krehbiel, Keith. "Institutional and Partisan Sources of Gridlock: A Theory of Divided and Unified Government." *Journal of Theoretical Politics* 8 (January 1996): 7–40.

———. *Pivotal Politics*. Chicago: University of Chicago Press, 1998.

Kreuger, Brian. "A Comparison of Conventional and Internet Political Mobilization." *American Politics Research* 34, no. 6 (2006): 759–76.

Krosnick, Jon A., and Donald R. Kinder. "Altering the Foundations of Support for the President through Priming." *American Political Science Review* 84 (1990): 497–512.

Kuo, David. *Tempting Faith: An Inside Story of Political Seduction*. New York: Free Press, 2006.

Kupchan, Charles A., and Peter L. Trubowitz. "Dead Center: The Demise of Liberal Internationalism in the United States." *International Security* 32, no. 2 (Fall 2007): 7–44.

Ladd, Everett Carll, Jr., with Charles Hadley. *Transformations of the American Party System*. New York: Norton, 1975.

Ladd, Jonathan McDonald. "Elections through the Lens of News Media Trust." Typescript, Georgetown University, 2009. http://www9.georgetown.edu/faculty/jml89/LaddMediaVoting.pdf (accessed July 23, 2009).

Lang, Robert, Thomas Sanchez, and Alan Berube. "The New Suburban Politics: A County-Based Analysis of Metropolitan Voting Trends since 2000." In *Red, Blue and Purple America: The Future of Election Demographics*, edited by Ruy Teixeira, 25–49. Washington, DC: Brookings Institution, 2008.

Laracey, Mel. *Presidents and the People: The Partisan Story of Going Public*. College Station: Texas A&M Press, 2002.

La Raja, Raymond J. "Why Soft Money Has Strengthened Parties." In *Inside the Campaign Finance Battle: Court Testimony on the New Reform*, edited by Anthony Corrado, Thomas E. Mann, and Trevor Potter. Washington, DC: Brookings Institution Press, 2003, 69–96.

———. *Small Change: Money, Political Parties, and Campaign Finance Reform*. Ann Arbor: University of Michigan Press, 2008.

Larson, John. *Internal Improvements: National Public Works and the Promise of Popular Government in the Early United States*. Chapel Hill: University of North Carolina, 2000.

Lawrence, Eric, John Sides, and Henry Farrell. "Self-Segregation or Deliberation? Blog Readership, Participation, and Polarization in American Politics." *Perspectives on Politics*, 2009.

Layman, Geoffrey. *The Great Divide: Religious and Cultural Conflict in American Party Politics*. New York: Columbia University Press, 2001.

Layman, Geoffrey C., and Thomas M. Carsey. "Party Polarization and Party Structuring of Policy Attitudes: A Comparison of Three NES Panel Studies." *Political Behavior* 24 (2002a September): 199–236.

———. "Party Polarization and "Conflict Extension" in the American Electorate." *American Journal of Political Science* 46 (2002b October): 786–802.

Lazarsveld, Paul F., Bernard R. Berelson, and Hazel Gaudet. *The People's Choice: How the Voter Makes up His Mind in a Presidential Campaign.* New York: Columbia University Press, 1948.

Leal, David, Matt Baretto, Jongho Lee, and Rodolfo O. De la Garza. "The Latino Vote in the 2004 Election." *Political Science and Politics* 38, no. 1 (2005): 41–49.

Leege, David C., and Lyman A. Kellstedt, ed. *Rediscovering the Religious Factor in American Politics.* Armonk, NY: M. E. Sharpe, 1993.

———, Kenneth D. Wald. "Religion, Culture, and Politics within American Culture Wars: The Autonomy of the Political." Paper presented at the Annual Meeting of the Society for the Scientific Study of Religion, Montreal, 1998.

———. Brian S. Krueger, and Paul D. Mueller. *The Politics of Cultural Differences: Social Change and Voter Mobilization Strategies in the Post-New Deal Period.* Princeton, NJ: Princeton University Press, 2002.

Leighley, Jan E. *Mass Media and Politics: A Social Science Perspective.* Boston, MA: Houghton Mifflin, 2004.

Lenski, Gerhard E. *The Religious Factor: A Sociological Study of Religion's Impact on Politics, Economics, and Social Life.* Garden City, NY: Doubleday, 1961.

Leuchtenburg, William E. *Franklin D. Roosevelt and the New Deal, 1932–1940.* New York: Harper and Row, 1963.

———. *The White House Looks South: Franklin D. Roosevelt, Harry S. Truman, and Lyndon B. Johnson.* Baton Rouge, LA: Louisiana State University Press, 2005.

LeVeaux, C., and J. C. Garand. "Race-Based Redistricting, Core Constituencies, and Legislative Responsiveness to Constituency Change." *Social Science Quarterly* 84, no. 1 (2003): 32–51.

Lien, Pei-te, M. Margaret Conway, and Janelle Wong. *The Politics of Asian Americans.* New York: Routledge, 2004.

Link, Arthur S., ed. *The Papers of Woodrow Wilson.* 69 vols. Princeton, NJ: Princeton University Press, 1984.

Linn, Suzanna, Jonathan Moody, and Stephanie Asper. "Explaining the Horse Race of 2008." *PS: Political Science & Politics* 42, no. 3 (2009): 459–66.

Liscio, Rebekah E., Jeffrey M. Stonecash, and Mark D. Brewer. "Unintended Consequences: Republican Strategy and Winning and Losing Voters." In *The State of the Parties.* 5th ed., edited by John C. Green. New York: Rowman and Littlefield, Forthcoming.

Lowi, Theodore J. *The End of Liberalism: The Second Republic in the United States.* New York: Norton, 1979.

———. *The Personal President: Power Invested, Promised Unfilled.* Ithaca, NJ: Cornell University Press, 1985.

Lubell, Samuel. *The Future of American Politics.* 2nd ed. rev. Garden City, NY: Doubleday Anchor Books, 1956.

Lublin, David. *The Republican South.* Princeton, NJ: Princeton University Press, 2004.

Lusane, Clarence. *No Easy Victories: Black Americans and the Vote.* New York: Franklin Watts, 1996.

Madison, James, Alexander Hamilton, and John Jay. *The Federalist Papers,* 1787–88. http://thomas.loc.gov/home/histdox/fedpapers.html.

Mahler, Jonathan. "After the Imperial Presidency." *New York Times Magazine,* November 9, 2008. http://www.nytimes.com/2008/11/09/magazine/09power-t.html.

Malbin, Michael J. "Small Donors, Large Donors and the Internet: The Case for Public Financing after Obama." (A Campaign Finance Institute working paper), April 2009. http://www.cfinst.org/pr/prRelease.aspx?ReleaseID=228.

Mann, Thomas E., and Norman Ornstein. *The Broken Branch: How Congress Is Failing America and How to Get It Back on Track.* New York: Oxford University Press, 2006.

Marshall, Bryan W., Brandon C. Prins, and David W. Rohde. "Majority Party Leadership, Strategic Choice, and Committee Power: Appropriations in the House, 1995–98." In *Congress on Display, Congress at Work,* edited by William Bianco, 69–99. Ann Arbor: University of Michigan Press, 2000.

Martin, William. *With God on Our Side: The Rise of the Religious Right in America.* New York: Broadway Books, 1996.

Marty, Martin E. *Righteous Empire: The Protestant Experience in America.* New York: Dial, 1970.

Mason, Robert. "Ronald Reagan and the Republican Party: Responses to Realignment." In *Ronald Reagan and the 1980s: Perceptions, Policies, Legacies,* edited by Cheryl Hudson and Gareth Davies. New York: Palgrave Macmillan, 2008, 151–73.

Massey, Douglas S. *Categorically Unequal: The American Stratification System.* New York: Russell Sage, 2007.

Mayhew, David R. *Congress: The Electoral Connection.* New Haven, CT: Yale University Press, 1974.

———. *Divided We Govern: Party Control, Lawmaking, and Investigations 1946–1990.* New Haven. CT: Yale University Press, 1991.

McAllister, Ted V. "Reagan and the Transformation of American Conservatism." In *The Reagan Presidency: Pragmatic Conservatism and its Legacies,* edited by W. Elliot Brownlee and Hugh Davis Graham. Lawrence: University Press of Kansas, 2003, 40–60.

McCarty, Nolan. "The Policy Effects of Political Polarization." In *The Transformation of American Politics: Activist Government and the Rise of Conservatism,* edited by Paul Pierson and Theda Skocpol, 223–55. Princeton, NJ: Princeton University Press, 2007.

———, Keith T. Poole, and Howard Rosenthal. *Polarized America: The Dance of Ideology and Unequal Riches.* Cambridge, MA: MIT Press, 2006.

McClain, Paula D., and Joseph Stewart Jr. *"Can We All Get Along?" Racial and Ethnic Minorities in American Politics.* 5th ed. Boulder, CO: Westview Press, 2010.

McCombs, Maxwell E., and Donald L. Shaw. "The Agenda-Setting Function of Mass Media." *Public Opinion Quarterly* 36 (1972): 176–87.

McCormick, Richard L. *The Party Period and Public Policy: American Politics from the Age of Jackson to the Progressive Era.* Oxford, UK: Oxford University Press, 1986.

McCormick, Richard P. "Political Development and the Second Party System." In *The American Party Systems: Stages of Political Development,* edited by William Nisbet Chambers and Walter Dean Burnham. New York: Oxford University Press, 1967, 90–116.

McDonald, Michael P. "Up, Up and Away! Voter Participation in the 2004 Presidential Election." *The Forum,* 2, no. 4 (2004): art. 4.

———. *Voter Turnout: United States Election Project,* 2005. http://elections.gmu.edu/voter_turnout.htm.

McGerr, Michael. *The Decline of Popular Politics: The American North, 1865–1928.* New York: Oxford University Press, 1986.

McGirr, Lisa. *Suburban Warriors: The Origins of the New Right.* Princeton, NJ: Princeton University Press, 2001.

McKee, Seth C. *Republican Ascendancy in Southern U. S. House Elections.* Boulder, CO: Westview Press, 2010.

McMahon, Kevin. *Reconsidering Roosevelt on Race: How the Presidency Paved the Road to Brown.* Chicago: University of Chicago Press, 2003.

McWilliams, Carey. The Anti-Federalists, Representation, and Party. *Northwestern University Law Review* 84, no. 1 (Fall 1989): 12–38.

Meckler, 2009. http://online.wsj.com/article/SB123487951033799545.html.

Mellow, Nicole. *The State of Disunion: Regional Sources of Modern American Partisanship.* Baltimore, MD: Johns Hopkins University Press, 2008.

Melnick, R. Shep. The Congress, Courts, and Programmatic Rights. In *Remaking American Politics*, edited by Richard A. Harris and Sidney M. Milkis. Boulder, CO: Westview Press, 1989, 188–212.

Meyers, Marvin. *The Jacksonian Persuasion: Politics and Belief.* Stanford, CA: Stanford University Press, 1957.

Milkis, Sidney M. *The Presidents and the Parties: The Transformation of the American Party System Since the New Deal.* Oxford: Oxford University Press, 1993.

———. *Political Parties and Constitutional Government: Remaking American Democracy.* Baltimore, MD: Johns Hopkins University Press, 1999.

———. "Franklin Roosevelt, the Economic Constitutional Order, and the New Politics of Presidential Leadership." In *The New Deal and the Triumph of Liberalism*, edited by Sidney M. Milkis and Jerome Mileur. Amherst: University of Massachusetts Press, 2002, 31–72.

———. "Parties versus Interest Groups." In *Inside the Campaign Finance Battle: Court Testimony on the New Reform*, edited by Anthony Corrado, Thomas E. Mann, and Trevor Potter. Washington, DC: Brookings Institution Press, 2003, 40–48.

———. "The Modern Presidency, Social Movements and the Administrative State: Lyndon Johnson and the Civil Rights Movement." In *Race and American Political Development*, edited by Joseph Lowndes, Julie Novkov, and Dorian Warren. New York: Routledge, 2008, 256–87.

———. *Theodore Roosevelt, the Progressive Party, and Transformation of American Democracy.* Lawrence: University Press of Kansas, 2009.

———. Jesse H. Rhodes. "George W. Bush, the Republican Party, and the 'New' American Party System." *Perspectives on Politics* 5, no. 3 (September 2007a): 461–88.

———. "George W. Bush, the Republican Party, and American Federalism." *Publius*, 37, no. 3 (2007b): 478–503.

———, Daniel J. Tichenor. "'Direct Democracy' and Social Justice: The Progressive Party Campaign of 1912." *Studies in American Political Development* 8, no. 2 (Fall 1994): 282–340.

Miller, Joanne M., and Jon A. Krosnick. "News Media Impact on the Ingredients of Presidential Evaluations: Politically Knowledgeable Citizens are Guided by a Trusted Source." *American Journal of Political Science* 44, no. 2 (2000): 295–309.

Moley, Raymond. 1949. *27 Masters of Politics.* Westport, CT: Greenwood Press, 1979.

Monroe, Nathan W., Jason M. Roberts, and David W. Rohde, eds. *Why Not Parties? Party Effects in the United States Senate.* Chicago: University of Chicago Press, 2008.

Mucchiaroni, Gary, and Quirk, Paul J. "Deliberations of a Compassionate Conservative: George W. Bush's Domestic Policy." In *The George W. Bush Presidency: Appraisals and Prospects,* edited by Colin Campbell and Bert A. Rockman, 175–200. Washington, DC: CQ Press, 2004.

Muir, William K. "Ronald Reagan: The Primacy of Rhetoric." In *Leadership in the Modern Presidency,* edited by Fred I. Greenstein. Cambridge, MA: Harvard University Press, 1988, 261–95.

Murphy, Andrew R. *Prodigal Nation: Moral Decline and Divine Punishment from New England to 9/11.* New York: Oxford University Press, 2009.

Murray, Charles. *Losing Ground.* New York: Basic Books, 1984.

Nagourney, Adam. "The Week Ahead: Politics," *New York Times,* May 9, 2004, http://www.nytimes.com/2004/05/09/weekinreview/the-week-ahead-politics.html?pagewanted=1.

———. "Dean Argues His 50-State Strategy Helped Obama Win," *The International Herald Tribune,* November 12, 2008.

Nathan, Richard. *The Administrative Presidency.* New York: Wiley, 1983.

National Public Radio. "Sen. Grassley's Twitter Broadside at Obama." June 8, 2009. http://www.npr.org/templates/story/story.php?storyId=105128505 (accessed July 23, 2009).

Neuhaus, Richard John. *The Naked Public Square: Religion and Democracy in America.* Grand Rapids, MI: Eerdmans, 1984.

New Republic. Editorial, "The Democrats as Legislators." September 2, 1916.

Nichols, Roy F. *The Invention of the American Political Parties: A Study of Political Improvisation.* New York: Free Press, 1967.

Obama, Barack. Announcement for President, February 10, 2007. www.barackobama.com.

Olson, Laura R. "Toward a Contextual Appreciation of Religion and Politics." In *Religion, Politics, and the American Experience: Reflections on Religion and American Public Life,* edited by Edith L. Blumhofer. Tuscaloosa: University of Alabama Press, 2002.

———, Wendy Cadge, and James T. Harrison. "Religion and Public Opinion about Same-Sex Marriage." *Social Science Quarterly* 87, no. 2 (June 2006): 340–60.

———, John C. Green. "The Worship Attendance Gap." In *Beyond Red State, Blue State: Electoral Gaps in the Twenty-First Century American Electorate,* edited by Laura R. Olson and John C. Green. Upper Saddle River, NJ: Prentice Hall, 2007.

Oppenheimer, Bruce I. "The Rules Committee: New Arm of Leadership in a Decentralized House." In *Congress Reconsidered,* edited by Lawrence C. Dodd and Bruce I. Oppenheimer, 96–116. New York: Praeger, 1977.

Ortiz, Hector L., and Jeffrey M. Stonecash. "The Class Gap." In *Beyond Red State, Blue State,* edited by Laura R. Olson and John C. Green. Upper Saddle River, NJ: Pearson / Prentice Hall, 2009.

Ostrogorski, M. *Democracy and the Organization of Political Parties.* New York: Macmillan, 1902.

Page, Benjamin I., and Lawrence R. Jacobs. *Class War: What Americans Really Think About Economic Inequality.* Chicago: University of Chicago Press, 2009.

Patterson, James T. *Congressional Conservatism and the New Deal: The Growth of the Conservative Coalition in Congress, 1933–1939*. Lexington: University of Kentucky Press, 1967.

Patterson, Thomas E. *Out of Order*. New York: Vintage, 1994.

Perlstein, Rick. *Before the Storm: Barry Goldwater and the Unmaking of the American Consensus*. New York: Hill and Wang, 2001.

———. *Nixonland: The Rise of a President and the Fracturing of America*. New York: Scribner, 2008.

Peters, Gerhard. "Voter Turnout in Presidential Elections, 1824–2004," at John Woolley and Gerhard Peters. *The American Presidency Project at US Santa Barbara, 1999–2009*. http://www.presidency.ucsb.edu/data/turnout.php (accessed October 1, 2009).

Petrocik, John R. "Issue Ownership in Presidential Elections, with a 1980 Case Study." *American Journal of Political Science* 40 (1996): 825–50.

———. *Party Coalitions: Realignments and the Decline of the New Deal Party System*. Chicago: University of Chicago Press, 1981.

Pew Forum on Religion & Public Life. "Religion and the 2006 Elections," 2006. http://pewforum.org/docs/index.php?DocID=174.

———. "U.S. Religious Landscape Survey," 2008. http://religions.pewforum.org/pdf/report-religious-landscape-study-full.pdf.

Piffner, James P. *Power Play: The Bush Presidency and the Constitution*. Washington, DC: Brookings Institution Press, 2008.

Phaelzer, Jean. *Driven Out: The Forgotten War Against Chinese Americans*. Berkeley: University of California Press, 2008.

Phillips, Kevin. *The Emerging Republican Majority*. New Rochelle, NY: Arlington House, 1969.

Philpot, Tasha S. *Race, Republicans, and the Return of the Party of Lincoln*. Ann Arbor: University of Michigan Press, 2007.

Piereson, James. "Party Government." *Political Science Reviewer* 12, no. 1 (Fall 1982): 2–52.

Pitkin, Hanna Fenichel. *The Concept of Representation*. Berkeley: University of California Press, 1967.

Plotke, David. *Building a Democratic Political Order: Reshaping American Liberalism in the 1930s and 1940s*. New York: Cambridge University Press, 1996.

Plutzer, Eric, and Michael McBurnett. "The 'Marriage Gap' Reconsidered." *Public Opinion Quarterly* 55 (1991): 113–27.

Polsby, Nelson. *How Congress Evolves: Social Bases of Institutional Change*. New York: Oxford University Press, 2004.

Pomper, Gerald M. *Passions and Interests: Political Party Concepts of American Democracy*. Lawrence: University Press of Kansas, 1992.

Poole, Keith T., and Howard Rosenthal. *Congress: A Political-Economic History of Roll Call Voting*. New York: Oxford University Press, 1997.

———. *Ideology and Congress*. New Brunswick, NJ: Transaction, 2007.

Prior, Markus. *Post-Broadcast Democracy: How Media Choice Increases Inequality in Political Involvement and Polarizes Elections*. New York: Cambridge University Press, 2007.

———. "The Immensely Inflated News Audience: Assessing Bias in Self-Reported News Exposure." *Public Opinion Quarterly* 73, no.1 (2009): 130–43.

Rae, Nicol C. *The Decline and Fall of the Liberal Republicans from 1952 to the Present.* New York: Oxford University Press, 1989.

———."Class and Culture: American Political Cleavages in the Twentieth Century." *Western Political Quarterly* 45 (September 1992): 629–50.

Ramakrishnan, Karthick. *Democracy in Immigrant America.* Stanford, CA: Stanford University Press, 2005.

———, Janelle Wong, Taeku Lee, and Jane Junn. "Race-Based Considerations and the Obama Vote: Evidence from the 2008 National Asian American Survey." *Du Bois Review: Social Science Research on Race* 6, no. 1 (2009): 219–38.

Ranney, Austin. *Channels of Power.* New York: Basic Books, 1983.

Reeher, Grant X. *Narratives of Justice.* Ann Arbor: University of Michigan Press, 1996.

Reichley, A. James. "The Rise of National Parties." In *The New Direction in American Politics*, edited by John E. Chubb and Paul E. Peterson. Washington, DC: Brookings Institution Press, 1985.

———. *The Life of the Parties.* New York: Free Press, 1992.

———. *Faith in Politics.* Washington, DC: Brookings Institution, 2002.

Reiter, Howard L. "The Building of a Bifactional Structure: The Democrats in the 1940s." *Political Science Quarterly* 116 (Spring 2001), 107–29.

———. "Factional Persistence within Parties in the United States." *Party Politics* 10, no. 2 (May 2004.): 251–71.

———, Jeffrey M. Stonecash. *Counter-Realignment: Political Change in the Northeast.* New York: Cambridge University Press, Forthcoming.

Remini, Robert V. *Andrew Jackson and the Bank War: A Study in the Growth of Presidential Power.* New York: Norton, 1967.

Republican National Committee (RNC). 2008. "2008 Republican Party National Platform." http://gop.com/2008platform/.

Reynolds, John F. 2006. *The Demise of the American Convention System.* Cambridge, UK: Cambridge University Press.

Ridout, Travis N., and Rob Mellen, Jr. "Does the Media Agenda Reflect the Candidates' Agenda?" *Harvard International Journal of Press/Politics* 12, no. 2 (2007): 44–62.

Riker, William. *The Strategy of Rhetoric.* New Haven, CT: Yale University Press, 1996.

Riordon, William L. *Plunkitt of Tammany Hall.* New York: E.P. Dutton, 1963.

Robinson, Carin. "Doctrine, Discussion, and Disagreement: Evangelical Protestant Interaction with Catholics in American Politics." PhD diss., Georgetown University, 2008.

Robinson, Edgar E. *They Voted for Roosevelt: The Presidential Vote, 1932–1944.* Stanford, CA: Stanford University Press, 1947.

Rochefort, David A., and Roger W Cobb. *The Politics of Problem Definition: Shaping the Policy Agenda.* Lawrence: University Press of Kansas, 1994.

Rogers, Daniel. "In Search of Progressivism." *Review of American History* 10 (December 1982): 114–23.

Rogers, Reuel R. *Afro-Caribbean Immigrants and the Politics of Incorporation.* New York: Cambridge University Press, 2006.

Rohde, David W. *Parties and Leaders in the Postreform House.* Chicago: University of Chicago Press, 1991.

Roosevelt, Franklin D. *The Public Papers and Addresses of Franklin D. Roosevelt*, edited by Samuel Rosenman, 13 vols. New York: Random House, 1938–50.

Roosevelt, Theodore. *The Works of Theodore Roosevelt*, 20 vols. New York: Scribner's, 1926.

Roozen, David A., and James R. Nieman. *Church, Identity, and Change: Theology and Denominational Structures in Unsettled Times.* Grand Rapids, MI: Eerdmans, 2005.

Rossiter, Clinton. *Parties and Politics in America.* Ithaca, NY: Cornell University Press, 1960.

Rove, Karl. Personal interview with Sidney M. Milkis (November 15, 2001).

Rovere, Richard A. "A Man For This Age Too." *New York Times Magazine*, April 11, 1965.

Rudalevige, Andrew. *The New Imperial Presidency: Renewing Presidential Power after Watergate.* Ann Arbor: University of Michigan Press, 2005.

Rutenberg, Jim. "Obama Nears Record for Spending on Ads," *New York Times*, October 18, 2008. http://www.nytimes.com/2008/10/18/world/americas/18iht-ads.1.17063320.html (accessed July 23, 2009).

———. "Obama Plans to Take Campaign to Republican Bastions," *The International Herald Tribune*, June 23, 2008. http://www.nytimes.com/2008/06/22/world/americas/22iht-obama.1.13881160.html.

Sabato, Larry J. *The Rise of Political Consultants: New Ways of Winning Elections.* New York: Basic Books, 1981.

Sack, Kevin. "Democrats in Political Debt for Black Turnout in South," *The New York Times*, November 6, 1998, A1.

Saslow, Eli. "Grass-Roots Battle Tests The Obama Movement," *The Washington Post*, August 23, 2009. http://www.washingtonpost.com/wp-dyn/content/article/2009/08/22/AR2009082202343.html.

Saunders, Kyle L., and Alan I. Abramowitz. "Ideological Realignment and Active Partisans in the American Electorate." *American Politics Research* 32 (2004 May): 285–309.

Savage, Barbara Dianne. *Your Spirits Walk Beside Us: The Politics of Black Religion.* Cambridge, MA: Belknap Press/Harvard University Press, 2008.

Schickler, Eric, and Kathryn Pearson. "Agenda Control, Majority Party Power, and the House Committee on Rules, 1937–1952." *Legislative Studies Quarterly* (2009)

———, Kathryn Pearson, and Brian D. Feinstein, "Shifting Partisan Coalitions: Support for Civil Rights in Congress from 1933–1972." *Journal of Politics* 2010, forthcoming..

Schier, Steven E. *Panorama of a Presidency: How George W. Bush Acquired and Spent His Political Capital.* Armonk, NY: M. E. Sharpe, 2009.

Schlesinger, Arthur M., Jr. *The Vital Center: The Politics of Freedom.* New York: Houghton Mifflin, 1949.

———. *The Politics of Upheaval.* Boston: Houghton Mifflin, 1960.

Schouten, Fredreka. "Obama Ads Overwhelm TV Presence of McCain," *USA Today*, October 28, 2008. http://www.usatoday.com/news/politics/election2008/2008-10-27-campaignadvertising_N.htm (accessed June 23, 2009).

Schudson, Michael. *The Power of News.* Cambridge, MA: Harvard University Press, 1996.

Sears, David O., Carl P. Hensler, and Leslie K. Speer. "'Whites' Opposition to Busing': Self-Interest of Symbolic Politics." *American Political Science Review* 73, no. 2 (1979): 369–84.

Seelye, Katherine Q. "Sarah Palin Calls Health Care Overhaul 'Downright Evil.'" *The Caucus*, August 8, 2009. http://thecaucus.blogs.nytimes.com/2009/08/08/sarah-palin-has-weighed-in-on/

Shafer, Byron E., and Richard Johnston. *The End of Southern Exceptionalism: Class, Race, and Partisan Change in the Postwar South*. Cambridge, MA: Harvard University Press, 2006.

Shapiro, Isaac, Robert Greenstein, and Wendell Primus. "Pathbreaking CBO Study Shows Dramatic Increases in Income Disparities in 1980s and 1990s" (May 31, 2001). Washington, DC: Center on Budget and Policy Priorities, 10. http://cbpp.org/cms/?fa=view&id=334.

Shaw, Daron R. "The Effect of TV Ads and Candidate Appearances on Statewide Presidential Votes, 1988–96." *American Political Science Review* 93, no. 2 (1999): 345–61.

———. *The Race to 270: The Electoral College and the Campaign Strategies of 2000 and 2004*. Chicago: University of Chicago Press, 2006.

———, Brian E. Roberts. "The Campaign, the Media, and the Prospects of Victory: The 1992 and 1996 US Presidential Elections." *British Journal of Political Science* 30 (2000): 259–89.

Shaw-Taylor, Yoku, and Steven A. Tuch. *The Other African Americans: Contemporary African and Caribbean Immigrants in the United States*. Lanham, MD: Rowman and Littlefield, 2007.

Shea, Daniel. "The Passing of Realignment and the Advent of the 'Baseless' Party System." *American Politics Quarterly* 27, no. 1 (January 1999): 33–57.

Shea, Danny. "Political Websites See Traffic Surge, Huffington Post Leads the Way." *The Huffington Post*, October 24, 2008. http://www.huffingtonpost.com/2008/10/24/political-websites-see-tr_n_137700.html (accessed June 23, 2009).

Shefter, Martin. *Political Parties and the State: The American Historical Experience*. Princeton, NJ: Princeton University Press, 1994.

———. *The Politics Presidents Make: Leadership from John Adams to Bill Clinton*. Cambridge, MA: Harvard University Press, 1997.

———.War, Trade, and U.S. Party Politics. In *Shaped by War and Trade*, edited by Ira Katznelson and Martin Shefter. Princeton, NJ: Princeton University Press, 2002, 113–33.

———. "Leadership by Definition: First Term Reflections on George W. Bush's Political Stance." *Perspectives on Politics* 3, no. 4 (2005): 817–31.

———"The Conservative Insurgency and Presidential Power: A Developmental Perspective on the Unitary Executive." *Harvard Law Review* 122, no. 8 (June 2009): 2074–2103.

Shepsle, Kenneth A., and Mark S. Bonchek. *Analyzing Politics*. New York: Norton, 1997.

Sherman, Gabriel. "The Scoop Factory: Inside Politico and the Brave New World of Post-Print Journalism," *The New Republic*, March 4, 2009. http://www.tnr.com/politics/story.html?id=82d8d496-d402-4863-b98d-8967de7cc6ab (accessed June 23, 2009).

Silbey, Joel. "From 'Essential to the Existence of Our Institutions' to 'Rapacious Enemies of Honest and Responsible Government': The Rise and Fall of American Political Parties, 1790–2000." In *The Parties Respond: Changes in American Parties and*

Campaigns. 4th ed., edited by L. Sandy Maisel. Boulder, CO: Westview Press, 2002, 1–18.

Simon, Adam F., and Jennifer Jerit. "Toward a Theory Relating Political Discourse, Media, and Public Opinion. *Journal of Communication* 57 (2007): 254–71.

Sinclair, Barbara. *Legislators, Leaders, and Lawmaking.* Baltimore: Johns Hopkins University Press, 1995.

———. *Party Wars.* Norman, OK: University of Oklahoma Press, 2006.

———. "Spoiling the Sausages: How a Polarized Congress Deliberates and Legislates." In *Red and Blue Nation?* vol. 2, edited by Pietro S. Nivola and David W. Brady, 55–87. Washington, DC: Brookings Institution Press, 2008.

Sitkoff, Harvard. *A New Deal for Blacks: The Emergence of Civil Rights as a National Issue.* Vol. 1, *The Depression Decade.* New York: Oxford University Press, 1978.

Skowronek, Stephen. *Building a New American State: the Expansion of National Administrative Capacities, 1877–1920.* Cambridge, UK: Cambridge University Press, 1982.

———. *The Politics Presidents Make: Leadership from John Adams to Bill Clinton.* Cambridge, MA: Harvard University Press, 1997.

———. "Leadership by Definition: First Term Reflections on George W. Bush's Political Stance." *Perspectives on Politics* 3, no. 4. (2005): 817–31.

Skowronek. Stephen. "The Conservative Insurgency and Presidential Power: A Developmental Perspective on the Unitary Executive." *Harvard Law Review* 122, no. 8 (June 2009): 2070–2103.

Smith, Christian. *American Evangelicalism: Embattled and Thriving.* Chicago: University of Chicago Press, 1998.

Smith, Mark A. *The Right Talk: How Conservatives Transformed the Great Society into the Economic Society.* Princeton, NJ: Princeton University Press, 2007.

Soss, Joe, Jacob S. Hacker, and Suzanne Mettler. *Remaking America: Democracy and Public Policy in an Age of Inequality.* New York: Russell Sage Foundation, 2007.

Speel, Robert W. *Changing Patterns of Voting in the Northern United States.* University Park, PA: The Pennsylvania State University Press, 1998.

Squire, Peverill, and Christina Fastnow. "Comparing Gubernatorial and Senatorial Elections." *Political Research Quarterly* 47, no. 3 (September 1994.): 705–20.

Stampp, Kenneth M. "The Concept of Perpetual Union." In Kenneth Stampp, *The Imperiled Union: Essays on the Background of the Civil War.* New York: Oxford University Press, 1980, 3–37.

Steensland, Brian, Jerry Z. Park, Mark D. Regnerus, Lynn D. Robinson, W. Bradford Wilcox, and Robert D. Woodberry. "The Measure of American Religion: Toward Improving the State of the Art." *Social Forces* 79, no. 1 (September 2000.): 291–318.

Stehr, Stephen. "Top Bureaucrats and the Distribution of Influence in Reagan's Executive Branch." *Public Administration Review* 57, no. 1 (1997): 75–82.

Stimson, James A. *Tides of Consent: How Public Opinion Shapes American Politics.* New York: Cambridge University Press, 2004.

Stokes, Donald E. "Some Dynamic Elements of Contests for the Presidency." *American Political Science Review,* 60 (1966): 19–28.

Stokes, Thomas. *Chip Off My Shoulder.* Princeton, NJ: Princeton University Press, 1940.

Stolberg, Sheryl Gay. "Obama Signs Equal-Pay Legislation," *New York Times,* January 20, 2009. http://www.nytimes.com/2009/01/30/us/politics/30ledbetter-web.html.

Stone, Deborah. "Welfare Policy and the Transformation of Care." In *Remaking America*, edited by Joe Soss, Jacob S. Hacker, and Suzanne Mettler, 183–202. New York: Russell Sage, 2007.

Stonecash, Jeffrey M. *Class and Party in American Politics*. Boulder, CO: Westview Press, 2000.

———. "Parties and Taxes: The Emergence of Distributive Issues, 1950-2000." Earlier version presented at the Midwest Political Science Association Meetings, April, 2001.

———. *Parties Matter: Realignment and the Return of Partisanship*. Boulder, CO: Lynne-Rienner, 2005.

———. *Inequality and the American Public: Report of the Maxwell Poll, 2007*. Syracuse, NY: The Campbell Institute, Maxwell School, Syracuse University, 2007.

———, Mark D. Brewer, and Mack D. Mariani. *Diverging Parties: Social Change, Realignment, and Party Polarization*. Boulder, CO: Westview Press, 2003.

Storing, Herbert. *What the Anti-Federalists Were For: The Political Thought of the Opponents of the Constitution*. Chicago: University of Chicago Press, 1981.

Streb, Matthew. *Rethinking American Electoral Democracy: Controversies in Electoral Democracy and Representation*. New York: Routledge, 2008.

Stroud, Natalie Jomini. "Media Use and Political Predispositions: Revisiting the Concept of Selective Exposure." *Political Behavior* 30, no. 3 (2008): 341–66.

Summers, Mark W. *The Plundering Generation: Corruption and the Crisis of the Union, 1849–1861*. Oxford, UK: Oxford University Press, 1988.

Sundquist, James L. *Dynamics of the Party System: Alignment and Realignment of Political Parties in the United States*. Washington, DC: Brookings Institution Press, 1983.

Taddeo, Lisa. "The Man Who Made Obama," *Esquire*, February 2, 2009. http://www.esquire.com/features/david-plouffe-0309?src=rss.

Tate, Katherine. *From Protest to Politics*. Cambridge, MA: Harvard University Press, 1993.

Taylor, Andrew J. "The Ideological Development of the Parties in Washington, 1947–1994." *Polity* 29, no. 2 (Winter 1996): 273–92.

Teles, Steve M. *Whose Welfare: AFDC and Elite Politics*. Lawrence: University Press of Kansas, 1998.

Tewksbury, David. "The Seeds of Audience Fragmentation: Specialization in the Use of Online News Sites." *Journal of Broadcasting and Electronic Media* 49, no. 3 (2005): 332–48.

Tichenor, Daniel J. *Dividing Lines: The Politics of Immigration Control in America*. Princeton, NJ: Princeton University Press, 2002.

Troy, Gil. *See How They Ran: The Changing Role of the Presidential Candidate*. Cambridge, MA: Harvard University Press, 1996.

———. *Morning in America: How Ronald Reagan Invented the 1980s*. Princeton, NJ: Princeton University Press, 2007.

Tuchman, Gaye. "Objectivity as a Strategic Ritual: An Examination of Newsmen's Notions of Objectivity." *American Journal of Sociology* 77, no. 4 (1972): 660–79.

Tulis, Jeffrey. *The Rhetorical Presidency*. Princeton, NJ: Princeton University Press, 1987.

Tygiel, Jules. *Ronald Reagan and the Triumph of American Conservatism*. New York: Longman, 2004.

Uhlaner, Carole J. and F. Chris Garcia. "Learning Which Party Fits: Experience, Ethnic Identity, and the Demographic Foundations of Latino Party Identification." In *Diversity in Democracy: Minority Representation in the United States*, edited by G. Segura and S. Bower, 72–101. Charlottesville, VA: University of Virginia Press, 2005.

U.S. Congress. Senate. *Secure America and Orderly Immigration Act of 2005*. 109, S.1033.

———. *Comprehensive Enforcement and Immigration Reform Act of 2005*. 109, 1438.

———. *Comprehensive Immigration Reform Act of 2006*. 109, 2611.

U.S. Census Bureau, Population Division. "Population Projections of the United States, by Age, Sex, Race, and Hispanic Origin: 1993–2050." In *Current Population Reports*, 1993.

———. "The Census Bureau on Prospects for U.S. Population Growth in the Twenty-First Century." *Population and Development Review* 26, no. 1 (2000): 4.

———. *Interim State Population Projections*. 2004.

Van Buren, Martin. Martin Van Buren to Thomas Ritchie. Martin Van Buren Papers (July 13, 1827). Washington, DC: Library of Congress.

———. *Inquiry into the Origin and Course of Political Parties in the United States*. New York: Hudson and Houghton, 1867.

Van Riper, Paul. *History of the United States Civil Service*. Evanston, IL: Row, Peterson, 1958.

Vavreck, Lynn. *The Message Matters: The Economy and Presidential Campaigns*. Princeton, NJ: Princeton University Press, 2009.

Verba, Sidney, Kay Lehman Schlozman, and Henry E. Brady. *Voice and Equality: Civic Voluntarism in American Politics*. Cambridge, MA: Harvard University Press, 1995.

Viorst, Milton. *Fall from Grace: The Republican Party and the Puritan Ethic*. New York: New American Library, 1968.

Wald, Kenneth D., Dennis E. Owen, and Samuel S. Hill. "Churches as Political Communities." *American Political Science Review* 82, no. 2 (June 1988): 531–48.

———. "Political Cohesion in Churches." *Journal of Politics* 52, no. 1 (February 1990): 197–215.

Wallstein, Peter. "Retooling Obama's Campaign Machine for the Long Haul," *Los Angeles Times*, January 14, 2008. http://articles.latimes.com/2009/jan/14/nation/na-obama-army14.

———, Tom Hamburger. "Obama's Army May Get Drafted," *Los Angeles Times*, November 14, 2008. http://articles.latimes.com/2008/nov/14/nation/na-transition14.

Walters, Ronald W. *Black Presidential Politics in America: A Strategic Approach*. Albany, NY: SUNY Press, 1988.

Walton, Hanes, Jr. *Black Political Parties: An Historical and Political Analysis*. New York: Free Press, 1972.

———, Robert C. Smith. *American Politics and the African American Quest for Universal Freedom*. New York: Longman, 2003.

Ware, Alan. *The Democratic Party Heads North, 1877–1962*. New York: Cambridge University Press, 2006.

Wattenberg, Martin P. *The Decline of American Political Parties: 1952–1988*. Cambridge, MA: Harvard University Press, 1990.

Weiss, Nancy J. *Farewell to the Party of Lincoln: Black Politics in the Age of FDR.* Princeton, NJ: Princeton University Press, 1983.

Welch, Susan, and Lee Sigelman. "The Politics of Hispanic Americans: Insights from National Surveys, 1980–1988." *Social Science Quarterly* 74 (1993): 76–94.

West, Darrell M. *Air Wars: Television Advertising in Election Campaigns, 1952–2004.* 4th ed. Washington, DC: CQ Press, 2005.

White, John K. *The Values Divide: American Politics and Culture in Transition.* New York: Chatham House, 2003.

———, and Daniel M. Shea. *New Party Politics: From Jefferson and Hamilton to the Information Age.* Boston: Bedford/St. Martin's, 2000.

Wiebe, Robert. *Self Rule: A Cultural History of American Democracy.* Chicago: University of Chicago Press, 1995.

Wilcox, Clyde, and Carin Larson. *Onward Christian Soldiers? The Christian Right in American Politics.* 3rd ed. Boulder, CO: Westview, 2006.

Wilde, Melissa J. *Vatican II: A Sociological Analysis of Religious Change.* Princeton, NJ: Princeton University Press, 2007.

Williams, Rhys H., ed. *Cultural Wars in American Politics: Critical Reviews of a Popular Myth.* New York: Aldine de Gruyter, 1997.

Wilson, James. Q. *The Amateur Democrat: Club Politics in Three Cities.* Chicago: University of Chicago Press, 1962.

Wilson, Scott, and Joshua Partlow. "On Afghanistan, Political Test for Obama," *Washington Post,* August 26, 2009. http://www.washingtonpost.com/wp-dyn/content/article/2009/08/25/AR2009082501312.html.

Wolfe, Alan. *One Nation, After All.* New York: Viking, 1998.

Wolfensberger, Donald R. "The Motion to Recommit in the House: The Creation, Evisceration, and Restoration of a Minority Right." In *Party, Process, and Political Change in Congress.* Vol. 2, *Further New Perspectives on the History of Congress,* edited by David W. Brady and Mathew D. McCubbins, 271–93. Stanford, CA: Stanford University Press, 2007.

Wong, Janelle. *Democracy's Promise: Immigrants and American Institutions.* Ann Arbor, MI: University of Michigan Press. 2006.

Wong, Kenneth K. *Funding Public Schools.* Lawrence: University Press of Kansas, 1999.

Woodrow-Lafield, Karen A. "Implications of Immigration for Apportionment." *Population Research and Policy Review* 20 (2001): 22.

Woodward, C. Vann. *Origins of the New South, 1877–1913.* Baton Rouge: Louisiana State University Press, 1951.

Wuthnow, Robert. *The Restructuring of American Religion: Society and Faith since World War II.* Princeton, NJ: Princeton University Press, 1988.

———, John H. Evans, eds. *The Quiet Hand of God: Faith Based Activism and the Public Role of Mainline Protestantism.* Berkeley: University of California Press, 2002.

Xenos, Michael, and Patricia Moy. "Direct and Differential Effects of the Internet on Political and Civic Engagement." *Journal of Communication* 57, no. 4 (2007): 704–18.

Zaller, John. *The Nature and Origin of Mass Opinion.* New York: Cambridge University Press, 1992.

Index